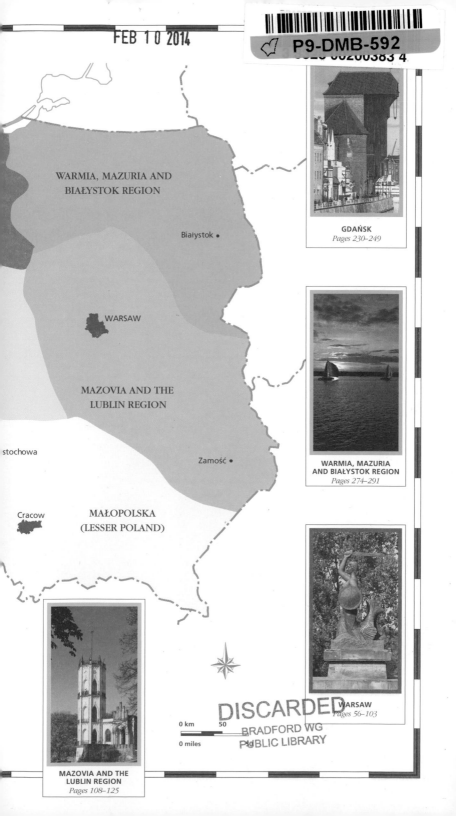

FEB 1 0 2014

WARMIA, MAZURIA AND
BIAŁYSTOK REGION

Białystok •

GDAŃSK
Pages 230–249

WARSAW

MAZOVIA AND THE
LUBLIN REGION

stochowa

Zamość •

**WARMIA, MAZURIA
AND BIAŁYSTOK REGION**
Pages 274–291

Cracow

MAŁOPOLSKA
(LESSER POLAND)

0 km   50

0 miles   50

WARSAW
Pages 56–103

**MAZOVIA AND THE
LUBLIN REGION**
Pages 108–125

EYEWITNESS TRAVEL

POLAND

EYEWITNESS TRAVEL

POLAND

Main contributors: Teresa Czerniewicz-Umer
Małgorzata Omilanowska
Jerzy S. Majewski

DK

LONDON, NEW YORK,
MELBOURNE, MUNICH AND DELHI
www.dk.com

Produced by Wydawnictwo Wiedza i Życie, Warsaw

CONTRIBUTORS Małgorzata Omilanowska, Jerzy S. Majewski
ILLUSTRATORS Andrzej Wielgosz, Bohdan Wróblewski,
Piotr Zubrzycki, Paweł Mistewicz
PHOTOGRAPHERS Krzysztof Chojnacki; Wojciech Czerniewicz, Stanisława
Jabłońska, Piotr Jamski, Euzebiusz Niemiec
CARTOGRAPHERS Ewa i Jan Pachniewiczowie,
Maria Wojciechowska, Dariusz Osuch (D. Osuch i spółka)

EDITOR Teresa Czerniewicz-Umer
DTP DESIGNERS Paweł Kamiński, Paweł Pasternak
PROOFREADER Bożena Leszkowicz
TECHNICAL EDITOR Anna Kożurno-Królikowska
DESIGNER Ewa Roguska i zespół
COVER DESIGN Paweł Kamiński

TRANSLATORS Mark Cole, Marian Dragon,
Teresa Levitt, Joanna Pillans, Vera Rich

Edited and typeset by Book Creation Services Ltd, London

Printed and bound by Malaysia by Vivar Printing Sdn Bhd

First American Edition, 2001
13 14 15 16 10 9 8 7 6 5 4 3 2 1

Published in the United States by
DK Publishing, 375 Hudson Street,
New York, New York 10014

Reprinted with revisions 2004, 2007, 2010, 2013

Copyright © 2001, 2013 Dorling Kindersley Limited, London

Published in the UK by Dorling Kindersley Limited, London.

A catalog record for this book is available from the Library of Congress.

ISSN 1542-1554
ISBN 978-0-75669-512-5

FLOORS ARE REFERRED TO THROUGHOUT IN ACCORDANCE WITH
EUROPEAN USAGE; IE THE "FIRST FLOOR" IS THE FLOOR ABOVE
GROUND LEVEL.

*Front cover main image: Niedzica Castle,
Pieniny National Park, Poland*

MIX
Paper from
responsible sources
FSC
www.fsc.org   FSC™ C018179

CONTENTS

INTRODUCING POLAND

The eagle, emblem of Poland, in
the Zygmunt Chapel, Cracow

WARSAW AREA BY AREA

Neo-Classical rotonda in the
Saxon Gardens, Warsaw

Horsedrawn carriages in Zakopane

Lion from Namiestnikowski
Palace, Warsaw

POLAND REGION
BY REGION

TRAVELLERS'
NEEDS

SURVIVAL
GUIDE

Wawel Royal
Cathedral, Cracow

INTRODUCING POLAND

DISCOVERING POLAND

Perched between East and West, Poland has had a varied history which has shaped it into the beguiling, delightful and refreshingly different mix of old and new that we see today. The chapters of this book have been divided into nine

Copernicus statue in Warsaw

colour-coded regions to reflect the diversity of Poland. Each region has its own special flavour: its own architecture, cuisine, customs and sights. The following pages aim to give a taste of these regions and show you what there is to see and do.

The picturesque square at the heart of Warsaw's Old Town

WARSAW

- **Postcard-pretty Old Town**
- **A Socialist Realist city**
- **Exciting nightlife**

Rebuilt to its original 13th-century design after being destroyed in World War II, Warsaw's **Old Town** *(see pp62–7)* is truly delightful. The city's controversial Socialist Realist architecture, embodied by the enormous **Palace of Culture and Science** *(see p89)*, reflects the capital's post-war history. Be sure to visit a few of the city's vibrant bars and clubs for a taste of Warsaw's nightlife.

MAZOVIA AND THE LUBLIN REGION

- **Renaissance Zamość**
- **Chopin and Żelazowa Wola**
- **Picturesque Vistula Valley**

The finely preserved town of **Zamość** *(see pp124–5)* was built in the 16th century according to the Renaissance concept of the ideal city.

The birthplace of Chopin, **Żelazowa Wola** *(see p114)* houses a fascinating museum dedicated to the great Polish composer. In the idyllic Vistula Valley, affluent **Kazimierz Dolny** *(see pp118–19)* is the unofficial capital of the area popular with Poland's New Rich.

CRACOW

- **Wonderful Old Town**
- **Historic Wawel Hill**
- **Cracow Jewish Festival**

Cracow's **Old Town** centres around the beautiful 13th-century market square *(see p130)*, which features many fine examples of Gothic and Renaissance architecture. The Old Town is overlooked by the glorious buildings on **Wawel Hill** *(see pp138–43)*, a symbol of national strength and patriotism. At the annual **Festival of Jewish Culture** *(see p33)*, you can enjoy music, art, theatre performances and much more.

MAŁOPOLSKA

- **Poland's painful past**
- **Wieliczka's salt mine**
- **Winter sports at Zakopane**

The tragedy of the Polish Jews can be witnessed at **Oświęcim (Auschwitz)** *(see p160)* where an estimated 1.1 million people died at the hands of the Nazis. This is now a UNESCO World Heritage Site. The old underground salt mine at **Wieliczka** *(see p162)* features a chapel, museum and a restaurant. A favourite retreat for many artists and intellectuals at the turn of the 20th century, Poland's winter capital **Zakopane** *(see p164)* attracts thousands of skiers every winter.

The ski resort at Zakopane, upgraded for the 2006 Olympics

SILESIA

- **Historic Wrocław**
- **Gold-digging in Złotoryja**
- **Getting away from it all in the Kłodzko Valley**

As well as a bustling Old Town, **Wrocław** *(see pp188–97)* is home to many of the country's more eclectic contemporary artists. **Złotoryja** *(see p180)* sits on the banks of the gold-rich Kaczawa River. Try your luck, then visit the Gold Museum or watch the experts at the International Gold Panning Championships. The majestic **Kłodzko Valley** *(see pp200–1)* is criss-crossed with hiking trails full of ancient churches and castles, and is famed for its mineral springs.

The Kłodzko Valley, a natural paradise for hikers

WIELKOPOLSKA

- **Industrial Łódź**
- **Poznań's beautiful churches**
- **Kórnik's castle island**

Built in the 1800s by a trio of mill owners, the industrial city of **Łódź** *(see pp228–9)* has many fascinating museums and a welcoming atmosphere, yet it remains almost untouched by tourism. The churches in **Poznań** *(see pp214–19)* are among the most delightful in Poland. The Gothic cathedral is the country's oldest, and the place where, allegedly, Poland's first king was christened. A visit to the island

The tranquil landscape of Pomerania's Kashubia region

castle at **Kórnik** *(see p211)*, inspired by Neo-Gothic English architecture and the Orient, is a splendid day out.

GDAŃSK

- **The cradle of Solidarity**
- **Westerplatte's WWII legacy**

In 1980 unemployed worker Lech Wałęsa climbed over a fence at a shipyard in **Gdańsk** *(see pp232–49)* and gave a speech that arguably led to the end of Communism. The story of Wałęsa and the Solidarity movement can be seen in Gdańsk's "Roads to Freedom" exhibition. On 1 September 1939, the opening shots of World War II were fired on the tiny **Westerplatte** peninsula *(see p249)*, which is now a pilgrimage site with burned-out bunkers, a memorial and a museum.

POMERANIA

- **Gothic Toruń**
- **Summer fun in Sopot**
- **Ethnic enclave in Kashubia**

Founded by the Teutonic Knights, **Toruń** *(see pp270–73)* features the second-largest ensemble of Gothic architecture in Poland. The birthplace of Nicolaus Copernicus, Toruń is also known as the traditional home of gingerbread. The seaside town of **Sopot** *(see p263)* is the country's unofficial summer capital and a non-stop party venue for the three hottest months of the year.

Kashubia *(see p262)*, known as the Polish Switzerland, is a gloriously peaceful area of lakes and rolling hills. The Kashubians are a distinctive ethnic group with their own language and culture.

WARMIS, MAZURIA AND THE BIAŁYSTOK REGION

- **Fun on the Mazurian Lakes**
- **Copernicus's Frombork**
- **The bison of Białowieża**

Sail or canoe on **Lake Śniardwy** *(see pp284–5)* and explore the beautiful scenery of eastern Poland, full of peaceful harbours and tiny villages. On the Baltic coast is sleepy **Frombork** *(see p278)*, where the astronomer Nicolaus Copernicus spent most of his life in the town's beautifully preserved 14th-century Gothic cathedral. For a spectacular nature holiday, head to **Białowieża National Park** *(see p291)*. A landscape of rivers and canals, where the last bison in Europe live, it is also a bird-watching paradise.

The exceptionally well-preserved Gothic cathedral at Frombork

Putting Poland on the Map

Poland covers an area of 312,685 sq km (120,696 sq miles) and is located in the centre of Europe. It borders Lithuania, Belarus and the Ukraine to the east, Slovakia and the Czech Republic to the south, and Germany to the west. In the north, Poland's coastline stretches for 528 km (330 miles) on the Baltic Sea and borders Kaliningrad, an enclave of Russia. Poland has a population of 38.6 million, making it the eighth most highly populated country in Europe. The capital, Warsaw, has over 1.7 million inhabitants.

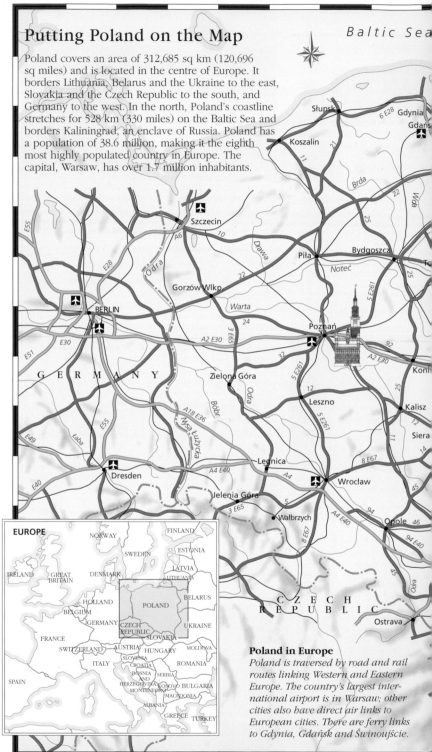

Poland in Europe
Poland is traversed by road and rail routes linking Western and Eastern Europe. The country's largest international airport is in Warsaw; other cities also have direct air links to European cities. There are ferry links to Gdynia, Gdańsk and Świnoujście.

KEY

✈ Airport

⚓ Port

▭ Motorway

▬ Major road

— Railway

—·— National border

A PORTRAIT OF POLAND

Growing numbers of tourists visit Poland every year. Even so, it is still a relatively unknown country. To travellers crossing the lowlands from Eastern to Western Europe, there may not appear to be the diversity in landscape and buildings seen in other European countries. The pages that follow show the visitor the variety that Poland has to offer, in terms of its culture, history and landscape.

Although it is situated in the plains of central Europe, Poland has a varied landscape. Alpine scenery predominates in the Tatra Mountains along the country's southern border, while the north is dominated by lakelands, which contrast with the landscape of the Baltic coast. For those who like unspoiled natural scenery, there are areas of primeval forests in Białowieża and extensive marshlands along the banks of the River Biebrza which are a haven for many rare bird and plant species. About 30 per cent of the area of Poland is woodland, including a number of vast forests covering more than 1,000 sq km (390 sq miles). Most of these consist of coniferous trees and mixed woodland, but there are also many forests of deciduous trees, mainly oak and hornbeam, or beech.

The Polish eagle

Many areas of great natural beauty are protected as national parks or reserves. Mountain lovers can make use of the well-developed infrastructure of hostels and other shelters, such as those found in the Beskid Sądecki or the Tatra Mountains; the more adventurous can explore the unfrequented and almost inaccessible Beskid Niski or Bieszczady. All areas have clearly marked hiking trails and well-equipped shelters *(schroniska)*. The countless lakes of Warmia and Mazuria, areas known as the Land of a Thousand Lakes *(Kraina Tysiąca Jezior)* are a haven for watersports enthusiasts, as are the waters of Pomerania and Wielkopolska. The lakes are popular with canoeists and in summer are dotted with rowing and sailing boats.

The Bzura, one of Poland's many unspoiled rivers

◁ A rural chapel in winter

A summer's day on a sandy Baltic beach

POPULATION AND RELIGION

Poland's inhabitants, who number almost 39 million, all but constitute a single ethnic group, with minorities accounting for less than 4 per cent of the population. The largest minorities are Belarussians and Ukrainians, who inhabit the east of the country, and Germans, who are concentrated mainly around the city of Opole in Silesia.

The vast majority of Poles are Catholic, but large regions of the country, such as Cieszyn Silesia, have a substantial Protestant population, and followers of other denominations are also widely dispersed. In the east of the country there are many Orthodox Christians; here, religious denomina-

Lacemaker from Koniakowo

tion does not necessarily coincide with ethnic identity, although Belarussians tend to be Orthodox while Ukrainians belong to the Greek Catholic (Uniate) Church. In the Białystok region there are villages where Catholics, Orthodox Christians and Muslims – the descendants of Tartar settlers – live side by side. As in Spain and Ireland, the fact that the majority of the population is Catholic continues to exert a major influence on the moral values of the country, as well as on its political life. An example of this is the many debates in the Sejm (the lower house of the Polish parliament) that have alternately limited and liberalized the right to abortion.

Religion, however, is not a major factor in the way that Poles vote, as election results show. The political scene is divided between the supporters of the right and the post-communist left. In the first decade of the 21st century, the Polish electorate showed itself to be quite unstable, with each elected government standing in opposition to the previous one.

Pump room at the spa of Polanica-Zdrój

Religious belief is outwardly expressed by a deep reverence for religious symbols and rituals. Wayside crosses and shrines to the saints or the Virgin Mary add charm to the Polish countryside. The main religious festivals – Christmas, Easter, Corpus Christi and Assumption, as well as All Saints' Day, when almost everyone in Poland, regardless of their religious denomination, visits the graves of relatives – are solemnly observed. An unusual cult surrounds the Virgin. For centuries, believers from all over Poland and further afield have made the pilgrimage to the image of the Black Madonna in Częstochowa *(see pp156–7)*. Indeed, throughout Poland there are shrines to the Virgin, to whom miraculous powers have been ascribed. Another famous pilgrimage is made by Orthodox Christians to the holy mountain of Grabarka *(see p291)*. Poland is also visited by Jews from all over the world who come in remembrance of the millions who died there during the Holocaust under German occupation of the country during World War II.

Corpus Christi procession

CULTURAL VARIETY AND SHIFTING BORDERS

Magnificent buildings bearing witness to past splendours can be seen at almost every step. Most of these monuments are in Małopolska, Lubelszczyzna, Wielkopolska and Lower Silesia. Not all of them, however, belong to Polish culture, since the country's frontiers have changed many times over the centuries. A particularly important change came at the end of World War II, when the Allies approved a westward shift of Poland's borders. As a result, the inhabitants of the eastern areas, lost to Poland after the war, were resettled, and many were sent to the western regions, inhabited by Germans – who were in turn displaced.

Restored market square of the Old Town, Wrocław

A poster by Maria Pałasińska dedicated to Solidarity

The legacy of more than 100 years of partition rule is still visible in Poland's cultural landscape today. Russian, Prussian and Austrian administration left their mark not only on rural and urban architecture but also on the customs and mentality of the Polish people.

DEMOCRATIC CHANGE AND ECONOMIC DEVELOPMENT

The fall of communism in Poland came about largely thanks to the efforts of the trade union Solidarity (Solidarność), which was founded in 1980 but forced to go underground after the imposition of martial law. When the democratic opposition won the elections to the Sejm and the Senate in 1989, Poland again became a country with a parliamentary democracy and a market economy. This was important enough in itself, but it had wider implications too: by tackling its inefficient, crisis-ridden socialist economy, Poland had set the standard for economic reform in Central and Eastern Europe as a whole. Many Polish industries were priva-

Logo of the Polish stock exchange

tized, and the drastic reforms that were carried through over a number of years accelerated Poland's GDP to make it the fastest-growing in Europe. By the end of the 1990s, the Polish economy had become largely resistant to crisis.

The country has a substantial foreign trade deficit, but this is balanced by the surplus produced by an unofficial cross-border trade. There are, however, negative aspects of the reforms – among them the budget deficit and unemployment. The latter continues to be high. The problem of unemployment is somewhat mitigated by the illegal employment of workers, although this is usually confined to small firms. There is an ambitious programme of privatization, but it has not yet been fully completed, and some enterprises are still state-owned.

Heavy industry tends to be outdated, unprofitable and economically inefficient. There is an ongoing systematic programme of coal-mine closure, and former mineworkers have been forced to look for work elsewhere.

Session of the Sejm, the lower house of the Polish parliament

The Pazim, the second-tallest building in Szczecin

Political and economic changes have had their impact on Poland's towns and cities. Old buildings are being renovated, attention is being paid to the environment, new shops have appeared, and large out-of-town supermarkets and modern petrol (gas) stations have sprung up. New buildings – though not always architecturally distinctive – are going up everywhere. Market squares and main streets in many Polish towns have been pedestrianized. In many of the old towns that suffered damage during World War II – including Szczecin, Kołobrzeg, Głogów and Elbląg – buildings are now being reconstructed. Smaller towns, too – swelled by sprawling apartment housing after the war – are now acquiring more traditional buildings. Nonetheless, the vast concrete housing developments typical of the communist era still dominate many Polish townscapes.

Not surprisingly, this has brought considerable social and economic problems in its wake.

The archaic farming system is another candidate for restructuring. Polish farming is still based on traditional family smallholdings consisting of no more than a few acres of land. It is seriously under-mechanized and requires a disproportionate amount of manpower.

A fundamental part of the reform process was Poland's drive to join Western military and economic structures. In 1999, Poland became a member of NATO, and then in 2004, it joined the European Union. This required harmonization of the Polish legal and economic systems with those of the EU countries, providing a further powerful incentive to change.

Many modern public buildings – mainly office blocks – are springing up, too. Much of the new development is centred on the capital, Warsaw, although commercial investment is now slowly beginning to filter through to other cities, among them Cracow, Katowice, the Baltic conurbation of Gdańsk, Sopot and Gdynia, and Wrocław, Poznań and Łódź as well.

The privatized Grupa Kęty SA metalworks

The Landscape of Poland

Poland's landscape is very varied. The south of the country is bounded by mountain ranges which, the further north you travel, gradually turn into areas punctuated by hills and low-lying ancient forests. Northern Poland, an area of great natural beauty, has been shaped by a succession of glaciers that moved southwards from Scandinavia. National parks and reserves have been established in many areas. The central regions of the country, consisting of lowlands, merge into picturesque lakelands and coastal plains.

A cabbage white on a meadow flower

FAUNA OF POLAND

The most typical Polish wildlife – including wild boar, deer and hare – is to be found in mixed and deciduous forests. Some species, such as bison and capercaillie, are found almost nowhere else in Europe. In the Carpathian and Sudety mountains, bears and lynxes may be seen.

Roman snail

MOUNTAINS

LAKELAND SCENERY

The Tatra Mountains *(see pp164–5)* are the highest in Central Europe. Though covering a small area, they provide breathtaking alpine scenery. The High Tatras *(Tatry Wysokie)* are mainly granite, with jagged, rocky peaks. At 2,499 m (8,200 ft) above sea level, Rysy is the highest peak in Poland. The Western Tatras *(Tatry Zachodnie)*, consisting of sedimentary rock and crystalline shale, are inhabited by such rare animals as brown bears, marmots and chamois.

Nutcracker

The lakelands that cover much of northern Poland consist of picturesque moraine woodland and thousands of lakes. Largest and most scenic are the Great Mazurian Lakes, in a district known as the Land of a Thousand Lakes *(Kraina Tysiąca Jezior)*. Abounding in forests, marshes and peat bogs, they are a haven for many bird species: the largest concentration of storks in Europe, swans, grebes, cranes and cormorants.

Crane

The crocus (Crocus satinus) *blooms in early spring in mountain valleys and alpine meadows, mainly in the Tatras and Babia Góra ranges.*

Bog arum (Calla palustra) *is a poisonous perennial plant with a characteristic white leaf below a globular flower. It grows in peat bogs.*

The silver thistle (Carlina acaulis) *is a protected plant. Its leaves form a rosette containing a basket-like flower with a covering of dry, silvery leaves.*

The great sundew (Drosera anglica), *an insect-eating plant found in peat bogs, is a protected species in Poland.*

Deer, *which live in herds, are a relatively common sight in Poland's deciduous and mixed forests. They are hunted as game animals.*

Marmots, *rodents of the beaver family, live in the Tatra Mountains. They 'whistle' when disturbed.*

Wild boar, *widespread in Poland, are the ancestors of the domestic pig. Deciduous and mixed forests are their principal habitat.*

Moose *live in large forests, marshes and peat bogs, even near large cities. Large populations of them can be seen in Kampinoski National Park and in the Białystok region.*

THE LOWLANDS

The apparent monotony of the lowlands is broken by elevations, meandering rivers, marshes and peat bogs. Most of the land is under cultivation, but there are also extensive forests. Białowieża Forest *(see p291)* shelters bison. Moose can be seen in the marshes and storks in the lakes.

Hoopoe

THE COAST

The sandy beaches of Poland's Baltic coast are among the finest in Europe. They are situated by sand dunes or cliffs, and were it not for river estuaries, it would be possible to walk along them for the entire length of the coast. Narrow sandy spits formed by the coastal currents and known as *mierzeje* are a characteristic feature of the shoreline.

Seagull

The corn poppy (Papaver rhoeas) *is becoming increasingly rare as it is weeded out from cereal crops.*

Lyme grass (Elymus arenarius) *grows on the sand dunes. It has pointed leaves and its roots bind the sandy subsoil.*

Toadflax (Linaria vulgaris) *has narrow leaves and yellow-orange flowers with a characteristic spur. It grows in ditches and on wasteland.*

Marram grass (Ammophila arenarea) *has narrow grey-green leaves, and flowers between June and August. Like lyme grass, it helps to bind the sand dunes where it grows.*

Early Polish Architecture

A Romanesque capital

Over the centuries, and particularly during World War II, Poland lost a great deal of its architectural heritage. However, major efforts on the part of both private individuals and the government have meant that many important buildings have been restored, and in some cases completely rebuilt. Royal and aristocratic palaces, churches, castles and entire streets of old towns can thus be admired today. Traditional wooden buildings are another interesting feature of Polish architecture.

Renaissance courtyard at Wawel Royal Castle

ROMANESQUE ARCHITECTURE

The Romanesque style of architecture seen in Polish cathedrals, palace chapels and monasteries flourished largely as a result of the country's conversion to Christianity in the 10th century. Unfortunately, few Romanesque buildings have survived intact. Among those that have are the collegiate church at Tum near Łęczyca *(see p229)* and the monastery at Czerwińsk *(see p114)*, both of which are decorated with stone carvings. The Romanesque style reached its apogee during the 12th century.

Semicircular presbytery

Triforium with decorative columns

Narrow windows that also served defensive purposes

The collegiate church at Tum near Łęczyca, *dating from the mid-12th century, is Poland's largest surviving Romanesque religious building.*

This 12th-century Romanesque doorway *is from the Cathedral of St Mary Magdalene (see p190).*

GOTHIC ARCHITECTURE

Gothic elements began to appear in late Romanesque architecture in the early 13th century; this transitional style can be seen in the abbeys at Wąchock, Sulejów and Koprzywnica. By the end of the century, the Gothic style was prevalent throughout Polish architecture. Many fortified castles were built at this time, more than 80 being founded by Kazimierz the Great. Notable examples are those at Będzin, Ogrodzieniec and Bobolice *(see pp158–9)*. Gothic churches and monasteries were also built throughout the country, fine examples surviving in Cracow and Wrocław. The oldest surviving wooden churches, such as that at Dębno, date from the same period. In Polish provincial architecture, the Gothic style persisted until the early 17th century.

The 15th-century church at Dębno (see p165) *is one of the oldest surviving wooden churches in Poland.*

The doorway of the early 15th-century Church of St Catherine *in Cracow has an ornamental stepped frame.*

THE RENAISSANCE AND MANNERISM

Renaissance architecture was introduced to Poland in the early 16th century by the Italian architect Bartolomeo Berrecci, who designed Wawel Royal Castle and the Zygmunt Chapel in Cracow. Many of the churches in Mazovia (as at Pułtusk and Płock) were influenced by the Italian Renaissance, as were the town halls in Poznań and Sandomierz. From the mid-16th century onwards, buildings in Pomerania were designed in the northern Mannerist style.

Decorative ceilings *such as those in the churches of Lubelszczyzna and Kalisz illustrate provincial interpretations of Renaissance and Mannerist forms.*

The Zygmunt Chapel (see p143) *is one of the finest examples of Renaissance architecture in Poland.*

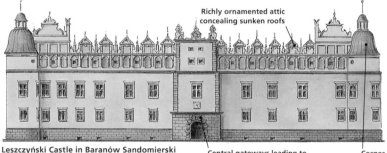

Richly ornamented attic concealing sunken roofs

Leszczyński Castle in Baranów Sandomierski (see p153) *is one of the few surviving late Renaissance buildings in Poland.*

Central gateways leading to a courtyard surrounded by cloisters

Corner lookout turret

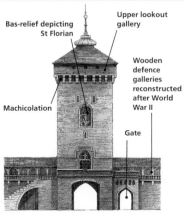

Upper lookout gallery

Bas-relief depicting St Florian

Wooden defence galleries reconstructed after World War II

Machicolation

Gate

The Florian Gate in Cracow (see p134), *a surviving city watchtower with Gothic fortifications, dates from the 13th to 15th centuries.*

ARCHITECTURE OF THE AGE OF THE TEUTONIC KNIGHTS

The Teutonic Knights, who ruled Eastern Pomerania and Prussia in the 13th and 14th centuries, left impressive brick-built Gothic buildings (such as those at Malbork, Gniew and Bytów) and city walls (as at Chełmno and Toruń), and founded numerous churches.

The imposing bulk of the Upper Castle, part of the Malbork Castle complex

Later Polish Architecture

Buildings dating from the Baroque era are quite a
common sight in Polish towns and cities. Many
distinctive 19th-century residences and architectural
ensembles are also noteworthy, as in Łódź;. Around
1900, at a period coinciding with that of Art Nouveau,
attempts to build in a Polish national style produced
particularly felicitous results. Folk architecture is
another area of great interest. The best way to
explore it is to visit the *skansens* (open-air museums)
which exist in each region of the country.

Baroque cartouche with
the emblem of Poland

BAROQUE ARCHITECTURE

In the first half of the 17th
century, architects of Italian
descent started to introduce the
early Baroque style to Poland.
Nobles built imposing residences,
chief among them Krzyżtopór
Castle in Ujazd *(see pp44–5 and
p152)*, in the Mannerist style,
and the fortified early Baroque
palace in Łańcut *(see pp172–3)*.
Italian architects were also
commissioned to design the
Royal Palace in Warsaw, the
country's new capital. The
destruction wrought during the
Polish-Swedish war was followed
by a period of building in the
late Baroque style. In Warsaw,
the renowned Dutch architect
Tylman van Gameren designed
a large number of buildings,
alongside Italian architects.
During the rule of the Saxon
kings in Poland, architects from
Dresden designed many new
buildings in Warsaw, as well
as palaces like the one at
Białystok *(see p290)*.

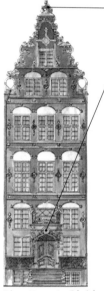

High gable framed
by volutes

Pediment decorated with
coat of arms

Edena House *in Gdańsk
is a fine example of the
Mannerist style.*

Kodeń Church, *with its broken
façade, is typical of the late
Baroque period.*

Steep broken
roof

Bay window with a
decorative gable

This country house in Koszuty (see p211) *is a
typical example of an aristocrat's country seat
in the Baroque style.*

Porch in front of
main entrance

Corner
turrets

NEO-CLASSICISM

Neo-Classicism appeared in Poland after the rule of Stanisław August Poniatowski, the country's last king. The Royal Palace and Łazienki Palace in Warsaw were built in the Neo-Classical style, as were many others including those at Lubostroń and Śmiełów. Features included landscaped gardens in the English manner.

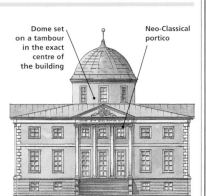

Dome set on a tambour in the exact centre of the building

Neo-Classical portico

The town hall in Łowicz *is an example of small-town public buildings in the Neo-Classical style of the early 19th century.*

Lubostroń Palace (see p221) *is a fine example of Palladianism, a refined Neo-Classical style imitating the work of the Italian Renaissance architect Andrea Palladio – in this case, his Villa Rotonda at Vicenza.*

HISTORICISM AND MODERNISM

The second half of the 19th century saw a proliferation of Neo-Gothic, Neo-Renaissance and Neo-Baroque buildings. In the 1880s there was a movement towards creating an architecture in the Polish national style, which gave rise to some very picturesque structures. Art Nouveau was short-lived in Poland, although it did leave a number of attractive buildings, primarily in Łódź.

The wooden chapel at Jaszczurówka *is an example of a building in the Polish national style.*

The Warsaw School of Economics *combines modern features and traditional elements.*

TRADITIONAL ARCHITECTURE

Fine examples of wooden architecture can be found today at most *skansens*. Log cabins, often with thatched roofs, can still be seen in many villages in Poland.

Painted interior of a peasant dwelling in Zalipie

Beehive in human form

Windmill at the *skansen* **(open-air museum) in Wdzydze Kiszewskie**

The Literature of Poland

Stanisław Wyspiański

Polish literature has always been inextricably linked to the historical development of the country, as the political situation, particularly over the last two centuries, has not always favoured freedom of speech. Many writers were forced to emigrate, while those who remained were often obliged to publish their works in other countries. Poland boasts four winners of the Nobel Prize for Literature: Henryk Sienkiewicz, Władysław S. Reymont, Czesław Miłosz and Wisława Szymborska.

THE MIDDLE AGES

Polish writing originates in the 11th century. The earliest works were in Latin, often written by people from other regions who copied hagiographies and holy chronicles. The oldest Polish chronicle, by the Benedictine monk Gall Anonim, dates from the beginning of the 12th century. Native Polish writers soon appeared, and Polish literature expanded into all the literary forms known in Europe at the time. The first work in the Polish language was written in the second half of the 13th century. The earliest religious song in Polish, *The Mother of God (Bogurodzica)*, was probably written at the end of the 13th century, although it is not found in manuscript until the 15th century. The Polish *Holy Cross Sermons (Kazania świętokrzyskie)* date from around 1450.

Jan Kochanowski writing *Treny*, a lament for his daughter's death

RENAISSANCE AND BAROQUE

The Renaissance is regarded as the Golden Age of Polish literature, when both prose and poetry flourished. Mikołaj Rej (1505–69), the first significant writer in the Polish language, is generally regarded as the father of Polish literature. The most prominent poet of the time was Jan Kochanowski (1530–84), who wrote the first Polish tragedy, entitled *The Dismissal of the Greek Envoys (Odprawa posłów greckich)*. He was also the author of the humorous *Trifles (Fraszki)* and the sorrowful *Laments (Treny)*, a lament in the form of a cycle of 19 poems. Other notable figures among Poland's early poets are Mikołaj Sęp Szarzyński (1550–81) and Szymon Szymonowic (1558–1629).

The ancient Sarmatian culture had a great influence on Polish Baroque literature. The greatest works of the period are by Jan Chryzostom Pasek (1636–1701), who wrote highly colourful accounts both of great historical events and of the everyday life of the Polish nobility in the reign of Jan III Sobieski.

Romantic poet Adam Mickiewicz by Walenty Wańkowicz

THE ENLIGHTENMENT AND THE 19TH CENTURY

The Enlightenment, and particularly the reign of the last king of Poland, Stanisław August Poniatowski, was an important period in the development of Polish literature. The first Polish novel, *The Adventures of Mikołaj Doświadczyński (Mikołaja Doświadczyńskiego przypadki)*, was written by Bishop Ignacy Krasicki (1735–1801), a moralist and satirical poet.

POLISH CINEMA

The first Polish feature film was made as early as 1902, but it was not until after World War II that Polish film-makers achieved international renown. The best-known Polish film directors include Andrzej Wajda, whose *Man of Iron* won the Palme d'Or at the 1981 Cannes Film Festival, Krzysztof Zanussi, Krzysztof Kieślowski *(Decalogue, Three Colours – Blue/White/Red)* and Roman Polański *(Chinatown)*, who has spent many years making films in the USA and France.

Scene from J. Hoffman's film *Colonel Michael*

Polish Romantic poetry played an important role in keeping nationalist sentiment alive. The outstanding writers of that time, Adam Mickiewicz, Juliusz Słowacki and Zygmunt Krasiński, wrote outside Poland. To this day, their work forms the canon of patriotic literature, whose jewel in the crown is Mickiewicz's *Pan Tadeusz*, which is both a nostalgic evocation of the vanishing traditions of the nobility and a vision of the emergence of more modern social attitudes. Also notable at this time was the comedy writer Aleksander Fredro, whose works include *Revenge (Zemsta)* and *Husband and Wife (Mąż i Żona)*. Another writer who holds a prominent place in the history of Polish Romantic literature is Cyprian Kamil Norwid, regarded as the precursor of modernism. Eliza Orzeszkowa (1840–1910) and Bolesław Prus (1847–1912) are the principal figures in the next phase of the development of the Polish novel. Another major writer of this time was Henryk Sienkiewicz (1846–1916), best known in Poland for his trilogy of historical novels describing events in 17th-century Poland and *The Teutonic Knights (Krzyżacy)*, which is devoted to the late 14th and early 15th centuries. Outside Poland, Sienkiewicz is better known for *Quo Vadis?*, which deals with the beginnings of Christianity and for which he was awarded the Nobel Prize for Literature in 1905.

20TH- AND 21ST-CENTURY LITERATURE

From 1900 onwards Young Poland *(Młoda Polska)*, a modern trend in Polish literature particularly associated with the artistic community of Cracow, began to emerge. A key role in this was played by Stanisław Wyspiański (1869–1907), author of the Symbolist play *The Wedding (Wesele)*, which was made into a film by Andrzej Wajda 70 years later. Also influential in Young Poland was a Bohemian group surrounding Stanisław Przybyszewski, a friend of Henrik Ibsen and Edvard Munch.

Another Nobel laureate was Władysław Reymont (1865–1925), who wrote society novels. He was awarded the Nobel Prize in 1924 for *The Peasants (Chłopi)*, which describes the lives of the inhabitants of a village near Łowicz. Between the wars, avant-garde writers such as Stanisław Ignacy Witkiewicz (called Witkacy, 1885–1939), Bruno Schulz (1893–1942) and Witold Gombrowicz (1904–69) came to prominence.

Wisława Szymborska receiving the Nobel Prize for Literature

Monument to Aleksander Fredro in Wrocław

Polish literature after World War II spawned many famous writers, several of whom wrote from abroad for political reasons. Stanisław Lem (1921–2006) wrote philosophical science fiction, which has been translated into many languages. His *Solaris* was made into a film twice – in 1972 by Andrei Tarkovsky and in 2002 by Steven Soderbergh. Tadeusz Różewicz, also well known as a poet, and Sławomir Mrożek are prominent playwrights. Hanna Krall and Ryszard Kapuściński (1932–2007) are known for their documentary-writing. Andrzej Szczypiorski, who wrote *A Mass for Arras (Msza za miasto Arras)* and *The Beginning (Początek)*, has also achieved international recognition. Contemporary poetry has a special place in Polish literature. Apart from Tadeusz Różewicz, its main exponents are Zbigniew Herbert, Ryszard Krynicki and Stanisław Barańczak. The best illustration of the achievements of contemporary Polish writers is the award of two Nobel Prizes: in 1980 to Czesław Miłosz and in 1996 to the Cracow poetess Wisława Szymborska.

Nobel Prize winner Czesław Miłosz

The Music of Poland

Poland has made a major contribution to the international music scene, as much through the works of great composers as through its renowned jazz musicians and colourful folk music. Polish classical composers such as Fryderyk Chopin (1810–49), Stanisław Moniuszko (1819–72), Karol Szymanowski (1882–1937) and Wojciech Kilar (born 1932) have often been inspired by folk music, as have modern jazz and rock musicians. Poland has also given the world such outstanding musical performers as the tenor Jan Kiepura and the pianists Artur Rubinstein and Witold Małcużyński.

Fryderyk Chopin in a portrait by Eugène Delacroix

EARLY MUSIC

Although they are not widely known, there is much of interest in the works of early Polish composers. Mikołaj z Radomia, a composer of the first half of the 15th century, produced both religious and secular works. In the Renaissance, composers such as Wacław of Szamotuły and Mikołaj Gomółka brought Polish music into the European mainstream. The first Polish opera stage was set up in the 17th century at the court of Władysław IV. Court and religious music flourished at that time, and the works of such composers as Adam Jarzębski, Stanisław S. Szarzyński and Marcin Mielczewski are still widely performed by Polish musicians today.

THE 19TH AND 20TH CENTURIES

The most prominent Polish composer of the Romantic era was undoubtedly Fryderyk Chopin (1810–49), who composed almost exclusively for the piano. Chopin contributed to the establishment of a Polish national style in music, and exerted a great influence on the development of European piano music. During his short life he composed a large number of preludes, mazurkas, polonaises, waltzes, études and other pieces. Many of Chopin's works contain elements of folk music. The Chopin Piano Competition, held in Warsaw, has been a regular event since 1927, and award-winners have gone on to become world-famous pianists.

Stanisław Moniuszko is regarded as the father of the Polish national opera. His most famous operas are *Halka*, inspired by highland folklore, and *The Haunted House (Straszny dwór)*, which evokes the traditions of the Polish nobility.

In the second half of the 19th century, the violinist Henryk Wieniawski and the pianist Ignacy Paderewski achieved world renown. The latter was also prominent in politics, serving for a time as Prime Minister of Poland.

Before World War I, the town of Zakopane was a major centre of Polish culture. It drew not only artists but also composers who sought inspiration from the landscape of the Tatra Mountains and the colourful folklore of the highland dwellers. Among composers associated with Zakopane is Mieczysław Karłowicz (1876–1909), noted especially for his symphonies. Karłowicz perished tragically in an avalanche in the Tatras at the young age of 33. Another frequent visitor to Zakopane was Karol Szymanowski, whose fascination with the folk music of the region inspired him to

Stanisław Moniuszko

compose a number of works, including the ballet *Harnasie*.

One of the best-known modern composers is Krzysztof Penderecki (b. 1933), whose oeuvre includes epic symphonies, oratorios and operas. His opera *The Devils of Loudun (Diabły z Loudun)* has been performed all over the world. Other prominent composers of international standing are Andrzej Panufnik (1914–91), Witold Lutosławski (1913–94) and Henryk Górecki (1933–2010), whose works include the outstanding Symphony No. 3, which has topped the classical music charts for years. Other major composers of symphonic music are Wojciech Kilar (b. 1932) and Zbigniew Preisner (b. 1955), most widely known for their film music.

Folk band outside the Cloth Hall (Sukiennica) in Cracow

The composer and conductor Krzysztof Penderecki

JAZZ

Jazz traditions in Poland go back to the time of the Second Republic. After World War II, jazz was deemed by the authorities to be "alien to the working class", and it was not until 1956 that jazz could be performed in public. An important jazz musician of that time was the pianist and composer Krzysztof Komeda (1931–69), who wrote the popular lullaby for Roman Polański's film, *Rosemary's Baby*.

During the 1960s, other jazz musicians came to prominence, including Adam Makowicz, Tomasz Stańko and Michał Urbaniak. Jazz clubs opened throughout the country, and the Warsaw Jazz Jamboree, first held in 1958, became the world's biggest jazz festival. Another renowned festival is Jazz on the Oder, held in Wrocław.

Many jazz musicians came to public recognition in the 1970s and 1980s, among them the pianist and saxophonist Włodzimierz Nahorny, the saxophonists Zbigniew Namysłowski and Janusz Muniak, and the pianist Sławomir Kulpowicz.

FOLK MUSIC

Polish folk music is unusually colourful. Every region has its own specific tradition, and the music of the Tatra Mountains is unique. Folk bands play quite a basic range of instruments, the main one being the fiddle, and sometimes bagpipes or drums and basses. Depending on the region these instruments are supplemented by clarinets, horns, accordions and occasionally dulcimers.

The best way of getting to know and enjoy Polish folk music is to attend some of the concerts traditionally held during the summer months, such as the Kazimierz or Zakopane festivals. Here there is a chance to listen to live music being played and to watch the dance groups that perform in colourful folk costumes.

Polish vocal and dance groups have brought worldwide popularity to Polish folk music. The Mazowsze group, for example, gives stage performances that are inspired by the folk traditions of various regions.

The Warsaw Jazz Jamboree

The Traditional Nobility

The tradition of the Polish nobility was dominated by the idea of Sarmatism, which was based on the myth that the Polish aristocracy were descended from a warrior people called the Sarmatians. Sarmatism was influential in shaping the ideology of the ruling class, as well as its customs and lifestyle. A Sarmatian embraced the old order, was patriotic and Catholic, and at the same time valued freedom and privilege, lived life as a landowner and upheld family traditions. Sarmatism played an important part in art and literature, particularly memoirs.

Aristocratic figurine in porcelain

A kulawka *was a special toasting goblet for drinking "bottoms up", as it could only be set down on its rim.*

Noblemen's houses *were typically single-storey buildings fronted by an imposing colonnade. Rooms flanked the central entrance hall.*

Turban

Headpiece with heron feathers

Kontusz in the style worn by ladies

Wyloty – slit sleeves rolled back and over the shoulder

A TRADITIONAL BEVERAGE

Mead was a favourite drink of the Polish aristocracy. It is made by fermenting wort, a solution of honey and water that has been flavoured with herbs. The most popular type of mead is *trójniak*, in which honey makes up one-third of the total wort. The rarest is *półtorak*, with two parts honey and one part water. Although mead is no longer widely drunk, it is still produced today.

Stolnik mead

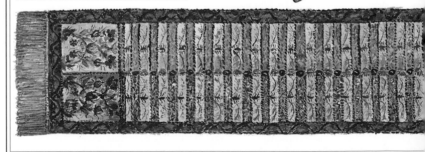

An election gathering, *at which the nobility elected the king, is portrayed here. This was one of the greatest privileges exercised by the gentry.*

COATS OF ARMS

The coats of arms of aristocratic families in Poland number no more than about 200. They were held in common by members of clans with different names. Aristocratic titles were not used at the time of the Republic (with the exception of the titles of Lithuanian princes), while magnate families looked to foreign rulers for titles. Polish heraldic symbols usually had their origins in individual symbols; they were therefore relatively simple and differed from those of Western Europe.

POLISH NATIONAL DRESS

Required attire of the nobility in the Baroque era, its main elements were the żupan *(a kind of shirt) and the* kontusz *(an outer garment tied with a waistband). Headgear took the form of either a* kołpak *(fur hat) or a square-bottomed* rogatywka. *Men wore their hair short and sported a moustache, and sometimes a beard.*

Kołpak

Żupan

Cielątkowa

Łodzia

Szreniawa

Wyloty

Kontusz sash

The kontusz was an outer garment with cutout sleeves, which were thrown over the shoulders.

Coffin portraits *of the deceased were painted in oils on metal plates cut to the shape of the cross-section of a coffin, to which they were attached during funerals.*

The karabela was a traditional sword that had a single-sided blade and a highly ornamented handle, often with inlaid precious stones.

Silk sashes known *as* kontusze *were an indispensable part of a nobleman's attire. Several yards in length, they were worn wrapped around the waist and tied in a decorative knot, allowing the tassels to hang downwards.*

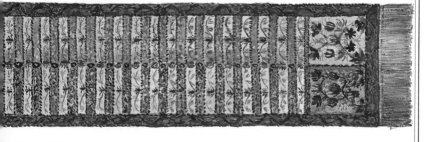

The Different Religions of Poland

Roadside shrine

Although the majority of the Polish population today is Roman Catholic, in the course of the country's history its inhabitants have adhered to a variety of faiths. Besides Roman Catholics, there have been Orthodox Christians, Uniates and Jews (most of whom lost their lives in World War II), and, since the 16th century, Lutheran and Calvinist Protestants. When the Polish borders were redrawn after World War II, a large section of the Eastern Orthodox population found itself in Belarus or the Ukraine. At the same time, the western border moved further westwards, incorporating many German Protestant churches. The wide variety of Poland's ecclesiastical architecture bears witness to the many cultures and religions that have existed there.

The Convent of the Old Believers at Wojnowo *is one of the few places where this religious group can still be found.*

Orthodox Christians *today are found mainly in the eastern parts of the country, where many of their historic churches still stand.*

The Evangelical Reform Church in Warsaw *was built after the Reformation and used by the small group of Calvinist believers in Poland.*

The Basilica of the Holy Cross and the Birth of the Holy Mother (*Bazylika Krzyża Świętego i Narodzenia Matki Boskiej*) has the second-tallest church tower in Poland.

The cemetery at Kruszyniany, *one of the few Muslim burial grounds in Poland, is used by people of Tartar descent.*

The 'Church of Peace' (Kościół Pokoju) *at Świdnica was one of three churches to be built specifically for Silesian Protestants after the Thirty Years' War, which ended in 1648.*

OTHER DENOMINATIONS

Some of Poland's historic churches have changed denomination over the years – for instance, when Polish Catholics took over disused Protestant churches. Although the original interiors have generally not survived, the exteriors have often been carefully conserved. Some religious denominations no longer have followers in Poland, although their places of worship remain. An example is the Mennonite chapel in Gdańsk.

Old Mennonite chapel in Gdańsk

Open-air altar

Pauline monastery

Judaic *artifacts in museums are poignant vestiges of the synagogues that were once so numerous in Poland. As a result of the Holocaust and the ensuing communist era, there are few Jews in Poland today.*

CZĘSTOCHOWA PILGRIMAGE

The Monastery of Jasna Góra in Częstochowa is the most important Catholic shrine in Poland – and one of the greatest in the Christian world. The image of Our Lady of Częstochowa, also known as the Black Madonna, draws pilgrims all year round. The main pilgrimage, which attracts hundreds of thousands of believers from Poland and beyond, is held in the meadows at the foot of the monastery on 15 August each year.

The picturesque wooden churches *of the Ukrainian Uniates, or Greek Catholics, built for the Lemk and the Boyk minorities, survive in the Carpathian Mountains. Their congregations were resettled in other areas during Operation Vistula after World War II.*

POLAND THROUGH THE YEAR

Tourists tend to visit Poland in the summer, between June and September. During that period, the most popular tourist spots are crowded, and a variety of open-air events, from street theatre festivals to re-enactments of medieval tournaments, take place throughout the country. The main music and drama festivals are held in spring and

Gingerbread heart

autumn. The best way of spending winter in Poland is skiing in the mountains. As the majority of Poles are Catholics, traditional Catholic feast days are the most important holidays. The celebrations that take place at Christmas, Easter, and Corpus Christi as well as other local church festivals are interesting spectacles for tourists.

SPRING

The official beginning of spring, 21 March, is an unofficial day of truancy among young people in Poland. The tourist season begins with the first warm days of spring.

MARCH

Topienie Marzanny (*23 Mar)* is the day when, in many areas, children throw small dolls – symbolizing winter – into rivers.
The International Poster Biennial *(even-numbered years)*, Warsaw.
Festival of Stage Songs, Wrocław. Polish and international performers take part.
International Dance Group Presentation, Kalisz.
International Festival of Alternative Theatre, Cracow.

Passion play in Kalwaria Zebrzydowska

APRIL

Palm Sunday (the Sunday before Easter) is the day when "palms" are blessed in the churches. The most colourful celebrations take place in villages in Kurpie and Małopolska – in particular Rabka, Lipnica Murowana and Tokarnia. During Holy Week (the week leading up to Easter), mystery plays are performed in churches around the country. The oldest and best-known spectacle is *Chwalebne Misterium Pańskie*, a passion play which has been performed in Kalwaria Zebrzydowska *(see p161)* since the 17th century. On **Holy Saturday**, Easter food is taken to church in baskets and blessed. Visits are also made to symbolic sepulchres in churches.
Easter Sunday is the most important Catholic holiday, when the grandest mass is held to mark the Resurrection.
Easter Monday *(Śmigus-dyngus)* is marked by the custom of people throwing water over one another.
Gdańsk International Guitar Festival *(every other year)*, Gdańsk.
Paka Cabaret Review, Cracow. A varied programme attracts large audiences to this festival of cabaret art.

A female entertainer performing at a festival in Cracow

Festival of Theatre Schools, Łódź. Performances are held in the town's major theatres, and there are also panel discussions and workshops.

MAY

International Labour Day *(1 May).*
3 May The most important public holiday, marking the adoption of the first Polish constitution of 1791.
Chamber Music Days *(first 2 weeks in May),* Łańcut. This is an international event.
International Book Fair *(last 2 weeks in May),* Warsaw. One of the largest events of its kind in Europe.
Kontakt Theatre Festival *(last 2 weeks in May),* Toruń.
Jazz on the Oder, Wrocław. Renowned jazz festival.
Poznań Jazz Fair, Poznań.
Short Film Festival, Cracow. The oldest film festival in the country.

AVERAGE HOURS OF SUNSHINE PER DAY

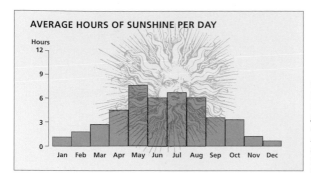

Hours
12 —
9 —
6 —
3 —
0 —

Jan Feb Mar Apr May Jun Jul Aug Sep Oct Nov Dec

Sunny days
The period from May to September has the greatest number of days of sunshine. April and September are often also sunny, while December has the least sunshine.

SUMMER

From the end of June to the beginning of September, open-air events are held all over the country. Theatrical life in the towns and cities, by contrast, tends to slow down. Most open-air events are held in tourist areas.

Corpus Christi procession in Spicimierz

JUNE

Festival of Polish Song *(early Jun)*, Opole.
Borderlands Theatre Festival *(first week in Jun)*, Cieszyn.
Corpus Christi *(variable)*. Solemn processions are held throughout the country.
Midsummer's Night *(23 Jun)*.
Fishermen's Sea Pilgrimage *(29 Jun)*. Decorated fishing boats sail into the port of Puck across the bay.
Mozart Festival *(late Jun–early Jul)*, Warsaw.

Malta – International Theatre Festival *(late Jun)*, Poznań.
Summer Film Festival *(late Jun)*, Łagów.
Festival of Folk Bands and Singers *(late Jun)*, Kazimierz Dolny.
Jewish Culture Festival *(Jun/Jul)*, Cracow.

JULY

Festival of Film Stars, Międzyzdroje.
Fireworks Festival, Ustka.
Viking Festival, Wolin. Viking battles. Most of the boats arrive from Scandinavia.
International Street Theatre Festival *(mid-Jul)*, Jelenia Góra. There is also street theatre in Jedlnia Zdrój, Szczawno Zdrój and Wałbrzych in Lower Silesia, and in the cities of Gdańsk, Toruń, Cracow and Warsaw.
International Organ Festival *(mid-Jul)*, Kamień Pomorski.
Singing Poetry Festival *(mid-Jul)*, Olsztyn Castle.
Piknik Country *(end of Jul)*, Mrągowo. International country music festival.

Street performers at the Dominican Fair in Gdańsk

AUGUST

Beskid Culture Week *(early Aug)*, Beskid region.
Dominican Fair *(first 2 weeks in Aug)*, Gdańsk.
Chopin Festival *(second week in Aug)*, Duszniki Zdrój.
FAMA *(Aug)*, Świnoujście. Student arts festival.
Złota Tarka Traditional Jazz Festival *(mid-Aug)*, Iława.
Feast of the Assumption *(15 Aug)*. This is a religious holiday, but it is also the day on which Poles commemorate their victory over the Bolsheviks in 1920.
International Song Festival *(late Aug)*, Sopot.

Fishermen's sea pilgrimage in the bay of Puck

AVERAGE PRECIPITATION

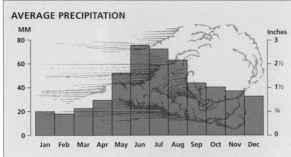

| | Jan | Feb | Mar | Apr | May | Jun | Jul | Aug | Sep | Oct | Nov | Dec |

MM: 0 / 20 / 40 / 60 / 80

Inches: 0 / ¾ / 1½ / 2½ / 3

Rainfall and snow
Although autumn showers are the most unpleasant, the heaviest rainfall occurs in summer. Heavy snow is usual in winter.

AUTUMN

Fine weather continues in Poland to the end of October. Autumn comes soonest in Pomerania, Warmia and Mazuria, as well as Suwalszczyna. The transition from September to October – when fallen leaves create a riot of colour – is known as the "golden Polish autumn". It is also a time when major cultural events take place, as well as the beginning of the new academic year.

SEPTEMBER

Festival of Polish Piano Music *(early Sep)*, Słupsk.
Warsaw Autumn *(mid-Sep)*, Warsaw. Contemporary music.
Wratislavia Cantans *(early Sep)*, Wrocław. Oratorio and cantata festival.
Festival of Science *(last 2 weeks in Sep)*, Warsaw.

Inauguration of the academic year

Programme for the Polish Feature Film Festival

Days of Julian Tuwim, Łódź. Various events, including poetry readings.
Archaeology gala, Biskupin.

OCTOBER

Konfrontacje Theatre Festival, Lublin.
Lemk Cultural Festival, Gorzów Wielkopolski.
Festival of Student Song, Cracow. Performances by the best student vocalists and accompanists.
Warsaw Film Festival, Warsaw.
Festival of Early Music *(late Oct)*. An international festival with venues in Warsaw, Cracow and other cities.
Polish Feature Film Festival *(end Oct)*. Gdynia.
Głogów Jazz Meeting *(late Oct)*. Głogów.

Lithuanian All Saints' Day, Puńsk. Poetry and music in memory of the dead.

NOVEMBER

All Saints' Day *(1 Nov)*. People visit the graves of their relatives and light candles there.
All Saints' Day Jazz Festival, Cracow. The first jazz festival in post-communist Europe.
Jazz Jamboree, Warsaw. The Jazz Jamboree is one of Europe's major jazz festivals.
"Etiuda" International Film Festival *(early Nov)*, Cracow.
Independence Day *(11 Nov)*. The biggest ceremonies in honour of Polish independence in 1918 take place in Warsaw.
St Martin's Day *(11 Nov)*. In Wielkopolska and Eastern Pomerania people traditionally cook a goose and bake pretzels and croissants on St Martin's Day. The holiday is marked by major ceremonies in Poznań, where St Martin is the patron saint.

Candles lit at a cemetery on All Saints' Day

AVERAGE TEMPERATURES

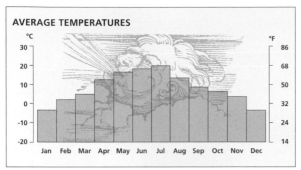

Temperatures
Temperatures are highest in the summer, when they can exceed 30° C (86° F). In winter, temperatures can fall below zero (32° F), although this is usually short-lived.

WINTER

The first snow can fall in November, although snowless winters are becoming more common. Subzero temperatures and hard frosts are not unusual. The coldest part of the country is Suwalszczyna, in the northeast corner.

DECEMBER

International Festival of Films for Children and Youth, Poznań.
Christmas Crib Competitions *(first week in Dec),* held in Cracow market square.
Christmas Eve *(24 Dec).* The beginning of Christmas is marked with a meat-free dinner and midnight mass.
Christmas *(25 and 26 Dec).* Public holidays, with masses held in all churches.
New Year's Eve *(31 Dec).* Throughout Poland, people see in the New Year at balls and parties, and at celebrations in the main squares of most towns.

Cribs being brought to Cracow's Christmas Crib Competitions

JANUARY

New Year *(1 Jan).* Public holiday. A carnival begins and the season of balls opens.
Orthodox Church Music Festival *(mid-Jan),* Cracow.

FEBRUARY

Feast of St Mary Gromniczna *(2 Feb).* Wax candles known as *gromnice* are lit in churches.

End of Carnival The last Thursday before Lent is marked by eating doughnuts or other fried delicacies known as *faworki.* Splendid balls, concerts and shows are put on throughout the country to mark the last Saturday of the carnival.
International Festival of Sea Shanties, Cracow.

PUBLIC HOLIDAYS

New Year's Day
(1 January)
Easter Monday
(variable)
May Day
(1 May)
Constitution Day
(3 May)
Corpus Christi
(variable)
Feast of the Assumption (15 August)
All Saints' Day
(1 November)
Independence Day
(11 November)
Christmas (25 and 26 December)

Winter cityscape, Gdańsk

THE HISTORY OF POLAND

Poland's borders have changed almost continuously with the course of history. The origins of the Polish nation go back to the 10th century, when Slav tribes living in the area of Gniezno united together under the Piast dynasty, which then ruled Poland until 1370.

Mieszko I, the first historic prince of this line, converted to Christianity in 966, bringing his kingdom into Christian Europe. The Piast dynasty ruled Poland with variable fortune and embroiled the nation in domestic quarrels for 150 years. After this dynasty died out, the great Lithuanian prince Jagiełło took the Polish throne and founded a new dynasty. The treaty with Lithuania signed at Krewo in 1385 initiated the long process of consolidation between these nations, culminating in 1569 with the signing of the Union of Lublin. In the 15th century the Jagiellonians achieved many military successes, forming the powerful Republic of Two Nations (Rzeczpospolita Obojga Narodów). After the Jagiellonian dynasty died out in 1572, the authorities introduced elective kings, with the nobility having the right to vote. Poland's political and

The Polish eagle

military weakness led to its partitioning by Russia, Prussia and Austria. In 1795 Poland was wiped off the map of Europe for more than 100 years. Attempts to wrest independence by insurrection were unsuccessful, and Poland did not regain its sovereignty until 1918. The arduous process of rebuilding and uniting the nation was still incomplete when, at the outbreak of World War II, a six-year period of German and Soviet occupation began. The price that Poland paid was very high: millions were murdered, including virtually its entire Jewish population. The country suffered devastation and there were huge territorial losses, which were only partly compensated by the Allies' decision to move the border westwards. After the war, Poland was subjugated by the Soviet Union and did not become a fully democratic nation until 1989.

Map of the Republic of Two Nations (Rzeczpospolita Obojga Narodów) in the 17th century

◁ Stanisław August Poniatowski, the last king of Poland

Poland under the Piast Dynasty

Crown of Kazimierz the Great

During the 6th century AD, Slav tribes began migrating from the east to what is today Polish territory. The Vistulanians (Wiślanie) settled around Cracow, and the Poles (Polanie) around Gniezno. The Polanie united under the rule of the Piast dynasty in the 10th century, and the conversion of Mieszko I (c. 960–92) to Christianity in 966 led to the formation of the Polish state. After Mieszko, Bolesław the Brave (992–1025) acquired significant new territories. Later Piast rulers reigned with variable fortune. On the death of Bolesław the Wry-Mouthed (1107–38), the nation was divided into districts, not to be reunified until the reign of Władysław the Elbow-High (1306–33). The country flourished under the rule of his son, Kazimierz the Great (1333–70).

POLAND IN THE YEARS 1090–1127

■ *Polish territory*

Prayer at the grave of St Wojciech
The Czech bishop Wojciech, who was martyred while on a mission to Prussia in 997, was the first Polish saint.

Bishop Stanisław of Szczepanów

Tomb of Henry IV
The Silesian prince Henry IV, the Good (Henryk IV Probus, 1288–90) tried to unite Poland but died, probably by poisoning. His tomb is a fine example of early 14th-century Gothic sculpture.

MARTYRDOM OF ST STANISŁAW
An embroidery of 1504 from the chasuble in Kmita depicts the murder of Bishop Stanisław of Szczepanów in 1079.

TIMELINE

997 Martyrdom of Bishop Wojciech while on a mission to Prussia

1000 Congress at Gniezno; convocation of the Polish church metropolis

1025 Coronation of Bolesław the Brave, first king of Poland

1124–1128 Bolesław the Wry-Mouthed initiates the conversion of Western Pomerania to Christianity

950	1000	1050	1100	1

966 Adoption of Christianity

Coin minted in the reign of Bolesław the Brave

1079 Martyrdom of Bishop Stanisław of Szczepanów

1138 Beginning of the division of Poland

Vistulanian Plate

This Romanesque floor laid with plaster c.1170, preserved in the collegiate church in Wiślica, depicts a scene of adoration.

Bolesław the Bold

Kazimierz the Great

This 14th-century sculpture from the collection in the Collegium Maius in Cracow depicts Kazimierz the Great, who "found Poland of wood, and left it in stone".

VESTIGES OF THE PIAST DYNASTY

The Piast dynasty witnessed the development of Romanesque and early Gothic architecture. Romanesque churches have survived in Tum *(see p229)*, Czerwińsk *(see p114)* and Tyniec *(see p145)*. The abbeys in Sulejów, Wąchock *(see p152)* and Koprzywnica date from the 13th century. Some of the Gothic castles of Kazimierz the Great can be seen in the Jura region – for example at Będzin, Olsztyn and Bobolice *(see pp158–9)*.

The Crypt of St Leonard *is a vestige of the Romanesque cathedral at Wawel Royal Castle in Cracow (see pp138–9).*

The castle at Będzin *is the best-preserved of all the Gothic castles built by Kazimierz the Great (see p205).*

Founding Document of the Cracovian Academy

Founded in 1364, the Cracovian Academy was the second university (after Prague) to be established in Central Europe.

1241 Defeat at the Battle of Legnica against the Mongols

1320 Coronation of Władysław the Elbow-High and the unification of the Polish state

1340–1366 Kazimierz the Great conquers western Ruthenia (Ruś Halicko-Wołyńska)

1200	1250	1300	1350

1226 Konrad Mazowiecki invites the Teutonic Order to Masovia

Coronation sword of Bolesław the Brave

The initials of Kazimierz the Great on the door of Wawel Cathedral

1370 Louis of Hungary (Ludwik Węgierski) seizes the Polish crown

Poland under the Jagiellonians

Jagiellonian coat of arms

The treaty signed in Krewo in 1385 uniting the Polish and the Lithuanian states proved to be a decisive moment in the history of Central Europe. The Grand Duke of Lithuania Władysław Jagiełło received the hand of Jadwiga, the young and beautiful ruler of Poland, and was crowned king of Poland. Jadwiga died in 1399, but the relationship between Poland and Lithuania established by the Union of Krewo was gradually strengthened. Jagiełło founded the Jagiellonian dynasty and, by the reign of Kazimierz the Jagiellonian in the mid-15th century, Poland and Lithuania had come to be the greatest power in central Europe. The Jagiellonian kings also ruled the Czech nations and Hungary.

REPUBLIC OF TWO NATIONS IN THE YEARS 1386–1434

- ☐ Poland
- ☐ Lithuania
- ☐ Feudal territories

Second Treaty of Toruń
Signed in 1466, the treaty concluded the Thirteen Years' War with the Teutonic Knights, who lost nearly half their territory to Poland.

Ulryk von Jungingen, Grand Master of the Teutonic Order

Chapel at Lublin Castle
Ruthenian paintings in the Catholic Chapel of the Holy Trinity founded by Władysław Jagiełło reflect the multicultural nature of the Polish-Lithuanian state.

Plate showing Filippo Buonaccorsi
This sculpture commemorating the Italian humanist and educator of the young royals, who died in 1496, is by the eminent late Medieval sculptor Veit Stoss.

TIMELINE

1399 Death of Queen Jadwiga

1411 First Treaty of Toruń, establishing peace with the Teutonic Knights

1413 Treaty of Horodło, strengthening the bond between Poland and Lithuania

1440 Formation of the Prussian Union, in opposition to the Teutonic Knights

1385	1400	1415	1430

1385 Union of Krewo joins Poland and Lithuania

1410 Battle of Grunwald

1415 At the Council of Constanz, Paweł Włodkowic proclaims the theory of the sovereignty of all Christian and non-Christian peoples

Queen Jadwiga's sceptre

Virgin from Krużlowa
*This statue, of around
1400, is a masterpiece of
late Gothic sculpture.*

Gothic Pax
*The skill of medieval
goldsmiths can be
seen in this finely
crafted cross.*

GOTHIC ARCHITECTURE

Many late Gothic buildings
have survived in Poland.
Among the most important
are the Collegium Maius
and the Barbican in Cracow
(see p133). After the
formation of Royal Prussia,
many parish churches
were built in the towns
lying within its territory,
the largest being the
Church of St Mary in
Gdańsk *(see pp238–9)*.

**Witold, the Grand
Duke of Lithuania**

The imposing twin-tower
façade of the Church of
St Mary *reflects Cracow's
former status (see p132).*

BATTLE OF GRUNWALD

In one of the greatest medieval battles, on
15 July 1410, Poland and Lithuania, with
their Ruthenian allies, routed the armies of
the Teutonic Knights, who never regained
their former might. The scene is depicted
in this painting by Jan Matejko of 1878.

**Deposition from
Chomranice**
*This Deposition of
Christ (c.1450) is
held to be the apogee
of Polish Gothic art.*

1445	1460	1475	1490

1454 Act incorpor-
ating Prussia into the
Crown of Poland

1473 Birth of
Nicolaus
Copernicus

1496 Piotrkowski
Statute restricts
the rights of
commoners to
acquire land

1444 Władysław of Varna
[d]ies at the Battle of Varna,
[f]ought against the Turks

1466 Second
Treaty of Toruń

1492 Death of Kazimierz
the Jagiellonian. First
general Sejm (parliament)

*Figure of St John by Veit Stoss, from the altar
in the Church of St Mary, Cracow*

Poland's Golden Age

Emblematic cockerel

In the 16th century the Republic of Two Nations (Rzeczpospolita) formed by Poland and Lithuania was one of the largest European powers. In the western territories of the Polish Crown there was peace, relative prosperity and – rare elsewhere – religious tolerance. Under the Jagiellonians, and later under the first elective kings, art, education and the economy flourished. In the political sphere there was a significant movement to improve the Republic and institute reforms.

The so-called real union between Poland and Lithuania was concluded in Lublin in 1569. At that time, in terms of language, nationality and religion, the Republic was the most diverse state in Europe.

REPUBLIC OF TWO NATIONS, EARLY 16TH CENTURY

▨ Poland	▨ Lithuania	
▨ Feudal territories		

Nicolaus Copernicus (1473–1543)
This Polish astronomer and humanist showed that the Earth revolves around the Sun.

Codex Behem
This illuminated manuscript of 1505 by Baltazar Behem, a writer and notary of Cracow, lists the city's privileges, statutes, and the guild laws.

Representatives of the peoples of the East and West

Nobleman who brought the news of the Chancellor's death

OPATÓW LAMENT
The Renaissance tomb of Chancellor Krzysztof Szydłowiecki in the collegiate church at Opatów features a bas-relief sculpture depicting the mourning of the deceased, installed after 1532 *(see p152)*. Around the table are friends of the Chancellor, humanists attached to the royal court and foreigners.

TIMELINE

	1505 Adoption of the constitutional law of *Nihil Novi*	**1520** Adoption of the Statute of Toruń, introducing serfdom	**1525** Secularization of the defeated Teutonic Order. The elector Albrecht Hohenzollern, Duke of Prussia, makes an oath of fealty to the Polish king, Zygmunt the Old, in Cracow	**1543** Copernicus famous trea is published
1500		**1520**		**1540**
	1518 Bona Sforza arrives in Poland and marries Zygmunt the Old (Zygmunt Stary)	**1521** The Polish army occupies Teutonic Prussia in the final war with the Teutonic Knights		

Renaissance oven tile

Tomb of Stefan Batory

Despite his short reign, Batory was one of the most illustrious of the elective monarchs.

Union of Lublin

The federation of Poland and Lithuania established under the Union of Lublin in 1569 provided for a joint Sejm (parliament), king and foreign policy. However, each country had its own government, army, treasury and judiciary.

Zygmunt the Old

Vice-chancellor Piotr Tomicki

Jan Tarnowski, the deceased's son-in-law

Dogs, symbolizing the loyalty of the dead man's friends

Tapestry with Satyrs

The collection of tapestries at Wawel Royal Castle (see p140) comprises over 160 splendid pieces. They were brought to the castle in the 16th century.

16TH-CENTURY ARCHITECTURE

The first instance of the Renaissance style in Poland dates from 1502. Often imitated but never equalled, the most splendid early Renaissance building was the Zygmunt Chapel in Wawel Cathedral *(see p143)*, completed in 1533.

This castle in Książ Wielki, *built by Santi Gucci between 1585 and 1589, is the most splendid example of Italian Mannerism in Poland.*

The collegiate church in Pułtusk (see p113), *built c.1560 by the architect Gianbattista of Venice, has barrel vaulting.*

1557 Outbreak of the war with Russia over Livonia

1563 Split of Polish Calvinists and isolation of the Polish Brethren, an extreme group of Reformationists

1564 Jesuits arrive in Poland

1587 Zygmunt III Vasa is elected king of Poland

Grotesque mask from Baranów Sandomierski

| 1560 | 1580 | 1600 |

1561 Secularization of the Livonian Branch of the Teutonic Order and incorporation of Livonia

1569 Union of Lublin

1579 The capture of Połock marks the start of Stefan Batory's victory in the war against Russia

1596 The capital is moved from Cracow to Warsaw

The "Silver" 17th Century

Statue of Jan III Sobieski

The 17th century was dominated by the wars that the Republic of Two Nations waged against the Swedes, Russia and the Ottoman Empire. An uprising in the Ukraine in 1648 marked the beginning of a series of catastrophes. In 1655 the Republic of Two Nations was invaded and largely occupied by the Swedes. Although it was short-lived, the Swedish occupation – known as the Deluge (*Potop*) – wreaked havoc. The final triumph of the Republic of Two Nations was the victory against the Turks at the Battle of Vienna in 1683, during the reign of Jan III Sobieski. The country eventually emerged from the wars without major territorial losses, but it was considerably weakened and its dominance was over.

REPUBLIC OF TWO NATIONS IN THE YEARS 1582–1648

- ■ Poland
- ■ Lithuania
- □ Feudal territories

A rebus on the main gate spells out "Krzyżtopór" with a cross (*Krzyż*) and an axe (*Topór*).

Siege of Jasna Góra, the Luminous Mountain
The run of Swedish victories ended in 1655 with the heroic Polish defence of the Pauline Monastery in Częstochowa.

Moat

Nobleman in a Dance with Death
The figure of a common Polish yeoman in traditional dress decorates the Chapel of the Oleśnicki family in Tarłów.

KRZYŻTOPOR CASTLE

In the first half of the 17th century, dazzling residences were built in the Republic of Two Nations. The most splendid was the eccentric castle in Ujazd. Built at great expense, it stood for barely 11 years. It was demolished in 1655 by the Swedes and remains in ruins to this day (*see p152*).

TIMELINE

1604 First Moscow expedition of the false Demetrius

1606 Zebrzydowski Rebellion

1629 Truce with Sweden in Altmark

1634 Władysław IV's victory over Russia, and peace in Polanów

16 Beginning the Swedi Delu

1600

1620

1640

1601 Outbreak of Northern War with Sweden

1620 Battle against the Turks and Tatars at Cecora

1632 Death of Zygmunt III Vasa

1648 Death of Władysław IV, start of the Chmielnicki Uprising in the Ukraine

Zygmunt III Vasa

Baroque Monstrance

This monstrance, at Pelplin Cathedral in Pomerania, dates from 1646.

Shrine of St Stanisław

Relics of the patron saint of Poland are preserved in a shrine that was installed in Wawel Cathedral between 1626 and 1629.

The cloister walls around the courtyard are painted with real and legendary ancestors of the Ossoliński family.

Bastions

Husaria

Charges by the famous Hussars, the best heavy cavalry in Europe, decided the outcome of many battles. Their greatest victory was against the Turks at the Battle of Vienna (1683).

17TH-CENTURY ARCHITECTURE

Many magnificent buildings in the late Mannerist and early Baroque styles were erected in the first half of the 17th century, during the reign of the Vasa dynasty. After the destruction wrought by the Swedish Deluge, there was no further artistic flowering until the reign of Jan III Sobieski. The early Baroque castles – for example, the Royal Palace in Warsaw *(see pp64–5)* – as well as numerous churches, of which the most impressive are the Jesuit churches in Cracow, Warsaw and Poznań, are all splendid examples of the architecture of this period.

The Bishops' Palace in Kielce (see p150) *is the best-preserved early Baroque residence.*

The Royal Chapel (see p239) *in Gdańsk, commissioned by Jan III Sobieski, was built by Tylman van Gameren and Andreas Schlüter in the Baroque style.*

1660 Peace treaty signed in Oliwa ends the Polish-Swedish War

1667 Turks invade the southeastern borderlands

1686 Signing of the Perpetual Peace with Russia

Pair of cherubs

| 1660 | 1680 | 1700 |

1658 Polish Brethren exiled from Poland

1668 Abdication of Jan Kazimierz

1683 Jan III Sobieski's victory over the Turks at the Battle of Vienna

1699 Peace of Karłowice with Turkey

Mannerist window frame

Poland in the 18th Century

Order of Military Virtue

In the first half of the 18th century, Poland was ruled by the Wettin dynasty of Saxony. Polish interests were gradually subordinated to those of neighbouring powers, and the election of Stanisław August Poniatowski as king, supported by the Tsarina Catherine the Great, sealed the nation's fate. Attempts to counteract Russian influence came to an end with the First Partition of Poland in 1772. The efforts of the patriotic faction and the achievements of the Four-Year Sejm changed little. The Second Partition followed in 1793, and when the uprising led by Tadeusz Kościuszko – the final attempt to save the country – was quashed, Poland lost its statehood for over 100 years.

REPUBLIC OF TWO NATIONS BEFORE THE PARTITIONS

- [ ] Poland
- [ ] Lithuania

Stanisław August Poniatowski

Rococo Statue from Lvov
In southeastern Poland, original altar statues by sculptors of the Lvov School can still be admired.

Rococo Secretaire
This desk incorporates a clock cabinet and is decorated with painted panels depicting mythological scenes.

Portrait of Maria Leszczyńska
After the Polish king Stanisław Leszczyński lost the throne, his daughter Maria settled in Nancy and married Louis XV of France.

TIMELINE

1697 Coronation of August II, the Strong	**1717** "Dumb Sejm"	**1733** Election of August III	**1740** Opening of Collegium Nobilium, Warsaw
1704 Coronation of Stanisław Leszczyński, supported by the king of Sweden	**1721** End of Northern War		
1700	**1720**		**1740**
1700 Outbreak of Northern War	**1709** August II, the Strong returns to the throne	**1733** Stanisław Leszczyński is re-elected king	

Casing of a grenadier's cap

Tadeusz Kościuszko
This man fought in the American War of Independence and led the insurrection against the Russians in 1794.

August III
This Saxon king of the Wettin dynasty was an ardent lover of porcelain. His likeness was reproduced in Meissen.

18TH-CENTURY ARCHITECTURE

During the 18th century – the era of the late Baroque and Rococo – artists and architects from Saxony joined those who had already come to Poland from Italy. Many palaces, including Radziwiłł, were built in Warsaw and the provinces, such as Białystok *(see p290)*. Thanks to the patronage of Stanisław August Poniatowski, many Neo-Classical buildings were created, among them Łazienki in Warsaw.

The Palace on the Water (see pp94–5) *in Warsaw was the royal summer residence.*

Hugo
Kołłątaj

Prince Józef
Poniatowski

Stanisław
Małachowski,
Speaker of
the Sejm

CONSTITUTION OF 3 MAY

The Constitution of 3 May 1791 was a radical experiment in democracy and reform – the first such in Europe. It was, however, soon annulled as a result of the Federation of Targowica and the Russo-Polish war. Jan Matejko's painting shows members of the Sejm (parliament) marching on Warsaw Cathedral to swear allegiance.

Hugo Kołłątaj
A leading intellectual of the Polish Enlightenment, Kołłątaj collaborated on the Constitution of 3 May.

1764 Coronation of Stanisław August Poniatowski

1773 Convocation of National Education Commission

Coat of arms of Stanisław August Poniatowski

1794 Insurrection against the Russians

1795 Third Partition of Poland

1760

1780

1800

1756 Outbreak of the Seven-Year War

1772 First Partition of Poland

1788–1792 Deliberations of the Four-Year Sejm

1791 Adoption of the Constitution of 3 May

1793 Second Partition of Poland

Poland under the Partitions

Eclectic detail

Deprived of its independence, Poland became a territory for exploitation as though it were a colony. The hopes vested in Napoleon proved illusory. The transitory Grand Duchy of Warsaw lasted only eight years. The failure of the successive November and January insurrections (1830 and 1863) led to further restrictions by the tsarist rulers: landed property was confiscated and cultural and educational institutions dissolved. Many Poles tried to help the country from abroad. The collapse of the partitioning empires in World War I enabled Poland to regain its independence in 1918.

REPUBLIC OF TWO NATIONS UNDER THE PARTITIONS

◼ *Russian partition*

◼ *Prussian partition*

◻ *Austrian partition*

Patrol of Insurgents
This painting by Maksymilian Gierymski of around 1873 shows a scene from the January Insurrection. Several insurgents are patrolling the land.

Henryk Sienkiewicz's House in Oblęgorek
The small palace was given to the Nobel laureate Henryk Sienkiewicz in 1900 to mark the occasion of 25 years of his work as a writer.

Beggar waiting for alms

Emperor Franz Josef enjoying the loyalty of his subjects.

TIMELINE

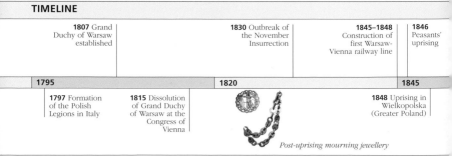

1807 Grand Duchy of Warsaw established

1830 Outbreak of the November Insurrection

1845–1848 Construction of first Warsaw-Vienna railway line

1846 Peasants' uprising

1795

1820

1845

1797 Formation of the Polish Legions in Italy

1815 Dissolution of Grand Duchy of Warsaw at the Congress of Vienna

1848 Uprising in Wielkopolska (Greater Poland)

Post-uprising mourning jewellery

Fryderyk Chopin
This genius of a composer and pianist was born in Żelazowa Wola and left Poland forever in 1830.

Stained-glass Window
The stained-glass windows designed by Stanisław Wyspiański for the Franciscan Church in Cracow are among the most beautiful works of Secessionist art in Poland.

THE GREAT EMIGRATION

In the 30 years following the November Insurrection, nearly 20,000 Poles left the country, the majority going to France. An important group of émigrés gathered around Prince Adam Czartoryski in Paris. Famous Poles in exile included the composer Fryderyk Chopin and poets Adam Mickiewicz, Zygmunt Krasiński, Juliusz Słowacki and Cyprian Kamil Norwid.

Prince Adam Czartoryski, *an exile in Paris, was considered the uncrowned king of Poland.*

The inhabitants of Cracow greet the emperor

EMPEROR FRANZ JOSEF ENTERS CRACOW
Juliusz Kossak produced a series of paintings to commemorate the emperor's visit to Cracow in 1880. The city's inhabitants received him with great enthusiasm.

Prince Józef Poniatowski
Bertel Thorvaldsen designed this monument to Prince Józef Poniatowski, who died in 1813. Poniatowski was considered a Polish national hero.

1861 Founding of the National Sejm in Galicia

1873 Founding of the Academy of Sciences in Cracow

1903 Marie Curie (Maria Skłodowska-Curie) receives the Nobel Prize for Physics

1905 Henryk Sienkiewicz receives the Nobel Prize for Literature

1870

1895

1864 Final abolition of serfdom

1863 Start of the January Insurrection

Secessionist wall painting

1915 Russian troops leave Warsaw

Poland from 1918 to 1945

Eagle – emblem of the reborn Poland

Poland regained its independence in 1918, but for several years afterwards battles raged over its borders. In 1920, independence was again threatened by the Red Army. Despite domestic conflicts, Poland made considerable economic progress. The territories of the three areas previously held by Russia, Austria and Prussia were consolidated. The country's brief period of independence ended in 1939 with the German and Soviet invasions. Poland was occupied and its population persecuted, terrorized and partially exterminated. About 6 million Poles were killed, including 3 million Polish Jews *(see p160)*. An underground state operated, with the Home Army answering to the government in exile. Polish soldiers fought the Germans on all fronts.

POLAND IN 1938

■ *Polish territory*

Volunteers fighting alongside the soldiers

Gdynia
Although Poland gained access to the sea, it had no port. Work on the construction of a port at Gdynia began in 1922.

Interior of the Silesian Sejm
The industrialized region of Silesia had its own parliament in the interwar years, a sign of its importance.

MIRACLE ON THE VISTULA

This was the name given to Marshal Józef Piłsudski's victory at the Battle of Warsaw on 13–16 August 1920, which halted the Soviet march westwards and shattered the Bolshevik hope of a proletarian revolution throughout Europe.

TIMELINE

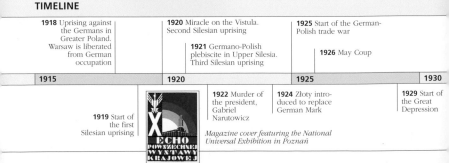

1918 Uprising against the Germans in Greater Poland. Warsaw is liberated from German occupation

1920 Miracle on the Vistula. Second Silesian uprising

1921 Germano-Polish plebiscite in Upper Silesia. Third Silesian uprising

1925 Start of the German-Polish trade war

1926 May Coup

1915	1920	1925	1930

1919 Start of the first Silesian uprising

1922 Murder of the president, Gabriel Narutowicz

1924 Złoty introduced to replace German Mark

1929 Start of the Great Depression

Magazine cover featuring the National Universal Exhibition in Poznań

ECHO POWSZECHNEJ WYSTAWY KRAJOWEJ

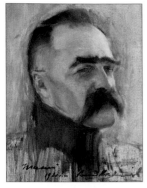

Józef Piłsudski
Józef Piłsudski led the legions which were set up in the Austrian sector then dispersed. In 1918 he became the first leader of an independent Poland.

Plaque to the Victims of Execution
One of many plaques in Warsaw marking places of execution during World War II.

WARSAW UPRISING
On 1 August 1944 the underground Home Army (Armia Krajowa) launched an uprising in Warsaw against the occupying Germans. Its aim was to liberate the capital before the arrival of the Red Army. The Russians were waiting on the left bank of the river, allowing the Germans to suppress the outburst. The uprising lasted over two months and led to the complete destruction of the city as well as the loss of tens of thousands of lives.

In his film *Kanał*, *the director Andrzej Wajda showed the insurgents struggling through sewers beneath German-occupied districts of Warsaw.*

Father Ignacy Skorupka leads soldiers into attack

Bolshevik soldiers flee the battlefield

Hanka Ordonówna
She was one of the most popular actresses between the wars.

Monument to Those Fallen and Murdered in the East
This monument honours all the Poles who were killed or deported after the Soviet invasion in 1939.

1935 Death of Marshal Piłsudski

1936 Start of the construction of the Central Industrial Region

1938 Poland annexes territory to the west of the River Olza

1942 Home Army formed. Anders' army evacuated from USSR

1943 Ghetto Uprising, Warsaw

Occupying forces demolish the statue of Adam Mickiewicz

1935	1940	1945

1939 Outbreak of World War II. German troops enter Poland, followed by Soviet forces. The Polish army is defeated and the country occupied

1940 The Russians murder Polish officers who were taken prisoner in Katyń

1944 Polish soldiers take the monastery at Monte Cassino, Italy. Warsaw Uprising. Formation of a pro-Soviet, Communist government in Lublin

Modern Poland

In 1945 the allies agreed that Poland should be included in the Soviet zone of influence. The Big Three (Britain, the USA and the Soviet Union) also decided to alter Poland's borders. After rigged elections in 1947, the Communists took complete control. Despite successes in rebuilding the country, the socialist economy proved ineffective. The formation of Solidarity (Solidarność) in 1980 accelerated the pace of change, which was completed when Poland regained its freedom after the 1989 elections.

1945 After the terrible devastation of the war, the country is hauled out of the ruins by the effort of the whole nation

1947 Communists falsify the results of elections to the Sejm (parliament)

1955 30,000 delegates from 114 countries take part in the World Festival of Youth in Warsaw. This is the first time that the Iron Curtain has been briefly lifted

1966 Celebrations marking the millennium of Christianity in Poland, organized separately by Church and State

1968 In March, conflicts occur between students and security forces. The authorities provoke incidents of an anti-Semitic and anti-intellectual nature

1945	1950	1955	1960	1965	1970	1975

1945	1950	1955	1960	1965	1970	1975

1945 End of World War II

1946 Rigged referendum on abolishing the Senate, introducing agricultural reforms, nationalizing industry and the western border

1953 Height of the persecution of the Catholic Church, trial of priests of the metropolitan curia of Cracow; Cardinal Stefan Wyszyński, Primate of Poland, is arrested

1956 In June, a workers' revolt in Poznań is bloodily suppressed. In October, after more demonstrations by students and workers, Soviet intervention is threatened. Władysław Gomułka becomes First Secretary of the Central Committee of the Polish United Workers' Party

1957 Premiere of *Kanał*, directed by Andrzej Wajda, one of the first films of the Polish School

1958 First International Jazz Jamboree in Warsaw

1968 Polish forces take part in the armed intervention in Czechoslovakia

1970 Bloody suppression of a strike and workers' demonstrations on the coast. Edward Gierek becomes First Secretary of the Central Committee of the Polish United Workers' Party

1976 Demonstrations against price rises, by workers in Radom and Ursus, are quashed. The opposition forms the Workers' Defence Committee. At the 21st Olympics in Montreal, Irena Kirszenstein-Szewińska wins gold for track and field sports for the third time

1979 First visit of John Paul II, the "Polish Pope", to his homeland. Both a religious and a political event, it rekindles Polish hopes of regaining freedom

1980 Agreements signed in Gdańsk on 31 August end the strikes and allow the formation of the first Independent Autonomous Trades Unions. Lech Wałęsa becomes their leader

2012 Poland and Ukraine host the UEFA Football Championship – Euro 2012

1990 Lech Wałęsa elected president of Poland

1981 Under the leadership of General Wojciech Jaruzelski, the Communist authorities introduce martial law. Solidarity goes underground

1997 The worst flood in a century devastates large areas of southern Poland

1999 Poland joins NATO

2002 Poland formally invited to join EU in 2004

2005 Death of John Paul II, the "Polish Pope"

1980	1985	1990	1995	2000	2005	2010	2015

1980	1985	1990	1995	2000	2005	2010	2015

1990 Official end of the Polish People's Republic, adoption of Leszek Balcerowicz's radical market reforms

1989 At round-table talks, the opposition negotiates with the authorities about legalizing Solidarity and calling an election, in which the "civic society" then wins a landslide victory

2004 Poland joins the EU

2000 Cracow is European City of Culture

2010 A tragic air crash kills 96 people, including President Lech Kaczyński and his wife; Bronisław Komorowski elected president of Poland

2007 Poland joins the Schengen Area

2005 Lech Kaczyński elected president of Poland

1984 Assassination of Father Jerzy Popiełuszko, Solidarity's pastor

1997 On a visit to Warsaw, US president Bill Clinton announces that Poland is to join NATO

The Rulers of Poland

At the time of its formation in 966, the Polish nation was ruled by the Piast dynasty. Bolesław the Brave, son of Mieszko I, was the first king of Poland. During the Period of Disunity from 1138, rulers bore only the title of prince. The first prince to be crowned king of Poland was Przemysław II. After the death of Kazimierz the Great, the Polish crown passed to Louis of Hungary of the Angevin dynasty. The marriage of his daughter Jadwiga to the Lithuanian duke Jagiełło in 1384 established the Jagiellonian dynasty. From 1572 the Republic of Two Nations was ruled by elective kings with no hereditary rights. The last king was Stanisław August Poniatowski.

1386–1434
Władysław II
Jagiełło

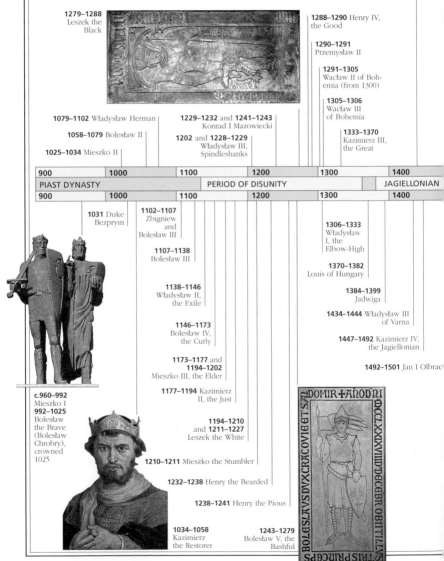

1279–1288 Leszek the Black

1288–1290 Henry IV, the Good

1290–1291 Przemysław II

1291–1305 Wacław II of Bohemia (from 1300)

1305–1306 Wacław III of Bohemia

1333–1370 Kazimierz III, the Great

1079–1102 Władysław Herman

1229–1232 and **1241–1243** Konrad I Mazowiecki

1058–1079 Bolesław II

1202 and **1228–1229** Władysław III, Spindleshanks

1025–1034 Mieszko II

900	1000	1100	1200	1300	1400
PIAST DYNASTY			PERIOD OF DISUNITY		JAGIELLONIAN
900	1000	1100	1200	1300	1400

1031 Duke Bezprym

1102–1107 Zbigniew and Bolesław III

1306–1333 Władysław I, the Elbow-High

1107–1138 Bolesław III

1370–1382 Louis of Hungary

1138–1146 Władysław II, the Exile

1384–1399 Jadwiga

1434–1444 Władysław III of Varna

1146–1173 Bolesław IV, the Curly

1447–1492 Kazimierz IV, the Jagiellonian

1173–1177 and **1194–1202** Mieszko III, the Elder

1492–1501 Jan I Olbrac

1177–1194 Kazimierz II, the Just

1194–1210 and **1211–1227** Leszek the White

1210–1211 Mieszko the Stumbler

c.960–992 Mieszko I
992–1025 Bolesław the Brave (Bolesław Chrobry), crowned 1025

1232–1238 Henry the Bearded

1238–1241 Henry the Pious

1034–1058 Kazimierz the Restorer

1243–1279 Bolesław V, the Bashful

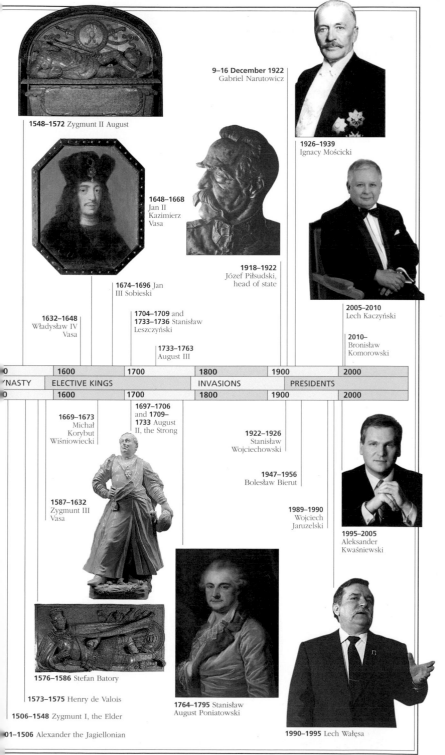

1548–1572 Zygmunt II August

9–16 December 1922
Gabriel Narutowicz

1648–1668
Jan II
Kazimierz
Vasa

1926–1939
Ignacy Mościcki

1918–1922
Józef Piłsudski,
head of state

1674–1696 Jan
III Sobieski

1704–1709 and
1733–1736 Stanisław
Leszczyński

2005–2010
Lech Kaczyński

1632–1648
Władysław IV
Vasa

1733–1763
August III

2010–
Bronisław
Komorowski

| 0 | 1600 | 1700 | 1800 | 1900 | 2000 |

| DYNASTY | ELECTIVE KINGS | | INVASIONS | PRESIDENTS | |

| 0 | 1600 | 1700 | 1800 | 1900 | 2000 |

1697–1706
and **1709–**
1733 August
II, the Strong

1669–1673
Michał
Korybut
Wiśniowiecki

1922–1926
Stanisław
Wojciechowski

1947–1956
Bolesław Bierut

1587–1632
Zygmunt III
Vasa

1989–1990
Wojciech
Jaruzelski

1995–2005
Aleksander
Kwaśniewski

1576–1586 Stefan Batory

1573–1575 Henry de Valois

1764–1795 Stanisław
August Poniatowski

1506–1548 Zygmunt I, the Elder

1501–1506 Alexander the Jagiellonian

1990–1995 Lech Wałęsa

WARSAW AREA
BY AREA

Warsaw at a Glance

Most places of interest are located in the centre of Warsaw. This area not only forms the geographical heart of the city, but is also Warsaw's largest municipality. It is made up of seven smaller districts, Śródmieście being the central one. In the pages that follow, however, Warsaw is divided into three parts: the Old and New Towns, the Royal Route and the City Centre. The most interesting historical features of Warsaw are located along the Royal Route (Trakt Królewski), a series of roads linking the Old Town (Stare Miasto) and the Royal Castle (Zamek Królewski) with the Water Palace (Łazienki) and Wilanów, the palace of Jan III Sobieski, which stands just outside the city.

The Old Town Square, *surrounded by town houses rebuilt after wartime destruction, is one of the most beautiful features of Warsaw. It teems with tourists and local people throughout the year. A statue of the Mermaid, symbol of Warsaw, is a prominent feature in the centre of the square.*

The Palace of Culture *is still the tallest building in Warsaw, despite the ongoing construction of skyscrapers in the city. The 30th floor has a viewing terrace as well as a multimedia tourist centre.*

The buildings on the north side of Theatre Square *now house banks and luxury shops, as well as the little church of St Albert and St Andrzej, which contains important works of art.*

0 m	500
0 yds	500

◁ **Royal Castle Square with Zygmunt's Column**

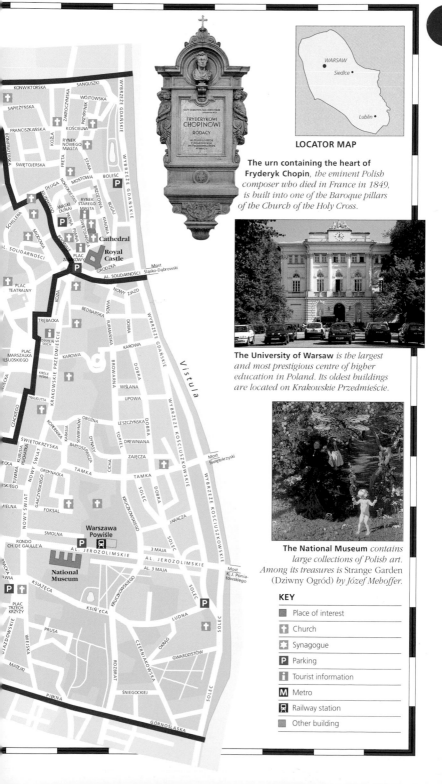

LOCATOR MAP

The urn containing the heart of **Fryderyk Chopin**, *the eminent Polish composer who died in France in 1849, is built into one of the Baroque pillars of the Church of the Holy Cross.*

The University of Warsaw *is the largest and most prestigious centre of higher education in Poland. Its oldest buildings are located on Krakowskie Przedmieście.*

The National Museum *contains large collections of Polish art. Among its treasures is* Strange Garden (Dziwny Ogród) *by Józef Mehoffer.*

KEY

▨	Place of interest
✠	Church
✡	Synagogue
P	Parking
i	Tourist information
M	Metro
▥	Railway station
▨	Other building

THE OLD AND NEW TOWNS

The Old Town (Stare Miasto), partially surrounded by medieval walls, is the oldest district in Warsaw. It was founded at the turn of the 13th and 14th centuries, growing up around the castle of the Mazovian princes. Its medieval urban layout survives to this day. The pride of the Old Town is the market square with colourful town houses. Also of major interest are the Cathedral of St John and the Royal Castle, which was destroyed by German forces in 1944 and rebuilt between 1971 and 1984. Next to the Old

Traditional house decoration

Town is the New Town (Nowe Miasto), which became a separate urban entity in 1408. The reconstruction of the Old Town and New Town, almost completely destroyed during the war, was an undertaking on a scale unprecedented in the whole of Europe. Today, these two districts are the most popular tourist attractions in Warsaw. The Old Town pulsates with life until late evening. There are many interesting little streets and an abundance of cafés, good restaurants and antique shops.

SIGHTS AT A GLANCE

Churches
Cathedral of St John p66 **3**
Church of the Holy Spirit **8**
Church of the Visitation of the Virgin Mary **15**
Church of St Jacek **11**
Church of St Kazimierz **14**
Church of St Martin **5**
Jesuit Church **4**

Historic Streets and Squares
New Town Square **13**
Old Town Square **6**
Ulica Freta **12**

Historic Buildings and Monuments
The Barbican and City Walls **7**
Monument to the 1944 Warsaw Uprising **10**
Raczyński Palace **9**
Royal Castle pp64–5 **2**
Zygmunt's Column **1**

GETTING THERE
Both Old and New Towns are pedestrianized. The nearest bus stops to the Old Town are on Plac Zamkowy for buses 116, 175, 178, 180, 195, 222 and 503, or at the beginning of the W-Z Route tunnel for trams 20, 23, 26 and 40 or bus 190. It is best to walk from the Old to the New Town. Alternatively, you can take buses 116, 175, 180 and 195 and get off at Plac Krasińskiego or Ulica Bonifraterska.

KEY
■ Street-by-Street map pp62–3

■ Street-by-Street map pp68–9

🛈 Tourist information

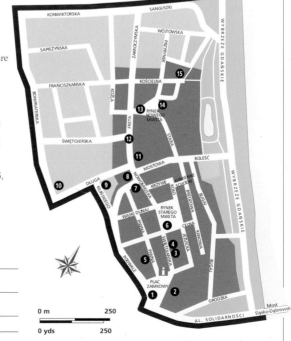

0 m 250
0 yds 250

◁ **The tower of the Church of St Martin overlooking the passage between Ulica Piwna and Ulica Świętojańska**

The Old Town

The Old Town Square (Rynek Starego Miasta) is surrounded on all sides by town houses, rebuilt after World War II with great devotion. Today it is one of the most attractive places in Warsaw. From spring to autumn it is filled with café tables, and also becomes an open-air gallery of contemporary art. On the square and in neighbouring streets, especially Piwna and Jezuicka, there are numerous restaurants and bars that are reputed to be the best in Warsaw. The whole of the Old Town is not only a tourist attraction but also a favourite place for local people, who go to walk there, and for lovers to meet.

Church of St Martin
This striking modern crucifix incorporates a fragment of a figure of Christ that was burned during the 1944 Warsaw Uprising **5**

★ **Cathedral of St John**
After suffering damage during World War II, the cathedral was rebuilt in the Gothic style **3**

Jesuit Church
The Baroque-Mannerist sanctuary of Our Lady of Mercy, patron saint of Warsaw, was rebuilt after World War II **4**

Zygmunt's Column
This is the oldest secular monument in Warsaw **1**

★ **Royal Castle (Zamek Królewski)**
This former royal residence, rebuilt in the 1970s, is today the symbol of Polish independence **2**

The Palace Under the Tin Roof was the first house in the city of Warsaw to have a tin, rather than tiled, roof.

Barbican and City Walls
This brick building once protected the northern approach to the city **7**

LOCATOR MAP
See Street Finder, map 2

The Historical Museum of Warsaw occupies the north side of the market square.

Statue of Zygmunt III Vasa at the top of Zygmunt's Column

Zygmunt's Column **1**

Plac Zamkowy. **Map** 2 D3. 116, 175, 178, 180, 190, 195, 222, 503. 20, 23, 26, 40.

Zygmunt's Column, in the centre of Plac Zamkowy, is the oldest secular statue in Warsaw. It was erected in 1644 by Zygmunt III's son Władysław IV. The monument, which stands 22 m (72 ft) high, consists of a Corinthian granite column supported on a tall plinth and topped with a bronze statue of the ruler, who is depicted with a cross in his left hand and a sword in his right. The figure is the work of Clemente Molli, and the whole monument was designed by Augustyn Locci the Elder and Constantino Tencalla, two Italian architects working for the king. This monument, unusual in European terms, glorifies the secular ruler in a manner which had until then been reserved for saints and other religious subjects. Despite repeated damage and repairs, the statue retains its original appearance. The column on which it stands, however, has already been replaced twice. An older, fractured shaft can be seen on the terrace near the south façade of the Palace Under the Tin Roof.

★ Old Town Square
The square pulsates with life until late in the evening **6**

Statue of the Mermaid

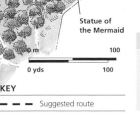

0 m   100
0 yds   100

KEY

– – – Suggested route

STAR SIGHTS

★ Royal Castle

★ Cathedral of St John

★ Old Town Square

Royal Castle ❷

Tabletop from 1777

The decision to build the Royal Castle (Zamek Królewski) was made when Zygmunt III Vasa moved the capital from Cracow to Warsaw in 1596. It was built in the early Baroque style by the Italian architects Giovanni Trevano, Giacomo Rodondo and Matteo Castelli between 1598 and 1619, incorporating the earlier castle of the Mazovian princes. Successive rulers remodelled the castle many times. The late Baroque façade overlooking the River Vistula dates from the time of August III, and the splendid interiors from that of Stanisław August. Completely destroyed by the Germans during World War II, the castle was reconstructed from 1971 to 1988.

★ Ballroom
Decorated with 17 pairs of golden columns, the ballroom is one of the castle's most elaborate interiors.

Royal Princes' Rooms
Historical paintings by Jan Matejko are displayed here.

Senators' Room
In this room, the Constitution of 3 May was formally adopted in 1791. The coats of arms of all the administrative regions and territories of the Republic are depicted on the walls. A reconstructed royal throne is also on show.

Main entrance

Zygmunt Tower
This tower, 60 m (197 ft) high, was built in 1619. It is crowned by a cupola with a spire. It is also known as the Clock Tower (Zegarowa), since a clock was installed in 1622.

STAR FEATURES

- ★ Ballroom
- ★ Marble Room
- ★ Canaletto Room

★ Marble Room

The interior dates from the time of Władysław IV. The magnificent portraits of Polish rulers by Marcello Bacciarelli are the only later additions.

The Lanckoroński Gallery on the second floor contains two paintings by Rembrandt: *Portrait of a Young Woman* and *Scholar at his Desk*.

VISITORS' CHECKLIST

Plac Zamkowy 4. **Map** 2 D3.
Tel 022 355 51 70.
Reservations 9am–2pm Tue–Fri
(institutions only). **Fax** 022
355 51 27. 116, 175, 178,
180, 190, 195, 222, 503.
20, 23, 26, 40. 10am–
4pm Tue–Sat, 11am–4pm Sun.
Royal and Grand Apartments
10am–6pm daily (from 11am
Mon & Sun). Oct–Apr: after
4pm & Mon, 1 Jan, Easter Sat
& Sun, 1 May, Corpus Christi,
1 Nov, 24, 25, 31 Dec. (free
on Sun except **Royal and
Grand Apartments**).
except Sun.
no flash.
www.zamek-krolewski.pl

Knights' Hall

The finest piece in this beautiful interior is the Neo-Classical sculpture of Chronos by le Brun and Monaldi.

Apartment of Prince Stanisław Poniatowski

The Rococo panelling, thought to be by the French cabinet-maker Juste-Aurèle Meissonier, was taken from the former Tarnowski Palace.

★ Canaletto Room

The walls of this room are decorated with scenes of Warsaw by Canaletto, the famous Venetian painter who was one of the most commercially successful artists of his day.

Cathedral of St John ❸

The Cathedral of St John started life as a parish church at the beginning of the 15th century, only acquiring cathedral status in 1798. Over the years, successive rulers endowed it with new chapels and other elements. Important ceremonies have taken place here, including the coronation of Stanisław August Poniatowski in 1764 and the oath of allegiance to the Constitution of 3 May in 1791. Many famous Poles are buried in the cathedral, among them the Polish primate, Cardinal Stefan Wyszyński. Having been seriously damaged in World War II, the cathedral was rebuilt; its new façade was designed by Jan Zachwatowicz in the spirit of Mazovian Gothic architecture.

VISITORS' CHECKLIST

ul. Świętojańska 8. **Map** 2 D3. *Tel* 022 831 02 89. 🚌 116, 175, 178, 180, 195, 222, 503. 🚃 20, 23, 26, 40. ⭕ 10am–1pm, 3–5:30pm Mon–Fri, 10am–1pm Sat, 2–5:30pm Sun. **Crypt** ⭕ as above but 3–5:30pm Sun. 📷 www.katedra.mkw.pl

Narutowicz Crypt
Gabriel Narutowicz, first president of the Polish Republic, is interred in the cathedral with other distinguished Poles.

Choir Stalls
The choir stalls are a copy of those donated as a votive offering after Poland's victory in 1683 at the Battle of Vienna.

Main entrance

Baryczkowski Crucifix
This crucifix, famed for its miraculous powers, dates from the start of the 16th century and contains natural human hair.

Małachowski Family Tomb
This monument, carved in white marble, is based on a design by the Danish Neo-Classical sculptor Bertel Thorvaldsen.

Jesuit Church ❹

ul. Świętojańska 10. **Map** 2 D3.
Tel *022 831 16 75.* 🚋 🚌 *same as Cathedral (p66).*

This Mannerist-Baroque church was built for the Jesuit order between 1609 and 1629, at the same time as the monastery. Although it had a somewhat chequered history, it survived without major changes until 1944, when it was completely destroyed. When it was rebuilt after World War II, the church's somewhat unusual architecture was restored on the basis of the original plans, which had survived. Located in a narrow space, it has a unique layout; especially original is the way in which the chancel is flooded by light falling from the lantern in the elliptical dome over the apse. The crypt, which contains a stone-cutter's workshop, is in the space once occupied by the basements of the Gothic town houses that stood on the site.

Jesuit church, dedicated to the Merciful Mother of God

Church of St Martin ❺

ul. Piwna 9/11. **Map** 2 D3. ***Tel*** *022 831 02 21.* 🚋 🚌 *same as Cathedral (p66).*

The existing post-Augustan Church is the result of two major reconstructions in the Baroque style, carried out in 1631–6 and in the first half of the 18th century. The latter phase of rebuilding took place under the direction of architect Kaȓol Bay, who

designed the undulating façade. The late Baroque decoration of the interior was destroyed in 1944. Only a partially burned crucifix survived. After the war, the interior was minutely restored to a design by Sister Alma Skrzydlewska and the crucifix incorporated into a modern design. In the 1980s, the church was a meeting place for the political opposition to the Communist government.

Old Town Square ❻

Map 2 D3. 🚋 🚌 *same as Cathedral (p66).* **Historical Museum of Warsaw** ***Tel*** *022 635 16 25.* ⏰ *9am–7pm Tue, 9am–6pm Wed–Fri, 10am–8pm Sat & Sun. A 20-min English-language film about Warsaw is screened at noon daily.* ● *Mon, pub hols & one weekend a month.* 🆓 *(free Sun).* 🌐 www. mhw.pl **Museum of Literature** ***Tel*** *022 831 40 61.* ⏰ *10am–4pm Mon, Tue & Fri, 11am–6pm Wed & Thu, 11am–5pm Sun.* ● *Sat & pub hols.* 🌐 www.muzeumliteratury.pl

Until the end of the 18th century, this rectangular market square was the most important place in Warsaw. The houses around the square were built by the most affluent members of the community. Most of them date from the 1600s, and it is these that give the square its period character. In the centre there was once a town hall, a weigh house and stalls, all demolished in 1817. In their place now stands a statue of the Mermaid *(Syrenka)*.

Each row of houses bears the name of one of the people involved in the Four-Year Sejm. On the north side is Dekerta – named after Jan Dekert, mayor of Warsaw in

the 18th century. All the houses are interconnected and now host the **Historical Museum of Warsaw**, which displays typical interiors of townspeople's homes and craftsmen's studios.

The Barbican, standing on the site of the former outer city gate

The Barbican and City Walls ❼

ul. Nowomiejska. **Map** 2 D2.

Warsaw is one of the few European capitals where a large portion of the old city wall survives. Construction of the wall began in the first half of the 14th century and continued in phases up to the mid-16th century. A double circumvallation, reinforced with fortresses and towers, encircled the town. The earliest part of the fortifications is the Barbican, erected around 1548 by Gianbattista of Venice. It was built on the site of an earlier outer gate and was intended to defend the Nowomiejska Gate (Brama Nowomiejska). The northern part of this defensive building, in the form of a dungeon reinforced by four semicircular towers, survived as the external wall of a town house. After World War II, parts of the wall were rebuilt and the Barbican, which had ceased to exist for a long period, was restored to its full scale.

Old Town Square, a favourite place both for local people and tourists

For hotels and restaurants in this region see pp298–9 and pp316–17

New Town

The New Town took shape at the beginning of the 15th century along the route leading from Old Warsaw to Zakroczym. Of interest here are the Pauline, Franciscan, Dominican and Redemptorist churches and the Church of the Holy Sacrament, which were all rebuilt after World War II, and the colourful reconstructed town houses. Ulica Mostowa, the steepest street in Warsaw, leads up to the fortress that defended one of the longest bridges in 16th-century Europe.

★ New Town Square
A town hall once stood in the centre of this irregularly shaped square ⓭

Church of the Holy Spirit
Every year, pilgrims gather at this Baroque church before setting off to Jasna Góra, in Częstochowa ❽

Ulica Freta
This is the main thoroughfare in New Town. Freta *means an uncultivated field or suburb* ⓬

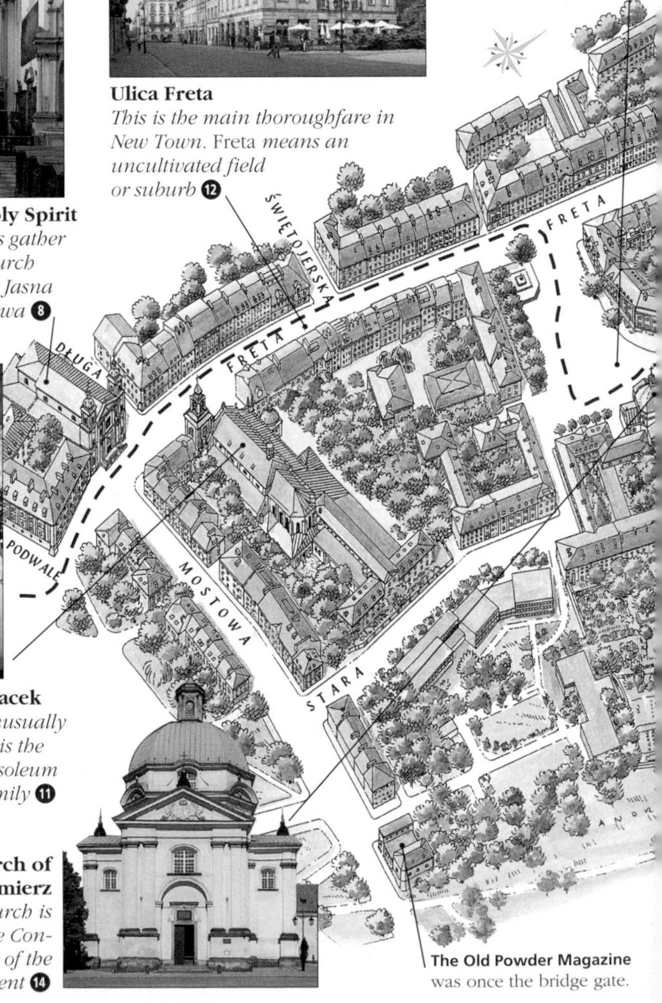

★ Church of St Jacek
A feature of the unusually elongated interior is the 17th-century mausoleum of the Kotowski family ⓫

★ Church of St Kazimierz
This beautiful church is connected to the Convent of the Order of the Holy Sacrament ⓮

The Old Powder Magazine was once the bridge gate.

LOCATOR MAP
See Street Finder, map 2

0 m   100
0 yds   100

Church of the Visitation of the Virgin Mary
The oldest surviving church in New Town, Princess Anna of Mazovia funded its construction in the early 15th century 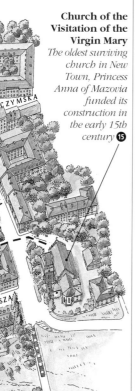 ⑮

STAR SIGHTS

★ Church of St Jacek

★ Church of St Kazimierz

★ New Town Square

KEY

– – – Suggested route

Church of the Holy Spirit ❽

ul. Nowomiejska 23. **Map** 2 D2. *Tel* 022 831 45 75. 🚌 116, 175, 178, 180, 195, 222. ◻ 6–8am, 4–6pm Mon–Sat, 6:30am–2pm, 4–7:30pm Sun. At other times, on request.

The little wooden Church of the Holy Spirit (Kościół św. Ducha) already existed in the 14th century. Repeatedly extended, it was burned down during the Swedish invasion in 1655. As the townspeople could not afford to rebuild the church, King Jan Kazimierz donated the site to the Pauline fathers from Częstochowa, who were renowned for defending their monastery at Jasna Góra *(see pp156–7)*. In return, and at their own expense, the monks built a wall that enclosed the church and the monastery within Warsaw's defences.

The present church was built in 1707–17, based on a design by the architect Józef Piola. The work was directed by Józef Szymon Bellotti and later Karol Ceroni. The interior was completed in 1725.

Rebuilt after war damage, the church is known today – as it has been since 1711 – as the main starting point for pilgrimages to the shrine of the Virgin Mary at Jasna Góra.

In Ulica Długa, a small Neo-Classical house abuts the church. It was built at the beginning of the 19th century on the smallest plot in Warsaw; it occupies only a few square metres and has its own registry number.

Church of the Holy Spirit, facing down Ulica Mostowa

Façade of Raczyński Palace, which today is the Old Records Archive

Raczyński Palace ❾

ul. Długa 7. **Map** 2 D2. *Tel* 022 635 45 32. 🚌 116, 175, 178, 180, 195, 222.

Raczynski Palace (Pałac Raczyńskich), rebuilt in 1786 to a design by the royal architect Jan Chrystian Kamsetzer, houses the Old Records Archive. The most beautiful feature of this former residence is the early Neo-Classical ballroom – damaged in the war but restored afterwards – which is decorated with stuccowork and allegorical paintings on the theme of Justice.

The subject of the paintings was manifestly at odds with the sentiments of the residence's owner, Kazimierz Raczyński, who held high office in the royal court and was considered a traitor to his country by his contemporaries. In the 19th century, the palace was the seat of the Government Justice Commission, and in the interwar period, of the Ministry of Justice.

Particularly tragic events occurred here during World War II. Bullet marks in the wall of the building are evidence of the street execution of 50 local inhabitants who were arrested at random on 24 January 1944. But the worst crimes were committed here during the Warsaw Uprising. On 13 August 1944 a tank-trap exploded, killing some 80 insurgents, and on 2 September the Nazi SS killed several hundred injured people in the building, which was being used as a hospital.

Monument to the 1944 Warsaw Uprising

Monument to the 1944 Warsaw Uprising ⑩

pl. Krasińskich. **Map** 1 C2.
🚌 116, 178, 180, 222, 503.

This monument, unveiled in 1989, commemorates the heroes of the historic Warsaw Uprising. It consists of sculptures by Wincenty Kućma placed in an architectural setting by Jacek Budyń. The sculptures represent soldiers – one group defending the barricades, the other going down into the sewers. (The insurgents used the sewer system to move around Warsaw during the uprising.) The entrance to one such sewer is still to be found near the monument.

It was in front of this monument, during the celebrations marking the 50th anniversary of the uprising, that the President of the Federal Republic of Germany, Richard Herzog, apologized to the Polish nation for the unleashing of World War II by the Third Reich and the bloody suppression of the Warsaw Uprising.

Church of St Jacek ⑪

ul. Freta 8/10. **Map** 2 D2.
Tel 022 635 47 00. 🚌 116, 178, 180, 222, 503.

At the beginning of the 17th century, while the Jesuits were building a Baroque church in Old Town, the Dominicans started work on a Gothic chancel for the Church of St Jacek (Kościół św Jacka). They returned to the Gothic style partly because of the conservatism of Mazovian buildings and partly in an attempt to endow the church with the appearance of age, so as to create an illusion of the age-old traditions of the order – which had in fact only been set up in Warsaw in 1603. When work was interrupted by a plague that raged in Warsaw in 1625, the few remaining monks listened to confessions and gave communion through openings drilled in the doors. The work

Church of St Jacek from Ulica Freta

was completed in 1639. Next to it was erected the largest monastery in Warsaw.

Interesting features inside the church, rebuilt after World War II, include the beautiful vaulting above the aisles, the Gothic chancel, decorated with stuccowork of the Lublin type, and the 17th-century tombstones shattered in 1944. The Baroque tomb of Adam and Małgorzata Kotowski, by the Dutch architect Tylman van Gameren, is also noteworthy. The domed chapel in which it stands is decorated with portraits, painted on tin plate, of the donors, who became prosperous and were ennobled despite their humble origins.

Ulica Freta ⑫

Map 2 D2. 🚌 116, 178, 180, 222, 503. **Maria Skłodowska-Curie Museum Tel** 022 831 80 92.
⏰ 8:30am–4:30pm Tue, 9:30am–5pm Wed–Fri, 10am–5:30pm Sat, 10am–5pm Sun. 🏛 📷

The main road in the New Town, Ulica Freta developed along a section of the old route leading from Old Warsaw to Zakroczym. At the end of the 1300s, buildings began to appear along it, and in the 15th century it came within the precincts of New Warsaw (Nowa Warszawa).

Several good antique shops and cafés are on this street. The house at No. 15, where Marie Curie was born, is now a museum dedicated to her. Films about her life and the history of chemistry are presented to groups on request at an extra charge.

MARIA SKŁODOWSKA-CURIE (1867–1934)

Maria Skłodowska (Marie Curie) was 24 years old when she left Warsaw to study in Paris. Within a decade she had become famous as the co-discoverer of radioactivity. Together with her husband, Pierre Curie, she discovered the elements radium and polonium. She was awarded the Nobel Prize twice: the first time in 1903, when she won the prize for physics jointly with her husband – becoming the first woman Nobel laureate – and the second in 1911 for chemistry.

The triangular-shaped New Town Square

New Town Square ⑬

Map 2 D2. 🚌 116, 178, 180, 222, 503.

The heart of the New Town is the market square (Rynek Nowego Miasta). Once rectangular, it acquired its odd triangular shape after reconstruction. When the town hall, which stood in the centre of the square, was demolished in 1818, a splendid view of the Baroque dome which crowns the Church of St Kazimierz was opened up. Destroyed in 1944, the church was rebuilt in a manner reminiscent of the 18th century, though not exactly replicating the original. The façades of many buildings around the square are covered with Socialist Realist murals. A charming 19th-century well is to be found near Ulica Freta.

Church of St Kazimierz ⑭

Rynek Nowego Miasta 2.
Map 2 D2. **Tel** 022 635 71 13.
🚌 116, 178, 180, 222, 503.
Convent ⬤ Church open to visitors.

The Church and Convent of the Order of the Holy Sacrament, designed by Tylman van Gameren, was built in 1688–92 by King Jan III Sobieski and Queen Maria Kazimiera. The remarkable domed building is distinguished by its clear Baroque architecture of classic proportions. The interior, which was damaged in he war, has since been renovated. Previously polychrome, it is now white. The most beautiful reconstructed feature is the tomb of Maria Karolina, Princesse de Bouillon, granddaughter of Jan III Sobieski. It was installed in 1746 by Bishop Andrzej Załuski and Prince Michał Kazimierz Radziwiłł, a well-known reveller who once, unsuccessfully, sought her hand in marriage. The tomb features a fractured shield and a crown falling into an abyss – references to the Sobieski coat of arms and the death of the last member of the royal line. At the rear of the convent a garden, unchanged since the 17th century, descends in tiers to the River Vistula below.

Tomb of Maria Karolina, Princesse de Bouillon

Church of the Visitation of the Virgin Mary ⑮

ul. Przyrynek 2. **Map** 2 D1.
Tel 022 831 24 73. 🚌 116, 178, 180, 222, 503.

The brick tower of the Church of the Visitation of the Virgin Mary (Kościół Nawiedzenia NMP) rises over the roofs of the houses on the bank of the River Vistula. This church is the oldest in the New Town. It was built at the beginning of the 15th century by the Mazovian princess, Anna, wife of Janusz I, the Elder, and is reputed to stand on the site of a pagan sacred spot.

Restoration carried out in the 19th century changed the building's appearance several times. Damaged during World War II, it was subsequently rebuilt in the 15th-century Gothic style. The vaulting above the chancel was completed by medieval methods: that is, it was filled by hand, without the use of pre-fabricated moulds.

In the cemetery next to the church there stands a modern statue of Walerian Łukasiński (1786–1868), founder of the National Patriotic Society.

From the terrace next to the church, there is a magnificent view of the Vistula valley.

Church of the Visitation of the Virgin Mary

THE ROYAL ROUTE

The Royal Route (Trakt Królewski) is so named because of the former royal residences that line it. It stretches from Belvedere Palace (Belweder), up to the Old Town, along Aleje Ujazdowskie, through Nowy Świat and on to Krakowskie Przedmieście. This part of Warsaw has been largely rebuilt after destruction suffered in World War II. On Aleje Ujazdowskie there are beautiful parks and little palaces surrounded by gardens, most of which now house embassies. The Neo-Classical Nowy Świat, its wide pavements decorated in summer with baskets of flowers, is lined with cafés and elegant shops. The most impressive buildings are on Krakowskie Przedmieście. This splendid location on the edge of the escarpment inspired powerful citizens to build large houses with gardens. Many churches and monasteries were also located here, as well as the president's residence and university buildings. In the street itself, there are statues of distinguished Poles. In summer, fêtes and bazaars are often organized along the Royal Route.

Cardinal Stefan Wyszyński

SIGHTS AT A GLANCE

Churches
Carmelite Church ❸
Church of the Holy Cross ❼
Church of St Anne ❶
Church of the Visitation ❺

Historic Buildings and Monuments
Gniński-Ostrogski Palace ❾
Namiestnikowski Palace ❹
Parliament ⓯
Staszic Palace ❽
Statue of Adam Mickiewicz ❷
University of Warsaw ❻

Streets and Squares
Nowy Świat ❿
Plac Trzech Krzyży ⓭
Aleje Ujazdowskie ⓮

Museums
National Museum pp80–81 ⓫
Polish Military Museum ⓬

GETTING THERE

You can get to the Royal Route by buses E-2, 102, 111, 116, 118, 160, 171, 174, 175, 178, 180, 195, 503, and on trams travelling along Aleje Jerozolimskie and the W-Z route.

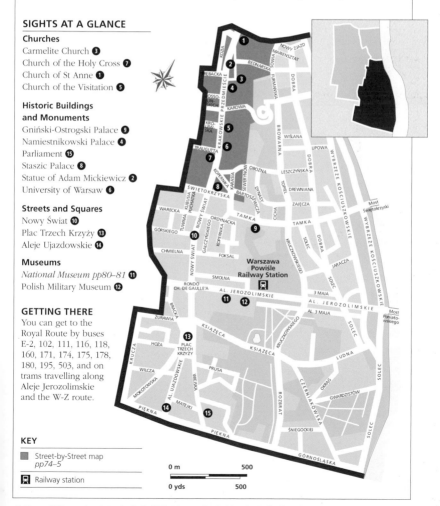

KEY

▨ Street-by-Street map *pp74–5*

🚇 Railway station

| 0 m | 500 |
| 0 yds | 500 |

◁ *Mermaid (Syrena)*, a statue by Ludwik Nitsche, on the Kościuszko Embankment

Krakowskie Przedmieście

Krakowskie Przedmieście is undoubtedly one of the most beautiful streets in Warsaw. Rebuilt after the war, the magnificent palaces that lie along it now generally house government departments. There are also pleasant restaurants, bars and cafés. The street is lined with trees, green squares and little palaces with courtyards. On weekdays, Krakowskie Przedmieście is one of the liveliest streets in Warsaw, as two great institutions of higher education are situated here: the University of Warsaw and the Academy of Fine Arts.

Church of the Visitation
Also known as the Church of St Joseph, this is one of the few churches in Warsaw that was not destroyed during World War II. Its interior features are intact ❺

Carmelite Church
The Church of Our Lady of the Assumption and St Joseph the Bridegroom has a splendid early Neo-Classical façade crowned with a green globe representing the earth ❸

Namiestnikowski Palace
This former palace, rebuilt in the Neo-Classical style for the tsar's governor in the Kingdom of Poland, is now the president's residence ❹

KAROWA

KRAKOWSKIE

BEDNARSKA

TREMBACKA

TOKARZEWSKIEGO

MIODOWA

KOZIA

★ **Church of St Anne**
The Neo-Classical façade of the church is reminiscent of the style of the 16th-century Italian architect Andrea Palladio ❶

Statue of Adam Mickiewicz
The unveiling of the statue in 1898 was a great manifestation of patriotism ❷

The Hotel Bristol, which overlooks the Namiestnikowski Palace, is the most luxurious, as well as the most expensive, hotel in Warsaw.

The statue of Nicolaus Copernicus is situated at the southern end of Krakowskie Przedmieście.

LOCATOR MAP
See Street Finder, map 2

Staszic Palace
This Neo-Classical palace now houses the Polish Academy of Sciences **8**

★ **Church of the Holy Cross**
Inside this church are urns containing the hearts of Fryderyk Chopin and Władysław Reymont, winner of the Nobel Prize for Literature **7**

★ **University of Warsaw**
The University of Warsaw is the largest educational institution in Poland. Only some of the faculties are situated at its main site on Krakowskie Przedmieście **6**

KEY

– – – Suggested route

STAR SIGHTS

★ Church of St Anne

★ Church of Holy Cross

★ University of Warsaw

0 m   100

0 yds   100

Church of St Anne **1**

ul. Krakowskie Przedmieście 68.
Map 2 D3. *Tel 022 826 89 91.*
116, 175, 178, 180, 195, 222, 503. 20, 23, 26, 40.

This Gothic church was built for the Bernardine order by Anna, widow of the Mazovian prince Bolesław III, in the second half of the 15th century. It was extended between 1518 and 1533. Destroyed during the Swedish invasion in 1655–60, it was rebuilt in a Baroque style to a design by Józef Szymon Bellotti. The Gothic chancel and the external walls were retained. The Neo-Classical façade, by Chrystian Piotr Aigner and Stanisław Kostka Potocki, is a later addition.

When the monastery was closed in 1864, the church became a religious academic institution, a role that it maintains to the present day. The relics of St Ładysław of Gielniów, one of the patron saints of Warsaw, are preserved in a side chapel. The magnificent interior of the church has polychrome paintings by Walenty Żebrowski and a series of Rococo altars. In the monastery, part of which dates from the 16th century, the crystalline vaulting in the cloisters has survived.

Crystalline vaulting in the cloister of the Bernadine monastery

Statue of Adam Mickiewicz ❷

ul. Krakowskie Przedmieście.
Map 2 D4.

This statue of Poland's most distinguished Romantic poet was unveiled in 1898, on the centenary of his birth. Erecting the statue during the period of intense Russification that followed the January Insurrection of 1863 was a great achievement on the part of the committee in charge of the project, led by Michał Radziwiłł and Henryk Sienkiewicz. The statue was designed by Cyprian Godebski, and the plinth by Józef Pius Dziekoński and Władysław Marconi. It was set up in a square off Krakowskie Przedmieście that was once lined with houses flanked by side streets. The houses were later demolished and the road widened. Only the statue of the Mother of God of Passau, dating from 1683, on the edge of the square, survives. It was made in the workshop of Szymon Belloti to a commission from Jan III Sobieski as an offering in thanks for a Polish victory at the Battle of Vienna and for the protection of the royal family.

Carmelite Church ❸

ul. Krakowskie Przedmieście 52/54.
Map 2 D4. 🚌 *116, 175, 178, 180, 195, 222, 503.*

The Baroque Church of Our Lady of the Assumption (Kościół Wniebowzięcia NMP) was built for the order of Discalced Carmelites in 1661–82, probably to a design by Józef Szymon Belloti, although the Neo-Classical façade is considerably later. Designed by Efraim Schroeger, it dates from 1782 and is one of the earliest examples of Neo-Classicism in Poland. Despite suffering war damage, the church,

The early Neo-Classical façade of the Carmelite Church

consisting of a nave with interconnecting side chapels and a transept, has many of its original features. The main altar, with sculptures by Jan Jerzy Plersch, is beautiful. Plersch also carved the sculptural group of the *Visitation of the Virgin*, a very sophisticated and Romantic piece which was transferred from an earlier Dominican church and can now be seen on the altar near the rood arch. Also noteworthy are the Baroque paintings, especially the two small works in the side altars near the chancel, by Szymon Czechowicz.
During the Northern War of 1705, Stanisław Leszczyński held peace negotiations with Charles XII in the church. From 1864, after the closure of the monastery, the monastic buildings housed a seminary.

Statue of Adam Mickiewicz

Namiestnikowski Palace ❹

ul. Krakowskie Przedmieście 46/48.
Map 2 D4. 🚌 *116, 175, 178, 180, 195, 222, 503.* ⬤ *to the public.*

The palace owes its elegant Neo-Classical form to refurbishment carried out by Chrystian Piotr Aigner in 1918–19. However, this work conceals much older walls, as a palace stood on this site as early as the mid-17th century.
Namiestnikowski Palace was home to several prominent familes, among them the Koniecpolskis, the Lubomirskis and, from 1685, the Radziwiłłs. From them the government of the Kingdom of Poland bought the palace in 1818 as the residence of the governor-general of the tsarist government. Among the people who lived here were General Józef Zajączek, viceroy of Tsar Alexander, and the much-hated General Iwan Paskiewicz. The wife of General Zajączek was a very colourful figure; she was a prima ballerina and shocked the town with her love affairs late into old age.
The palace escaped serious damage during World War II. After refurbishment, it was designated the seat of the Council of Ministers and witnessed many important political events: the signing of the Warsaw Pact in 1955, the treaty normalizing relations with Germany in 1970, and the Round Table Talks in 1989. Since 1994 the palace has been the residence of the president of the Republic of Poland.

Namiestnikowski Palace with a statue of Józef Poniatowski

For hotels and restaurants in this region see pp298–9 and pp316–17

Baroque ebony tabernacle in the Church of the Visitation

Church of the Visitation ❺

ul. Krakowskie Przedmieście 34.
Map 2 D4. 🚌 116, 175, 178, 180, 195, 222, 503.

The Order of the Visitation was brought to Poland by Maria Gonzaga, wife of Jan Kazimierz. Work on the Church of the Visitation (Kościół Wizytek) began in the same year but was interrupted, and not resumed until the 18th century, when the architect Karol Bay took control of the project. The façade, by Efraim Schroeger, was completed in 1763. The church suffered no war damage, so its interior features have survived intact. The most splendid of these are the Rococo pulpit in the form of a ship and the sculptures on the high altar. Many fine paintings have also survived, including *The Visitation* by Tadeusz Kuntze-Konicz, *St Luis Gonzaga* by Daniel Szulc and *St Francis of Sales* by Szymon Czechowicz. The ebony tabernacle, decorated with silver plaques by Herman Pothoff, was commissioned by Ludwika Maria and completed in 1654. Next to the church, the Baroque convent building and garden are still used by the Nuns of the Visitation today.

University of Warsaw ❻

ul. Krakowskie Przedmieście 26/28.
Map 2 D5. **Tel** 022 552 00 00. 🚌 116, 175, 178, 180, 195, 222, 503.

The nucleus of the University of Warsaw (Uniwersytet Warszawski) grew from a summer palace known as the Villa Regia. In the first half of the 17th century, the palace belonged to the Vasa dynasty. From then on it underwent many phases of refurbishment, and in 1816 was chosen to house what was then the new university. After further alteration, the former palace acquired the late Neo-Classical appearance that it has today – as did the outbuildings to each side (designed by Jakub Kubicki in 1814–16), the main school (Corrazzi, commenced 1841), and the lecture hall and the former Fine Arts Department (both by Michał Kado, 1818–22). After the January Insurrection – when the university was run by the Russian

authorities – a library was added (Stefan Szyller and Antoni Jabłoński, 1891–4). The Auditorium Maximum was built when the university passed back into Polish hands after the country regained its independence.

Today, the University of Warsaw is Poland's largest educational establishment. The complex around Kazimierz Palace (Pałac Kazimierzowski), which houses several buildings, is now mainly used as its administrative centre.

Church of the Holy Cross ❼

ul. Krakowskie Przedmieście 3. **Map** 2 D5. **Tel** 022 556 88 20. 🚌 116, 175, 178, 180, 195, 222, 503.

The original Church of the Holy Cross (Kościół św Krzyża, 1626) was destroyed during the Swedish Deluge of the 1650s. The current Baroque missionaries' church was designed by Giuseppe Simone Bellotti and built between 1679 and 1696. The façade was completed in 1760.

The church is a splendid example of Varsovian church architecture of the late 17th century. During World War II, it suffered major damage and most of its interior was destroyed. The most interesting surviving feature is the altar in the south wing of the transept, designed by Tylman van Gameren. Many important ceremonies have taken place in the church, including the funerals of political thinker Stanisław Staszic (1755–1826), composer Karol Szymanowski (1882–1937) and painter Leon Wyczółkowski (1852–1936). Urns containing the hearts of composer Fryderyk Chopin (1810–49) and novelist Władysław Reymont (1867–1925) are built into a pillar of the nave.

Statue of Christ, Church of the Holy Cross

SVRSVM CORDA

Monument to Nicolaus Copernicus in front of Staszic Palace

Staszic Palace ⑧

ul. Nowy Świat 72. **Map** 2 D5.
🚌 *111, 116, 125, 151, 175, 180, 195, 222, 503.*

Contrary to what its name suggests, Staszic Palace (Pałac Staszica) never belonged to Stanisław Staszic, nor did he ever live here – although he did fund it. The palace was built by Antonio Corazzi between 1820 and 1823 in the late Neo-Classical style, as the headquarters of the Royal Society of Friends of Science. Since World War II it has housed the Polish Academy of Science and the Warsaw Scientific Society. The monument to astronomer Nicolaus Copernicus that stands in front of the building is by Bertel Thorvaldsen. It was unveiled in 1830.

Gniński-Ostrogski Palace ⑨

ul. Okólnik 1. **Map** 4 D1. *Tel 022 441 62 51.* 🚌 *102, 111, 116, 151, 174, 175, 178, 180, 195, 503.*
◻ *11am–8pm Tue–Sun.* 🎫 🎭 📷
Concerts. www.chopin.museum/en

Built after 1681, Gniński-Ostrogski Palace (Pałac Gnińskich-Ostrogskich) is one of Tylman van Gameren's grand masterpieces. The pavilion was erected on an elevated terrace above a cellar. According to legend, a golden duck lived under the palace, guarding its treasures.
   Today the palace is home to the Fryderyk Chopin Museum (Muzeum Fryderyka Chopina), which houses portraits, letters and autograph manuscripts, as well as the grand piano at which Chopin composed during the last two years of his life. It is also the home of the Chopin Society, and regular performances of Chopin's music take place here.

Nowy Świat ⑩

Map 3 C1, 3 C2, 4 D1. 🚌 *E-2, 111, 116, 151, 175, 180, 195, 222, 503.* 🚊 *7, 8, 9, 22, 24, 25.*

The street known as Nowy Świat (New World) is a stretch of the medieval route leading from the castle to Czersk and on to Cracow, and thus forms part of the Royal Route. Buildings started to appear along a section of the road at the end of the 18th century. First came a small number of Neo-Classical palaces; by the beginning of the 19th century they had been joined by late Neo-Classical town houses. At the end of the 19th century, Nowy Świat was an elegant street of restaurants, cafés, summer theatres, hotels and shops. After serious damage in World War II, only the Neo-Classical buildings were reconstructed, although later buildings were given pseudo-Neo-Classical features to preserve a uniformity of style.
   Today, Nowy Świat is one of the most attractive streets in Warsaw, with wide pedestrian areas and cafés with pavement gardens. Blikle, the café at No. 33, boasts a 130-year tradition and the best doughnuts (*pączki*) in town. Kossakowski Palace, at No. 19, was remodelled by Henryk Marconi in 1849–51. Strolling along Nowy Świat it is worth turning down Ulica Foksal, where there are a number of 19th-century houses and small palaces. The most beautiful, at Nos. 1/2/4, was built for the Zamoyski family by Leandro Marconi in 1878–9. Today, it houses an up-market art gallery and the Association of Architects of the Polish Republic. At the roundabout on the intersection of Nowy Świat and Aleje Jerozolimskie stands the huge building of the former Polish United Workers' Party Central Committee. Transformed after the fall of communism into a "den of capitalism", it now houses banks, the Polish stock exchange and the offices of various companies.

Nowy Świat, a street of elegant shops and cafés

National Museum

See pp80–81.

Polish Military Museum ⑫

Aleje Jerozolimskie 3. **Map** 4 D2 and 6 E1. **Tel** 022 629 52 71/2. 🚃 111, 117, 158, 507, 517, 521. 🚋 7, 8, 9, 22, 24, 25. 🕙 10am–5pm Wed, 10am–4pm Thu–Sun. 🎟 (free on Sun). 🎫 **Outdoor exhibition** ⬜ until dusk, free admission. ⬜ ⬜ **www.**muzeumwp.pl

The Polish Military Museum (Muzeum Wojska Polskiego), established in 1920, contains a collection of Polish arms and armour spanning more than 1,000 years. The most interesting aspect of the permanent exhibition is the collection of armour from the Early Middle Ages to the end of the 18th century. It includes a rare gilded helmet that belonged to a Polish chieftain of the Early Christian era and numerous pieces relating to the greatest medieval battles fought on Polish territory.

Among the more unusual exhibits are medieval jousting armour and an impressive collection of 17th-century armour of the Husaria, the famous Polish cavalry, with eagle wings, leopardskins and a mounted cavalryman in full regalia. Heavy weapons from the two World Wars are displayed in the park outside.

Plac Trzech Krzyży ⑬

Map 3 C2, 3 C3. 🚃 E-2, 108, 116, 118, 151, 166, 171, 180, 195, 222, 503.

Plac Trzech Krzyży (Three Crosses Square) is something of a misnomer. Mounted on top of Baroque columns, two gilded crosses, commissioned by August II and made by Joachim Daniel Jauch in 1731, mark the beginning of Droga Kalwaryjską (Road

of Calvary). The third cross is held by St John Nepomuk, whose statue was erected in 1752 by Grand Crown Marshal Franciszek Bieliński to mark the completion of the project to pave the streets of Warsaw. A fourth cross crowns the dome of the 19th-century Church of St Alexander (Kościół św. Aleksandra).

The oldest buildings around the square are two 18th-century town houses: No. 1 Nowy Świat, with an early Neo-Classical façade, and No. 2 Plac Trzech Krzyży, part of the complex of the Institute of the Deaf and Blind, established in 1817. Other buildings erected round the square in the 20th century have restored something of its urban character.

Statue of St John Nepomuk

Aleje Ujazdowskie ⑭

Map 3 C3, 3 C4, 3 C5. 🚃 116, 138, 151, 166, 180, 182, 187, 188, 195, 502, 503, 514, 520, 523, 525.

Aleje Ujazdowskie is one of the most beautiful streets in Warsaw – a good place for a stroll in the summer. While the east side is bordered by parks, the west is lined with elegant houses originally built for Warsaw's ruling classes but now largely occupied by embassies. There are also palatial houses; No. 17

and No. 19, by architect Stanisław Grochowicz, are especially splendid. No. 17, built in 1903–4, has an eclectic façade. No. 1, formerly a barracks, houses the offices of the Council of Ministers.

Parliament ⑮

ul. Wiejska 2/4/6. **Map** 4 D3, 4 D4. **Tel** 022 694 25 00. 🚃 E-2, 107, 108, 116, 118, 151, 159, 166, 171, 180, 195, 222, 503. 🕙 by prior arrangement.

The parliamentary tradition in Poland dates from 1453, but it was interrupted by the loss of Polish sovereignty in the late 1700s. Only after the restoration of Poland's independence in 1918 was its two-chamber parliament – comprising the Sejm and the Senate – reconvened. Lacking a suitable building, representatives and senators gathered for a time in the former Institute for the Education of Young Ladies.

In 1925–8, a lofty semi-circular hall was built, with a debating chamber for the Sejm. It was designed by Kazimierz Skórewicz and decorated with Art Deco bas-reliefs by Jan Szczepkowski. After damage suffered in World War II, the parliamentary buildings were significantly extended in the spirit of the comparatively refined Socialist Realist style, to a design by Bohdan Pniewski.

In 1989, after the first free elections since World War II, the upper parliamentary chamber, abolished under communist rule, was restored.

In 1999, a monument in honour of the Home Army was unveiled in front of the Sejm.

The semicircular parliament (Sejm) building, with Art Deco bas-reliefs

National Museum ⓫

The National Museum (Muzeum Narodowe) was originally the Museum of Fine Arts, acquiring its present status in 1916. Despite wartime losses, today it has a large collection of works of art covering all periods from antiquity to modern times. Due to lack of space, not all the exhibits are on permanent display.

W. Szymanowski, The Kiss

★ Virgin and Child
This important painting by Sandro Botticelli is the only work by the artist in Polish collections.

★ St Anne Fresco
This fresco of St Anne is one of the 10th-century wall paintings discovered by Polish archaeologists in Faras, Sudan.

Battle of Grunwald, a painting by Jan Matejko *(see pp40–41)*, is the most famous in the Gallery of Polish Art.

Greek Vase
Some of the Greek vases displayed in the Gallery of Ancient Art are partly from a private collection.

KEY

- ▪ Ancient Art
- ▪ Faras Collection
- ▪ Medieval Art
- ☐ 19th-century Art
- ▪ 20th- and 21st-century Art
- ☐ 15th- to 18th-century European Paintings
- ☐ 15th- to 19th-century Polish and European Portraits
- ▪ Polish Decorative Art
- ▪ European Decorative Art
- ▪ L. Kronenberg Silver Room
- ▪ Temporary exhibitions
- ☐ Non-exhibition areas

Ground f

Virgin from Wrocław
This "Beautiful Madonna" is an early 15th-century sculpture that exemplifies the International Gothic style.

The Raising of Lazarus
This painting by Rembrandt pupil Carel Fabritius is one of his finest, and the most important exhibit in the Foreign Art Gallery.

VISITORS' CHECKLIST

al. Jerozolimskie 3. **Map** 4 D2.
Tel 022 629 30 93. 🚌 *E-2,
111, 117, 158, 517, 521.* 🚊 *7,
8, 9, 22, 24, 25.* ⬜ 10am–6pm
Tue, Wed & Fri–Sun, 10am–9pm
Thu. ● Mon, 1 Jan, Easter Sun,
1 and 3 May, Corpus Christi, 15
Aug, 1 Nov, 24–26 Dec. 🎟 free
Tue. 🏠 🚻 📷 🖥 📷 🔌 ♿
📹 **Films.www**.mnw.art.pl

Furniture
This bedroom designed by Karol Tichy in 1909 reflects the utilitarian aspect of 20th-century design. It is on display in the Decorative Arts Gallery.

Second floor

Banquet
The painter and mathematician Leon Chwistek developed a theory of "zonism", according to which various areas of a painting are dominated by certain shapes and colours, as in this scene.

First floor

★ Polish Hamlet
This portrait of the aristo-crat and politician Aleksander Wielopolski painted by Jacek Malczewski in 1903, is in the style of the Polish Symbolist school.

STAR PAINTINGS

★ Virgin and Child

★ Polish Hamlet

★ St Anne Fresco

GALLERY GUIDE
The collections are arranged on three floors. On the ground floor are the Galleries of Ancient Art, the Faras Collection and the Gallery of Medieval Art. On the first floor is the collection of Polish art. Foreign paintings can be seen on the first and second floors.

THE CITY CENTRE

rom the late 18th to the mid-19th century, the area around Ulica Senatorska and Plac Teatralny was the commercial and cultural centre of Warsaw. Imposing Neo-Classical buildings with impressive colonnades are still to be seen there. The Grand Theatre (Teatr Wielki) on Plac Teatralny is one of the largest buildings of its type in Europe. The Saxon Gardens (Ogród Saski), stretching through the centre of the district, are what remains of a former royal park that adjoined the residence of the Saxon king August II. In the second half of the 19th

Nike Monument

century, the city's commercial centre moved to the area around Ulica Marszałkowska, prompted by the opening in 1845 of Warsaw's first railway station at the junction with Aleje Jerozolimskie. The city centre was completely transformed after the damage inflicted during World War II. Today, its principal landmark is the Palace of Culture and Science (Pałac Kultury i Nauki). The western part of the city centre is dominated by tower blocks. For tourists, the eastern side is of most interest. Here, several historic buildings have survived, dating from the 18th up to the early 20th century.

SIGHTS AT A GLANCE

Places of Worship
Capuchin Church **3**
Evangelical Church of the Augsburg Confession **12**
Nożyk Synagogue **15**

Buildings and Historic Monuments
Arsenal **6**
Branicki Palace **2**
Krasiński Palace **5**
Pac Palace **4**
Palace of Culture and Science **14**
Primate's Palace **1**
Przebendowski-Radziwiłłów Palace **7**

Monuments and Commemorative Sites
Monument to the Heroes of the Ghetto **18**
Monument to those Fallen and Murdered in the East **19**
Umschlagplatz Monument **17**

Streets and Squares
Plac Bankowy **8**
Plac Teatralny **9**

Parks
Saxon Gardens **10**

Museums and Galleries
Ethnographical Museum **13**
Pawiak Prison **16**
Zachęta **11**

KEY

▪ Street-by-Street map
   pp84–5

Ⓜ Metro

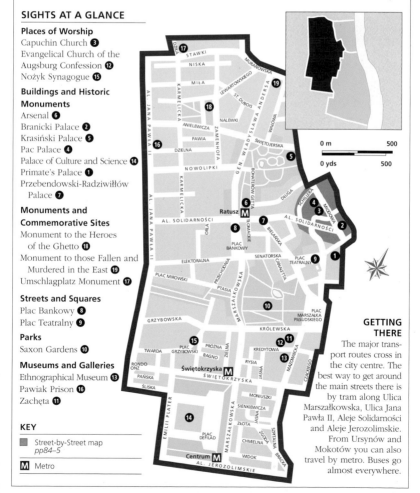

GETTING THERE

The major transport routes cross in the city centre. The best way to get around the main streets there is by tram along Ulica Marszałkowska, Ulica Jana Pawła II, Aleje Solidarności and Aleje Jerozolimskie. From Ursynów and Mokotów you can also travel by metro. Buses go almost everywhere.

◁ **The Palace of Culture and Science by night, seen from Ulica Złota**

Ulica Miodowa

Ulica Miodowa lies just outside the much-visited Old Town. Tourists rarely venture here, but it holds many attractions nonetheless. The street has three Baroque churches and several palaces – including the Neo-Classical Primate's Palace and the Rococo Branicki Palace – set behind spacious courtyards. The former Collegium Nobilium, the most famous Polish school for the children of the nobility in the 18th century, now houses the Academy of Dramatic Arts.

The Basilian church is hidden behind the palace façade. Byzantine-Ukrainian masses are celebrated here.

★ **Pac Palace**
The 19th-century interiors are decorated in the Gothic, Renaissance, Greek and Moorish styles ④

Nike Monument

AL. SOLIDARNOŚCI

★ **Capuchin Church**
In accordance with the rule of poverty of the Capuchin order, the altars in this church have no gilt or polychrome decoration ③

SENATORSKA

MIODOWA

SCHILLERA

MIODOWA

Branicki Palace
Rebuilt after World War II, the palace was crowned with sculptures derived from paintings by Canaletto ②

The Field Cathedral of the Polish Armed Forces was built in the 17th century as a church for the Piarist order.

KEY

– – – Suggested route

0 m   50

0 yds   50

STAR SIGHTS

★ Capuchin Church

★ Pac Palace

The Primate's Palace, a building in the Neo-Classical style

Primate's Palace ❶

ul. Senatorska 13/15. **Map** 2 D3.
***Tel** 022 829 66 67.* 111, 116, 175, 180, 195. ● *to the public.*

The present-day appearance of the Primate's Palace (Pałac Prymasowski) reflects the refurbishments carried out by Efraim Schroeger in 1777–84 for the Primate of Poland, Antoni Ostrowski. Schroeger's work was then continued by Szymon Zug for the next primate, Michał Poniatowski. The unusual arrangement of the building, with its semicircular wings, is reminiscent of the designs of the most celebrated architect of the Italian Renaissance, Andrea Palladio (1508–80).

The Primate's Palace is generally considered to be the first Neo-Classical palace built in Poland. It was destroyed during World War II, then was rebuilt in 1949–52. Today it is used as an office building.

The superb Great Hall (Sala Wielka) is decorated with Ionic columns and delicate Neo-Classical stuccowork.

Branicki Palace ❷

ul. Miodowa 6. **Map** 2 D3. 116, 180, 195. ● *to the public.*

Branicki Palace (Pałac Branickich) was built for Jan Klemens Branicki, adviser to August III. This powerful magnate was known both as a distinguished soldier and a connoisseur of fine art. Work began on the palace in 1740, to a design by Jan Zygmunt Deybel, and was completed by Giacopo Fontana.

Following almost complete destruction during World War II, this Rococo palace was rebuilt in 1947–53. The reconstruction was based on detailed historical research and 18th-century paintings.

Capuchin Church ❸

ul. Miodowa 13. **Map** 1 C3. 116, 174, 175, 180, 195.

The Capuchin Church (kościół Kapucynów), or Church of the Transfiguration, was built by Jan III Sobieski in gratitude for the Polish victory over the Turks at the Battle of Vienna in 1683. Building began in the same year under the direction of Izydor Affaita – probably to designs by Tylman van Gameren and Agostino Locci the Younger – and was completed by Carlo Ceroni in 1692. The modest façade recalls the Capuchin church in Rome. The church houses urns containing the heart of Jan III and the ashes of the Saxon king, August II. In the crypt, there is a nativity scene with emotive figures.

Sarcophagus with the heart of Jan III Sobieski in the Capuchin church

Pac Palace ❹

ul. Miodowa 15. **Map** 1 C3.
Tel 022 634 96 00. 🚌 116, 175,
180, 195. ◯ occasionally.

The Baroque Pac Palace
(Pałac Paca), formerly the
residence of the Radziwiłł
family, was designed and
built by Tylman van Gameren
in 1681–97. One of the
palace's 19th-century owners,
Ludwik Pac, commissioned
the architect Henryk Marconi
to redesign it; work was completed in 1828. The interiors
were decorated in the Gothic,
Renaissance, Greek and
Moorish styles, and the
façade remodelled in the
Palladian manner. The
palace gate was modelled
on a triumphal arch and
decorated with Classical bas-
relief sculptures – the work of
Ludwik Kaufman, a pupil of
the celebrated Neo-Classical
sculptor Antonio Canova.
Today the palace houses
the Ministry of Health.

**Neo-Classical medallion on the
façade of Pac Palace**

Krasiński Palace ❺

pl. Krasińskich 5. **Map** 1 C2.
Tel 022 531 02 00. 🚌 116, 178,
180, 222. ◯ during exhibitions.

Krasiński Palace (Pałac
Krasińskich), in the Baroque
style, is regarded as one of
the most beautiful late 17th-
century buildings in Warsaw.
It was designed by Tylman
van Gameren and built
between 1687 and 1700 for
the mayor of Warsaw,
Jan Dobrogost Krasiński.
   A triangular pediment
features ornamental reliefs
depicting the heroic deeds
of the Roman patrician
Marcus Valerius (known
as Corvinus), a legendary

Krasiński Palace seen from the palace gardens

ancestor of Jan Dobrogost
Krasiński. The reliefs are the
work of Andreas Schlüter,
an outstandingly gifted
sculptor and architect who
later designed the Arsenal
and Royal Castle in Berlin.
Rebuilt after war damage,
the palace now houses a
collection of antique prints
and manuscripts from the
National Library.

Arsenal ❻

ul. Długa 52. **Map** 1 B3. **Tel** 022 831
15 37. 🚌 E-2, 107, 111, 127, 160,
171, 180, 195, 410, 503, 520, 522.
🚋 4, 15, 18, 20, 23, 26, 35.
Ⓜ Ratusz. **www.pma.pl**
Archaeological Museum
◯ 9am–4pm Mon–Thu & Sat,
10am–4pm Sun. ◯ 3rd Sun in the
month. 🎟 (free on Sun). 🎫

The arsenal was built in
1638–47, in the Baroque
style, by Władysław IV Vasa.
There, during World War II,
boy scout soldiers of the
Grey Ranks (the Szare
Szeregi, who were actively
involved in the resistance
movement) released 21 prisoners from the hands of the
Gestapo; this brave action is
commemorated by a plaque.
   The Arsenal now houses
the Archaeological Museum,
with exhibits from excavations carried out within both
the country's pre-war and
present day borders. Also on
display are objects from other
European countries, Asia, the
Americas and Africa. The exhibition on prehistoric Poland
is highly recommended. By
prior arrangement, younger
visitors may make clay pots
using prehistoric methods.

Przebendowski-Radziwiłłów Palace ❼

al. Solidarności 62. **Map** 1 C3.
Tel 022 826 90 91. 🚌 E-2, 107,
111, 160, 171, 175, 190, 195, 410,
503, 512, 522, 527. 🚋 13, 18, 23,
26, 32, 35, 36. Ⓜ Ratusz.
Independence Museum (Muzeum
Niepodległości) ◯ 10am–5pm Tue–
Fri, 10am–4pm Sat & Sun.
🎟 (free on Sun). 🎫 **www**.muzeum
niepodleglosci.art.pl

Before World War II, this
Baroque palace was in a
narrow shopping street. When
the East-West (W-Z) route was
constructed (1948–9), it was
suddenly surrounded by a
major traffic artery. The palace,
which has the most beautiful
mansard roofs in Warsaw and
an oval bow-fronted façade,
was built in 1728 to a design
by Jan Zygmunt Deybel. Since
1990 it has housed the Independence Museum (Muzeum
Niepodległości), which features
a collection of documents
relating Poland's history.

**The Baroque Przebendowski-
Radziwiłłów Palace**

For hotels and restaurants in this region see pp298–9 and pp316–17

Plac Bankowy ❽

Map 1 B3 and 1 B4. ▦ *E-2, 107, 111, 127, 171, 180, 195, 410, 522.* ▦ *13, 18, 23, 26, 32, 35, 36.* Ⓜ *Ratusz.* **John Paul II Collection** pl. Bankowy 1. *Tel 022 620 27 25.* ◯ *10am–5pm (4pm in winter) Tue–Sun.* ▦

Today Plac Bankowy (Bank Square) is one of the busiest places in Warsaw. Once a quiet little square, it was radically altered after the construction of the East–West route and Ulica Marszałkowska. A statue of Feliks Dzierżyński, the founder of the Soviet security service, was erected here, and the square was renamed in his honour. In 1989, to the joy of local inhabitants, the statue was removed and the square's original name restored. Plac Bankowy was once the site of the largest synagogue in Warsaw. It was demolished after the collapse of the Ghetto Uprising of 1943. A tower block now stands on the site. The most interesting buildings are on the west side of the square. The group of Neo-Classical buildings zealously rebuilt after World War II were designed by Antonio Corazzi. The most impressive is the three-winged palace of the Commission for Revenues and Treasury, which today serves as a town hall. From the junction with Ulica Elektoralna, the fine building of the former Bank of Poland (Bank Polski) and Stock Exchange (Giełda) can be admired. The building now houses the John Paul II Collection, donated by Janina and Zbigniew Porczyński. It consists of over 450 works by famous artists and is arranged thematically.

Neo-Classical frieze on the façade of the Grand Theatre

Plac Teatralny ❾

Map 1 C4. ▦ *111.*

Before 1944, Plac Teatralny (Theatre Square) was the heart of Warsaw. The enormous Neo-Classical Grand Theatre (Teatr Wielki) on the south side was designed by Antonio Corazzi and Ludwik Kozubowski and completed in 1833. The façade is decorated with a Neo-Classical frieze by Paweł Maliński depicting Oedipus and his companions returning from the Olympian Games. The theatre was rebuilt and greatly enlarged after suffering war damage. Two statues stand in front of the building: one depicts Stanisław Moniuszko, the father of Polish opera *(see p26)*, and the other Wojciech Bogusławski, who instigated the theatre's construction. Today it is the home of the National Opera and the National Theatre.

In 1848, the Russian composer Mikhail Glinka (1803–57) lived and worked in the house at No. 2 Ulica Niecała, just off Plac Teatralny.

Bogusławski Monument

Opposite the theatre, on the north side of the square, stood the small Church of St Andrew and the enormous, repeatedly extended Jabłonowski Palace, which was refashioned as the town hall in 1817–19. Close by was Blank's Palace, a late Baroque building, which was owned by Piotr Blank, a banker at the time of Stanisław August Poniatowski (1764–95). At the beginning of the Nazi occupation of Poland, the Germans arrested Stefan Starzyński, the heroic mayor of Warsaw, in this building. During the Warsaw Uprising, the poet Krzysztof Kamil Baczyński died amid its ruins. In the years after World War II, only Blank's Palace was rebuilt; Jabłonowski Palace and the church – now the Church of St Brother Albert and St Andrew – were rebuilt at the end of the 20th century. The Nike Monument, which once stood in Plac Teatralny in memory of Warsaw's resistance against the Nazis, was moved to a different site near the East-West route, where it stands on a high plinth.

Municipal government buildings on Plac Bankowy

Tomb of the Unknown Soldier in the Saxon Gardens

Saxon Gardens ⑩

Map 1 C4, 1 C5. 📷 *107, 160, 171, 174, 178.* 🚋 *15, 18, 35, 36.*

The Saxon Gardens (Ogród Saski) were laid out between 1713 and 1733 by August II, the Strong, to a design by Jan Krzysztof Naumann and Mateus Daniel Pöppelmann. Originally the royal gardens adjoining Morsztyn Palace, they became the basis for a Baroque town planning project in Warsaw known as the Saxon Axis (Osią Saską). In 1727 the Saxon Gardens became the first public park in Poland, and for two centuries they served as an alfresco "summer salon" for Varsovians. At the time of August III, Karol Fryderyk Pöppelmann built a Baroque summer theatre here; this stood until 1772. Between 1816 and 1827, James Savage refashioned the gardens in the English style. In 1870 they were graced by an enormous wooden summer theatre, which was destroyed in September 1939, at the start of World War II. The gardens are now adorned with 21 Baroque sandstone statues made by sculptors including Jan Jerzy Plersch in the 1730s. There were once many more statues here; some were removed to St Petersburg by Marshal Suvorov, who recaptured Warsaw during

Baroque sculpture from the Saxon Gardens

the uprising led by Tadeusz Kościuszko in 1794.

Saski Palace was destroyed at the end of 1944. All that remains today is the Tomb of the Unknown Soldier, where the body of a soldier who fell in the defence of Lvov (1918–19) was interred on 2 November 1925. Plans are afoot to restore the palace to its former glory.

Zachęta ⑪

pl. Małachowskiego 3. **Map** 1 C5. *Tel 022 556 96 00.* 📷 *E-2, 174, 410.* 🕐 *noon–8pm Tue–Sun.* 🎟️ *(free on Thu).* **www**.zacheta.art.pl

The Zachęta building – now the National Gallery of Contemporary Art – was built in 1899–1903 for the Society for the Promotion of Fine Arts. It was designed by Stefan Szyller, the leading architect of Warsaw's Revival period, a 19th- and early

20th-century architectural movement. It was conceived as a monumental building in the Neo-Renaissance style, with four wings (only completed in 1995) and a glass-roofed inner courtyard.

In order to promote the work of contemporary Polish artists, the Society organized exhibitions and competitions, and purchased works of art. The Zachęta's permanent collections were transferred to the National Museum, and the building, as before, now serves as a venue for temporary exhibitions of modern art.

It was here in 1922 that Gabriel Narutowicz, the first president of the newly independent Polish Republic, was assassinated by Eligiusz Niewiadomski, a Polish painter, critic and fanatic.

Evangelical Church of the Augsburg Confession ⑫

pl. Małachowskiego 1. **Map** 1 C5. *Tel 022 556 46 60.* 📷 *174, 410.*

The Evangelical Church of the Augsburg Confession (Kościół św Trójcy) was designed by Szymon Bogumił Zug and built in 1777–81. The Neo-Classical building is crowned by a dome 58 m (189 ft) high. For a long time the church was the highest building in Warsaw, and bore witness to the religious tolerance of the Polish nation and of Stanisław August Poniatowski (1764–95), the last king of Poland. The church is reminiscent of the

Façade of the Zachęta building (National Gallery of Contemporary Art)

The interior of the Evangelical Church of the Augsburg Confession

Pantheon in Rome; however, this ancient model was merely a starting point from which Zug developed a unique design. The interior of the church features a vast barrel-vaulted nave with rectangular transepts. The west front features a massive Doric portico which emphasizes the severity of the façade, regarded as one of the outstanding examples of Neo-Classical architecture in Poland. The interior, with its double tier of galleries supported by columns, has excellent acoustics and is used for choral and other concerts.

Ethnographical Museum ⓭

ul. Kredytowa 1. **Map** 1 C5. **Tel** 022 827 76 41/5. 🚌 125, 150, 160, 506. ⭘ 10am–6pm Tue–Thu, 10am–4pm Fri, 10am–5pm Sat, noon–5pm Sun. 🔵 public hols. 🖼 (free on Sat). 🔼 🏛🧑‍🦽🎫📷

The Ethnographical Museum (Muzeum Etnograficzne) is housed in a Neo-Renaissance building on the south side of Plac Małachowski. The former head office of the Land Credit Association, it was built in 1854–8, to a design by Henryk Marconi, an Italian architect who settled in Warsaw. It recalls the Libreria Sansoviniana in Venice, and is one of the city's finest 19th-century buildings. The museum con-

Sacred figure, Ethnographical Museum

tains permanent displays of Polish folk costumes, folklore and arts and crafts, and collections of ethnic and tribal art from around the world, including Africa, Australia, the Pacific and Latin America. It also mounts occasional temporary exhibitions.

In a neighbouring building on Ulica Mazowiecka, behind a gate with bullet marks, is the glass-fronted Artist's House (Dom Artysty), which contains a modern art gallery. Also on Ulica Mazowiecka are several bookshops, the best of which are at the intersection with Ulica Święto-krzyska. Up until the beginning of World War II, Ziemiańska, a very famous café, was to be found at No. 22 Ulica Mazowiecka. This was where the cream of society and the artistic community met to exchange ideas and gossip over coffee.

Palace of Culture and Science ⓮

pl. Defilad 1. **Map** 3 A1, 3 B1. **Tel** 022 656 76 00. 🚌 109, 117, 118, 125, 127, 128, 130, 131, 150, 158, 160, 171, 174, 175, 210, 275, 422, 501, 504, 507, 510, 517, 519, 520, 521, 525. 🚋 4, 7, 8, 9, 10, 15, 17, 22, 24, 25, 35, 36. Ⓜ Centre (Centrum). **Viewing platform** ⭘ 10am–6pm daily. 🖼 🔼 🧑‍🦽 www.pkin.pl

Queen Juliana of the Netherlands is reputed to have described the Palace of Culture and Science (Pałac Kultury i Nauki) as "modest but tasteful". This enormous building – a gift for the people of Warsaw from the nations of the USSR – was built in 1952–5 to the design of a Russian architect, Lev Rudniev. At the time, this monument to "the spirit of invention and social progress" was the second tallest building in Europe. It resembles Moscow's Socialist Realist tower blocks, and although it has only 30 storeys, with its spire it is 230 m 68 cm (750 ft) high. Its volume is over 800,000 cubic m (28 million cubic ft) and it contains 40 million bricks. It is said to incorporate many architectural and decorative elements taken from stately homes after World War II. Despite the passage of time, this symbol of Soviet domination still provokes extreme reactions, from admiration to demands for its demolition.

Palace of Culture and Science, reminiscent of a Socialist Realist tower block

Interior of Nożyk Synagogue

Nożyk Synagogue ⑮

ul. Twarda 6. **Map** 1 A5. **Tel** 022
620 43 24. 🚌 109, 151, 160.
Jewish Historical Institute ul.
Tłomackie 3/5. **Tel** 022 827 92 21.

Nożyk Synagogue was
founded by Zelman and
Ryfka Nożyk. In 1893 they
donated the land on which
it was to be built. Later they
left half of their estate to the
Orthodox Jewish community.
The synagogue was built
between 1898 and 1902. The
interior has an impressive
portico, crowned by a metal
dome bearing the Star of
David, which contains the Ark
of the Covenant. In the centre
of the nave is a raised pulpit
known as a bema. The nave
is surrounded by galleries that
were originally intended for
female worshippers.

Today, this is the only
active synagogue in Warsaw.
When it was built, it was
hidden away in the heart of a
housing estate, surrounded by
high-rise tenement buildings.
After the war, few of these
were still standing. During
the Nazi occupation, the

synagogue was closed for
worship and the German
forces used it as a warehouse.
Reopened in 1945, it was
eventually (1977–83) restored
to its original condition.

Of a total population of
no more than 1,300,000,
there were about 400,000
Jews in Warsaw before
World War II; the city had
the second largest Jewish
population after that of New
York. The northern part of
Warsaw, which was inhabited
predominantly by Jews, was
densely built up, with many
tenement blocks. The
languages spoken in the area
were Yiddish, Hebrew and
also Russian, spoken by Jews
who had fled Russia.

Those interested in Jewish
history and culture should
also visit the historic – though
somewhat overgrown –
cemetery on Ulica Okopowa.
The museum of the Jewish
Historical Institute (Żydowski
Instytut Historyczny), with a
library, archives and Judaic
museum, is also worth a visit.

Pawiak Prison ⑯

ul. Dzielna 24/26. **Map** 1 A2.
Tel 022 831 13 17. 🚌 107, 111,
180, 510. 🚃 4, 15, 16, 17. ⏰
9am–5pm Wed, 9am–4pm Thu &
Sat, 10am–5pm Fri, 10am–4pm Sun.
📷 ✍ ♿ 🏛 👫

Pawiak Prison was built
in the 1830s by Henryk
Marconi. It became notorious
during the Nazi occupation,
when it was used to imprison
Poles and Jews arrested by
the Germans. Now in ruins,
Pawiak serves as a museum.
In front of the ruin stands
a long-dead tree, covered
with obituary notices for
prisoners who died there.

Tree with obituary notices in
front of Pawiak Prison

Umschlagplatz Monument ⑰

ul. Stawki. **Map** 1 A1.
🚌 157. 🚃 4, 15, 16, 17, 33.

The Umschlagplatz
Monument, unveiled in
1988, marks the site of a
former railway siding on

Umschlagplatz Monument on the Path of Remembrance

Ulica Dzika. It was from here that some 300,000 Jews from the Warsaw Ghetto and elsewhere were loaded onto cattle trucks and dispatched to almost certain death in the extermination camps. Among them was Janusz Korczak and his group of Jewish orphans. Living conditions in the Ghetto were inhuman, and by 1942 over 100,000 of the inhabitants had died. The monument, on which the architect Hanna Szmalenberg and the sculptor Władysław Klamerus collaborated, is made of blocks of black and white marble bearing the names of hundreds of Warsaw's Jews.

Between the Monument to the Heroes of the Ghetto and the Umschlagplatz Monument runs the Trail of Jewish Martyrdom and Struggle, unveiled in 1988. It is marked by 16 blocks of granite bearing inscriptions in Polish, Hebrew and Yiddish and the date 1940–43. The site of a bunker, in which the uprising's commanders blew themselves up has been specially marked. Each block is dedicated to the memory of the 450,000 Jews murdered in the Warsaw Ghetto in the years 1940–43, to the heroes of the Ghetto Uprising in 1943 and to certain key individuals from that time.

Stone on the Path of Jewish Remembrance

Monument to the Heroes of the Ghetto ⑱

ul. Zamenhofa. **Map** 1 B2. 🚌 *111, 157, 180.*

The Monument to the Heroes of the Ghetto (Pomnik Bohaterów Getta) was erected in 1948, when the city of Warsaw still lay in ruins. Created by the sculptor Natan Rapaport and the architect Marek Suzin, it symbolizes the heroic defiance of the Ghetto Uprising of 1943, which was planned not as a bid for liberty but as an honourable way to die. It lasted one month.

Reliefs on the monument depict men, women and children struggling to flee the burning ghetto, together with a procession of Jews being driven to death camps under the threat of Nazi bayonets.

In front of this monument, on 7 December 1970, Willy Brandt, Chancellor of

Monument to the Heroes of the Ghetto (detail)

West Germany, knelt in homage to the murdered victims. Today, people come here from all over the world to remember the heroes of the Uprising.

In 2013 a museum dedicated to the history of Polish Jews opened near the monument, within the former ghetto area of the city.

Monument to those Fallen and Murdered in the East ⑲

ul. Muranowska. **Map** 1 C1. 🚌 *116, 178, 222, 316, 503.* 🚊 *4, 6, 15.*

This emotionally stirring monument, designed by Mirosław Biskupski, has the form of a typical railway wagon in which Poles were deported from the country into the depths of the Soviet Union. It is filled with a pile of crosses symbolising the hundreds of thousands of Poles carted off to the East in cattle vans and murdered in Soviet prison camps.

GHETTO UPRISING

The Nazis created the Jewish ghetto on 16 November 1940. The area was carefully isolated with barbed wire fencing, which was later replaced with brick walls. Over 450,000 people were crowded into the ghetto: Jews from Warsaw and other parts of Poland as well as gypsies. In March 1942 the Germans began to liquidate the ghetto, deporting over

300,000 people to the death camp in Treblinka. The Ghetto Uprising, which began on 19 April 1943 and lasted one month, was organized by the secret Jewish Fighting Organization. Following the suppression of the Uprising, the Nazis razed the whole area to the ground.

Further Afield

There are many places of interest outside the centre of Warsaw. The most important lie along the Royal Route stretching from the Royal Castle in the north to Wilanów in the south, and also on the edges of the escarpment that runs down to the left bank of the River Vistula; here there are several country mansions with extensive parks. Most can be reached by tram or by bus.

Grave of Father Jerzy Popiełuszko, Church of St Stanisław Kostka

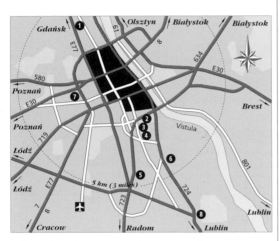

SIGHTS AT A GLANCE

Belvedere Palace **4**
Centre for Contemporary Art **2**
Church of St Anthony **6**
Church of St Stanisław Kostka **1**
Królikarnia Palace **5**
Łazienki Palace **3**
Warsaw Rising Museum **7**
Wilanów **8**

KEY

■	City centre
▬	Main road
═	Other road
─	River
✈	Airport

Church of St Stanisław Kostka **1**

ul. Hozjusza 2. **Tel** 022 839 45 72.
🚌 114, 116, 122, 157, 181, 185, 195, 503. 🚋 6, 15.

The Modernist Church of St Stanisław Kostka (Kościół św. Stanisława Kostki), set among the villas of Żoliborz, is the burial place of Father Jerzy Popiełuszko, the pastor of the Solidarity movement, and because of this it is a place of pilgrimage for Poles. Popiełuszko was a national hero, renowned for his courageous sermons in defence of Poland's freedom. He was eventually murdered in 1984 by communist security agents. His grave is in the church cemetery; it is covered with a stone cross and surrounded by linked rocks arranged in the manner of a rosary. The church itself is distinguished by its openwork twin towers. Inside, there are Baroque paintings by the Silesian artist Michael Willmann.

Centre for Contemporary Art **2**

Jazdów 2. **Map** 3 C5. **Tel** 022 628 12 71. 🚌 E-2, 116, 138, 151, 166, 180, 182, 187, 188, 195, 411, 502, 503, 514, 520, 523, 525. 🕙 noon–7pm Tue–Sun (to 9pm Fri). 🎫 (free on Thu). 🚗 📷 🏛 🛗 ♿ 🍴

The Centre for Contemporary Art (Centrum Sztuki Współczesnej) organizes exhibitions of the work of artists from all over the world on a scale unequalled elsewhere in Europe. The centre

Ujazdowski Castle, the home of the Centre for Contemporary Art

is housed in Ujazdowski Castle, an early Baroque fortification built at the beginning of the 17th century for Zygmunt III Vasa and his son Władysław IV. The castle's layout was spacious – it had an internal cloistered courtyard and four towers – but its splendour was destined to be short-lived; the Swedish army sacked it in 1655 and it later changed hands repeatedly, being rebuilt many times. During World War II, Ujazdowski Castle was destroyed by fire. The ruins were completely removed in 1953 and rebuilding of the castle only began in the 1970s.

Refreshments are available in a room called the Qchnia Artystyczna, which is decorated in an original – if perhaps mad – manner and which commands exquisite views from the escarpment.

Łazienki Palace **3**

See pp94–95.

Belvedere Palace ④

ul. Belwederska 52. 🚌 116, 166, 180, 195, 503. ⬤ to the public; access to exhibition with prior reservation – call 022 695 19 53.

The history of Belvedere Palace (Belweder) goes back to the 17th century. Its present appearance, however, dates from 1818, when it was refashioned by Jakub Kubicki for the Russian governor general Prince Constantine (the much hated brother of Tsar Alexander I) and his Polish aristocrat wife. On the night of 29 November 1830, a detachment of cadet officers, together with a number of students, attacked the palace, starting the November Insurrection.

After 1918, Belvedere Palace became the official residence of the presidents of Poland, including Marshal Józef Piłsudski (1867–1935), to whom an exhibition situated in the palace is devoted.

To the south of the palace, on the former site of the Ujazdowski Church, a terrace was built with a landscaped park at the foot of the escarpment. It was adorned with canals, a pool and several romantic pavilions in Greek, Egyptian and Gothic styles. These grounds are now part of Łazienki Park.

Królikarnia Palace ⑤

ul. Puławska 113a. **Tel** 022 843 15 86. 🚌 210, 218. 🚊 10, 31. ⬤ 10am–6pm Tue–Sun. 🎟 (free on Thu). 🚫 🅿 📷 no flash. ♿ www.krolikarnia.mnw.art.pl

Królikarnia Palace (Pałacyk Królikarnia) owes its name ("rabbit hutch") to the fact that it stands on the site of a rabbit farm that belonged to August II in the 1700s. It is a square building covered with a dome, recalling Andrea Palladio's masterpiece, the Villa Rotonda, near Vicenza. This exquisite little Neo-Classical palace is set in a garden on the slope of the escarpment in the district of Mokotów. It was designed by Dominik Merlini for Karol de Valery Thomatis, the director of Stanisław August Poniatowski's royal theatres.

Today the palace houses the Xawery Dunikowski Museum, dedicated to this contemporary Polish sculptor.

Fatum, a sculpture by Xawery Dunikowski in Królikarnia Park

Church of St Anthony ⑥

ul. Czerniakowska 2/4. **Tel** 022 842 03 71. 🚌 131, 159, 162, 180, 185, 187. ⬤ by appt only, or during ceremonies.

Baroque Church of St Anthony at Czerniaków

The Baroque Church of St Anthony (Kościół św Antoniego), built between 1687 and 1693 by the monks of the Bernardine order, was designed by Tylman van Gameren. The church stands on the site of the former village of Czerniaków, which belonged to Stanisław Herakliusz Lubomirski, the Grand Crown Marshal.

The relatively plain façade of this church belies its ornate interior, which includes trompe l'oeil paintings, stuccowork and altars by the painter Francesco Antonio Giorgiolo and the renowned sculptor Andreas Schlüter, among others. The main theme of the paintings is the life of St Anthony of Padua.

Warsaw Rising Museum ⑦

ul. Grzybowska 79. **Tel** 022 539 79 05. 🚌 105, 109, 159. 🚊 1, 8, 22, 24. ⬤ 8am–6pm Mon, Wed–Fri (to 8pm Thu), 10am–6pm Sat & Sun. 🎟 (free on Sun).

One of the most popular museums in Warsaw opened in 2004 to commemorate the 60th anniversary of the Warsaw Rising in 1944. A tribute to those who fought and died for Poland's independence, the museum recreates the atmosphere during those 63 days of military struggle, but it also conveys what everyday life was like under Nazi occupation.

Façade of the Neo-Classical Belvedere Palace, looking onto the gardens

Łazienki Palace ❸

Łazienki Park is part of a great complex of heritage gardens. In the 17th century there was a royal menagerie along the foot of the escarpment. In 1674, Grand Crown Marshal Stanisław Herakliusz Lubomirski acquired the park and, engaging the services of Tylman van Gameren, he altered the southern part of the menagerie, building a hermitage and a bathing pavilion on an island. The pavilion gave the park its name (Łazienki meaning "baths"). In the second half of the 18th century, the park was owned by Stanisław August Poniatowski, who commissioned Karol Ludwik Agricola, Karol Schultz and later Jan Christian Schuch to lay it out as a formal garden. Lubomirski's baths were refashioned into a royal residence, Łazienki Palace, or Palace on the Water, which is now a museum.

Peacock
Just as in Stanisław August Poniatowski's time, visitors to Łazienki Park can admire the peacocks and take a boat ride on the lake, which is full of carp.

Old Orangery
In 1774–8, Dominik Merlini created the Stanisławowski Theatre in the Old Orangery. It is one of the few remaining 18th-century court theatres in the world.

Monument to Chopin
This Secessionist monument was sculpted in 1908 by Wacław Szymanowski but not unveiled until 1926. Positioned at the side of a lake, it depicts Poland's most celebrated composer sitting under a willow tree, seeking inspiration from nature.

0 m   100
0 yds   100

Temple of the Sibyl
This Neo-Classical building, based on an ancient Greek temple, dates from the 1820s. It is made of wood.

STAR SIGHTS

★ Palace on the Water

★ Theatre on the Island

★ **Palace on the Water**
*Stanisław Lubomirski's 17th-century
baths were converted (1772–93) into
the Palace on the Water, Stanisław
August Poniatowski's summer home.*

Myślewicki Palace
*Dominik Merlini designed the early
Neo-Classical Myślewicki Palace in 1775–84
for Stanisław August Poniatowski's nephew,
Prince Józef Poniatowski.*

★ **Theatre on the Island**
*The stage of the Theatre on the Island has a
permanent backdrop imitating the ruins of a
temple in the ancient city of Baalbek, Lebanon.*

New Orangery
*This building in
cast iron and glass
was designed by
Józef Orłowski and
Adam Loewe in
1860–61.*

Wilanów ⑧

Detail from Glory

Wilanów Palace was built at the end of the 17th century as the summer residence of Jan III Sobieski. This illustrious monarch, who valued family life as much as material splendour, commissioned Augustyn Locci to build a modest country house. Later the palace was extended and adorned by renowned architects and artists including Andreas Schlüter and Michelangelo Palloni.

Chinese Pavilion
This small building stands in the English-style garden on the north side of the palace.

Great Crimson Room
Originally a three-room apartment, the Great Crimson Room was reconstructed in 1900 to house the museum's array of foreign paintings.

Main Gateway
Dating from the time of Jan III Sobieski, the Main Gateway is crowned with allegorical figures of War and Peace.

★ Poster Museum
A former riding school rebuilt in the 1960s now houses the Poster Museum, the first of its kind in Europe.

★ Rose Garden

This section of Wilanów's garden was created in the 19th century to the south of the palace.

VISITORS' CHECKLIST

ul. SK Potockiego 10/16. **Tel** 022
842 25 09. ▥ E-2, 116, 117, 130,
139, 164, 180, 519, 522, 700, 710,
724. **Palace** ◯ 9:30am–4pm
Mon–Sat (6pm Mon & Sat, 8pm
Wed), 10:30am–6pm Sun; Oct–
Apr: closes at 4pm. ● Jan, Tue
(Oct–Apr). (free Sun). **Park** ◯
9am–dusk.
www.wilanow-palac.art.pl

★ Queen's Antechamber

The walls are covered with original Baroque fabric while the ceiling has allegorical paintings.

0 m   50
0 yds   50

Rear Façade of the Palace

Open perspectives allow the rear façade of the palace to be seen from across the park, and even from the adjoining fields of Morysin.

King's Bedchamber

The bed canopy is made of fabric brought back by Jan III Sobieski from his victory against the Turks at the Battle of Vienna in 1683.

STAR FEATURES

★ Queen's Antechamber

★ Poster Museum

★ Rose Garden

WARSAW STREET FINDER

The coordinates given along-side the names of buildings and attractions in Warsaw refer to the street plan on pages 100–3. Map coordinates are also given alongside information about Warsaw hotels (see pp298–9) and restaurants (see pp316–17). The first digit indicates the relevant page number;

Tourists in Warsaw

the letter and following number are grid references. On the plan opposite, Warsaw is divided into four sectors corresponding to the four maps on pages 100–103. The symbols that appear on the maps are explained in the key below. The plan of the city identifies the most important monuments and places of interest.

KEY

■	Important monument
■	Place of interest
■	Other building
🚉	Railway station
Ⓜ	Metro
🅿	Parking
ℹ	Tourist information
✚	Hospital or first aid station
🚓	Police station
✝	Church
✡	Synagogue
✉	Post office
🚕	Taxi rank
=	Railway line
→	One-way street
▬	Pedestrianized street

Summer café garden in the Old Town

Marathon runners on Krakowskie Przedmieście

Façade of the Neo-Classical Grand Theatre designed by Antonio Corazzi, on Plac Teatralny

0 m	500
0 yds	500

Church of the Holy Spirit from Ulica Freta

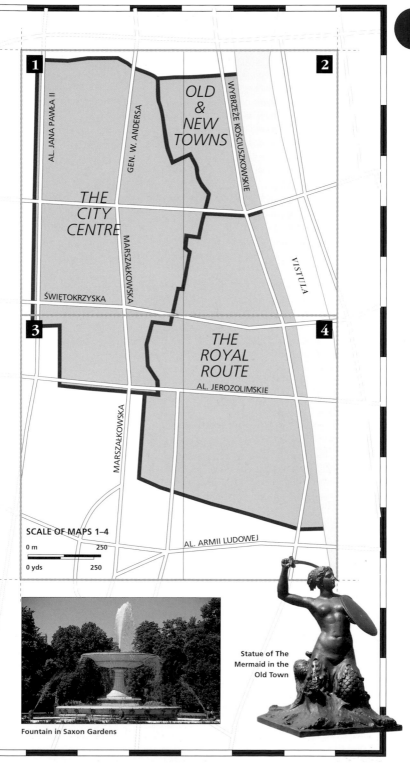

1

2

OLD & NEW TOWNS

AL. JANA PAWŁA II

GEN. W. ANDERSA

WYBRZEŻE KOŚCIUSZKOWSKIE

THE CITY CENTRE

MARSZAŁKOWSKA

VISTULA

ŚWIĘTOKRZYSKA

3

4

THE ROYAL ROUTE

AL. JEROZOLIMSKIE

MARSZAŁKOWSKA

SCALE OF MAPS 1–4

0 m — 250
0 yds — 250

AL. ARMII LUDOWEJ

Fountain in Saxon Gardens

Statue of The Mermaid in the Old Town

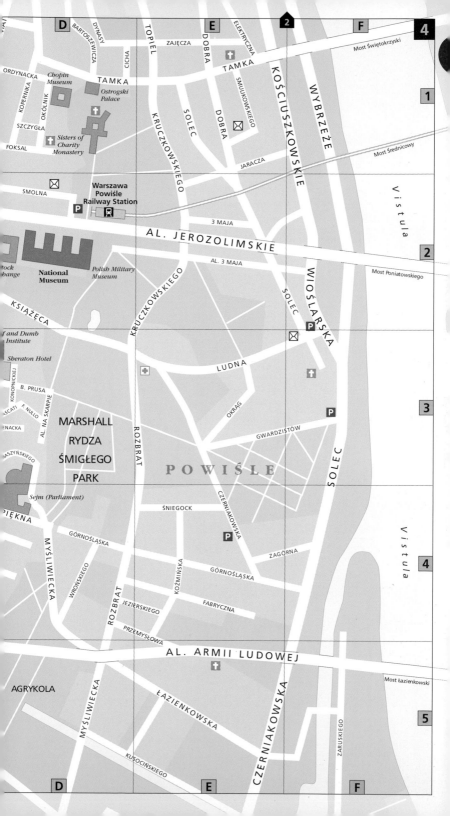

POLAND REGION BY REGION

Poland at a Glance

While southern Poland consists of a band of mountains and uplands, Central Poland is a land of endless plains. In the north, a post-glacial landscape dominates, and the Baltic coast, though fairly cool, has beautiful sandy beaches. Its provinces also offer unblemished natural landscapes. The Tatra Mountains, the highest in Poland, are traversed by well-marked footpaths, from which fine views and a pure alpine environment can be enjoyed. For admirers of manmade structures, many historic buildings have survived in regional Poland, despite the country's stormy history.

The Gdańsk Crane (see p237) *is one of the largest European cranes dating from the Middle Ages. Restored after war damage, it stands as a symbol of the city's former commercial might.*

GDAŃSK
(See pp230–49)

POMERANIA
(See pp250–73)

Many of the attractive sandy beaches (see p259) *on the Baltic Sea are backed by cliffs, which are vulnerable to storm damage.*

WIELKOPOLSKA (GREATER POLAND)
(See pp206–29)

SILESIA
(See pp174–205)

CRACOW
(See pp126–4

Raczyński Palace (see pp212–13) *at Rogalin is one of the most splendid residences in Greater Poland. The late Baroque palace now houses a museum of interiors and a valuable collection of paintings. It is surrounded by a beautiful park with ancient oaks.*

The town hall in Wrocław (see p191) *is one of the most interesting late Medieval buildings in Central Europe. It is crowned with unusual finials and fine stone sculptures.*

| 0 km | 75 |
| 0 miles | 75 |

◁ Panorama over the Vistula from Kazimierz Dolny

The Mazurian Lake District (see pp284–5), *known as "The Land of a Thousand Lakes", is a wilderness, with great forests, extensive woods and marshlands, and brick-built houses, Gothic churches and castles. Its pure character, unspoilt by civilization, is appreciated by storks: more nest here than anywhere else in Europe.*

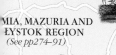

MIA, MAZURIA AND ŁYSTOK REGION
(See pp274–91)

In Kazimierz Dolny (see p119), *under the Renaissance colonnades of the town houses in the market square, paintings are on display and wicker baskets offered for sale. Fortune-telling gypsies mingle among the tourists.*

WARSAW
(See pp56–103)

MAZOVIA AND THE LUBLIN REGION
(See pp108–25)

AŁOPOLSKA (SER POLAND)
(ee pp146–73)

The Cloth Hall in Cracow (see p131), *an unusual building in the centre of Main Market Square, once contained market stalls. Today it is filled with shops selling souvenirs and local folk art, and popular cafés. On the first floor there is a splendid gallery of 19th-century Polish art.*

Krasiczyn Castle (see p170), *dating from the early 17th century, is defended by sturdy towers. The walls have elaborate parapets.*

MAZOVIA AND THE LUBLIN REGION

*I*n the nostalgic lowland landscape of Mazovia, sandy roads wind through the fields, lines of windswept willows stand in isolation, and meadows stretch to the edge of valleys where swift rivers flow. For centuries, Podlasie was the borderland between the Poles and the eastern Slavonic peoples. The hilly Lublin region has many excellent examples of Renaissance and Baroque architecture.

For centuries, Mazovia was, both culturally and economically, one of the least developed areas of the ethnically Polish lands of the Commonwealth of Two Nations. In the early Middle Ages it was the homeland of the Mazowie tribe. It was united with the state of the Polanie under Prince Mieszko I (963–92). The Principality of Mazovia came into existence in 1138, during the division of Poland, and it preserved its independence for nearly 400 years. Mazovia was incorporated into the Kingdom of Poland in 1526 after the death of the last Mazovian princes, and in 1596, Sigismund III Vasa moved the capital of the Commonwealth of Two Nations from Cracow to Warsaw, in Mazovia.

Mazovia's cultural distinctiveness has been influenced by the presence of a politically active yet conservative petty yeoman-gentry. Even today, in the east of the region and in Podlasie, farmsteads, with humble cottages built in the style of mansions, can be seen.

Apart from Warsaw, the towns of Mazovia have always been modest, and this is evident even today in more recent buildings and modern urban planning.

After the Congress of Vienna (1815), Mazovia and the Lublin region formed part of the Congress Kingdom, under Russian rule. In 1918, the whole area was returned to the reborn Poland.

The Lublin area differs considerably from Mazovia, in both landscape and culture. Its architectural jewel is the delightful town of Kazimierz Dolny, on the banks of the Vistula.

Mazovia – a region famous for its orchards

◁ Neo-Gothic mansion of Zygmunt Krasiński in Opinogóra

Exploring Mazovia and the Lublin Region

The Kampinoska Forest (Puszcza Kampinoska), a national park, extends out from the suburbs of Warsaw. There are also large tracts of woodland, with wild animals, in the north and south of Mazovia. The Lublin region has a more diverse landscape. The gorge of the Vistula, around the town of Kazimierz Dolny, is one of the region's most beautiful sights. Roztocze and Zamość, widely described as the "pearl of the Renaissance", are also very picturesque. In Mazovia, the ruins of brick-built castles can be seen, and in both regions there are many country mansions. Żelazowa Wola is Frédéric Chopin's birthplace and nearby Łowicz is a well-known centre of folklore.

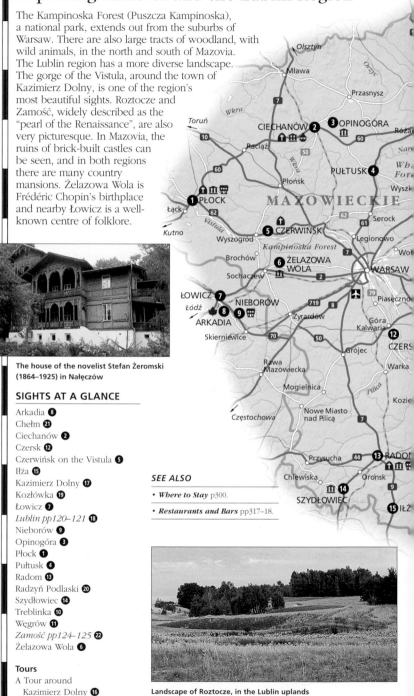

The house of the novelist Stefan Żeromski (1864–1925) in Nałęczów

Landscape of Roztocze, in the Lublin uplands

SIGHTS AT A GLANCE

SEE ALSO

- *Where to Stay* p300.
- *Restaurants and Bars* pp317–18.

KEY

━━━	Main road
═══	Minor road
─╫─	Main railway
───	Minor railway
▬▬	International border
▬▬	Regional border

Detail of the Romanesque portal of the church in Czerwińsk on the Vistula

GETTING AROUND

Warsaw, the chief city of Mazovia, has regular air links to major cities worldwide and to principal towns in Poland. All the larger towns in both regions have rail links. Travelling by express from Warsaw to Lublin takes a little over two hours. All places recommended in this guidebook are accessible by bus. However, many of the smaller ones are more easily reached by car. Highway E30 crosses Mazovia from east to west. From Warsaw, take highway E77 for Radom and highway 17 for Lublin.

Białystok

Ostrów Mazowiecka

10 TREBLINKA

Stara Wieś

11 WĘGRÓW

Liw

Kałuszyn

Siedlce

Łosice

Kobrin

Biała Podlaska

Łuków

Międzyrzec Podlaski

Żelechów

20 RADZYŃ PODLASKI

Kock

LUBELSKIE

Włodawa

16 A TOUR AROUND KAZIMIERZ DOLNY

Lubartów

19 KOZŁÓWKA

Polesian National Park

Puławy

Nałęczów

17 KAZIMIERZ DOLNY

18 LUBLIN

Łęczna

21 CHEŁM

Krasnystaw

Kraśnik

Wyżyna Lubelska

Hrubieszów

Janów Lubelski

Szczebrzeszyn

22 ZAMOŚĆ

Rzeszów

Biłgoraj

Tomaszów Lubelski

Tanew

Lviv

0 km — 25
0 miles — 25

The nave of the Renaissance cathedral in Płock

Płock ❶

Road map D3. 126,000.
ul. Stary Rynek 8
(024 367 19 44). **www**.ump.pl

This city, beautifully situated on the high Vistula Bluff, is best known today for its large petrochemical plants. Its history, however, goes back many centuries. From 1075, Płock was the seat of the bishopric of Mazovia. Under Władysław I (1079–1102) and his heir Bolesław III Wrymouth (1102– 1138), Płock was the capital of Poland and the favoured royal seat. From 1138 to the end of the 15th century, Płock was the place of residence of the Mazovian and Płock princes. In the 12th century, it was an important centre of political and cultural life in Poland.

The buildings of old Płock are relatively modest, although the small Neo-Classical houses, now restored, make a picturesque ensemble. Particularly noteworthy is the Neo-Classical **town hall,** built in 1824–7 to a design by Jakub Kubicki. Here, on 23 September 1831 during the uprising against Russian rule, the final session of the insurgent Sejm of the Kingdom of Poland was held.

Another notable building is the large Neo-Gothic cathedral (1911–19) of the Mariavite Church of Poland. Also worth seeing are the Baroque church, the Classical toll-gates and the remains of the Gothic city walls.

❶ Cathedral of Our Lady of Mazovia

ul. Tumska 3. **Tel** 024 262 34 35.
10am–5pm Mon–Sat, 11am–2pm Sun (use the side entrance).

The most interesting part of Płock is Tum Hill (Wzgórze Tumskie), with its Renaissance **Cathedral of Our Lady of Mazovia** and **castle** remains. The cathedral, built in 1531–5 was the first large Renaissance church in Poland. It was raised by Andrzej Krzycki, Bishop of Płock, later Primate of Poland and a noted scholar and poet. Giovanni Cini and Bernadino Zanobi de Gianotisa were the architects, with later rebuilding by Gianbattista of Venice. The interior of the cathedral is full of Renaissance and Baroque tombstones. A marble sarcoph-agus in the Royal Chapel hosts the remains of Władysław I and his son Bolesław III. The grand Neo-Renaissance façade of the cathedral, with its twin towers, was built at the start of the 20th century to a controversial design by Stefan Szyller, who was in charge of the restoration work.

🏛 Diocesan Museum

ul. Tumska 3a. **Tel** 024 262 26 23.
May–Sep: 10am–3pm Tue–Sat, 11am–4pm Sun & public hols; Oct–Apr: 10am–1pm Wed–Sat, 11am–2pm Sun & public hols.
www.mdplock.pl

The Diocesan Museum (Muzeum Diecezjalne) contains a rich collection of cathedral treasures. Especially note-worthy are the gold vessels and liturgical textiles, particu-larly the chasubles, the oldest of which date from the 1400s. The museum also possesses

The Neo-Classical town hall in the Old Market Square in Płock

woven sashes from the old court dress of the nobility (see pp28–9). Sashes were often made into vestments.

🏛 Museum of Mazovia

ul. Tumska 8. **Tel** 024 364 70 71.
1 May–14 Oct: 10am–5pm Tue–Sun; 15 Oct–30 Apr: 10am–4pm Tue–Sun. (free on Thu).

The Museum of Mazovia (Muzeum Mazowieckie) is located in a former monastery and houses one of the largest collections of Art Nouveau in the world. Exhibits include reconstructions of domestic interiors, with works of art, furniture, textiles, and everyday objects of the period.

Environs

There are sports facilities on **Lake Włocławek**, a reservoir on the Vistula, and a stud farm at **Łąck**, 9 km (5 miles) from Płock.

Tum Hill from the Vistula, with the cathedral and Benedictine abbey

Ruins of the Gothic Castle of the Mazovian princes in Ciechanów

Ciechanów ❷

Road map E3. 🏘 *47,000.* 🚊 🚌
ℹ️ *ul. Warszawska 34.*

On the edge of the town stand the Gothic ruins of the red-brick **Castle of the Mazovian princes**, built around 1420–30. After Mazovia was incorporated into the Kingdom of Poland, the widowed Queen Bona often stayed here. Today, the castle accommodates one of the exhibitions of the **Museum of the Mazovian Nobility** (Muzeum Szlachty Mazowieckiej).

In the town itself is the Gothic **Church of the Annunciation**, founded in the first half of the 16th century and rebuilt in the 17th, the parish **Church of the Nativity of the Blessed Virgin Mary**, dating from the 16th century, and the modest Neo-Gothic **town hall**, designed by Henryk Marconi in the mid-19th century. The low-rise apartment blocks with gable roofs near the railway station were built during the Nazi occupation. After the fall of Poland in September 1939 and the annexation of northern Mazovia to the Third Reich, the Nazis planned to settle German colonists in many towns here. Except for the castle and parish church, they intended to demolish the whole of Ciechanów and build it anew.

🏛 **Museum of the Mazovian Nobility**
ul. Warszawska 61a. **Tel** 023 672 53 46. ⏰ 8am–4pm Tue–Sun (Jul–Aug: 10am–6pm). 🏷 (free one day a week, usually Sat).
www.muzeumciechanow.pl

Opinogóra ❸

Road map E3. 🏘 *580.* 🚊 🚌

Opinogóra is closely associated with Count Zygmunt Krasiński (1812–59), a leading poet of the Romantic movement. The tiny Neo-Gothic mansion, situated in an extensive landscaped park, was built as a wedding present for him. According to the locals, it was designed by the French architect Eugène Emmanuel Viollet-le-Duc, although art historians attribute it to Henryk Marconi. Today, the mansion houses the **Museum of Romanticism** (Muzeum Romantyzmu).

The romantic park in which the mansion is set also contains the parish church, with the mausoleum of the Krasiński family where the poet is buried. Noteworthy too is the marble tomb of Count Zygmunt's mother, Maria Krasińska, by Luigi Pampaloni, dating from 1841.

🏛 **Museum of Romanticism**
ul. Krasińskiego 9. **Tel** 023 671 70 25. ⏰ 10am–6pm Tue–Sun (Oct–Apr: 8am–4pm). 🏷

Pułtusk ❹

Road map E3. 🏘 *18,600.* 🚌
ℹ️ *Wieża Ratuszowa 11 (023 692 51 32).* **www**.pultusk.pl

Of all the small towns in Mazovia, Pułtusk has the most beautiful setting. Its historic centre, located on an island formed by an arm of the River Narwa, has one of the longest market squares in Europe. The town hall, with its Gothic brick tower, houses the small

Regional Museum. Of equal interest is the Gothic-Renaissance **collegiate church**, with barrel vaulting over the nave executed by Gianbattista of Venice in 1551 and 1556.

To the south of the market square rise the walls of the castle of the bishops of Płock. Destroyed and rebuilt a number of times, it incorporates Renaissance, Baroque and Neo-Classical elements. After restoration work in the 1980s the **House of the Polish Diaspora** (Dom Polonii) was set up here. Visitors can stay in the hotel and enjoy tennis, canoeing, rowing, horse riding and winter sledging parties. The old-time Polish kitchen, which serves home-made fruit and berry liqueurs and home-baked sourdough bread, is recommended. Also worth seeing in the old town is the 18th-century Jesuit Church of Saints Peter and Paul.

🏛 **Regional Museum**
Rynek 41. **Tel** 023 692 51 32. ⏰ 10am–4pm Tue–Sun & public hols. 🏷 (free on Thu).

Environs
Near the town, on the right bank of the Narwa are water meadows and the **White Forest** (Puszcza Biała), which has a rich variety of plants and wildlife, including over 200 species of birds.

The town hall at Pułtusk, in one of Europe's longest market squares

The twin-towered basilica in
Czerwińsk on the Vistula

Czerwińsk on the Vistula ❺

Road map E3. 🏃 1,200. 🚌

The church and monastery
in Czerwińsk on the
Vistula, formerly owned by
the Canons Regular and now
by the Salesian order, are
among the oldest buildings in
Mazovia. The monastery was
in existence by 1155 and the
Romanesque **basilica** was
probably built in the time of
Bishop Aleksander of Płock
in the mid-12th century. In
spite of later Gothic and
modern alterations, the main
body of the building largely
retains its original appearance. The basilica's nave and
aisles each end in an apse –
a characteristic feature of
Romanesque churches. In
1410, the massed armies of
Małopolska, Lithuania and
Ruthenia gathered around the
Gothic bell tower on their
march to war against the
Teutonic Knights.

Environs
A few miles west of Czerwińsk
is the poor but nonetheless
charming little town of
Wyszogród, overlooking the
Vistula. In the Middle Ages it
had a castle (demolished at the
end of the 18th century) and
was the seat of a castellany.
Evidence of the town's past
glory survives in the church
and partially preserved former
Franciscan friary, founded
in 1406 and rebuilt several
times in the 17th and 18th
centuries. There is also a
Baroque parish church
dating from 1779–89.

Żelazowa Wola ❻

Road map E3. 🏃 60. 🚌

The romantic manor set in
a verdant, well-tended park
is the birthplace of the
composer Fryderyk Chopin
(1810–49). At the time of his
birth, however, it was no more
than a thatched outbuilding
in which Chopin's parents,
Mikołaj and Justyna Tekla,
rented a few rooms. In
1930–31, the building was
converted into the **Chopin
Museum** (Muzeum – Dom
Urodzenia Fryderyka Chopina)
and the park around it planted
with trees and shrubs donated
by horticulturalists from all
over Poland. Inside were
assembled all kinds of objects
associated with the composer.
During the German occup-
ation, many of these were
looted by the Nazis, the music
of Chopin was banned and all
pictures and busts of the
composer were destroyed.
After World War II, the manor
was rebuilt, and in 1948 the
museum was finally reopened
once more to the public.

Concerts of Chopin's music
are given in the house and
garden, providing visitors with
a unique opportunity to hear
the music of the most inspired
composer of the Romantic
period in the atmosphere of an
early 19th-century mansion.

Near Żelazowa Wola lies
the village of **Brochów**, on
the edge of the Kampinoska
Forest (Puszcza Kampinoska).
Fryderyk Chopin was
christened in the fortified
Renaissance church here.

🏛 **Chopin Museum**
Tel 046 863 33 00. ⏰ May–Sep:
9:30am–5:30pm Tue–Sun;
Oct–Apr: 10am–4pm Tue–Sun.
Concerts May–Sep: noon Tue–Sun
(Sun also 3pm). 🎟

Woman from Łowicz dressed in
regional costume

Łowicz ❼

Road map D3. 🏃 29,600. 🚉 🚌
ℹ Stary Rynek 3 (046 830 91 51).
www.lowicz.eu

The relatively small town
of Łowicz, established in the
13th century, was the seat of
one of the oldest castellanies
in Poland. For several
centuries, its castle (which is
no longer standing) was the
residence of the bishops of
Gniezno, primates of Poland.
The **collegiate church**, which
was founded in the Middle
Ages and rebuilt in the 17th
century, contains many notable
works of art. It also houses a
number of tombs, the most

The manor in Żelazowa Wola, birthplace of Frédéric Chopin

illustrious occupant of which was Primate Jakub Uchański (d. 1581). His tomb's most noteworthy features are a 16th-century alabaster carving by Jan Michałowicz of Urzędów and an early Neo-Classical frame by Ephraim Schroeger, dating from 1782–3.

The magnificent late Baroque high altar was made between 1761 and 1764 by Jan Jerzy Plersch to a design by Schroeger. It is considered by many to be one of the most original altars in Poland. The altar painting, crowned by an aureole and enclosed between the pilasters of a narrow frame, makes a great impression on churchgoers and tourists alike.

Near the collegiate church is the old **Piarist church** (kościół Pijarów) – the Piarists were a Catholic order. Its late Baroque undulating façade, which dates from around 1729, is extremely eye-catching. The interior of the building has Baroque altars by Jan Jerzy Plersch.

On the other side of Old Market Square, in the buildings of a former monastery and seminary for missionaries, is the **Łowicz Regional Museum** (Muzeum Ziemi Łowickiej) devoted to the folklore of the Łowicz area. Its exhibits include characteristic Łowicz costumes of the 19th and early 20th centuries, decorative paper cutouts and folk embroidery.

In the former chapel, built in 1689–1701 to designs by Tylman van Gameren and decorated with frescoes by Michelangelo Palloni, objects from the prehistoric Sarmatian culture are on display.

Łowicz comes alive at Corpus Christi, when in honour of this celebration local people dress in colourful traditional costumes to take part in a splendid procession that winds its way through the centre of town.

🏛 **Łowicz Regional Museum**
Stary Rynek 5/7. **Tel** 046 837 39 28.
◷ 10am–4pm Tue–Sun. ● Mon
& pub hols. 🔲 (free on Sat).
www.muzeumlowicz.pl

🏠 **Collegiate Church**
Stary Rynek 27. **Tel** 046 837 67 08.

Temple of Diana in Arkadia, the landscaped park near Łowicz

Arkadia ❽

Road map D3. 🏛 250. 🚌

Not far from Łowicz, on the road to Nieborów, lies Arkadia, a sentimentally romantic landscaped park. Laid out in 1778 by Princess Helena Radziwiłłowa, Arkadia's attractions include a lake with two islands and a number of romantic pavilions fancifully designed on historical or mythological themes by Szymon Bogumił Zug and Henryk Ittar.

Among ancient trees stand the Temple of Diana, the High Priest's Cottage, the Margrave's Cottage with Greek arch, the Gothic Cottage, the Grotto of the Sybil and the Aqueduct.

On some of the pavilion walls, fragments of decorative carving and stonework salvaged from the destroyed Renaissance bishops' castle in Łowicz are mounted.

Nieborów ❾

Road map E3. 🏛 950. 🚌

The Baroque palace in Nieborów was built by Tylman van Gameren between 1690 and 1696 for Primate Michał S. Radziejowski, Archbishop of Gniezno. Radziejowski was a noted connoisseur of literature, music, art and architecture, and as such was a client worthy of Tylman. A symmetric garden was also laid out. Around 1766, at the wish of a later owner, Prince Michał K. Ogiński, the building's façade was adorned with a Rococo figure portraying a dancing Bacchus, with a bunch of grapes and a garland on his head. Ogiński is also famous for the construction of a canal, which, via the river system, linked the Black Sea to the Baltic.

Between 1774 and 1945, Nieborów Palace was the property of the aristocratic Radziwiłł family. It is famous for its fine furnishings, which include Antoine Pesne's portrait of the famous beauty Anna Orzelska, who was the natural daughter of August II (1697–1733), and the antique head of Niobe, praised in the poetry of Konstanty Ildefons Gałczyński (1905–53). This Roman head, which was carved in white marble after a Greek original of the 4th century BC, was presented to Princess Helena Radziwiłłowa by Catherine the Great.

A grand interior at Nieborów Palace

Monument to the victims of the death camps at Treblinka

Treblinka ❿

Road map F3. 🏃 270. 🚉 🚌

In 1941, the Nazis established a labour camp, Treblinka I, and in 1942 a death camp, Treblinka II. Around 800,000 people, mainly Jews from liquidated ghettos, were murdered here. Those brought to Treblinka II were taken off the trains and herded, without even being registered, to the gas chambers. Up until March 1943, the victims were buried in mass graves. After March 1943, the graves were dug up and the bodies burned. Thereafter all bodies were burned. In November 1943, Treblinka II was closed and the ground ploughed over and seeded. Today, the **Treblinka Museum of Struggle and Martyrdom** stands as a reminder of the past.

In 1964, two monuments were erected on the site of the camp. The monument at Treblinka II spreads over 13 ha (30 acres). It gives an impression of "hundreds of thousands of human beings, coming from nowhere, in a spectral pilgrimage, going to their deaths". It is the work of the architect Adam Haupt and the sculptors Franciszek Duszenko and Franciszek Strynkiewicz.

🏛 **Treblinka Museum of Struggle and Martyrdom**
Kosów Lacki 76. **Tel** 025 781 16 58. ⬤ 9am–6:30pm daily (Nov–Mar: to 4pm). 📷 🖼
www.muzeum-treblinka.pl

Węgrów ⓫

Road map F3. 🏃 12,600. 🚌

Węgrów is a small town situated on the historical boundary between Mazovia and Podlasie. Its large, rectangular marketplace is distinguished by the Gothic-Baroque **parish church**, dating from 1703–6. Its interior is decorated with paintings by Michelangelo Palloni and fine Baroque images. The sacristy contains a mirror with a Latin inscription indicating that the legendary Pan Twardowski – the Polish Faust, who reputedly flew to the Moon on the back of a cockerel – used it in his practice of the black arts. Nearby stands a somewhat neglected **post-Reformation church**, dating from 1693–1706. Inside is an impressive Baroque monument to the founder, Jan Bonawentura Krasiński,

Armour, Museum of Arms, Liw

depicting Chronos and a female figure pointing to the spot where Krasiński is buried.

Environs
At **Liw**, 6 km (4 miles) west of Węgrów, are the remains of a Gothic castle erected in the 15th century. The castle was surrounded by marshes, and the gates could be reached only by a causeway. It was twice stormed by Swedes in the 17th century. In 1782, a small house was erected on the rubble for the county chancellery. Today it houses a **Museum of Arms** (Muzeum Zbrojownia), which besides a display of weaponry contains portraits by the 18th-century Sarmatian School.

In **Stara Wieś** to the north is the palace of the Krasiński-Golicyny family, which has the finest examples in Poland of interiors in the English Gothic style.

🏛 **Museum of Arms**
Liw, ul. Batorego 2. **Tel** 025 792 57 17. ⬤ 10am–4pm Tue–Sat, 11am–4pm Sun & public hols (May–Sep: 11am–6pm Sat & Sun). 📷 🖼

Czersk ⓬

Road map E4. 🏃 400. 🚌

Today, Czersk is no more than a small village; in the distant past it was the capital of Mazovia. By 1413 – most probably due to a change in the course of the Vistula, which had suddenly moved away from Czersk – that role had passed to Warsaw. The spectacular ruins of the princely **castle** tower over the Vistula. The road to the fortress crosses a bridge over the moat. Here, three high towers still stand. In the 12th century, Prince Konrad Mazowiecki used one of its dungeons to imprison the small boy who later became Prince Bolesław the Shy of

Ruins of the castle at Czersk

Cracow and Prince Henryk the Bearded of Wrocław.

Environs
Góra Kalwaria, 3 km (2 miles) north of Czersk, was once an important place of pilgrimage. Interesting features include the **market square**, with the **Church of the Exaltation of the Holy Cross** and the small Neo-Classical trade halls. The present **parish church** once belonged to the Bernardines. Before World War II, many Jews lived in Góra Kalwaria. Today, the Jewish cemetery serves as a memorial to that time.

An exhibit at the Centre for Polish Sculpture in Orońsk

Radom ⑬

Road map E4. 225,000. 🏠 ul. Traugutta 3 (048 360 06 10). **www**.radom.pl

This comparatively large town was at one time best known for its arms industry, but today it is more readily associated with the workers' protests of 1976, which took place four years before the founding of Solidarity. Although Radom was rebuilt in the 19th century, several of its older buildings can still be viewed. Nothing, however, remains of the old town itself, which until 1819 was surrounded by a wall.

The most interesting feature of Radom is the Gothic **parish church** in Ulica Rwańska, which was built in 1360–70 and later remodelled. Two Baroque buildings – Esterka and Gàska – at Nos. 4 and 5 Rynek – house the **Gallery of Contemporary Art**; beside them stands the arcaded **town hall**, by Henryk Marconi. Also worth visiting are the **Bernardine monastery** and **church**,

which contain 30 tombs and memorial plaques, the oldest of which dates from the 1500s. Wooden cottages, windmills and two 18th-century manors are displayed in the skansen at **Radom Rural Museum**.

🏛 Radom Rural Museum
ul. Szydłowiecka 30. **Tel** 048 332 92 81. 🕘 8am–5pm Tue–Fri, 10am–6pm Sat & Sun (winter: to 3pm). 🌑 public hols. **www**.muzeum-radom.pl

Environs
In parkland at **Orońsk**, 17 km (11 miles) from Radom, is the mansion of **Józef Brandt** (1841–1915), the noted painter of battle scenes. It is open to visitors, for whom a display of objects relating to the artist's life and work has been laid out. Another attraction is the **Centre for Polish Sculpture,** housed in a modern building within the park. International exhibitions and a sculpture biennale are held here.

Centre for Polish Sculpture
ul. Topolowa 1, Orońsk. **Tel** 048 618 45 16. 🕘 Apr–Oct: 8am–4pm Tue–Fri, 10am–6pm Sat & Sun; Nov–Mar: 7am–3pm Tue–Fri, 8am–4pm Sat & Sun. **www**.rzezba-oronsko.pl

Szydłowiec ⑭

Road map E4. 11,800. **www**.szydlowiec.pl

The most significant features of this small town are the late Renaissance **town hall** and the Gothic-Renaissance **castle**, set on an island. The castle was built in 1510–16 and remodelled in the 17th century. Of its rich interior decoration, only traces remain. Of greater interest is the **Museum of Folk Musical**

Late Renaissance town hall in Szydłowiec

Instruments, the only museum of its kind in Poland.

🏛 Museum of Folk Musical Instruments
ul. Sowińskiego 2. **Tel** 048 617 17 89. 🕘 9am–4pm Tue–Fri, 10am–5pm Sat & Sun (Oct–Mar: 9am–4pm Tue–Sun). 🌑 public hols. 📷 (free on Sat).

Environs
In **Chlewiska**, 11 km (7 miles) west of Szydłowiec, are the remains of an early 19th-century ironworks. A palace stands nearby.

Tower of the castle of the bishops of Cracow in Iłża

Iłża ⑮

Road map E4. 5,100.

Although the castle of the bishops of Cracow has been in ruins since the beginning of the 19th century, its tower still dominates the town. It was built in the 14th century by Bishop Jan Grot. Later owners transformed it into an elegant Renaiss-ance residence. In 1637, Władysław IV came here in disguise. Hiding in the crowd, he wanted to get a secret look at the bride he had married by proxy, Cecilia Renata, daughter of Leopold II of Austria. Dazzled by her beauty, he quickly made his presence known. Unfortunately, the marriage did not prove a happy one.

A Tour around Kazimierz Dolny ⑯

The environs of Kazimierz Dolny are renowned for their picturesque landscapes and rich heritage of historic buildings. Here the Vistula valley is cut by deep ravines, while from the gentle hills magnificent views unfold. It is tempting to linger in Nałęczów, with its popular spa, and in Puławy, where Czartoryski Palace stands in a landscaped park. The journey from Kazimierz Dolny to Janowiec can only be made by ferry; this provides an excellent opportunity for photographing both banks of the Vistula.

Gołąb ⑥
The Mannerist-Baroque church, which dates from 1628–36, has brick walls and fantastic decoration; beside it stands the Lorentine Chapel.

Sieciechów ⑦
The late Baroque Church of the Assumption of the Blessed Virgin towers over the buildings of the former Benedictine abbey. It was built between 1739 and 1769, though the walls contain Romanesque remains. The interior is adorned with paintings by Szymon Mankowski in the Rococo-Neo-Classical style.

Czarnolas ⑧
This was the home of Jan Kochanowski (1530–84), the greatest poet of the Polish Renaissance. Little is left of his wooden manor, and the museum devoted to the poet's life and work is housed in the 19th-century mansion.

0 km   5

0 miles   5

Janowiec ①
The extensive ruins of the castle that was built for the Firlej family in the 16th century now house a museum. It includes a small *skansen* where several wooden buildings, including an 18th-century manor and storehouse, have been re-erected.

TIPS FOR DRIVERS

Tour length: 150 km (94 miles).
Stopping-off points: Good cafés and restaurants are in Kazimierz Dolny, Nałęczów and Puławy. The ferry from Kazimierz to Janowiec runs from Apr to Nov, every 30 mins.

Bochotnica ④
In this hamlet stand the ruins of a 14th-century castle that, according to legend, Kazimierz the Great (1333–70) built for Esterka, the beautiful Jewish girl who became his mistress.

Puławy ⑤
The former residence of the Czartoryski family is set in a large landscaped park, now sadly neglected. Many small ornamental buildings, such as the Temple of the Sybil and the Gothic House, are to be seen here.

Nałęczów ③
This health resort also has a spa park, with a pump room, baths and Baroque palace. The wooden cottage housing the museum of the novelist Stefan Żeromski (1864–1925) is open to visitors.

Kazimierz Dolny ②
During the summer, Kazimierz Dolny swarms with tourists. It is a popular weekend destination for Varsovians. The town is well provided with guesthouses, good restaurants and cafés. There are also handicraft stalls and young artists offering their work for sale.

KEY

■ Tour route

■ Other road

⁂ Viewpoint

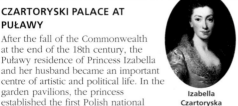

CZARTORYSKI PALACE AT PUŁAWY

After the fall of the Commonwealth at the end of the 18th century, the Puławy residence of Princess Izabella and her husband became an important centre of artistic and political life. In the garden pavilions, the princess established the first Polish national museum, called the Shrine of Memory. After the November Insurrection of 1831 failed, Puławy was deserted. The Czartoryskis went into exile abroad and their property was confiscated by the Russians.

Izabella Czartoryska

St Christopher, House of Krzysztof Przybyła, Kazimierz Dolny

Kazimierz Dolny ⓱

Road map F4. 🏚 *3,400.* 🚌
ℹ️ *Rynek 27 (081 881 00 46).*
🎪 *Festival of Folk Bands and Singers (Jun); Film Summer (Aug).*
www.kazimierzdolny.pl

This delightful little town, the favourite holiday resort of poets and painters, was probably founded by Kazimierz the Great. In the 16th and 17th centuries, it grew rich from the grain trade. The ruins of a Gothic **castle** with a high tower dominate the town. At its foot can be seen the Renaissance **Parish Church of Saints John the Baptist and Bartholomew** built in 1610–13, which incorporates the walls of an earlier Gothic church. The interior has provincial stuccowork decoration in the vaulting and early Baroque chapels.

The most attractive part of town is the **market square**, flanked by several Mannerist houses, with rich ornamental coverings. Particularly attractive are the **House of Mikołaj Przybyła** and **House of Krzysztof Przybyła**, at Nos. 12 and 13, dating from around 1615. There are also some 16th-century houses in Ulica Senatorska, which leads down to the Vistula, including the **Celej House**, which dates from around 1635. While strolling through the town, note the former synagogue, dating from the 18th century, the granaries on the banks of the Vistula, and the pre-war villas.

Lublin ⑱

Mannerist window frame

Lublin, the largest city in southeastern Poland, is well-endowed with historic buildings. It is also an important centre of academic life; its best-known seat of learning is the Catholic University of Lublin. Before World War II, the only Jewish college of higher education in Poland was located here. In 1944, after Lublin had been liberated from the Nazis, Poland's first communist government, convened at Stalin's behest, arrived here on the tanks of the Red Army.

mason Jan Wolff. The main street in Lublin, Krakowskie Przedmieście, is now a pedestrian precinct lined with elegant shops. In Plac Unii Lubelskiej are the **Capuchin church** (kościół Kapucynów) and the **Church of Our Lady Victorious** (Kościół Matki Boskiej Zwycięskiej), founded by Władysław Jagiełło (1386–1434) to commemorate his victory over the Teutonic Knights at the Battle of Grunwald in 1410 *(see pp40–41)*.

The Jewish **cemetery** adjoining Ulica Kalinowszczyna, established in 1555, is evidence of the Jewish community that existed in Lublin for many centuries, celebrated in the novels of Nobel laureate Isaac Bashevis Singer (1904–91).

🏛 Museum of the History of the Town Hall and Crown Tribunal of the Kingdom of Poland
Rynek 1. *Tel* 081 532 68 66.
◯ 9am–4pm Wed & Sat, 9am–5pm Sun. 📷

Historic houses round the Market Square in Lublin

Exploring Lublin

The most attractive district of Lublin is the **Old Town** (Stare Miasto), situated on the edge of the escarpment. It is reached through **Cracow Gate** (Brama Krakowska), which has become a symbol of the city. This old part of Lublin is a maze of romantic lanes and alleys. The façades of the houses are decorated with Mannerist and Baroque ornamentation and have splendid attics. Many of the buildings have Socialist Realist paintings dating from 1954, when the whole town was renovated to celebrate the tenth anniversary of the establishment of the communist Lublin Committee *(see p51)*.

Cracow Gate, one of Lublin's symbols

At the centre of the Old Town is the **Market Square**, with Lublin's town hall. Here, the Crown Tribunal of the Kingdom of Poland once had its seat. In the 18th century, the town hall was rebuilt by Dominik Merlini in the Neo-Classical style. Today it houses the **Museum of the History of the Town Hall and Crown Tribunal of the Kingdom of Poland**. The most magnificent place of worship in the Old Town is the **Dominican church** (kościół Dominikanów), founded in 1342 and rebuilt in the 17th and 18th centuries. The finest of its 11 chapels is the mid-17th-century Mannerist-Baroque Firlej Chapel. Its ribbed dome is an ambitious confection ascribed to the

Interior of the dome of the Firlej Chapel in the Dominican church

🔒 Cathedral of Saints John the Baptist and John the Evangelist
ul. Królewska 10. *Tel* 081 532 11 96.
The interior of this former Jesuit church is a triumph of Baroque art. Trompe l'oeil frescoes painted by Joseph Mayer in 1756–7 depict scenes set against a background of illusory architecture. The most beautiful frescoes are those in the cathedral treasury, depicting *Heliodorus Expelled from the Temple*.

Neo-Gothic façade of Lublin Castle

♣ Lublin Castle

pl. Zamkowy 1. **Muzeum Lubelskie**
Tel 081 532 50 01. 9am–4pm
Tue, Thu–Sat, 9am–5pm Wed & Sun
(Jun–Aug: 10am–5pm Tue–Sat,
10am–6pm Sun).
www.zamek-lublin.pl

Lublin's most important historic
building is the **Chapel of the
Holy Trinity** (Kaplica Świętej
Trójcy). It forms part of Lublin
Castle, which was built in the
14th century and remodelled in
the Gothic style in 1823–6 for
use as a prison. The interior of
this Catholic chapel *(see p40)*
is covered with Byzantine
frescoes painted in 1418 by
Orthodox artists. Among the
saints and angels is a portrait
of Władysław Jagiełło, the
chapel's founder. The chapel
is evidence of the cultural
diversity of the Kingdom of
Poland and the coexistence

at this time of the Roman
Catholic and Orthodox faiths.

In the museum laid out
in the rest of the castle are
exhibitions of Polish and
foreign paintings, folk art
and weaponry.

**Frescoes in the Chapel of the
Holy Trinity**

⛪ Majdanek State Museum

Droga Męczenników Majdanka 67.
Tel 081 710 28 33. 9am–5pm
daily (Nov–Mar: to 4pm). public
hols. **www**.majdanek.pl

In 1941, the Nazis established
a camp at Majdanek for Soviet
prisoners of war; it later
became a death camp. Of
the half million people who
passed through Majdanek,
360,000 were murdered. The
camp has been preserved as
a museum and memorial to
the victims of extermination.

⛪ Lublin Rural Museum

Aleja Warszawska 96. **Tel** 081 533
31 37. Apr, Oct: 9am–5pm daily;
May–Sep: 10am–6pm daily; Nov,
Dec: 9am–3pm Fri–Sun; Jan–Mar:
by appt (call 081 533 85 13).
Rural buildings from villages,
small towns and manorial
estates, together with their furnishings, are to be seen here.

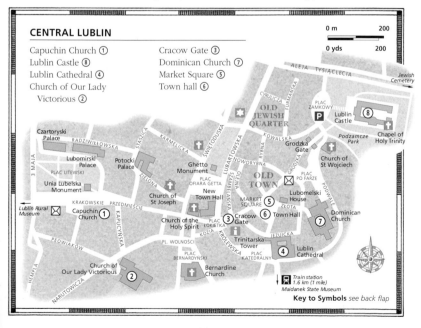

CENTRAL LUBLIN

Capuchin Church ①
Lublin Castle ⑧
Lublin Cathedral ④
Church of Our Lady
Victorious ②
Cracow Gate ③
Dominican Church ⑦
Market Square ⑤
Town hall ⑥

0 m 200
0 yds 200

Key to Symbols *see back flap*

Kozłówka ⑲

Road map F4. 🏛 800. 🚌

The magnificent palace at Kozłówka is one of the best-preserved aristocratic residences in Poland. Built between 1735 and 1742 in the Baroque style by Giuseppe Fontana, its first owner was Michał Bieliński, Palatine of Chełm, who at the wish of August II was married – albeit briefly – to one Aurora Rutkowska, who happened to be the king's illegitimate daughter by a Turkish lady named Fatima.

Kozłówka Palace later passed to the famous Zamoyski family, and was rebuilt in the Empire style and renamed **Zamoyski Palace**. In 1903, Konstanty Zamoyski established what in property law is called an "entail", in order to ensure that the palace would remain the undivided inheritance of the Zamoyski family.

Zamoyski was regarded by contemporaries as a "handsome man, outstanding for his good companionship and sense of humour". He was a great collector, a lover of music and a connoisseur of painting. He was educated in the France of Louis-Napoleon, and the style of the Second Empire is clearly visible in the rich décor of the palace interior, with its Neo-Rococo stuccowork, enormous ceramic stoves, chimneypieces in coloured

Picture gallery and White Staircase, Kozłówka Palace

marble, huge chandeliers, lambrequins, curtains, and furniture decorated with inlays and bronze – mainly excellent copies in Louis XV and Louis XVI style from the best French workshops.

Today, the palace is a **museum**. Its entire contents have been preserved, making it Poland's finest collection not only of 19th-century art but also of everyday objects. (Do not miss the early 20th-century bathroom, which is

most elegantly equipped, or the palace kitchens.)

Most impressive of all the exhibits is the collection of some 1,000 paintings, which almost completely cover the walls. These are not original works but high-quality copies of the masterpieces of European painting – the largest collection in Poland of its kind.

The palace chapel – which was modelled on the Royal Chapel at Versailles – was built between 1904 and 1909 by Jan Heurich junior, the pioneer of modern architecture in Poland. It contains a copy by Lorenzo Bartolini of the tomb of Zofia Zamoyska in the Church of Santa Croce in Florence.

An annexe of Kozłówka Palace is occupied by a unique gallery housing Socialist Realist art. The building is surrounded by a park that extends over 190,000 sq m (47 acres).

🏛 **Zamoyski Palace and Museum**
Tel 081 852 83 00. ⬤ Apr–Nov: 10am–4pm Tue–Sun (to 5pm in summer). 🖥 **www**.muzeum zamoyskich.pl

---

SOCIALIST REALIST ART, KOZŁÓWKA

Socialist Realism was a doctrinal art style that was developed in the Soviet Union in the Stalinist era. In Poland, it was current after World War II, from about 1949 to 1955. Its theoretical principles were unclear, and in practice what counted were the instructions given to the artists. The heroes of Socialist Realist works were party apparatchiks, buxom peasant women and muscular workers. A great number of such works, which were often to be seen on the roofs of public buildings and museum storehouses, can be seen in Kozłówka, where the largest collection in Poland of Socialist Realist art has been assembled.

Exhibition at Kozłówka

For hotels and restaurants in this region see p300 and p317–18

Radzyń Podlaski 20

Road map F4. 16,000.
station 8 km (5 miles) from the town. ul. Jana Pawła II 4 (083 352 73 14).

In its splendour, **Potocki Palace** rivals Branicki Palace in Białystok, the "Versailles of Podlasie" *(see p290)*. It was built for the ambitious Eustachy Potocki, who later became a general in the Lithuanian artillery. The palace was to be dazzling. It was reconstructed in 1750–58, in the Rococo style, by Giacopo Fontana and his talented team of artists. The painted decoration is by Jan Bogumił Plersch and the carving by Michał Dollinger and Chrystian Redler. The appearance of the palace, like the career of its owner, was calculated to have a great effect. With its elongated wings, it was different not only in form but also in character. Viewed from the courtyard, the unusual monumental wing, with its imposing gate-tower (visible even from the town), looks almost like a single-storey outbuilding. Similarly, the main block of the palace, which looks modest from the courtyard, overwhelms with its richness when viewed from the garden.

Dynamic Rococo carvings decorate the palace and adjacent orangery. The most interesting are the four groups of Hercules and the Lion, the Hydra, the Minotaur, and the Dragon.

Today, the palace houses various institutions.

In Radzyń Podlaski itself is the **Church of the Holy Trinity** (Kościół Świętej Trójcy), built in 1641 by Jan Wolff, the illustrious mason of the Zamoyski family. The church contains the imposing red marble Renaissance tomb of Mikołaj Mniszech and his wife Zofia, possibly the work of Santi Gucci.

Chełm 21

Road map G4. 67,600.
ul. Lubelska 63 (082 565 36 67).
International Choral Meetings (Apr). **www**.itchelm.pl

The most interesting aspect of Chełm is its network of underground tunnels, the remains of **chalk mines** (Podziemia). The tunnels are on three levels and descend to a depth of 30 m (100 ft); visitors may walk along them, candle in hand. In the 17th century, as many as 80 houses had an entrance to the workings. Mining ended in the 1800s. Above ground, the town's most impressive building is the **Piarist church**. It was built by Paolo Fontana in 1753–63 and has an undulant façade, elliptic nave and imposing dome. The Baroque interior is decorated with paintings by Joseph Mayer.

Interior of the Piarist church in Chełm

The best view of Chełm is from Castle Hill (Góra Zamkowa), where remains of a 13th-century princely castle can be seen. From here, the towers of Roman Catholic churches, the onion domes of a Greek Catholic and an Orthodox **church**, and a fine Baroque **synagogue** can be made out. A Jewish community, one of the earliest in Poland, settled here in the 12th century.

Chalk Mines
ul. Lubelska 55a.
Tel 082 565 25 30.
visits at 11am, 1pm and 4pm daily. public hols.

Environs
The **Polesian National Park** (Poleski Park Narodowy) lies 40 km (25 miles) northwest of Chełm. It forms part of the Łęczyńsko-Włodarskie Lake District and has many swamps, peat bogs and small lakes.

Rococo carvings on the orangery at Potocki Palace, Radzyń Podlaski

Zamość ㉒

Detail from building, Zamość

Zamość is one of the best-preserved Renaissance towns in Europe. It was one of the first to be planned and built from scratch according to Italian concepts of the ideal town. The moving force behind this project was Jan Zamoyski (1541–1605), chancellor and commander-in-chief of the Crown, one of the most powerful and enlightened magnates of Poland's Golden Age, and the owner of Zamość. Bernardo Mornando was the architect and work began in 1581, continuing for more than ten years. A programme of restoration was carried out in the 1970s, and in 1992 UNESCO declared the town a World Heritage Site. Today, theatrical performances and many other cultural events take place in the Main Square.

★ **Town Hall**

With its fine ornamental tower and imposing fan staircase, the Town Hall is the focal point of Zamość.

★ **Cathedral**

The cathedral, designed by Bernardo Morandi in 1587, was completed in the 1630s. It was rebuilt in 1824–6. It has an unusual Mannerist façade and distinctively decorated vaulting.

Arsenal

The Arsenal, closely connected with the town's formidable fortifications, is today the Polish Army Museum.

Franciscan Church

In the 19th century, this large church was turned into a barracks and its Baroque gables pulled down.

VISITORS' CHECKLIST

Road map G5. 👥 67,000. 🚉
🚌 ℹ *Rynek Wielki 13 (084 639 22 92).* **Regional Museum** *ul. Ormiańska 30.* **Tel** *084 638 64 94.* 🕐 *9am–4pm Tue–Sun.* 📷 🎿 🎷 *Jazz on the Borderlands (May); International Meeting of Jazz Vocalists (Jul).* www.zamosc.pl

Bastion Fortifications

The fortifications around Zamość allowed the town to resist a Cossack siege as well as the Swedish Deluge of the 1650s.

Former Church and Monastery of the Order of St John of God

★ **Main Market Square**

The Main Market Square (Rynek Wielki) is surrounded on all four sides by arcaded houses two storeys high. They were built to a unified design, but many of their façades have unusual and elaborate decorations with an Oriental flavour.

Church of St Nicholas
This church, built for the Greek Catholic Basilian order, is now Roman Catholic, demonstrating the multi-ethnic character of old Zamość.

STAR SIGHTS

★ Main Market Square

★ Town Hall

★ Cathedral

Doorway of the Old Rectory

This magnificent rectory, adjoining the cathedral, is one of the oldest houses in Zamość.

CRACOW

*C*racow is one of the most beautiful cities in Europe. Over the centuries, many important artists and architects came to work here, among them Veit Stoss from Germany, Bartolomeo Berrecci and Giovanni Maria Padovano from Italy, and Tylman van Gameren from Holland. Cracow has been spared major destruction, so it preserves the largest assemblage of historic buildings and monuments in Poland.

The earliest mention of Cracow in the historical records dates from the middle of the 10th century; it had certainly been incorporated into the Kingdom of Poland before 992. In 1000 it became a see, and around 1038 it assumed the importance of a capital. Wawel Hill became the seat of government, and from 1257, when Bolesław the Chaste gave the city a municipal charter, it began to spread and flourish at the foot of the hill. In 1364 the Cracow Academy was founded, increasing the city's importance on the European stage. During the 14th and 15th centuries, large sums of money were spent on the development of the city, as can be seen from the numerous Gothic churches and secular buildings that survive to this day.

At the beginning of the 16th century, Cracow came under the influence of the Renaissance. The Wawel Royal Castle, the Cloth Hall in the Main Market Square, and many private houses and mansions in the city were rebuilt in the Renaissance style. Cracow gradually lost its significance, and in 1596 the capital was moved to Warsaw, but it was in Wawel Cathedral that successive kings of Poland were crowned and entombed, and the city continued to acquire many magnificent buildings. Under the Partition of Poland *(see pp46–9)*, Cracow came under Austrian rule, which nevertheless permitted a relatively large degree of local autonomy. Hence it began to assume the role of the spiritual capital of all Poles, both in their native country and abroad. Cracow escaped significant damage during the two World Wars, and in 1978 UNESCO declared it a World Heritage site.

Memorial to Adam Mickiewicz, Poland's national poet, outside the Cloth Hall in the Main Market Square

◁ Wawel Cathedral's Zygmunt Chapel, "the Pearl of the Renaissance north of the Alps„

Exploring Cracow

As most places of interest in Cracow are located in its fairly compact historic centre, the city is best seen on foot. A good place to start is Wawel Hill (Wzgórze Wawelskie), with its imposing Wawel Royal Castle and Gothic cathedral, in the crypt of which many kings of Poland are interred. North of Wawel Hill lies the old city of Cracow with its attractive market, the Church of St Mary, the picturesque Cloth Hall and many interesting old houses. To the south of Wawel Hill is the Kazimierz district, with its preserved Jewish quarter. Outlying parts of the city are served by an extensive bus and tram network.

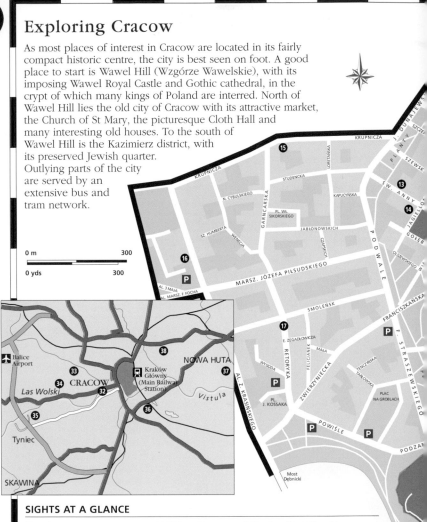

0 m   300

0 yds   300

SIGHTS AT A GLANCE

Churches

Benedictine Abbey in Tyniec **35**
Camaldolite Monastery in
   Bielany **34**
The Cathedral pp142–3 **27**
Church of Corpus Christi **29**
Church of St Anne **13**
Church of St Mary pp132–3 **3**
Church of Saints Peter
   and Paul **20**
Cistercian Abbey in
   Mogiła **37**
Dominican Church **5**
Franciscan Church **18**
Pauline Church on the
   Rock **28**
Piarist Church **11**
Premonstratensian Church **32**

Buildings, Squares and Streets

Barbican **8**
City Hall Tower **2**
Decjusz Villa **33**
Fortifications on the Wawel **23**
Medical Society Building **6**
Plac Matejki **7**
Plac Szczepański **12**
Ulica Floriańska **9**
Ulica Grodzka **19**
Ulica Kanonicza **21**
Ulica Retoryka **17**

Museums and Galleries

Cathedral Museum **24**
Cloth Hall **1**
Collegium Maius **14**
Józef Mehoffer Museum **15**

"Lost Wawel"
   Exhibition **25**
Museum of the Polish
   Air Force **38**
National Museum **16**
Princes Czartoryski
   Museum **10**
Rynek Underground **4**
Schindler's Factory **36**
Stanisław Wyspiański
   Museum **22**
*The Wawel Royal Castle
   pp140–41* **26**

Synagogues and Cemeteries

Old Synagogue **30**
Remuh Cemetery and
   Synagogue **31**

For additional map symbols *see back flap*

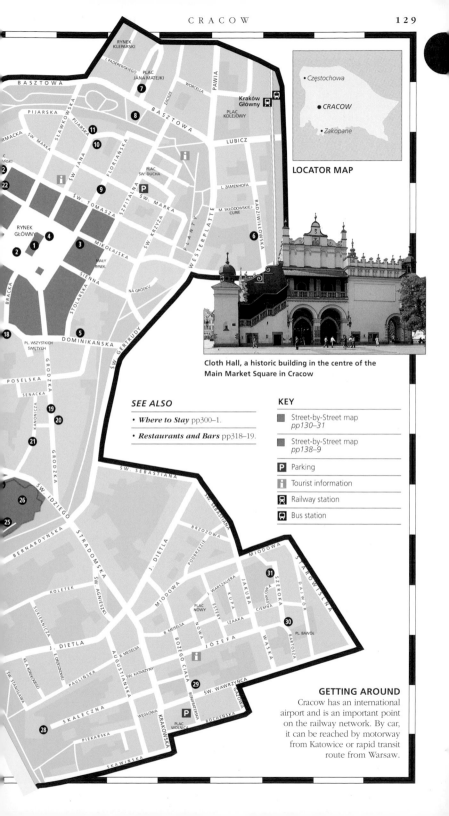

LOCATOR MAP

- Częstochowa
- CRACOW
- Zakopane

Cloth Hall, a historic building in the centre of the
Main Market Square in Cracow

SEE ALSO

- *Where to Stay* pp300–1.
- *Restaurants and Bars* pp318–19.

KEY

Street-by-Street map
pp130–31

Street-by-Street map
pp138–9

P Parking

i Tourist information

Railway station

Bus station

GETTING AROUND

Cracow has an international
airport and is an important point
on the railway network. By car,
it can be reached by motorway
from Katowice or rapid transit
route from Warsaw.

Main Market Square

This huge market square (Rynek Główny) was laid out when Cracow received its new municipal charter in 1257. One of the largest in Europe, it seethes with life all year round. In summer, pedestrians find themselves negotiating the maze of café tables that fill the square, along with a host of shops, antique dealers, restaurants, bars and clubs. There are also many interesting museums, galleries and historic sights, including some splendid Renaissance and Baroque houses and mansions.

★ **Church of St Mary**
The façade of this church has for centuries stood as a symbol of Polish architecture ❸

Rynek Underground ❹

★ **Cloth Hall**
This beautiful Renaissance building replaced an earlier Gothic market hall. The upper floor houses part of the National Museum ❶

RYNEK GŁÓWNY

City Hall Tower
The Gothic tower is the only remaining part of the former City Hall. A café has been opened in the basement ❷

St Wojciech is a small but splendid Romanesque church. One of the oldest stone churches in Poland, it pre-dates the planning of this vast square and is all but lost in it.

KEY

━ ━ ━ Suggested route

LOCATOR MAP
See pp128–9.

The Church of St Barbara, dating from the late 14th century, contains many treasures, including a 15th-century Gothic pietà.

House known as "At the Sign of the Lizards"

0 m   50
0 yds   50

STAR SIGHTS

★ Church of St Mary

★ Cloth Hall

Cloth Hall ❶

Rynek Główny 1/3. 🚌 *103, 124, 152, 502.* 🚊 *3, 4, 5, 13, 14, 15, 18, 19.* **Gallery of Polish Painting Tel** *012 424 46 03.* ☐ *10am–8pm Tue–Sat, 10am–6pm Sun.* 🌐 *(free on Thu).* 🚫 🗋 📷 ⛰

Set in the centre of the Main Market Square, the Cloth Hall (Sukiennice) replaces an earlier Gothic trade hall dating from the second half of the 1300s. Destroyed in a fire, then rebuilt by Giovanni Maria Padovano, it owes something of its present appearance to Tomasz Pryliński's Romantic-style restoration (1875–9). The ground floor is filled with cafés and souvenir shops, while on the upper floor is the Gallery of Polish Painting. Its collection of 19th-century works includes art by Jan Matejko, Marcello Bacciarelli and Piotr Michalowski.

City Hall Tower ❷

Rynek Główny 1. 🚌 *103, 124, 152, 502.* 🚊 *3, 4, 5, 13, 14, 15, 18, 19.* **Branch of the Historical Museum of Cracow Tel** *012 619 23 18.* ☐ *Apr–Oct: 10:30am–6pm daily.* ● *1, 3 May & 15 Aug.* 🌐 ↻

The Gothic tower, crowned by a Baroque cupola, that dominates the Main Market Square is the only remaining vestige of the City Hall, built in the 14th century and pulled down in the first half of the 19th. The tower houses a branch of the Historical Museum. Aspects of the city's history are also documented in the Museum of the History of the Market, in the crypt of the neighbouring Church of St Wojciech.

Church of St Mary ❸

See pp132–3.

Rynek Underground ❹

Rynek Główny 1. ☐ *Apr–Oct: 10am–10pm daily (to 8pm Mon, to 4pm Tue); Nov–Mar: 10am–8pm daily (to 4pm Tue).* ● *1st Tue of month.* 🌐 *(free on Tue).*

This high-tech museum, tracing the story of the city, is located under the Main Market Square. The underground vaults contain displays on transportation and trade, as well as archaeological finds such as the remains of an 11th-century cemetery and ancient coins and clothing. The museum cleverly blends modern technology with interactive exhibits and more traditional displays.

Dominican Church ❺

ul. Stolarska 12. **Tel** *012 423 16 13.* 🚊 *1, 3, 6, 8, 18.* ☐ *6:30am–8pm daily.*

The origins of the Dominican Church (kościół Dominikanów) go back to the second half of the 13th century. Rebuilt a number of times, by the middle of the 1400s it had become the magnificent Gothic building that still stands today. A number of mortuary chapels were also added; many of them are major works of Renaissance and Baroque art in their own right, with rich decorations and furnishings. Of particular note are the Baroque chapel of the Zbaraski family, at the west end of the north aisle, and the Mannerist chapel of the Myszkowski family, in the first bay of the south aisle. The church was badly damaged by a great fire that swept through the city in 1850, destroying most of its wooden furnishings, although it was promptly restored.

Shrine of St Jack in the Dominican church

Church of St Mary ❸

The imposing Church of St Mary (Kościół Mariacki) was built by the citizens of Cracow to rival the Royal Cathedral on Wawel Hill. Building began in 1355, but work on the vaulting and the chapels continued until the mid-15th century, and the lower tower was not completed until the early 16th. At this time, sermons were preached in German. This great basilica, with its rows of side chapels, contains an exceptional number of important works of art.

★ **Crucifix**
The large sandstone crucifix by Veit Stoss is a fine example of 15th-century sculpture.

Hejnał Tower
The famous trumpet call – the Hejnał – is sounded hourly from the tower. The call is unfinished, in memory of a medieval trumpeter, shot while sounding the alarm. The Hejnał is broadcast live by Polish radio daily at noon.

Main entrance

Baroque Porch
This pentagonal porch was built in the mid-18th century to a design by Francesco Placidi.

Ciborium
This large ciborium, in the form of a Renaissance church, was made by Giovanni Maria Padovano in about 1552.

STAR SIGHTS

★ Altarpiece of Veit Stoss

★ Crucifix

**Gothic
stained-glass
window made
around 1370**

**Visitors'
entrance**

★ Altarpiece of Veit Stoss
*This polyptych – the world's
largest Gothic altarpiece – is
11 m (36 ft) wide and 13 m
(42 ft) high. It was carved
by Veit Stoss in 1477–89.*

**Stained-glass window, Medical
Society Building**

Medical Society Building ❻

ul. Radziwiłłowska 4. **Tel** 012 422
75 47. 🚊 1, 3, 9, 10, 13, 19, 22. ⬜
10am–3pm Mon–Fri (stained glass by
appt). www.tlk.cm-uj.krakow.pl

The Medical Society Building
(Gmach Towarzystwa
Lekarskiego) was designed by
Władysław Kaczmarski and
Józef Sowiński and built in
1904. It would hardly merit
mention were it not for its
interior decor, the creation of
Stanisław Wyspiański, one of
the most talented artists of the
Young Poland movement. He
was responsible for the interior
decoration of individual rooms
and furnishings inspired by
folk art, as in the magnificent
stained-glass window *Apollo*
and *The Solar System*.

Plac Matejki ❼

🚌 105, 129, 130, 179, 502.
🚊 1, 8, 14, 15, 18.

This typical Cracovian
square was laid out
at the end of the
19th century. The
Church of St Florian
(Kościół św.
Floriana), on the
corner of Ulica
Warszawska, is
considerably
older. Its present
appearance is the
result of frequent
rebuilding – in
particular a
Neo-Baroque
reconstruction

in the early years of the 20th
century. The original church
on this site was built in the
early 13th century. At the
end of the 19th century,
huge monumental public
buildings and splendid
private houses were erected
around the square. The
Academy of Fine Arts, at
No. 13, designed by Maciej
Moraczewski and built
between 1879 and 1880,
is particularly impressive.

The Grunwald Monument
in the centre of the square
was unveiled in 1910 to mark
the 500th anniversary of the
Battle of Grunwald (see p41),
in which the armies of the
Teutonic Knights were
routed. The huge sculpture
of Władysław Jagiełło is by
Antoni Wiwulski.

Barbican ❽

ul. Basztowa. 🚌 124, 152, 502.
🚊 3, 4, 5, 13, 15. ⬜ Apr–Oct:
10:30am–6pm daily. 🚫

The Barbican (Barbakan)
is one of the remaining
elements of Cracow's
medieval fortifications.
The double ring of walls
that once surrounded the
city was built in stages
from 1285 to the beginning
of the 15th century. Most of
the circumvallation was
pulled down in the 19th
century. The Barbican
was built in 1498–9, when
the city's defences were
strengthened in response
to advances in military tactics
and equip-ment. It protected
the Florian Gate, to which
it was con-nected by an
underground passage. The
latter's route is indicated
by a change in the colour
of the paving stones.

The 15th-century Barbican, based on Arab designs

The Florian Gate, Ulica Floriańska

Ulica Floriańska ❾

🚌 105, 124, 129, 152, 179, 424, 502, 512. 🚊 2, 4, 5, 12, 13, 14, 15, 24. **Matejko's House Tel** 012 422 59 26. ⬭ 10am–6pm Tue–Sat, 10am–4pm Sun. 🖼 (free on Sun). 🔲 ⚒

This charming street in the old town is full of restaurants, cafés and shops. It leads from the Main Market Square to the Florian Gate and was once part of the Royal Route, along which rulers would ride on their way from Warsaw to their coronation in Cracow.

At No. 41, **Matejko's House** (Dom Matejki) is the birthplace of the painter Jan Matejko (1838–93). He spent most of his life here. On display is a collection of his paintings – also his studio, full of artist's materials. A little further on, at No. 45, is **Jama Michalika**, a café that was extremely fashionable in the late 19th to early 20th centuries. The fine Art Nouveau decor by Karol Frycz can still be seen.

The **Florian Gate** at the end of the street, is one of the few surviving remnants of the city's medieval fortifications, along with a section of the city wall and three towers.

Princes Czartoryski Museum ❿

ul. św. Jana 19. **Tel** 012 422 55 66. 🚌 124, 152, 424, 502, 512. 🚊 2, 4, 5, 12, 13, 14, 15, 24. ⬭ check website for details. 🖼 📷 🔲 ⚒ **www**.muzeum-czartoryskich. krakow.pl

This relatively small museum has one of the most interesting art collections in Poland. Assembled in Puławy at the end of the 18th century by Izabella Czartoryska (see p119), it was the private collection of the Czartoryski

Leonardo da Vinci, Lady with an Ermine, Czartoryski Museum

family. The collection was later taken to Paris and then to Cracow, where it was put on public view. It includes remarkable examples of handicrafts and carving, but most significant are the paintings – foremost among them Leonardo da Vinci's Lady with an Ermine (c.1485) and Rembrandt's Landscape with Good Samaritan (1638).

Piarist Church ⓫

ul. Pijarska 2. **Tel** 012 422 22 55. 🚌 124, 152, 502. 🚊 3, 4, 5, 13, 15, 19. ⬭ during services only.

The exceptionally beautiful Rococo façade of the Piarist church (kościół Pijarów), which stands at the top of Ulica św Jana, was built to the design of Francesco Placidi between 1759 and 1761. It conceals the façade of the older Baroque church of 1718–28 designed by Kacper Bażanka. The interior has stuccowork by Chrystian Bol and paintings by Franz Eckstein.

Plac Szczepański ⓬

🚌 124, 179, 424, 502. 🚊 2, 4, 5, 12, 13, 14, 15, 24. **Fine Arts Society Building Tel** 012 422 66 16. ⬭ 8:15am–6pm Mon–Fri, 10am–6pm Sat & Sun. 🖼 **The Bunker of Arts Tel** 012 422 10 52. ⬭ 11am–6pm Tue–Sun. 🖼

Plac Szczepański is always full of cars. Nonetheless, it contains a number of interesting buildings that house the arts and is well worth exploring.

At No. 1, the **Old Theatre** (Teatr Stary) is the oldest theatrical building in Poland. It opened in 1798 and has since been rebuilt twice – most recently between 1903 and 1905, when it was remodelled by Franciszek Mączyński and Tadeusz Stryjeński in the Art Nouveau style. The frieze on the façade is by Józef Gardecki.

Exhibitions are regularly held at the **Fine Arts Society Building** (Pałac Sztuki) at No. 4. Built by Franciszek

Mączyński in 1901, this too is in the Art Nouveau style. Interesting exhibitions of contemporary art are also on display for viewing at **The Bunker of Arts** (Bunkier Sztuki), a Brutalist building erected in the 1960s, located at No. 3a.

Baroque shrine of St John of Cantinus in the Church of St Anne

Church of St Anne ⑬

ul. św. Anny 11. *Tel* 012 422 53 18. 🚌 124, 152, 424, 502. 🚊 2, 4, 8, 14, 15, 18. ◯ *during services.*

In the narrow Ulica św. Anny, it is impossible to miss the imposing Baroque façade of the twin-towered Church of St Anne (Kościół św Anny). The architect was Tylman van Gameren. In designing the façade, he took into account the fact that any view of it would be acutely foreshortened by virtue of the narrowness of the street.

The church building was erected between 1689 and 1703, although work on the decoration was not completed until much later.

The interior has murals by Karol and Innocenti Monti and a fine high altar by Baldassare Fontana. The painting of St Anne that adorns it is by Jerzy Eleuter Siemigonowski. Also notable

are the Baroque choir stalls, decorated by Szymon Czechowicz, and the pulpit, which was carved by Antoni Frączkiewicz.

In the south transept is the shrine and reliquary of St John of Cantinus, a 15th-century theologian and the patron of St Anne's. The church was built after the saint's beatification.

Collegium Maius ⑭

ul. Jagiellońska 15. *Tel* 012 422 05 49. 🚌 124, 152, 424, 502. 🚊 2, 4, 8, 13, 14, 15, 18. ◯ *10am–2.20pm Mon–Sat (Mar–Oct: to 5:20pm Tue & Thu).* 🎟 *(free 3–4pm Tue).* 🎫 ♿ 🖥 www.maius.uj.edu.pl

The Collegium Maius is the oldest surviving college of the Jagiellonian University, which grew from the Cracow Academy established by Kazimierz the Great in 1364. Queen Jadwiga, wife of Władysław Jagiełło, bequeathed her personal fortune to the Academy in 1399. In the second half of the 15th century the Collegium Maius acquired new premises, which incorporated the walls of several older buildings. Its present appearance is largely due to a 19th-century restoration in a Romantic style, although the building's Gothic structure survives. Copernicus *(see p273)* undoubtedly walked in the cloistered courtyard when he was a student here. In the **Jagiellonian University Museum** are numerous exhibits documenting the rich history of the university.

Auditorium of the Collegium Maius, with Renaissance coffered ceiling

Józef Mehoffer Museum ⑮

ul. Krupnicza 26. *Tel* 012 421 11 43. 🚊 2, 4, 8, 12, 13, 15, 24. ◯ *10am–4pm Wed–Sun.* 🎟 *(free on Sun).* 🎫

This small museum is located in the house where Józef Mehoffer (1854–1946), the leading Art Nouveau stained-glass artist, lived. It contains furnishings made by Mehoffer, as well as examples of his artistic output, including the captivating *Portrait of the Artist's Wife.* The well-known artist and writer Stanisław Wyspiański (1869–1907) also lived in the house.

National Museum ⑯

al. 3 Maja 1. *Tel* 012 295 55 00. 🚌 103, 144, 152, 173, 179, 192, 512. 🚊 15, 18. ◯ *10am–6pm Tue–Sat, 10am–4pm Sun.* 🎟 *(free on Sun).* 🏠 ♿ 🖥 🖥 www.muzeum. krakow.pl

Model of the Monument to Adam Mickiewicz in the National Museum

The enormous edifice that dominates this part of the city is the main building of Cracow's National Museum. Building began in the 1930s but was not finished until 1989.

The exhibits are divided into three main sections. The first is devoted to the applied arts. The second comprises an interesting collection of militaria and objects of historical interest, such as the military jacket of Józef Piłsudski *(see p51).* The third has an important collection of 20th-century painting and sculpture. The work of the artists of the Young Poland movement is particularly well represented. The display also features pieces by schools that were active in the interwar years, and some fine examples of the art of the postwar period.

Ulica Retoryka **⓱**

🚋 103, 144, 152, 164, 173, 179, 192. 🚊 15, 18.

Take a walk down Ulica Retoryka and it is impossible to miss the remarkable houses that were designed and built here by Teodor Talowski (1857–1910) in the late 19th century. The architect had an exuberant imagination and a lively sense of humour; the houses that he designed are in an unusual mixture of the Neo-Gothic and Neo-Mannerist styles. They have startling ornamentation, sometimes artificially damaged so as to bestow a patina of age.

At No. 1, for example, is the house **"At the Sign of the Singing Frog"**. Close by is the house **"At the Sign of the Donkey"**, with a motto in Latin that translates as "Every man is master of his own fate". The architect gave to his own house the motto "Festina lente", or "Make haste slowly".

"At the Sign of the Singing Frog"

Franciscan Church **⓲**

pl. Wszystkich Świętych 5. *Tel* 012 422 53 76. 🚋 103, 124, 179, 192, 424, 502. 🚊 1, 3, 6, 8, 18. ◷ 6am–7:45pm daily. ● during services. **www**.franciszkanska.pl

The origins of the Gothic Franciscan church go back to the 13th and 15th centuries, although rebuilding

Stained-glass window in the Franciscan church

in the 17th and 19th centuries has considerably altered its appearance. The church, however, is renowned more for its interior decoration than for its architecture and attracts many visitors from all over the world.

A number of interesting features from different ages have been preserved, although the most notable are the Art Nouveau murals and stained-glass windows by Stanisław Wyspiański, dating from around 1900. The chancel and transept are decorated with a vertiginous scheme featuring entwined flowers, heraldic motifs and religious scenes. The stained-glass windows are monumental compositions of great expressive power and represent one of the highest achievements of the Secessionist stained-glass movement. Particularly noteworthy is *Let there be Light (see p49)*, which shows the figure of God the Father creating the world.

The cloisters are lined with murals that include the Gallery of Cracovian Bishops, in which the finest portrait is that of Bishop Piotr Tomicki, painted by Stanisław Samostrzelnik some time before 1535.

Ulica Grodzka **⓳**

🚊 1, 3, 6, 8, 10, 18, 40.

Many interesting buildings give this picturesque, winding street leading from the Main Market Square to the Wawel a historical atmosphere. At No. 53 is the cloistered courtyard of the **Collegium Iuridicum**, a law college founded in the 15th century and rebuilt in 1718. A little further along rises the façade of the Church of Saints Peter and Paul, with the white stone tower of the 13th-century Romanesque **Church of St Andrew** (Kościół św Andrzeja) gleaming behind it. The walls of the latter conceal an earlier, late 11th-century

The Church of St Andrew in Ulica Grodzka

building. The interior was radically altered around 1702 by Baldassare Fontana.

The adjacent Baroque building is the former Catholic **Church of St Martin** (Kościół św Marcina). Built between 1637 and 1640 for the Discalced Carmelites, it is now in the hands of the Evangelical Church of the Augsburg Confession.

Church of Saints Peter and Paul **⓴**

ul. Grodzka 54. *Tel* 012 422 65 73. 🚊 1, 6, 7, 8, 10, 12, 18. ◷ 9am–7pm Mon–Fri, 9am–5:30pm Sat, 1:30–5:30pm Sun; also during services. 📷

The Church of Saints Peter and Paul (Kościół św Piotra i Pawła) is one of the most beautiful early Baroque churches in Poland. It was built for the Jesuits soon after their arrival in Cracow.

Work began in 1596, but after a structural disaster in 1605, the church was almost completely rebuilt to the design of an architect who remains unknown to this day.

The church is enclosed by railings topped with the twelve figures of the apostles dating from 1715–22. The interior of the building contains fine stuccowork by Giovanni Battista Falconi and rich Baroque furnishings. The high altar and the organ screen, designed by Kacper Bażanka, are particularly noteworthy.

Among the many funerary monuments, the most striking is the black and white marble tomb of Bishop Andrzej Tomicki, dating from 1695–6.

Baroque façade of the Jesuit Church of Saints Peter and Paul

Ulica Kanonicza ㉑

🚋 1, 6, 8, 10. **Archdiocesan Museum** *Tel* 012 421 89 63. ◐ 10am–4pm Tue–Fri, 10am–3pm Sat, Sun. **www**.muzeumkra.diecezja.pl
Ukrainian Art Gallery *Tel* 012 421 99 96. ◐ 11am–4pm Thu–Sat.
Cricoteka *Tel* 012 422 83 32. ◐ 10am–1pm Mon–Fri (to 6pm Tue). **www**.cricoteka.com.pl

Ulica Kanonicza is named after the canons of the Cracow Chapterhouse, who once had their houses here. Most of the houses were established in the Middle Ages, but in the course of later rebuilding they were embellished with Renaissance, Baroque and Neo-Classical elements. They constitute one of the most important groups of historical buildings in Cracow today.

The finest of these houses is considered to be the **Deanery**, at No. 21. Its present form dates from the 1580s – a rebuilding project probably undertaken by the Italian architect Santi Gucci that preserved the arcaded courtyard and the mysterious decoration of the façade.

During the 1960s, Karol Wojtyła – later Pope John Paul II – lived in this house. The adjacent house at No. 19, with a modest Neo-Classical façade, contains the **Arch-**

diocesan Museum, which has many valuable religious artifacts and a reconstruction of the room at No. 21 where the future pontiff lived.

The house at No. 15 also dates from the 14th century, although its present form is a result of rebuilding during the Renaissance era. The house is the headquarters of the **Ukrainian Art Gallery**, and an interesting collection of icons from disused Greek-Catholic and Orthodox churches in southeastern Poland can be seen here.

A visit to **Cricoteka**, at No. 5, is a different kind of artistic experience. Cricoteka was the home of the famous avant-garde theatre group Cricot 2, founded by Tadeusz Kantor (1915–90) in 1956. A painter, stage-set designer and producer of "happenings", Kantor was an extremely versatile artist, and the shows he staged at Cricoteka – for example, *Wielopole, Wielopole* and *The Dead Class* – brought him universal renown. His company continued his work after his death. The Gothic house contains no stage – just archives and documents that relate the history of the theatrical company.

Helenka, a pastel portrait by Stanisław Wyspiański

Stanisław Wyspiański Museum ㉒

ul. Szczepańska 11. *Tel* 012 292 81 83. 🚋 2, 4, 6, 8, 12, 13, 14, 15, 24. ◐ 9am–6pm Tue–Sat, 9am–4pm Sun. 📷 (free on Sun).

Admirers of the splendid stained glass in the Franciscan church and the Medical Society Building should also visit this museum. Many of Stanisław Wyspiański's works are here; designs for stained-glass windows, stage sets, textiles and pastels.

Monumental portal of the Deanery in Ulica Kanonicza

The Wawel

On the Wawel, the Vistulanians built a citadel. It was replaced by a series of buildings, including the Renaissance castle and Gothic cathedral that stand there today. Once the site of coronations and royal burials, the Royal Cathedral is regarded by Poles as a spiritual shrine. The Wawel Royal Castle beside it, once the hub of cultural and political life in Poland, is a symbol of national identity.

★ Wawel Royal Castle (Zamek Królewski)
The Wawel Royal Castle, once home to the Jagiellonian kings, has survived without major damage. It incorporates the walls of older Gothic buildings **26**

Fortifications on the Wawel
The Wawel's systems of fortification have been demolished and renewed several times since the Middle Ages – right up to the 20th century
23

★ Cathedral
The Gothic cathedral, lined with royal burial chapels from different ages, has some extraordinarily valuable furnishings **27**

Cathedral Museum
On display are important artifacts from the cathedral treasury, including the magnificent robe of Stanisław August Poniatowski (1764–95) **24**

KEY

– – – Suggested route

Visitor Centre

LOCATOR MAP
See pp128–9.

"Lost
Wawel"
Exhibition
*On display
are various
finds from
archaeological
excavations on the
Wawel hill* ㉕

```
0 m          50
0 yds        50
```

STAR SIGHTS

★ Wawel Royal Castle

★ Cathedral

Fortifications on the Wawel ㉓

Wawel. 🚋 *3, 6, 8, 10, 18, 40.*
Sandomierska Tower ☐ *May–Sep: daily; Oct: Sat & Sun.* 🌀

The Wawel was fortified from early times. Only fragments of the oldest Gothic fortifications remain, but three towers raised in the second half of the 1400s survive; they are known as the Sandomierska Tower, the Senators' Tower and the Thieves' Tower. Of the fortifications dating from the 16th to the 17th centuries the most interesting is the Vasa Gate. Since 1921 it has been crowned with a monument to the 18th-century national hero Tadeusz Kościuszko. The Wawel continued to play a defensive role into the 19th century, and a relatively well-preserved system of fortifications dating from the late 18th to mid-19th centuries can still be seen today.

Sandomierska Tower, one of three towers on the Wawel

Cathedral Museum ㉔

Wawel 3. **Tel** *012 429 95 16.* 🚋 *3, 6, 8, 10, 18, 40.* ☐ *9am–5pm Mon–Sat (Oct–Mar: to 4pm).* ● *1 Jan, Easter, Corpus Christi, 15 Aug, Christmas.* 🌀

This museum is located in buildings near the cathedral and contains a valuable collection of pieces from the cathedral treasury. Here visitors can admire liturgical vessels and vestments; one of the finest is the chasuble of Bishop Piotr Kmita, which dates from 1504 and is ornamented with

Embroidered hood of Bishop Trzebicki's cope, Cathedral Museum

quilted embroidery depicting scenes from the life of St Stanisław *(see pp38–9).* The museum also contains replicas of funeral regalia, royal swords and trophies from battles won.

"Lost Wawel" Exhibition ㉕

Wawel 5. **Tel** *012 422 51 55.*
🚋 *3, 6, 8, 10, 18, 40.* ☐ *Apr–Oct: 9:30am–1pm Mon, 9:30am–5pm Tue–Fri, 10am–5pm Sat & Sun; Nov–Mar: 9:30am–4pm Mon–Sat, 10am–4pm Sun.* 🌀 *(free on Mon Apr–Oct; on Sun Nov–Mar).*
www.wawel.krakow.pl

For anyone who is interested in archaeology, this exhibition is a real delight. The display charts the development of the Wawel over a considerable period of time, and includes a virtual image of the Wawel buildings as they existed in the early Middle Ages, archaeological finds from Wawel hill, and a partially reconstructed pre-Romanesque chapel dedicated to the Blessed Virgin (Saints Felix and Adauctus).

Built at the turn of the 11th century, the chapel was discovered during research work carried out in 1917.

Chapel of the Blessed Virgin, part of the "Lost Wawel" exhibition

The Wawel Royal Castle ㉖

One of the most magnificent Renaissance residences in Central Europe, the Wawel Royal Castle was built for Zygmunt I, the penultimate ruler of the Jagiellonian dynasty. The four-winged palace, built in 1502–36 but incorporating the walls of a 14th-century building that stood on the site, was designed and constructed by the Italian architects Francisco Fiorentino and Bartolomeo Berrecci.

Head in the Audience Hall After the royal court was transferred from Cracow to Warsaw, the palace fell into neglect, and during the era of the Partitions it served as a barracks. At the beginning of the 20th century the castle was given to the city of Cracow, which started a restoration programme and turned into a museum.

Royal Treasury and Armoury
The Royal Armoury has a rich collection of arms and armour. The Royal Treasury has many precious objects, including this chalice from the abbey at Tyniec.

CASTLE GUIDE
The area open to visitors consists of part of the ground floor of the Royal Castle, where items from the Royal Treasury and Royal Armoury are displayed, as well as the halls on the first and second floors of the east and north wings. The castle's Oriental collection fills the first floor of the west wing.

Senators' Hall

Senators' Staircase

1st floor

The Castle Courtyard
A mix of architectural styles can be found at the castle. One of the highlights is the beautiful Renaissance-style courtyard, which was built in the 16th century.

KEY

- ☐ Royal Apartments
- ☐ Royal Treasury
- ☐ Royal Armoury
- ☐ Oriental Collection
- ☐ Non-exhibition space

Entrance to courtyard

Entrance to Royal Treasury and Royal Armoury

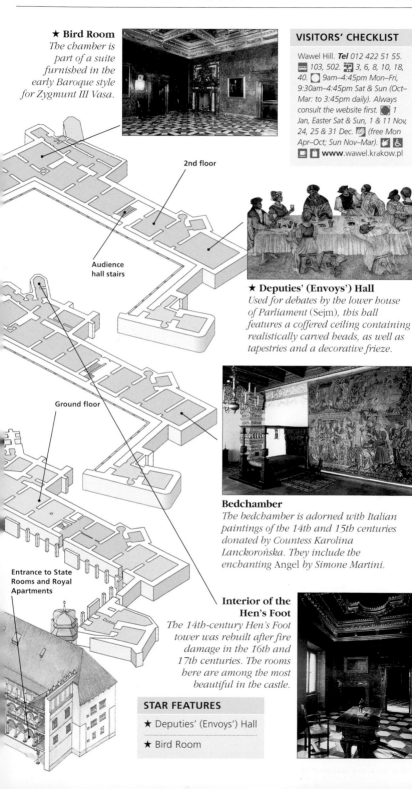

★ **Bird Room**
The chamber is part of a suite furnished in the early Baroque style for Zygmunt III Vasa.

VISITORS' CHECKLIST

Wawel Hill. *Tel* 012 422 51 55.
🚌 103, 502. 🚃 3, 6, 8, 10, 18,
40. ◯ 9am–4:45pm Mon–Fri,
9:30am–4:45pm Sat & Sun (Oct–
Mar: to 3:45pm daily). Always
consult the website first. ◐ 1
Jan, Easter Sat & Sun, 1 & 11 Nov,
24, 25 & 31 Dec. 🎫 (free Mon
Apr–Oct; Sun Nov–Mar). 📷 ♿
📧 🖼 www.wawel.krakow.pl

2nd floor

**Audience
hall stairs**

★ **Deputies' (Envoys') Hall**
Used for debates by the lower house of Parliament (Sejm), this hall features a coffered ceiling containing realistically carved heads, as well as tapestries and a decorative frieze.

Ground floor

Bedchamber
The bedchamber is adorned with Italian paintings of the 14th and 15th centuries donated by Countess Karolina Lanckorońska. They include the enchanting Angel by Simone Martini.

**Entrance to State
Rooms and Royal
Apartments**

**Interior of the
Hen's Foot**
The 14th-century Hen's Foot tower was rebuilt after fire damage in the 16th and 17th centuries. The rooms here are among the most beautiful in the castle.

STAR FEATURES

★ Deputies' (Envoys') Hall

★ Bird Room

The Cathedral ㉗

The Cathedral of Saints Stanisław and Wacław, which stands on the Wawel in Cracow, is one of the most important churches in Poland. Before the present cathedral was erected (1320–64), two earlier churches stood on the site. The cathedral has many fine features, including a series of chapels founded by rulers and bishops, the most beautiful being the Renaissance Zygmunt Chapel. There are royal tombs in both the cathedral and the Crypt of St Leonard, a remnant of the Romanesque Cathedral of St Wacław begun in 1038.

The top of the clock tower is decorated with statues of saints.

Zygmunt Bell
This is the largest bell in Poland. It was made in 1520, weighs almost 11 tonnes and has a diameter of over 2 m (6 ft).

Main entrance

★ Tomb of Kazimierz the Jagiellonian
This royal tomb in the Chapel of the Holy Cross, completed in 1492, is one of the last commissions that the German sculptor Veit Stoss fulfilled in Poland.

Shrine of St Stanisław
The silver coffin containing the relics of St Stanisław, the bishop of Cracow to whom the cathedral is dedicated, was made in 1669–71 by Pieter van der Rennen, a goldsmith from Gdańsk.

Crypt of the Pauline Church on the Rock, pantheon to Polish creativity

VISITORS' CHECKLIST

Wawel 3. *Tel* 012 429 95 16 (ext. 291). 🚋 3, 6, 8, 10, 18, 40. ⬜ 9am–5pm Mon–Sat, 12:30–5pm Sun (Oct–Mar: 4pm). 🎧 ♿ 🏛

Stalls

The early Baroque oak stalls in the chancel were made around 1620.

High altar

★ Zygmunt Chapel

The chapel containing the tombs of the two last Jagiellonian kings is the jewel of Italian Renaissance art in Poland. The tomb of Zygmunt the Old was made after 1530 by Bartolomeo Berrecci. That of Zygmunt August was made in 1574–5 by Santi Gucci.

Pauline Church on the Rock ㉘

ul. Skałeczna 15. *Tel* 012 421 72 44. 🚌 103, 124, 128, 144, 164, 169, 173, 179, 184, 194, 502. 🚋 8, 10, 18, 19, 22. ⬜ 8am–6pm daily. **Crypt of Honour** ⬜ Apr–Oct: 9am–5pm daily; Nov–Mar: by appt. 🎧

The impressive Baroque Pauline Church on the Rock (Kościół Paulinów na Skałce), with its adjoining monastery complex, was built in 1733–42 by Gerhard Müntzer in collaboration with Antoni Solari. The present church was preceded by two earlier buildings. It was at the foot of the altar of the Romanesque church, the first to be built on the site, that St Stanisław, Bishop of Cracow, was murdered (*see pp38–9*).

The interior includes Baroque stuccowork by Jan Lehnert. The crypt was converted by Teofil Żebrawski into a pantheon to Polish writers and artists. Among the eminent people who lie here are the painters Jacek Malczewski (1854–1929) and Henryk Siemiradzki, the writers and poets Józef Ignacy Kraszewski, Adam Asnyk (1839–97) and Wincenty Pol (1807–72), and the artist and writer Stanisław Wyspiański.

Return along Ulica Skałeczna towards Ulica Augustiańska and take a look at the beautiful Gothic Convent and Church of St Catherine (Kościół św Katarzyny), begun in the mid-14 century. It once belonged to the Augustinian order, but was deconsecrated and used as a warehouse. Of the original features only the high altar remains. The 15th-century Hungarian Chapel (Kaplica Węgierska) next door is connected by a covered bridge over Ulica Skałeczna to the Baroque Augustinian convent.

Royal tombs

These Baroque sarcophagi were made for members of the royal Vasa dynasty. The cathedral is the final resting place of most of the Polish kings, as well as national heroes and revered poets.

STAR FEATURES

★ Tomb of Kazimierz the Jagiellonian

★ Zygmunt Chapel

Church of Corpus Christi ㉙

ul. Bożego Ciała 26. **Tel** *012 430 62
90.* 🚮 *502.* 🚊 *3, 6, 8, 10, 18.*
⭘ *9am–6pm daily.*

The mighty Gothic Church
of Corpus Christi was built
as the parish church of the
town of Kazimierz, which
was founded to the south
of the castle by Kazimierz
the Great in the 14th
century. Work on the
church began around 1340,
continuing into the early
15th century. The basilica-
like interior contains some
fine works of art in the
Baroque style, including
the magnificent high altar
of 1634–7 with the painting
of *The Birth of Christ* by
Tomasso Dolabella, a fine
mid-18th-century pulpit,
and stalls dating from 1632,
originally built for the monks
(although the church has
been in the care of canons
since the 15th century). The
monastery is on the north
side of the church.

Old Synagogue ㉚

ul. Szeroka 24. 🚮 *184, 198.*
🚊 *3, 9, 13.* **Museum of Jewish
History Tel** *012 422 09 62.*
⭘ *Apr–Oct: 10am–2pm Mon,
9am–5pm Tue–Sun; Nov–Mar:
10am–2pm Mon, 9am–4pm Tue–
Thu, Sat & Sun, 10am–5pm Fri.*
🎟 *(free on Mon).* **www**.mhk.pl

**Gothic-Renaissance bema in the
Old Synagogue**

Built by Matteo Gucci in the
mid-16th century in the Renaissance style, the Old Synagogue
replaced an earlier Gothic
synagogue that burned down
in 1557. In the Hall of Prayer
you will find a reconstructed
bema and Ark of the Covenant.

The synagogue houses
a branch of the Historical
Museum. The displays within
consist of some artifacts used
in Jewish rituals, and documents relating to the history
of Cracovian Jews and their
martyrdom during the Nazi
occupation in World War II.

**Tomb in Remuh Cemetery from
the first half of the 17th century**

Remuh Cemetery and Synagogue ㉛

ul. Szeroka 40. **Tel** *012 429 57 35.*
🚮 *184, 198.* 🚊 *3, 9, 13.* ⭘ *9am–
6pm Sun–Fri.* 🅿 **Eagle Pharmacy**
*(Apteka pod Orłem) Plac Bohaterów
Getta 18. **Tel** 012 656 56 25.* ⭘
*Apr–Oct: 10am–2pm Mon, 9:30am–
5pm Tue–Sun; Nov–Mar: 10am–2pm
Mon, 9am–4pm Tue–Thu & Sat,
10am–5pm Fri.* 🎟 *(free Mon).*

The humble prayer house
known as the Remuh is one
of two synagogues in Cracow
that are still in use. It was
built around 1557 by Izrael
ben Józef for his son Mojżesz
Isserles, a famous scholar,
rabbi and reputed miracle
worker, known as Remuh.
Inside, the Renaissance Ark
of the Covenant and the
bema, rebuilt as a replica of
the original, have survived.
Behind the synagogue is one
of the most important Jewish
cemeteries in Europe. Despite

the damage that the cemetery
suffered during World War II,
many of the tombstones
have survived. Fragments of
shattered tombstones have
been built into the cemetery
wall abutting Ulica Szeroka.

This part of town was
immortalized in Steven Spiel-
berg's film *Schindler's List*.
The district now has shops
and kosher restaurants; the
family home of Helena Rubinstein, founder of the cosmetics
business, is also here.

On the other side of the
Vistula is the **Eagle Pharmacy**,
which played a vital role as a
shelter and communication
hub for the inhabitants of the
ghetto during War World II. It
now houses an exhibition on
the history of Cracow's Jews.

Premonstratensian Church ㉜

ul. Kościuszki 88. **Tel** *012 427 13 18.*
🚊 *1, 2, 6, 100, 101, 109, 209, 229,
239, 249, 259, 269, 409.*

This church (Kościół Norber-
tanek) and convent on the
banks of the Vistula at Zwi-
erzyniec was founded in 1162.
The present appearance of the
small nave church is due to
rebuilding in 1595–1604. The
extensive convent also dates
from the early 17th century.

The Chapel of St Margaret
(Kaplica św Małgorzaty), an
octagonal building in the early
Baroque style, is on nearby
Ulica św Bronisława. Behind
the chapel is the Church of Our
Saviour (Kościół Najświętszego
Salwatora). Built in the second
half of the 12th century, it was
remodelled at the beginning of
the 17th, when it was reduced
to a small nave church with a
tower at the west end.

Decjusz Villa ㉝

al. 28 Lipca 1943 r. 17a. **Tel** *012 425
36 38.* 🚮 *102, 134, 152, 192. For
details of the cultural programme,
visit the website* **www**.villa.org.pl

In the charming residential
district of Wola Justowska
stands the Decjusz Villa, a
manor house whose origins go
back to the late Middle Ages.

Decjusz Villa from the garden, the arcaded loggia flanked by towers

It was rebuilt around 1530 in the Renaissance style for Justus Ludwik Decjusz, and acquired its present shape around 1620, when Stanisław Lubomirski, Palatine of Cracow, had it extended and remodelled in the early Baroque style.

Visitors who want to make sure they get the best view of the Decjusz Villa, an impressive three-storey arcaded loggia that is flanked by towers, should view it from the garden. Today the villa houses the European Academy. There is a good restaurant in the basement.

Camaldolite Monastery in Bielany ㉞

ul. Konarowa 1–16. **Tel** 012 429 76 10. 🚌 109, 209, 239, 249, 269. ⭕ to men: during services; to women: 2 and 7 Feb, 25 Mar, Easter, Whitsun, 19 Jun, the first Sun after 15 Aug, 8 Sep, 25 Dec.

Seen from afar, this monolithic Mannerist-Baroque monastery set on Srebrna Góra (Silver Mountain) appears to be a tempting tourist attraction. However, the monks, who are the monastery's sole inhabitants, are committed to absolute silence and no contact with the outside world. Visits are therefore severely restricted, especially for women.

The monastery was founded in the early 17th century by Valentin von Säbisch and completed by Andrea Spezza. It is richly adorned with Baroque features, and from the windows of the chapel it is possible to glimpse the monks' dwellings, to which visitors are not admitted.

Benedictine Abbey in Tyniec ㉟

ul. Benedyktyńska 37. **Tel** 012 688 54 50. 🚌 112, 203. ⭕ daily for morning services & 1–6:30pm. **www**.tyniec.mm.com.pl

This impressive abbey is set on a high chalky outcrop overlooking the River Vistula. The history of the abbey goes back to the mid-11th century. Originally, a Romanesque basilica stood on the site. It was replaced in the 15th century by a Gothic church. The present Baroque abbey was built in 1618–22.

Although in the course of its stormy history the church has lost many fine and valuable features, it still retains its monumental Baroque altars. Some elements of the original Romanesque building have survived in the underground parts of the abbey adjacent to the church.

Benedictine abbey, Tyniec, on a chalky outcrop above the Vistula

Schindler's Factory ㊱

ul. Lipowa 4. 🚊 3, 6, 7, 9, 11, 13, 20, 23, 24, 50, 51. **Tel** 012 257 10 17. ⭕ Apr–Oct: 10am–8pm daily (to 4pm Mon, to 2pm first Mon of month); Nov–Mar: 10am–6pm daily (to 2pm Mon). 🎟 free Mon. 📷 **www**.oskarschindlersfactory.com

Located in the former industrial district of Zabłocie, Schindler's Factory is a symbol of humanitarian courage. In 1943, the factory's German owner, Oskar Schindler, protected his Jewish workers by claiming that they were essential to

the running of his business. The factory, part of the Historical Museum of Cracow (see p131), features an interactive exhibition on the occupation of 1939–45.

Cistercian Abbey in Mogiła ㊲

ul. Klasztorna 11. **Tel** 012 644 23 31. 🚌 113, 123, 153, 174. 🚊 15, 17. ⭕ 6am–7pm.

Behind the fine Baroque façade of the church, which was designed and erected by Franciszek Moser in 1779–80, lies a much older interior. Founded by Bishop Iwo Odrowąż, the Cistercian abbey was built in the 13th century; the church was consecrated in 1266. The interior of the early Gothic basilica, which contains a number of Renaissance paintings by Stanisław Samostrzelnik, has survived alongside later, mainly Baroque, features.

Other interesting parts of the abbey are the Gothic cloisters and the chapter house, which has paintings by the 19th-century artist Michał Stachowicz. These depict the legend of Wanda, whose patriotism led her to throw herself into the Vistula. Her tomb, situated under a tumulus, is located nearby.

Museum of the Polish Air Force ㊳

al. Jana Pawła II 39. 🚊 5, 9, 10, 15, 40, 73. **Tel** 012 640 99 60. ⭕ 9am–5pm Tue (outdoor exhibition only) & Wed–Sun. 🎟 (free on Tue). 📷 **www**.muzeumlotnictwa.pl

This museum is located on the historic Rakowice-Czyżyny airfield, one of the oldest military airfields in Europe (established in 1912). The collection consists of more than 200 aircraft, including pre-war Polish fighter planes, Spitfires, German Albatrosses and Soviet Kakaruzniks. Also in the museum are 22 rare aeroplanes that were once part of Hermann Göring's personal collection.

MAŁOPOLSKA (LESSER POLAND)

Małopolska is the country's most picturesque and varied region. Attractions such as the ski resort of Zakopane, hiking trails in the Tatra Mountains, the magical Black Madonna of Często-chowa and a lively folk tradition make it Poland's most popular tourist destination. Cracow, not only the regional capital but the spiritual and historic capital of the nation, is one of the noblest cities in Europe.

In the 9th century, the Vistulanian tribe established a state in Małopolska. Their capital was Cracow, or Wiślica. In 990, Małopol-ska became part of the Polanian duchy of Mieszko I, and in 1039, Prince Kazimierz the Restorer made Cracow the centre of his realm of power. For centuries, Małopolska was the heart of Poland. However, its importance began to wane at the end of the 16th century, when the capital of the Republic was moved to Warsaw.

After the Partitions of Poland, Małopolska went into a gradual decline. While Galicia, its southern part, came under Austrian rule, its northern part was incorporated into the Russian empire. When Galicia gained autonomy within the Austro-Hungarian Empire, Galician towns, and especially Cracow, became important centres of Polish culture, retaining their iden-tity despite a succession of annexations. Not until 1918, when Poland at last regained its indepen-dence, did Małopolska again become part of the Polish state.

The Małopolska region is dotted with picturesque towns, ruined castles, palaces, country mansions, great monasteries and pretty wooden churches. The eastern fringes of the region are distinguished by their Uniate Orthodox churches. There are also many monuments to the Jewish population that was present in Małopolska before 1945.

In many parts of the region, folk cus-toms survive and flourish, nowhere more than in the Podhale region; in Zakopane, the regional capital of Podhale, folklore and folk art are a local industry.

The Galician small town of Stary Sącz, at the foot of the Sądecky Beskidy Mountains

◁ Wooden house in the forest, beneath the towering Tatra Mountains

Exploring Małopolska

Małopolska, in the south of Poland, is the country's main tourist region. Apart from Cracow, the greatest attractions for visitors are the mountain ski resort of Zakopane, which is the winter sports capital, and the picturesque Tatra Mountains. In summer many hikers are drawn to the region, and its mountains are traversed by well-marked hiking trails. There are numerous welcoming hostels for those in need of overnight shelter. Parts of the Beskid Niski Mountains are almost without human habitation, so that it is still possible to walk for several hours without encountering a single living soul. Spiritual relief can be found deep within the forests, where walkers may be surprised to encounter pretty wooden churches.

Interior of a cottage in Zalipie, with traditional decoration

GETTING AROUND

Cracow and Rzeszów can be reached by air. The larger towns all have good rail links with the rest of the country. Some small villages can only be reached by bus or car. The E77 highway goes north and south from Cracow, while the E40 goes eastwards through Tarnów, Rzeszów and Przemyśl. Parallel to it, but further south, major road 28 connects Nowy Sącz with Biecz, Krosno and Sanok.

SEE ALSO

- *Where to Stay* pp301–3.

- *Restaurants and Bars* pp319–21.

KEY

═══	Motorway
━━━	Main road
┅┅┅	Minor road
╾╼╾	Main railway
────	Minor railway
▬▬▬	International border
▬▬▬	Regional border
△	Peak

A detail of Neo-Classical decorative moulding in the palace at Łańcut

SIGHTS AT A GLANCE

Niedzica Castle overlooking the artificial lake on the Dunajec

The Henryk Sienkiewicz Museum in Oblęgorek

Oblęgorek ❶

Road map E5. 🚶 950. 🚌

The writer Henryk Sienkiewicz *(see p25)* received a small manor house in the village of Oblęgorek as a gift from the nation in 1900. It is an eclectic building with a tall circular tower. The interior remains as it was when Sienkiewicz lived and worked here. Today it houses the **Henryk Sienkiewicz Museum**.

Sienkiewicz is the best-known Polish novelist. He received the Nobel Prize for Literature for his historical novel *Quo Vadis?* in 1905.

🏛 **Henryk Sienkiewicz Museum**
Tel 041 303 04 26. ⏱ 9am–4pm Tue–Sun. 🎟

Kielce ❷

Road map E5. 🚶 205,000.
🚉 🚌 ℹ *pl. Niepodległości 1 (041 348 00 60). Tel* 041 345 86 81.
www.um.kielce.pl

In a city whose beauty has been defaced by buildings that went up after World War II, the **Bishops' Palace** stands out like a jewel. It is an exceptionally fine example of a well-preserved aristocratic town house of the first half of the 17th century *(see p45)*. The early Baroque façades with four corner towers have been preserved almost intact, as has the decoration of the

rooms on the first floor. The marble doorways and beamed ceilings are original.

The palace was built in 1637–41, probably by the royal architect Giovanni Trevano, under the direction of Tomasso Poncino, for the Bishop of Cracow, Jakub Zadzik. During the reign of Zygmunt III, this exceptional clergyman was in charge of the Republic's foreign policy, successfully making peace with Russia and establishing a long-standing ceasefire with Sweden. His role as a bishop, however, was inglorious. He contributed to the shameful decision to condemn the Polish Brethren during the Sejm of 1641. These

events are illustrated on the palace ceilings, which were painted in 1641.

The period interiors form part of the **National Museum** in the palace. There is also an excellent gallery of Polish painting here.

Next to the palace is the **cathedral**, built on the site of an earlier church of 1632–5, the time of Bishop Zadzik.

Several dozen wooden village buildings from the area around Kielce are laid out over an area of 4.2 sq km (1.6 sq miles) in the **Kielce Rural Museum**.

🏛 **National Museum**
pl. Zamkowy 1. *Tel* 041 344 40 15.
⏱ 10am–6pm Tue–Sun. 🎟 (free on Sun). 🔌 www.muzeumkielce.net

🏛 **Kielce Rural Museum**
Temporary exhibition ul. Jana Pawła II 6. *Tel* 041 344 92 97.
⏱ 9am–5pm Tue–Sun. 🎟 (free on Sun). 🔌 www.mwk.com.pl
Skansen **in Tokarnia** *Tel* 041 315 41 71. ⏱ Apr–Oct: 10am–6pm Tue–Sun; Nov–Mar: 9am–3pm Tue–Sun. 🎟 ♿ 🎟 🍴 🚻

Environs
The ruins of a 13th-century castle dominate the town of **Chęciny**, 15 km (9 miles) to the west of Kielce. **Paradise Cave** (Jaskinia Raj), to the north of Chęciny, contains spectacular stalactites and stalagmites.

The Dining Hall in the Bishops' Palace in Kielce

Holy Cross Mountains ❸

Road map E5. 🚗 🚌 🛈 *041 367 64 36 or 367 60 11.*

In geological terms, the Holy Cross Mountains (Góry Świętokrzyskie) – part of the Małopolska uplands – are among the oldest in Europe. Eroded over many thousands of years, they are neither high nor steep, but they are except-ionally rich in minerals, which have been exploited since ancient times. The remains of prehistoric mines and furnaces have been found here. The Łysogóry range, with Mount Łysica at a mere 612 m (2,000 ft), the highest peak in the mountains, lies within the

Broken rock on the Łysogóry slopes, Świętokrzyski National Park

Świętokrzyski National Park. The primeval forest of fir trees that once covered the range was seriously damaged by acid rain in the 1970s and 1980s, so that only vestiges remain today. In ancient times Łysa Góra, the second-highest peak in the Holy Cross Mountains, was a pagan place of worship. Its slopes are covered with *gołoborza*, heaps of broken rock. Legend tells of the witches' sabbaths that are said to have taken place here.

The **Benedictine abbey in Święty Krzyż** on the summit of Łysa Góra was built in the 12th century and extended during the rule of the Jagiell-onian dynasty. The church, which replaces an earlier Romanesque church, was built in 1782–9 and has predom-inantly Baroque and Neo-Classical features. The interior is decorated with paintings by the 18th-century artist Franciszek Smuglewicz. The cloisters and vestry, with late Baroque frescoes, date from the 15th century. The domed chapel of the Oleśnicki family, dating from the 17th century, is the abbey's most outstanding feature. Kept in the chapel since 1723, the relic of the Holy Cross attracts crowds of pilgrims. In the crypt beneath

Ruins of the Baroque Bishops' Palace at Bodzentyn

the chapel is a glass coffin containing the supposedly mummified body of Prince Jeremi Wiśniowiecki. In his novel *With Fire and Sword* Henryk Sienkiewicz portrayed this magnate as a saviour, and hero of the battles against Ukrainian insurgents in 1648. History judges him less kindly: a seasoned soldier, an unimag-inative politician and a brute, who by passing sentences of impalement earned himself the nickname Palej (The Impaler).

Bodzentyn, north of Łysogóry, is worth a visit for its 18th-century Gothic parish church. The Renaissance altar comes from Wawel Cathedral in Cracow. The stately ruins of the Bishops' Palace can also be seen in the town.

ŚWIĘTOKRZYSKI NATIONAL PARK

The Łysogóry range constitutes the major part of the park. Natural features of particular interest include *gołoborza*, created by the fragmentation of quartzite sandstone, and vestiges of the primeval fir forest. On Chełmowa Góra, native Polish larch can be seen.

KEY

- – – Hiking trail
- ▬ Road
- 🅿 Car park
- 🛈 Tourist information
- ☆ Viewpoint

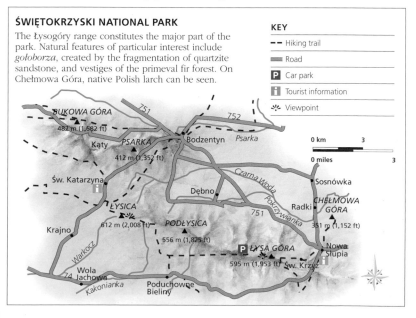

BUKOWA GÓRA 482 m (1,582 ft) · Katy · PSARKA 412 m (1,352 ft) · Bodzentyn · Psarka · Św. Katarzyna · 751 · 752 · Czarna Woda · Dębno · Sosnówka · ŁYSICA 612 m (2,008 ft) · Krajno · PODŁYSICA 556 m (1,825 ft) · Radki · CHEŁMOWA GÓRA 351 m (1,152 ft) · Pokrzywianka · 751 · Warkocz · ŁYSA GÓRA 595 m (1,953 ft) · Św. Krzyż · Nowa Słupia · Wola Jachowa · Poduchowne Bieliny · Kakonianka

0 km   3
0 miles   3

Wąchock ❹

Road map E4. 🏛 *3,300.* 🚉 🚌
Cistercian Abbey ul. Koscielna 14.
Tel *041 275 02 00.* ◯ *daily.*

Wąchock is a neat town with a well-preserved **Cistercian abbey**. It was founded in 1179 by Gedko z Gryfitów, Bishop of Cracow. The church, built in the early 13th century, has Romanesque and Gothic features. Although the architect is unknown, the inscription "Simon" that can be seen on the façade is thought to be his signature. The interior is decorated with mural paintings. The most important Romanesque interiors of the abbey – those of the chapter house and the rooms off the cloisters – have been preserved almost intact. The abbey was remodelled in the 1600s, the façade being given the appearance of a palace with the addition of arcades and an enormous tower.

Opatów ❺

Road map E5. 🏛 *7,100.* 🚌

The collegiate church of St Martin (Kolegiata św. Marcina), built in the first half of the 12th century, is among the best-preserved Romanesque churches in Poland. The façade has two quadrilateral towers and representations of dragons and plants on its borders. The interior contains interesting tombs, the most eminent being the one with the bronze effigy of Krzysztof Szydłowiecki, the royal chancellor who became the

Collegiate Church of St Martin in Opatów

owner of Opatów. The tomb dates from 1533–6 and bears a relief known as the Opatów Lament *(see pp42–3)*. The marble tombstone of Anna Szydłowiecka carved by Bernardino de Gianoti in 1536 is also noteworthy.

The curious holes and ruts in the walls of the church are an unusual mark of the past. Noblemen would use the church walls to sharpen their sabres, which they would often do on horseback. This explains why the holes are so high.

Ujazd ❻

Road map E5. 🏛 *1,600.* 🚌 🛈
077 463 70 37. **Krzyżtopór Castle**
Tel *015 860 11 33.* **www.**ujazd.pl

The main attraction in Ujazd are the ruins of **Krzyżtopór Castle**, built for the palatine

Krzysztof Ossoliński, probably by Agostino Locci the Elder in 1621–44. It is one of the most eccentric residences of its time in Europe *(see pp44–5)*. Having been attacked during the Swedish Deluge *(see p44)*, the castle fell into neglect. The palace was enormous, and for 300 years its walls provided the surrounding villages with vast amounts of building material. However, the magnificent ruins are still extremely impressive.

Environs
Ossolin, situated 15 km (9 miles) to the east of Ujazd, is the town from which the Ossoliński family came. The historic remains here are much more modest. It survived an explosion in 1816, inflicted by subsequent owners who sought to blow it up in search of the treasure rumoured to be hidden there.

The stately ruins of Krzyżtopór Castle in Ujazd

For hotels and restaurants in this region see pp301–3 and pp320–21

The Mannerist and Baroque collegiate church in **Klimontów**, 13 km (8 miles) east of Ujazd, and begun in 1643, is something of an architectural curiosity. The elliptical nave with galleries is an unusual combination, and the columns sunk into niches hollowed out in the pillars make a mockery of the principles of tectonics.

Sandomierz ❼

Road map F5. 🏘 *23,000.* 🚉 🚌
ℹ️ *PTTK, Rynek 12 (015 832 26 82).* **Underground Tourist Route** ul. Oleśnickich 1. **Tel** *015 832 30 88.* ⭕ *10am–6pm daily (Apr: to 5pm, Oct–Mar: to 4pm).*
www.sandomierz.pl

The best view of this small, ancient town is from the River Vistula. In 1138, Sandomierz became the capital of an independent duchy, and from the 14th century until the Partitions of Poland it was a regional capital. The **Underground Tourist Route**, a network of underground passages that runs beneath the town, dates from the 15th to 17th centuries.

The main entrance to the old town is **Opatów Gate**. The charming, slightly sloping **Market Square** is surrounded by elegant houses. In the centre stands the 14th-century town hall, with its splendid Renaissance parapet. It houses the **Regional Museum**. The most important building in the town is the **cathedral**, built around 1360 on the site of an earlier Romanesque cathedral and later altered. The 15th-century Ruthenian-Byzantine frescoes in the chancel depict scenes from the lives of Christ and the Virgin, and there are also some beautiful carvings.

The **Church of St James** (Kościół św Jakuba) is an exceptionally fine late Romanesque aisled basilica. Built in brick, it was begun in 1226. Its ceramic decoration and beautiful portal are evidence that it was built by master craftsmen from Lombardy. The remains of 49 Dominican friars murdered by Tartars in 1260 lie in the Martyrs' Chapel.

Opatów Gate, defending the old town of Sandomierz

🏛 Diocesan Museum
ul. Długosza 9. **Tel** *015 833 26 70.* ⭕ *9am–4pm Tue–Sat, 1:30–4pm Sun (Nov–Mar: to 3:30pm).* 📷
The museum is in the Gothic house of Jan Długosz (1415–80), the celebrated chronicler of Poland. It features religious paintings and sculptures from the Middle Ages to the 19th century, including *Madonna with the Christ Child* and *St Catherine* by Lucas Cranach the Elder.

🏛 Regional Museum
Castle Tel *015 644 57 57/58.* ⭕ *9am–4pm Tue–Fri, 9am–3pm Sat, 10am–3pm Sun (May–Sep: 10am–5pm Tue–Fri, 10am–6pm Sat & Sun).* **Town Hall** *Rynek 10.* **Tel** *693 378 799.* ⭕ *9am–4pm Tue–Fri, 9am–3pm Sat, 10am–3pm Sun (May–Sep: 10am–5pm Tue–Fri, 9am–5pm Sat & Sun).* 📷
The Regional Museum is split between the town hall and

the refurbished Gothic and Renaissance castle. The museum contains archaeological, ethnographic and historical displays.

Baranów Sandomierski ❽

Road map E5. 🏘 *1,500.* 🚉 *3 km (2 miles) from the centre.* 🌐 **www**.baranow.com.pl

Leszczyński Castle, built in Baranów Sandomierski for the Leszczyński family in 1591–1606, is one of the finest examples of Mannerist architecture in Poland. The castle consists of four wings arranged around a rectangular arcaded courtyard. The grand exterior staircase and the façades, with their elaborate attics giving the impression of a massive (but in fact delicate) curtained wall, are striking. The square tower in the central façade serves a purely decorative purpose. On account of its architectural ornamentation, featuring spheres, rosettes and strange creatures, the castle is thought to have been designed by Santi Gucci. The **Sulphur Basin Museum** on the ground floor contains furniture, suits of armour and other objects from the castle's heyday, as well as exhibits relating to the history of sulphur exploitation in the huge quarries nearby.

🏛 Sulphur Basin Museum
ul. Zamkowa 20. **Tel** *015 811 80 40.* ⭕ *9am–7pm Tue–Sun (Nov–Mar: to 4pm; Apr & Oct: to 5pm).* 📷 *(compulsory, every hour).*

Staircase in the courtyard of Leszczyński Palace in Baranów Sandomierski

The Camaldolite church in Rytwiany

Rytwiany ⑨

Road map E5. 🏃 950. �" 🚌

The main attraction of Rytwiany is the early Baroque **Camaldolite church** that stands next to the monastery. It was built in 1624–5 by the Tęczyński family and is considered to be one of the finest examples of Camaldolite architecture in Europe. In accordance with the rules of the order, the entrance to the sanctuary leads through a narrow passageway, with the tiny houses of the monks lying behind the monastery walls. The clock in the church tower marked the times for different activities in the monastery. The modest appearance of the façade contrasts with the exuberant interior: stuccowork is complemented by colourful frescoes painted by the prior, Venante da Subiaco. The church is hidden deep in the forest in a vast clearing, unfortunately beyond the reach of most tourists.

The ruins of the 15th-century Gothic castle of Wojciech Jastrzębiec, Archbishop of Gniezno, which stand on the edge of the village, are also worth visiting.

Kurozwęki ⑩

Road map E5. 🏃 840. 🚌 ℹ *ul. Zamkowa 3 (015 866 74 07).* **Castle** *Tel 015 866 72 71.* ☐ *Tue–Sun.*

The 14th-century Gothic **castle** that once stood in the small village of Kurozwęki was one of the earliest stone fortresses in Małopolska. Today, only vestiges remain, incorporated in the large Rococo-Neo-Classical **castle** that now stands on the site, surrounded by a neglected park. The castle was built for a Poraj family, who were at the height of their power in the times of Zawisza, Chancellor and Bishop of Cracow (died c.1382), known for his sumptuous lifestyle.

Environs
In **Raków**, 12 km (7 miles) north of Kurozwęki, is the Protestant church of the Polish Brethren. It is contemporary with the establishment of Raków Academy in the 1600s.

Szydłów ⑪

Road map E5. 🏃 1,100. 🚌 ℹ *ul. Targowa 3 (041 354 53 13).* 🎠 *Jousting tournament (early Jun).* **www**.szydlow.pl

This attractive medieval town is reached by crossing a bridge over a moat and passing through one of the old town gates. In the 16th century this was a flourishing town, and in 1528 it even had its own sophisticated water supply. By the mid-17th century, however, it was falling into decline. Features of interest are the **town walls**, 2 m (6 ft) thick and 680 m (2,230 ft) long, with spiked battlements, and the Market Square, dominated by the **Church of St Władysław** (Fara św Władysława), initially in the Gothic style but rebuilt in the 17th century.

Also worth a visit are the Gothic **castle** of Kazimierz the Great, with its **Regional Museum**, and the 16th-century **synagogue**, with Baroque wall paintings.

🏛 Regional Museum
ul. Szkolna 8. **Tel** *041 354 53 13.* ☐ *10am–7pm daily (Oct–Mar: to 5pm Mon–Fri, to 3pm Sat & Sun).* ⬤ *Mon & Wed in summer.*

Cracow Gate, the Gothic south gate into the old town of Szydłów

Grabki Duże ⑫

Road map E5. 🏃 410. 🚌

Between 1742 and 1750, the architect Francisco Placidi built a Rococo palace here for the castellan Stanisław Rupniewski. At the time, the unusual shape of the building aroused suspicions that the castellan intended it to be for a harem. Rupniewski loved women, so did nothing to contradict the gossip.

The nucleus of the "harem" is a central hall covered with a fanciful roof. This is surrounded by four single-storey

The castle in Kurozwęki, with its severe Neo-Classical façade

For hotels and restaurants in this region see pp301–3 and pp320–21

The palace of Stanisław Rupniewski in Grabki Duże, said to be for a harem

wings that once contained small apartments. The design of the palace is not dissimilar to that of a windmill.

Busko Zdrój ⓭

Road map E5. 🚶 18,400. 🚌 🚉
ℹ️ ul. Waryńskiego 4a (041 378 48 83). 🎵 K. Jamroz Music Festival (Jun, Jul). **www**.busko.com.pl

Springs with healing properties were discovered here in 1776, but it was not until the beginning of the 19th century that they began to be exploited. In 1836 a sanatorium was opened and a **park** laid out. The Neo-Classical **bath house** dates from 1836–8; visitors may sample the waters in the pump room. The spa itself is valued for its rare sulphur and salt springs and for its therapeutic mud.

Wiślica ⓮

Road map E5. 🚶 610. 🚌

This sleepy village may have been the capital of the Vistulanians in the 11th century. The Market Square, which is planted with trees, is unexpectedly dominated by the enormous Gothic **collegiate church**, founded by Kazimierz the Great after 1350. The chancel is decorated with Ruthenian-Byzantine frescoes dating from 1397–1400 which are now barely visible. The floor is that of an earlier Romanesque church; the figures engraved within it date from the second half of the 12th century and may perhaps represent the Piast princes *(see p39)* who founded the church.

Pińczów ⓯

Road map E5. 🚶 12,400. 🚌
ℹ️ ul. Piłsudskiego 2a (041 357 24 72). 🎵 Days of Ponidzie (Jun). **www**. muzeumitpinczow.eu

In the 16th century, the town of Pińczów was an important centre of artistic and intellectual life. It is dominated by the castle built in the 15th century for Cardinal Zbigniew Oleśnicki. Oleśnicki was a politician and confidant of Władysław II and Kazimierz IV, as well as being a patron of the medieval Polish chronicler Jan Długosz. During the Renaissance, the castle was remodelled for the Myszkowski family by Santi Gucci. It was dismantled before 1799, the result being that little remains today.

Between 1556 and 1586, the humanistic Calvinist college was active in Pińczów – just as the printing house of the Polish Brethren was to be a few decades later. A beautiful Renaissance house decorated with sgraffito is sometimes identified as the Polish Brethren's printing house: it is not, but it still merits the visitor's attention.

The **Chapel of St Anne** (Kaplica św Anny), on the top of the hill, is an unusual Mannerist building. It was founded in 1600 by Zygmunt Myszkowski and built, it is thought, by Santi Gucci.

In nearby Mirów, the **Franciscan church** and the 17th-century Mannerist-Baroque **parish church**, which has early Baroque vaulting and rich furnishings, are both worth a visit. In the vestibule of the parish church, a marble tombstone of a middle-class woman, Anna Jakubczyńska, who died in 1618, attracts the visitor's attention.

Also worth seeing is the late Renaissance **synagogue**, which is the last remaining trace of the Jews who once lived in Pińczów.

The parish and Franciscan church in Mirów, near Pińczów

Częstochowa ⑯

The monastery of Jasna Góra in Częstochowa is the most famous shrine of the Virgin in Poland and the country's greatest place of pilgrimage – for many, its spiritual capital. The image of the Black Madonna of Częstochowa, to which miraculous powers are attributed, is Jasna Góra's most precious treasure. Founded in 1382 by Pauline monks who came from Hungary at the invitation of Władysław, Duke of Opole (who probably brought the image of the Black Madonna to Częstochowa), the monastery withstood several sieges, including the legendary 40-day siege by the Swedes in 1655 *(see p44)*.

Knights' Hall
The hall contains a series of late 17th-century paintings depicting major events in the monastery's history.

Refectory
The ceiling is decorated with rich frescoes by the 17th-century painter Karl Dankwart. In 1670, a wedding reception was held here for the Polish king Michał Korybut Wiśniowiecki and his bride, Eleanor.

Bastion of St Roch (belonging to Morsztynowie)

The 600th Anniversary Museum has an impressive display of artifacts made by concentration camp inmates.

Arsenal

Stations of the Cross
The 14 Stations of the Cross standing on artificial rocks in the moat were created by the architect Stefan Szyller and the sculptor Pius Weloński in 1900–13. Every day, groups of pilgrims attend a religious service here.

STAR FEATURES

★ Black Madonna

★ Basilica of the Holy Cross and the Nativity of the Virgin Mary

★ Black Madonna

The most important icon of the Catholic faith in Poland, depicting the Virgin with the Christ Child, was probably painted in 1434 on top of an older Byzantine icon – the original Black Madonna, which was damaged by robbers in 1430.

VISITORS' CHECKLIST

Road map D5. 🏘 *245,000.* 🚉
🚌 ℹ️ *al. Najświętszej Marii Panny 65 (034 368 22 50);* **Jasna Góra, Pauline Monastery** *ul. Kordeckiego 2 (034 365 38 88).* **Jasna Góra** ⭕ *5am–9:30pm.* **Black Madonna of Częstochowa** *(unveiling times) 6am–noon daily (to 1pm Sat & Sun), 3–9:30pm (May–Sep: from 2pm). Times may vary.* **Treasury, Arsenal, 600th Anniversary Museum** ⭕ *9am–4pm daily (May–15 Oct: to 6pm).* 🎭 *"Gaude Mater" International Festival of Religious Music (early May).* **www**.*czestochowa.pl*

Outdoor altar, where services are held for the crowds of pilgrims.

Treasury

Gold and silver vessels, church vestments, tapestries and votive offerings are among the items on display.

Chapel of the Last Supper

This chapel was designed by Adolf Szyszko-Bohusz in the 20th century.

Confessional

Monastery Gates

The Lubomirski Gate, the Stanisław August Gate, the Gate of the Sorrowful Virgin Mary and the Bank (or Jagiellonian) Gate all lead to the monastery hill.

★ Basilica of the Holy Cross and the Nativity of the Virgin Mary

The present basilica dates from 1692–1728. The Baroque decoration of the high altar and of the ceiling, the latter by Karl Dankwart, is rich in detail.

Eagles' Nests Trail ⑰

The Cracow-Częstochowa upland is a limestone mountain range formed in the Jurassic period. Perched on rocky outcrops, some of the castles, most of which were built in the Middle Ages and ruined during the Swedish Deluge of the 1650s *(see p44)*, resemble eagles' nests. Ojców National Park, with Pieskowa Skała Castle, encompasses some of the most beautiful upland areas. This castle was once the stronghold of kings, but at the end of the Middle Ages it passed into the hands of bandits – Piotr Szafraniec and his son Krzysztof – who lured rich merchants to their deaths. Today all is peaceful: tourist trails, rock-climbing and beautiful scenery.

Olsztyn ①
Every autumn, thousands of spectators gather to watch as a magnificent firework display and laser show illuminate the stately ruins of the castle.

Mirów ②
The castle once belonged to the Myszkowski family. It is perched on a rocky ridge, turning the natural lie of the land to defensive advantage.

0 km _____ 5
0 miles _____ 5

TIPS FOR WALKERS

Length of trail: 190 k m (118 miles).
Stopping-off points: Many bars and restaurants are to be found along the trail. There is a restaurant and café in Pieskowa Skała Castle.

Bobolice ③
Today, jousting tournaments and outdoor games take place in the surroundings of the splendid ruins of the castle built by Kazimierz the Great in the 14th century.

Ogrodzieniec ④
In the 16th century the castle belonged to the Boner family of Cracow. With its gate, towers and galleries, it is one of the most picturesque castles on the trail.

Błędowski Desert ⑤
This miniature desert is 320 sq km (123 sq miles) of drifting sand and dunes. Unique in Central Europe, it is slowly becoming choked with vegetation.

Olkusz ⑥
The town is well endowed with historic buildings.It owes its prosperity to silver and lead mining.

Pieskowa Skała ⑦
The well-preserved castle with its arcaded courtyard and bastions dominates the Prądnik valley. It is situated on an inaccessible rock surrounded by spectacular scenery.

Ojców National Park ⑧
The Prądnik valley has a karst landscape; there are outcrops of limestone, a multitude of gorges and caves with bats. The most famous rock is the pillar known as Hercules' Club.

Grodzisko ⑨
The obelisk with a stone elephant is an unusual monument. It was made in 1686 and stands next to the Church of the Assumption.

Imbramowice ⑩
This small village has a late Baroque Premonstratensian convent built in the 18th century.

KEY

- ▬ Trail
- ▬ Other road
- ☆ Viewpoint

Map labels: 794 · 78 · 790 · Pilica · Podzamcze · 794 · Wolbrom · MIECHÓW · 791 · Klucze · 783 · 773 · 778 · 778 · CRACOW · 6 · 7 · 8 · 9 · 10

Gate and unloading platform, Birkenau extermination camp

Oświęcim (Auschwitz) ⓲

Road Map D5. 🏠 *43,000.* 🚆 🚌
ℹ️ *033 843 00 91.*

Although the name Oświęcim means little to foreigners, its German equivalent, **Auschwitz**, evokes fear in almost everyone. It was here that the Nazis established their largest concentration and extermination camp. Auschwitz is synonymous with death, cruelty, the annihilation of the Jews and the Holocaust. No visitor can leave unmoved.

The Auschwitz camp, known as Auschwitz I, opened in June 1940 when the first Polish political prisoners arrived. In March 1941 a much larger camp at **Birkenau** (Brzezinka in Polish), Auschwitz II, was started, 3km (2 miles) from Oświęcim. Auschwitz III, a labour camp, was built nearby in Monowice in 1943. The Nazis brought in people, overwhelmingly Jews, from all over Europe. The gas chambers, which had the capacity to kill thousands daily, started working ceaselessly in 1942. Trains drew up to the ramp where people would be herded out for selection for extermination (the fate of the majority), forced labour or medical experiments. Those selected for extermination would be gassed and their bodies incinerated in one of the four crematoria. Apart from Jews, a number of Poles, Soviet prisoners of war, gypsies and homosexuals died here too.

For the Poles, Auschwitz is a particular symbol of their own suffering. It was here that St Maksymilian Kolbe died from starvation after volunteering his life for that of a fellow prisoner, who survived. Soviet forces liberated the camp in January 1945. They found 7,650 sick and dying prisoners when they arrived.

Above the entrance to Auschwitz are inscribed the words "Arbeit macht frei" ("Work makes you free"). The camp has been preserved as a memorial, and the prison blocks that survive have been turned into a **museum** charting the history of the camp and of persecution in wartime Poland. In all, between 900,000 and 1.5 million Jews and others were murdered in the extermination camps here. The camp is a UNESCO World Heritage Site.

🏛 **Oświęcim-Brzezinka Museum**
ul. Więźniów Oświęcimia 20.
Tel 033 844 80 55. ⬭ Dec–Feb: 8am–3pm; Mar & Nov: 8am–4pm; Apr & Oct: 8am–5pm; May & Sep: 8am–6pm; Jun–Aug: 8am–7pm. 📷
📶 www.auschwitz.org.pl

Bielsko-Biała ⓳

Road Map D6. 🏠 *174,000.* 🚆 🚌
ℹ️ *Plac Ratuszowy 4 (033 819 00 50).* www.bielsko.pl

The city was created by joining the Silesian town of Bielsko and the Galician town of Biała. It was once an important centre for the production of textiles and wool, as an interesting early 20th-century complex of buildings testifies. Many streets contain miniature versions of old Viennese houses. The **Castle of the Sułkowski princes**, built in the Middle Ages and altered in the 19th century, is also of interest. The unusual hilltop Church of St Nicholas (Kościół św Mikołaja) began as a modest 15th-century Gothic church and was extensively remodelled in 1907–10.

Bielsko-Biała is a good starting point for excursions into the Beskid Śląski Mountains. The chair lift from the suburbs takes visitors to the Szyndzielnia peak, 1,026 m (3,365 ft) up.

Żywiec ⓴

Road Map D6. 🏠 *32,000.* 🚌
🚆 ℹ️ *ul. Zamkowa 2 (033 861 43 10).* www.zywiec.pl

The town of Żywiec is associated with one of the best Polish brands of beer, which is brewed locally. It is

Lake Żywiecki, a man-made reservoir on the River Soła

Arcaded courtyard of the Renaissance castle in Żywiec

also a good starting point for excursions into the Beskid Żywiecki Mountains. Lake Żywiecki, with its water-sports facilities, is another tourist attraction. This is also a town of thriving folk traditions; a particular high point is Corpus Christi, when women dressed in traditional costumes take part in a festive procession. Local monuments include the **Market Square**, surrounded by old houses, the 19th-century **town hall** and the **Church of the Nativity of the Virgin Mary** (Kościół Narodzenia Najświętszej Marii Panny), built in 1582–3. Not far from the Market Square is the **Gothic Church of the Holy Cross** (Kościół św Krzyża).

The most important buildings in the town are the Renaissance **castle** and the 19th-century **palace**, started in the 16th century for Mikołaj Komorowski. In the mid-17th century, Jan Kazimierz, King of Poland, was the owner of Żywiec. When he abdicated in 1668, he lived here briefly before leaving Poland.

In the early 19th century, the town became the property of the Habsburgs, who built a palace next to the castle. Marrying into the Polish aristocracy, the last of the Habsburgs were strongly connected with Poland.

🏛 **Town Museum**
ul. Zamkowa 5. **Tel** 033 861 21 24.
◯ 9am–3:30pm Tue–Fri, 10am–3pm Sat & Sun (Oct–Mar: 9am–4pm Tue–Sun). **www**.muzeum-zywiec.pl

Wadowice ㉑

Road Map D6. 🏘 19,400. 🚉 🚌
ℹ ul. Koscielna 4 (033 873 23 65).
www.it.wadowice.pl

Karol Wojtyła, who became Pope John Paul II in 1978, was born in Wadowice in 1920. His childhood home is now the **Museum of the Holy Father John Paul II**, with objects relating to his early life. He was christened in the late Baroque **Church of the Presentation of the Virgin Mary** (Kościół Ofiarowania NMP), near the Market Square. The church, built in 1791–8, replaces an early Gothic church, of which only the chancel remains. The tower, with Baroque cupola, was built by Tomasz Pryliński in the late 19th century.

🏛 **Museum of the Holy Father John Paul II**
ul. Kościelna 7. **Tel** 033 823 26 62.
◯ 9am–4pm daily (May–Oct: to 5:45pm). ♿

Kalwaria Zebrzydowska ㉒

Road Map D6. 🏘 4,400. 🚉 🚌
ℹ 033 876 63 04. 📷 🏛 **www**.kalwaria.eu

Kalwaria Zebrzydowska is the oldest **calvary** in Poland and one of the most unusual. It was commissioned in 1600 by

Herod's Palace, one of the stations of Kalwaria Zebrzydowska

Mikołaj Zebrzydowski, the ruler of Cracow and an ardent Catholic, whose plan it was to replicate the layout of Jerusalem.

The calvary (built 1605–32) consists of 40 chapels, set on the surrounding hills. The most distinctive are the work of the Flemish architect and goldsmith Paul Baudarth. Some have unusual shapes: the House of the Virgin Mary takes the form of the Mystic Rose, and the House of Caiaphas that of an ellipsis. Their façades have Dutch ornamentation. The large Baroque monastery church dates from 1702; the monastic buildings were constructed by Baudarth and Giovanni Maria Bernadoni in 1603–67.

The calvary attracts thousands of pilgrims every year. Passion plays are performed here during Holy Week, and the Feast of Assumption is celebrated in August.

Bernardine church in Kalwaria Zebrzydowska

The underground Chapel of St Kinga in the salt mine at Wieliczka

Wieliczka ㉓

Road map D5. 🏃 *19,000.* 🚉 🚌

Wieliczka is famous for its ancient **salt mine**, which was opened 700 years ago and is still being exploited today. Unique in the world, it has been listed by UNESCO as a World Heritage Site.

Only 2 km (1½ miles) of the network of underground galleries and chambers are open to the public. They reach a depth of 135 m (442 ft) and have a stable temperature of 13–14° C (55–57° F). The two-hour visit takes in ancient underground chambers, saline lakes, wooden mining machines and underground buildings. The most impressive of these is the Chapel of St Kinga, with altarpieces, chandeliers and sculptures made of salt. Additional figures carved in salt, the oldest dating from the 17th century, can be seen in other chambers. The Staszic Chamber has the highest ceiling, at 36 m (115 ft). At the end of the German occupation, the Nazis tried to establish an aircraft factory in the mines. There is also an underground sanatorium where respiratory diseases are treated.

The Salt Mine Castle at Ulica Zamkowa 8 is also worth a visit. From the 13th century right up until 1945 it was a base for the management of the salt mine. Today it houses a museum with – among other things – a splendid collection of antique salt mills.

Salt Mine
ul. Daniłowicza 10. **Tel** *012 278 73 02.* ☐ *Apr–Oct: 7:30am–7:30pm; Nov–Mar: 8am–5pm.* ● *1 Jan, Easter, 1 Nov, 24–26 Dec, 31 Dec.* 📷 🎦 🎧 🍴 🛍 **www**.kopalnia.pl

Niepołomice ㉔

Road map E5. 🏃 *8,500.* 🚉 🚌
www.niepolomice.com

In the 14th century, the **royal castle** at Niepołomice was the hunting base of Kazimierz the Great. Between 1550 and 1571 it was converted into a Renaissance palace by Zygmunt August. The entrance gate, dating from 1552, was once decorated with a Jagiellonian eagle; the plaque, with the Latin inscription "May the King Win and Live", hints at its former splendour. The monarchs loved hunting in the **game**

park nearby. In 1525 Zygmunt I brought "in a wooden trunk a great bear from Lithuania". The bear hunt ended unhappily. Confronted by the angry animal, the pregnant Queen Bona Sworza turned and fled, falling from her horse and suffering a miscarriage.

At the castle in 1551, Queen Bona Sworza's son, Zygmunt August, sat at the deathbed of his sweetheart wife, Barbara Radziwiłłówna. Their marriage had caused a moral and political scandal, and Queen Bona was unjustly suspected of poisoning her daughter-in-law.

Today, the forest is much smaller than it was in the time of the Jagiellonians. It is still, however, a sizeable nature reserve with plenty of secluded areas, and bison are raised there.

Zalipie ㉕

Road map E5. 🏃 *710.* 🚌
🚉 *6 km (4 miles) from the village.*

Zalipie has a unique folk art tradition: cottages, barns, wells and fences are painted with colourful floral, animal, geometric and other motifs. Domestic interiors and furnishings are also decorated. The painters are predominantly the women of the village. Every year in June, a competition called the Painted Cottage is organized and exhibitions of paintings are held.

Painted cottage in Zalipie

The Gothic-Renaissance town hall in Tarnów

Tarnów ㉖

Road map E5. 👤 *118,000.*
🚌 🚊 ℹ *Rynek 2 (14 688 90 90).*
www.it.tarnow.pl

Tarnów received its municipal charter in 1330; the medieval layout of the old town is perfectly preserved and many ancient houses are still standing. Those around the arcaded **Market Square** are among the finest. The **town hall**, in the centre, dates from the 15th century and was remodelled in the second half of the 16th century by Giovanni Maria Padovano. The Renaissance attics and elegant portal date from that time.

The late Gothic **Cathedral of the Nativity of the Virgin Mary** (Katedra Narodzenia NMP) was built in 1400 and has been extended many times. It is the grandest building in Tarnów, its Gothic portal decorated with sophisticated iconography. Its **Diocesan Museum** is worth a visit.

The monuments, stalls, epitaphs and tombstones within are mostly those of the Tarnowski family, who at one time owned the town. The large tombs belonging to Grand Hetman Jan Tarnowski and his son Jan Krzysztof were fashioned by Giovanni Maria Padovano between 1561 and 1570.

The portraits of the deceased are remarkable. The marble bas-reliefs depict Jan Tarnowski's victories in battle at Orsza, Obertyn and Starodub. Tarnowski, a friend of the poet Jan Kochanowski, was known as a charismatic and witty commander as well as a renowned author of military theory.

🏛 **Diocesan Museum**
pl. Katedralny 6. **Tel** 014 621 99 93. 🕙 *10am–3pm Tue–Sat, 9am–2pm Sun.* **www**.muzeum.diecezja.tarnow.pl

The castle in Dębno, which houses a Museum of Period Interiors

Dębno near Brzeska ㉗

Road map E6. 👤 *1,400.* 🚌

This small, well-proportioned castle surrounded by a moat was built in 1470–80 for the castellan and royal chancellor Jakub Dębiński. It survives in an excellent state of preservation. The **Museum of Period Interiors** installed in the castle re-creates the atmosphere of noble houses of the 15th to 18th centuries. Not only the living quarters but also the castle's kitchen, pantry and wine cellar are included in the exhibition.

🏛 **Museum of Period Interiors**
Tel 014 665 80 35. 🕙 *Mar–Dec: 9am–4pm Tue–Fri, 11am–3pm Sat & Sun.* 🔴 *Jan, Feb.* 📷 📹
www.muzeum.tarnow.pl

Nowy Wiśnicz ㉘

Road map E6. 👤 *1,900.* 🚌

The enormous **castle** and the **Monastery of the Discalced Carmelites** overlook this town from the hills above. The **parish church** stands in the Market Square below. Each of these early Baroque buildings was raised by Stanisław Lubomirski, Palatine of Cracow, in the 17th century. This rich and wise magnate earned renown in the Battles of Chocim against the Turks, and grew so strong that he "felt more powerful than the king". Twice the emperor bestowed a dukedom on him. The castle, which previously belonged to the Kmita family, was extended by Lubomirski after 1615. It has corner towers, an arcaded courtyard and an unusual entrance gate, framed by enormous volutes. Now a prison, the monastery is not open to visitors. The façade of the parish church is one of the most unusual pieces of architecture in Poland, combining Baroque elements in a Mannerist way.

Lubomirski Castle, towering above the town of Nowy Wiśnicz

Old cottages along the main street of Chochołów

Chochołów ㉙

Road Map D6. 🏘 *1,100.* 🚌

Along the main street of the 16th-century village stand traditional wooden cottages, the best examples of highland architecture in the whole Podhale region. One of the cottages, at No. 75, is open to the public. It dates from 1889 and has "white" and "black" rooms, a vestibule and a cellar. It also houses the **Museum of the Chochołów Insurrection**, which took place in 1846 against Austrian rule.

Chochołów has a curious local custom that involves cleaning the walls of the building once a year until they are white.

🏛 Museum of the Chochołów Insurrection
Chochołów 75. ☐ *10am–2pm Wed–Sun.*

Zakopane ㉚

Road Map D6. 🏘 *27,000.* 🚗 🚌
ℹ *ul. Kościuszki 17 (018 201 22 11).* 🎭 *Autumn in the Tatras; International Festival of Mountain Folklore (end Aug).* **www**.zakopane.pl

For over 100 years, the Polish people have regarded Zakopane as their country's winter capital, on a par with alpine resorts as an upmarket winter sports and leisure centre.

Many tourists also appreciate Zakopane in the summer. While some go hiking in the mountains, most are content to admire the scenery from the windows of their cable cars gliding to the summit of Mt Kasprowy Wierch or from the funicular railway

Entrance to the Villa Koliba Museum

Zakopane, cable-car line from Kuźnice to Kasprowy Wierch

ascending Mt Gubałówka. Later in the day, many tourists gather in Krupówki, the town's central pedestrianized area, which is lined with cafés, restaurants, exclusive souvenir shops and art galleries.

Walking down Krupówki it is impossible to resist the market near the funicular railway station. On sale can be found leather *kierpce* (traditional moccasins), woollen pullovers, wooden *ciupagi* (sticks with decorative axe-like handles), and *bryndza* and *oscypek* (regional cheeses made from sheep's milk).

Villa Atma, the wooden house where the composer Karol Szymanowski *(see p26)* lived from 1930 to 1936, is now a museum dedicated to this eulogist of the Tatra Mountains. It is worth a visit since it is in typical Zakopane style.

In 1992, the Polish and Slovakian national parks in the Tatra Mountains were jointly designated a biosphere reserve by UNESCO. The

PANORAMA FROM MOUNT GUBAŁÓWKA

The finest panorama of the Tatra Mountains from the northern, Polish side of the range is from Mt Gubałówka or Głodówka pod Bukowiną. The Tatras, the highest mountains in Central Europe, with alpine landscapes, lie within Polish and Slovak national parks. The main attractions for tourists include the excursion to the Lake Morskie Oko (Eye of the Sea) and the ascent by cable car to the summit of Mount Kasprowy Wierch. In summer, hikers can follow the many designated trails. In winter, the mountains offer favourable conditions for skiing.

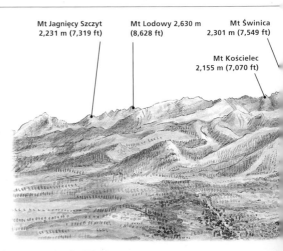

Mt Jagnięcy Szczyt 2,231 m (7,319 ft)

Mt Lodowy 2,630 m (8,628 ft)

Mt Świnica 2,301 m (7,549 ft)

Mt Kościelec 2,155 m (7,070 ft)

Tatra National Park can be accessed from Zakopane.

🏠 **Villa Atma**
ul. Kasprusie 19. **Tel** 018 201 34 93.
◯ 10am–4pm Tue–Sun (summer 2–6pm Fri).

Dębno Podhalańskie ③

Road Map E6. 🚶 790. 🚌

The picturesque larch timber **Parish Church of St Michael the Archangel** (Kościół parafialny św Michała Archanioła) is one of the most highly regarded examples of wooden Gothic architecture in Europe. The ceiling, walls and furnishings are covered with colourful geometric, figural and floral motifs painted in around 1500. A magnificent domed tower rises over the church. The church is still used for religious services.

Wooden Gothic church in Dębno Podhalańskie

The Convent of the Order of St Clare in Stary Sącz

Dunajec Raft Ride ③

See pp166–7.

Stary Sącz ③

Road Map E6. 🚶 8,800. 🚆 🚌
ℹ️ ul. Szwedzka 2, 018 443 55 97.
🎵 Early Music Festival (Jun–Jul).
www.sacz.pl

This charming Galician town has a cobbled Market Square surrounded by small houses that in summer are bedecked with flowers. Were it not for the presence of cars, tourists and modern shops, one might imagine that time had stood still here. The town's finest buildings include the **Convent of the Order of St Clare** (Klasztor Sióstr Klarysek), founded in 1208 by the Blessed Kinga. The Gothic church was consecrated in 1280 and the vaulting dates from the 16th century. Its altars, with stucco-work ornamentation made by Baldassare Fontana in 1696–9, and a pulpit from 1671 showing a depiction of the Tree of Jesse, complement the modern decoration of the church.

Environs
Nowy Sącz is situated 8 km (5 miles) northeast of Stary Sącz. In the large **Market Square** stands the Neo-Baroque **town hall** of 1895–7. The town's major buildings are the old collegiate church, now the parish Church of St Marguerite (Kościół parafialny św Małgorzaty), founded by Zbigniew Oleśnicki in 1466, and a fine synagogue.

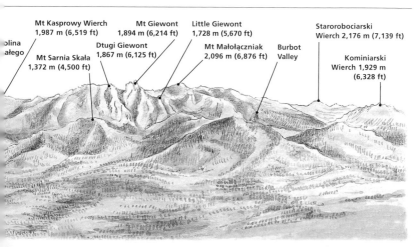

Mt Kasprowy Wierch
1,987 m (6,519 ft)

Mt Giewont
1,894 m (6,214 ft)

Little Giewont
1,728 m (5,670 ft)

Starorobociarski Wierch 2,176 m (7,139 ft)

Dtugi Giewont
1,867 m (6,125 ft)

Mt Małołączniak
2,096 m (6,876 ft)

Burbot Valley

Kominiarski Wierch 1,929 m (6,328 ft)

olina ałego

Mt Sarnia Skała
1,372 m (4,500 ft)

Dunajec Raft Ride ㉜

The Pieniny mountains form a small range famous for its spectacular landscapes cut through by the Dunajec valley. The raft ride on the river that flows through the limestone mountain gorges is one of the best-known tourist attractions in Poland. At first the rafts move with deceptive calm, but as they approach the gorge behind the cloister ruins the water becomes rougher as the river twists and winds. This lasts for about 8 km (5 miles), after which the water once again flows more slowly. The exhilarating ride ends in Szczawnica, a well-known health resort.

Czorsztyn Castle ①
The castle was built in 1330 for the Hungarian Berzevicy family. It now houses the Museum of the Spisz Region.

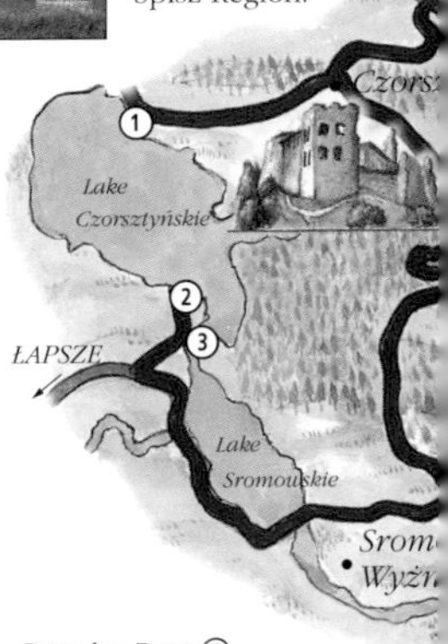

Niedzica Castle ②
The castle once guarded the Polish border with Hungary. Its ruins perch on a precipitous outcrop of rock.

0 km 1

0 miles 1

KEY

- Raft ride route
- Tour route
- Other road
- Viewpoint

Dunajec Dam ③
Despite protests, the building of this dam went ahead. On the day of its opening in 1997, it saved the Dunajec valley from a disastrous flood.

Krynica ㉞

Road map E6. *11,000.* *ul. Piłsudskiego 4 (018 471 51 07).* *concerts by spa orchestras (all year round).* **www**.krynica.pl

Well-equipped with sanatoria and pump rooms, Krynica is one of the largest health resorts in Poland. Fashionable and luxurious pre-war boarding houses stand next to old wooden villas. The best known is "Patria", built by Bohdan Pniewski in the Art Nouveau style, and owned by singer Jan Kiepura (1902–66). The **New Sanatorium** near the pedestrian promenade (Deptak) is also worth a visit. Completed in 1939, it retains its original furnishings and décor. The Great Pump Room nearby is always very popular with visitors.

One of Nikifor's paintings on view at the Nikifor Museum

The town is surrounded by tree-covered mountains. Mt Jaworzyna, at 1,114 m (3,654 ft) the highest peak in the area, can be reached by cable car, departing from Czarny Potok. In winter, the mountain turns into a skier's paradise. The local ski trails are the longest in Poland. Remote areas of the mountains are inhabited by lynxes, wolves and bears, so caution should be exercised away from the established trails.

The work of amateur painter Nikifor (d. 1968) is displayed in the "Romanówka" villa, now the **Nikifor Museum**.

Nikifor Museum
Bulwary Dietla 19. ***Tel*** *018 471 53 03.* *10am–1pm and 2–5pm Tue–Sun.*

Biecz ㉟

Road map E6. *4,500.* *City bus from Gorlice.* *Pogórze Folklore Days.*

In the 16th century this small town was one of the most important centres of cloth manufacture in Poland. It is dominated by the **town hall tower**, built in 1569–81, and the **Parish Church of Corpus Christi** (Kościół farny Bożego Ciała). One of the most magnificent late Gothic churches in all of Małopolska, it was built at the turn of the 15th century in a style that seeks to reconcile the Gothic tradition with the new canons of the Renaissance. The first pharmacy in the Carpathian foothills was located in the **Renaissance house** at Ulica Węgierska 2, dating from 1523; it now houses a division of the **Regional Museum**.

Regional Museum
ul. Kromera 3. ***Tel*** *013 447 10 93.* *8am–6pm Tue–Fri, 10am–6pm Sat & Sun (Oct–Apr: 8am–3pm Tue–Sat, 9am–2pm Sun).*

Szczawnica ⑧

This well-known health resort is mainly a centre for the treatment of respiratory diseases. It is also the disembarkation point for the Dunajec river raft ride.

Ostra Skała ⑦

After Ostra Skała (Sharp Rock) the River Dunajec turns sharply as it flows through the narrowest part of the gorge.

TIPS FOR VISITORS

Raft ride: *21/4–23/4 hours.*
Length: *18 km (11 miles) to Szczawnica; 23 km (14 miles) to Krósicienko.* **Tel** *018 262 97 21 or 262 97 93.***Starting point:** *Sromowce Wyżne – Kąty. Apr–Nov: daily.* 🖼 *www.*flisacy.com.pl

STARY SĄCZ

Krościenko on the Dunajec

969

THREE CROWNS

Sromowce Średnie Niżne

Trzy Korony ⑥

Trzy Korony (Three Crowns) is the most beautiful massif in the Pieniny range. In 1287, the Blessed Kinga took refuge from the Tartars in the Castle of the order of St Clare, whose ruins stand on one peak.

Cerveny Kláštor ⑤

The ruins of the Red Monastery can be seen on the Slovak side of the Dunajec.

Kąty ④

Departure point for the raft ride.

View of the Parish Church of Corpus Christi in Biecz

Environs

In the village of **Harklowa** is a late Gothic wooden church dating from the turn of the 15th century.

Krosno ㊱

Road map F6. 🏘 49,000. 🚌 🚐
🛈 *ul. Rynek 5 (013 432 77 07).*
🎭 *Krosno Fair (Jun); Krosno Music Autumn (Oct).*

Krosno was once the centre of the Polish oil industry, but there is more to the town than its industrial past. The finest historical monument is the Oświęcim Chapel in the Gothic Franciscan church. Completed in 1647, the chapel is decorated with exquisite stuccowork by Giovanni Battista Falconi. It contains the tombs of the half-siblings Anna and Stanisław, whose love ended in tragedy. The Market Square is surrounded by old arcaded houses, the most interesting of which is No. 7, with its Renaissance doorway.

Environs

In **Odrzykoń**, 10 km (6 miles) north of Krosno, stand the ruins of Kamieniec Castle. Kamieniec was the setting for *Revenge* (1834), the most popular comedy by the 19th-century writer Count Aleksander Fredro (*see p25*), the plot of which involves a dispute over the hole in the wall dividing the courtyard of the castle.

In the **geological park** not far from the castle stands a group of sandstone and shale structures known as Prządki (The Spinners), which have unusual, sometimes quite startling shapes.

Iwonicz Zdrój and **Rymanów**, 15 km (9 miles) east of Krosno, are very popular health resorts. At **Dukla** are the Baroque Mniszcha Palace, which today houses a historical museum, and the 18th-century Bernardine church with the charming Rococo tomb of Maria Amalia Brühla Mniszkowa, with its peaceful effigy.

In **Bóbrka**, 12 km (7 miles) south of Krosno, an industrial *skansen* has been created in what is certainly one of the oldest oil wells in the world, established in 1854.

Bieszczady Mountains Tour ㊲

The Bieszczady mountains, together with the neighbouring Beskid Niski, are the wildest in Poland. Tourists return with blood-curdling tales of encounters with bears and wolves, or the discovery of a skeleton in the forest undergrowth. Needless to say, these stories are often exaggerated. Before World War II, the region was densely populated by Ukrainians and ethnic groups known as the Boyks and the Lemks. After the war, because of fighting and resettlements, it became deserted, and farming largely disappeared from the region by the 1970s. Pastures and burnt-out villages became overgrown as the forest encroached and wild animals returned to the mountains.

Komańcza ⑦
Cardinal Stefan Wyszyński, Primate of Poland, was sent into exile to this village, deserted after World War II. He was interned by the communist authorities in 1955–6.

SAN

Połonina Wetlińska ⑥
Known as "połoniny", these elongated ranges with picturesque alpine meadows above forest level are a characteristic feature of the Bieszczady Mountains. The most interesting, 1,250 m (4,100 ft) up, are Caryńska and Wetlińska.

TYLAWA

Bieszczady National Park ⑤
The highest and wildest part of the mountains falls within Bieszczady National Park, which covers an area of 2,700 sq km (1,042 sq miles). In summer, many tourists walk the hiking trails. The main tourist base is in the small village of Ustrzyki Górne.

BIESZCZADY MOUNTAIN ANIMALS

The lynx, emblem of Bieszczady National Park, is not the only feline to make its home in these mountains. Wildcats also live here. They are rarely seen because they are very shy, concealing themselves in the forest undergrowth. Carpathian deer, with a population of 5,000, are more often encountered. Roe deer are also abundant and relatively tame. Wolves, a protected species numbering about 100 here, are more cautious. Bison, kings of the Polish forest, number up to 120, and brown bear may also be seen. The Bieszczady Mountains are also popular with ornithologists for the many species of birds of prey: eagles, including the golden eagle, falcon and hawk.

A wild mountain wolf

Zagórz ①
Zagórz, dominated by the ruins of the 18th-century Baroque fortified Church of Discalced Carmelites, is the starting point of hiking trails into the Bieszczady Mountains.

Równia ④
The most beautiful Orthodox churches in the Bieszczady Mountains are vestiges of the numerous villages of the Boyks and the Lemks.

TIPS FOR DRIVERS

Tour length: 106 km (66 miles).
Stopping-off points:
Restaurants, boarding houses and inns can be found in Polańczyk, Lesko, Wetlin, Ustrzyki Dolne and Ustrzyki Górne. In the summer season, bars also open.

Solina ③
The highest dam in Poland – 82 m (269 ft) high and 664 m (2,178 ft) long – was built at Solina. The reservoir that was created is ideal for sailing. The dam is surrounded by magnificent forests with nature reserves.

Lesko ②
This charming town has many fine buildings, including a castle and a 16th-century parish church. The Baroque synagogue houses a museum, and the Jewish cemetery is also of interest.

KEY

▬ Tour route

▬ Other road

☼ Viewpoint

0 km   5

0 miles   5

The Divine Tower, one of four towers in Krasiczyn Castle

Krasiczyn ⏏

Road map F6. 🏰 440. 🚌 **Castle**
Tel 016 671 83 21. ⏰ 9am–4pm
daily. 🎫 📷 compulsory. 🍴 🏨
www.krasiczyn.pl

Krasiczyn Castle is one of the most magnificent castles in the old Ruthenian territories of the Polish crown. Building began in 1592 on the site of an earlier castle by Stanislaw Krasicki, castellan of Przewór. It was continued by his son Marcin and completed in 1608. The architect was Galeazzo Appiani.

The castle takes the form of an arcaded courtyard, with a tall clock tower over the gate and four stout cylindrical towers at the corners. The Divine Tower contains a chapel. The Papal Tower is crowned by a dome and decorated with a parapet symbolizing the papal tiara. The Royal Tower has a crown-shaped dome, and the Tower of the Gentry is topped with sword pommels.

The Baroque sgraffito on the walls is striking. Mythological scenes are depicted on the upper tier; the central tier is filled with portraits of the kings of Poland from the 14th-century Jagiellonian monarchs to Jan III Sobieski, King of Poland at the time, as well as portraits of nobles. In the lowest tier are medallions with the busts of Roman patricians. Little of the original decoration of the interior survives, as it was destroyed

by fire in 1852, on the eve of the marriage of a later owner, Duke Leon Sapieha. The castle is open to visitors; the residential section contains a hotel and restaurant.

Environs
In Krzywcza, 10 km (6 miles) west of **Krasiczyn** stand the ruins of the castle of the Kącki family. About 12 km (7 miles) south of Krasiczyn, in **Posada Rybotycka**, can be seen the only stone fortified Uniate church in Poland. In **Kalwaria Pacławicka**, the 18th-century Franciscan monastery has about a dozen chapels marking the Stations of the Cross. Passion plays are performed here on Good Friday and many processions and plays are organized during the year for different church festivities.

The funeral of the Virgin enacted in a passion play in Kalwaria Pacławicka

Przemyśl ⏏

Road map F6. 🏰 67,000. 🚉 🚌
ℹ️ ul. Grodzka 1 (016 675 21 63).
🛶 Canoe rally (Apr, May); Gitariada International Festival (Jul).
www.przemysl.pl

The history of Przemyśl, picturesquely laid out on a hill and the banks of the River San, goes back to prehistoric

times. In the Middle Ages it was a regional capital and lay on a busy trade route. The object of dispute between Poland and Ruthenia, it became part of Poland in 1340, later passing into Austrian control.

During World War I, the strongly fortified city successfully held out against the besieging Russian army. The **fortifications** from that time survive. From 1939 to 1941 the River San, which flows through the city, constituted a border between territory held by the Soviet Union and Germany.

The city's Catholic and Orthodox churches, together with its synagogues, are evidence of its multicultural history. Today, a Ukrainian minority lives alongside the city's Polish population.

The **cathedral**, remodelled in 1718–24, is predominantly in the Baroque style; of its earlier Gothic form only the chancel remains. Notable features of the interior include the Renaissance tomb of Bishop Jan Dziaduski, by Giovanni Maria Padovano, and the late Gothic alabaster figure of the Virgin from Jacków. Near the cathedral are the Baroque Church of the Discalced Carmelites and the former Jesuit church, now Uniate, dating from 1627–48. The castle, founded by Kazimierz the Great in the 1340s, stands on a hill above the city. The top of its tower offers a panorama of the city and the San valley.

Przemyśl, on the banks of the River San

Orsetti House, a palace in the Renaissance style, in Jarosław

Jarosław 40

Road map F5. 🏛 *41,000.* 🚆 🚌
Jarosław Museum in the Orsetti House *Tel 016 621 54 37.* ◯ *10am–2pm Wed–Sun (Jul & Aug: 9am–5pm Wed–Fri, 10am–4pm Sat & Sun).* 🎟 *(free on Sun)* 🎵 *Early Music Festival (Aug).* **www**.jaroslaw.pl

The city of Jarosław owes its wealth to its location on the River San and the trade route linking the east with western Europe. In the 16th and 17th centuries, the largest fairs in Poland were held here. When Władysław IV attended a fair in Jarosław, he mingled with an international crowd and conversed with merchants from as far away as Italy and Persia. The **Orsetti House**, built in the style of an Italian Renaissance palazzo, testifies to the wealth of the city's merchants. Built in the 16th century and extended in 1646, it is crowned with a Mannerist parapet. The **town hall**, with coats of arms on the corner towers, stands in the centre of the broad **Market Square**.

Leżajsk 41

Road map F5. 🏛 *14,500.* 🚆 🚌
ℹ *ul. Rynek 1a (017 787 70 67).* 🎵 *Organ recitals in the basilica (Jun–Sep: 7pm; booking required).* **www**. lezajsk.um.gov.pl

The major attractions of Leżajsk are its Bernardine basilica and monastery, built by the architect Antonio Pellacini and the organ recitals that take place in the basilica, which was built in 1618–28. Its interior decoration and the furnishings, such as the oak stalls, pulpit and high altar, are mostly the work of the monks themselves. The basilica was established by Łukasz Opaliński, who earned renown by his defeat of the lawless magnate Stanisław Stadnicki in mortal combat.

The west end of the nave is filled with the complex organ, completed in 1693 and said to be the finest in Poland. The central theme of the elaborate Baroque casing is Hercules' fight with the Hydra, the nine-headed monster of Greek mythology. Not only is this a symbol of the age-old struggle of virtue against vice but also of Polish victory over the Turks, who were threatening Europe at the time.

The Jewish cemetery in Leżajsk is a place of pilgrimage for Jews from all over the world, who come to visit the tomb of Elimelech, the great 18th-century Orthodox rabbi.

Łańcut 42

See pp172–3.

Rzeszów 43

Road map F5. 🏛 *165,000.* 🚆
🚌 🚶 ℹ *ul. Asnyka 6 (017 852 46 11).* **www**.erzeszow.pl/en

The dominant building in this town is the Gothic **Church of Saints Stanisław and Adalberg** (Kościół św św Stanisława i Wojciecha), dating from the 15th century and with a later Baroque interior. The former Piarist **Church of the Holy Cross** (Kościół św Krzyża), extended in 1702–07 by Tylman van Gameren, and the Baroque monastery and **Bernardine church** of 1624–9 are also worth a visit. The latter contains the unfinished mausoleum of the Ligęz family, with eight alabaster statues carved by Sebastian Sala around 1630.

The remains of the old **castle** of the Ligęz family can still be seen. It later passed into the ownership of the Lubomirskis, who surrounded it with bastions in the 17th century. The Market Square, with an eclectic town hall remodelled in 1895–8, is another interesting feature.

Highlights of the **Muzeum Miasta Rzeszowa** include the gallery of 18th- to 20th-century Polish painting and the collection of glass, china and faïence.

🏛 **Muzeum Miasta Rzeszowa**
ul. 3 Maja 19. *Tel 017 853 52 78.*
◯ *9am–3pm Tue–Thu, Sun; 10am–5:30pm Fri.* 🎟 *(free on Sun).*

Fair in Leżajsk, a centre of folk pottery

Łańcut ⓶

The town of Łańcut was purchased by Stanisław Lubomirski in 1629. Securing the services of the architect Maciej Trapola and the stuccoist Giovanni Battista Falconi, this powerful magnate went about building a fortified residence in the town. It was completed in 1641. After 1775 the palace, by then owned by Izabella Lubomirska, was extended and the interiors remodelled. The Neo-Classical Ballroom and the Great Dining Room were created during this period, and the magnificent gardens with their many pavilions laid out. In the 19th century, ownership of the palace passed to the Potocki family. From 1889 to 1914, the penultimate owners, Roman and Elżbieta Potocki, modernized the residence. The palace, now a museum, attracts numerous visitors.

★ Column Room
The statue in this room is that of the young Henryk Lubomirski, carved by Antonio Canova in around 1787.

Mirror Room
The walls are lined with Rococo panelling brought back to Łańcut by Izabella Lubomirska – probably from one of her visits to France.

Library

Carriage
The largest collection of carriages in Poland is displayed in the coach house. It comprises 120 different types of coaches, carriages and other horse-drawn vehicles.

STAR FEATURES

★ Theatre

★ Ballroom

★ Column Room

★ Theatre

The small court theatre was built around 1800. Its present appearance is the result of remodelling carried out by the eminent Viennese workshop of Fellner & Helmer.

Sculpture Gallery

Many pieces, mostly 19th-century, make up the collection on display; among them is this statue of Psyche carried by Zephyrs, a copy of a piece by John Gibson.

Corner tower known as the Hen's Foot

The main entrance

Neo-Rococo Clock

This typically French Neo-Rococo gilt clock is mounted in the mirror that hangs over the fireplace in the Billiard Room.

★ Ballroom

The Neo-Classical ballroom was designed by Christian Piotr Aigner in 1800. The stuccowork is by Fryderyk Baumann.

Façade

The palace façades are fundamentally Baroque. The rustication of the lower storey, however, is typical of French Renaissance style – part of the remodelling that the palace underwent at the end of the 19th century.

SILESIA

*S*ilesia's great wealth of architectural monuments, its eventful history and its beautiful and varied landscape distinguish it from other regions of Poland. The region's well-preserved historic towns and the many hiking trails in the picturesque Sudeten Mountains make it an area that invites long exploration.

The stormy history of Silesia (Śląsk) and the great variety of cultural influences that have flourished here have given this region a rich heritage. It belonged initially to the Bohemian crown and passed into Polish control around 990. When Poland split into principalities, Silesia began to gain independence. Divided into smaller independent duchies, it returned to Bohemian rule in the 14th century. After 1526, together with other Bohemian territories, it became part of the Habsburg Empire. During the Reformation, many of its inhabitants were converted to Lutheranism. The Thirty Years' War (1618–48) inflicted devastation on Silesia, bringing in its wake the repression of Protestantism. While Jesuits and Cistercians erected magnificent Baroque monasteries at that time, under the terms of the Peace of Westphalia of 1648, Protestants were limited to building the three "peace churches,". The Habsburgs lost Silesia to Prussia in 1742. Although the main language was German, many areas, especially the Opole region and Upper Silesia, were inhabited by an influential Polish minority. After World War I, as a result of the Silesian Uprisings of 1919–21, the eastern part of Upper Silesia, together with Katowice, was included within Polish borders. After 1945, nearly all of historical Silesia joined Poland, and its German population was deported. Poles who had been resettled from Poland's eastern provinces (which had been annexed by the Soviet Union) took their place.

Silesia is an enchanting region, not only for the breathtaking beauty of its mountain landscapes but also for its outstanding architecture. The medieval castles built to defend ancient borderlands, the grand Renaissance manor houses and impressive Baroque residences, the great Gothic churches and stately monasteries – all these provide ample attractions and a historic atmosphere.

A hint of spring: melting snow in the Karkonosze Mountains

◁ **Książ Castle (seat of the Hochberg family) near Wałbrzych**

Exploring Silesia

The most attractive part of the region is
Lower Silesia. A good starting point for
exploration is Wrocław, the provincial
capital and a city full of historic
buildings as well as interesting
20th-century architecture. From
here, the area of Kotlina Kłodzka,
with the fantastically shaped Table
Mountains, is within easy reach.
Not far away lies Jelenia Góra,
a good base for hiking in the
Karkonosze Mountains in summer
or for skiing on the nearby slopes
in winter. The visitor to Silesia
will also find beautiful palaces
and churches in almost every
village. Many fine residences,
however, are gradually falling into ruin.

**Sheep in the alpine pastures of the
Beskid Śląski Mountains**

SEE ALSO

KEY

▬▬	Motorway
▬▬	Major road
▬▬▬	Minor road
▬▬	Main railway
▬▬	Minor railway
▬▬	International border
▬▬	Regional border

Map labels: Gorzow Wlkp., Oder (Odra), Krosno Odrzańskie, Sulechów, Gubin, Zielona Góra, LUBUSKIE, Cottbus, Nowa Sól, Wsch, Żary, ŻAGAŃ ①, GŁOGÓW ②, Szprotawa, Iłowa, Polkowice, Chocianów, Lubi, Bolesławiec, LEG, Zgorzelec, GRODZIEC ⑧, Lubań, LWÓWEK ŚLĄSKI ⑨, LEGNICK, POL, Dresden, ZŁOTORYJA ⑦, CZOCH CASTLE ⑩, Pilchowice, JAWOR, LUBOMIERZ ⑪, Świny, JELENIA GÓRA ⑭, BOLKÓW ⑮, Szklarska Poręba, Cieplice, Wałbrz, KSIĄ, ⑫, Karpacz, KARKONOSZE MOUNTAINS, KRZESZ, ⑤⑬, Hradec, Kudov Zdr

SIGHTS AT A GLANCE

GETTING AROUND

There are rail links between all the major Silesian cities, so that is possible to travel by train from Wrocław to Jelenia Góra, Legnica, Głogów, Świdnica, Wałbrzych and Kłodzko. There are also good connections between Katowice, Opole and Wrocław, and trains also stop in Brzeg. Although smaller towns are accessible by bus, the service can be very infrequent, so that outside the major cities the best way to travel is by car. The A4 motorway links several major cities, while smaller roads provide more scenic routes.

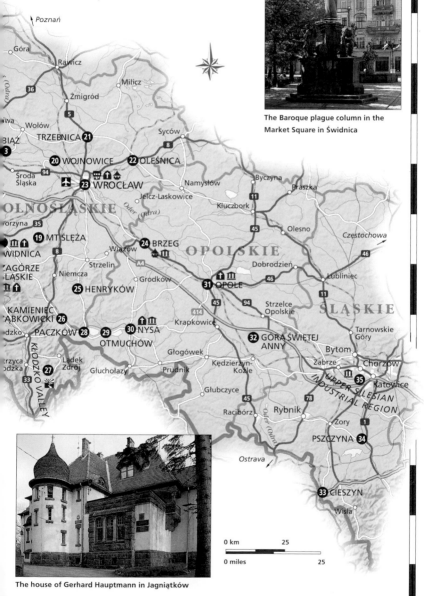

The Baroque plague column in the Market Square in Świdnica

The house of Gerhard Hauptmann in Jagniątków

0 km   25

0 miles   25

The Baroque-Neo-Classical palace of the Talleyrand family in Żagań

Żagań ❶

Road map B4. 🏛 26,000. 🚗 🚌
ℹ️ *ul. Szprotawska 4 (068 477 01).*
www.um.zagan.pl

The origins of Żagań go back as far as the 13th century. A particularly happy episode in the history of this pretty town on the River Bóbr was the period from 1845 to 1862, thanks to the beautiful Dorothea Talleyrand-Périgord, the youngest daughter of Peter Biron, Duke of Kurland.

Dorothea was something of a social magnet. She was a friend of Maurice Charles de Talleyrand, one of Louis Napoleon's ministers, and his nephew's wife. Her circle attracted the most eminent composers and writers of the day, among them Franz Liszt and Giuseppe Verdi. Her residence was the **palace** built for Albrecht von Wallenstein, a commander in the Thirty Years' War (1618–48). Dorothea had alterations made, and the palace's present Neo-Classical appearance and the layout of the rooms were commissioned by her in the mid-19th century. It now houses the **Cultural Institute**.

Other prominent buildings in the town are the Franciscan **Church of Saints Peter and Paul** (Kościół św Piotra i Pawła), built in the Gothic style and dating from the 14th century. The enormous **Church of the Assumption** (Kościół Wniebowzięcia NMP), which once belonged to the Augustinians, also merits attention. It was built in stages from the late 13th to the early 16th century, although the finely furnished interior dates from the 1830s. The library of the

monastery next to the church contains works by the 18th-century painter George Wilhelm Neunhertz and items connected to the German astronomer Johannes Kepler, who worked in Żagań between 1628 and 1630.

🏛 **Cultural Institute**
ul. Szprotawska 4. **Tel** 068 477 64 75. ◻ 8am–8pm daily. 📷

⛪ **Church of Saints Peter and Paul**
ul. Łużycka.

⛪ **Church of the Assumption**
pl. Klasztorny 2. **Tel** 068 377 29 82.

Głogów ❷

Road map B4. 🏛 69,000. 🚗 🚌
ℹ️ *ul. Poczdamska 1 (076 726 34 51).* 🎭 *Jazz in Głogów (Oct, Nov).*
www.glogow.pl

This town on the Odra River was established about 1,000 years ago but fell into ruin during World War II. Two Gothic churches, the

Architecture old and new: a street in the old town in Głogów

collegiate Church of the Assumption, set on an island in the Odra, and the Church of St Nicholas in the old town, have not been rebuilt. However, the beautiful Jesuit Baroque **Church of Corpus Christi** (Kościół Bożego Ciała), built in 1694–1724 to a design by Giulio Simonetti, has been reconstructed. Its original twin-tower façade was added in 1711 by Johann Blasius Peintner. The picturesque town hall with its slender tower owes its present form to remodelling carried out by Augustus Soller in 1831–4. It too has been reconstructed. On the bank of the Odra stands the castle of the dukes of Głogów, with an original 14th-century medieval tower and Gothic cellars, and later Baroque walls. It houses the **Archaeological and Historical Museum**. Among the exhibits are a collection of instruments of torture.

🏛 **Archaeological and Historical Museum**
ul. Brama Brzostowska 1.
Tel 076 834 10 81.
◻ 10am–5pm Wed–Sun.

⛪ **Church of Corpus Christi**
ul. Powstańców. **Tel** 076 833 36 01.

Lubiąż ❸

Road map B4. 🏛 2,300. 🚗
Malczyce. 🚌 **Abbey. Lubiąż Foundation Tel** 071 322 21 29.
◻ Apr–Oct: 9am–6pm daily; Nov–Mar: 10am–3pm daily. 📷

The gigantic Cistercian monastic complex situated on the high bank of the River Odra comes into view from a great distance. Cistercian monks first settled in Lubiąż in 1175. They built a Romanesque church followed by a Gothic basilica, of which the twin-tower façade and ducal chapel remain. The present abbey dates from 1681–1715. After World War II, it was used as a warehouse for unsold books, mostly works by Lenin. Its restoration began in the mid-1990s. An exhibition of Silesian sculpture as well as certain rooms of the monastery, including the

Refectory of the Cistercian Abbey in Lubiąż

🏛 **Copper Museum**
ul. Partyzantów 3. **Tel** 076 862 49
49. ⬜ 11am–5pm Tue–Sat. 🎫
(free on Sat and one Wed a month).
www.muzeum-miedzi.art.pl

🔒 **Parish Church of John the Baptist**
ul. Partyzantów 25.
Tel 076 862 29 95.

🔒 **Church of the Virgin Mary**
pl. Mariacki 1. **Tel** 076 854 34 40.
⬤ to the public.

🔒 **Cathedral of Saints Peter and Paul**
pl. Katedralny 6. **Tel** 076 724 42 71.

Legnickie Pole ❺

Road map B4. 🚶 1,300. 🚌

It was at Legnickie Pole that
a great battle between the
Poles, led by Henry II, the
Pious, and the Tartars took
place on 9 April 1241. Despite
the Turks' defeat of the Poles
and the death of their
commander, Poland prevented
westward Tartar expansion.
The **Museum of the Battle
of Legnica** details this event.

The Benedictine abbey,
dating from 1727–31 and built
by Kilian Ignaz Dientzenhofer
in the Baroque style, is the
greatest attraction of this small
village. The abbey church,
dedicated to St Jadwiga,
has an elliptical nave and
undulating vaulting covered
with trompe l'oeil paintings
by Cosmas Damian Asam. Its
furnishings are equally fine.

🏛 **Museum of the Battle
of Legnica**
Tel 076 858 23 98. ⬜ 11am–5pm
Wed–Sun. 🎫 (free on Wed).

refectory and the Ducal Hall,
are now open to the public.

The ceiling of the refectory
is decorated with paintings
by Michael Willmann, whose
work is also to be seen on
the altars of the parish church
in Lubiąż. The great Ducal
Hall is a magnificent example
of the late Baroque style, its
purpose being to glorify the
faith and the feats of the
Habsburg dynasty.

Legnica ❹

Road map B4. 🚶 105,000. 🚉
🛈 Rynek 25 (076 722 00 10).
www.portal.legnica.eu

Legnica, after Wrocław
and Opole Silesia's third-
largest city, became the
capital of the independent
duchy of Legnica in the 13th
century. Today it is a large
administrative centre and
copper-mining town, as
evidenced by the displays
in the **Copper Museum**.

The **Parish Church of John
the Baptist** (Fara św Jana
Chrzciciela) is one of
the most beautiful Baroque
shrines in Silesia, built for

the Jesuits in 1714–27. The
presbytery of the original
church was converted into
a chapel, the Mausoleum of
the Silesian Piasts (1677–8).

In the northern part of
the old town stands the
Dukes' Castle. It has
medieval origins and was
remodelled many times.
The fine Renaissance gate
was added by George von
Amberg in 1532–3. From
here, Ulica Mariacka leads
to the Gothic **Church of the
Virgin Mary** (Kościół NMP),
dating from the 14th century
and remodelled in the first
half of the 15th.

In the Market Square stand
the Baroque town hall of
1737–46, which houses a
theatre, and the Gothic
**Cathedral of Saints Peter
and Paul** (Katedra św Piotra
i Pawła), built in the 14th
century and preserving a
13th-century baptismal font.
In the centre of the Market
Square are eight narrow
arcaded houses known
as the **Herring Stalls** and,
at No. 40, a 16th-century
house known as **By the
Quail's Nest House**, with
sgraffito decoration.

The Baroque façade of the Benedictine abbey church in Legnickie Pole

Tower of the Baroque Church of Peace in Jawor

Jawor ❻

Road map B4. 👥 24,000. 🚉 🚌
ℹ️ Rynek 3 (076 870 33 71).

The capital of an independent duchy in the Middle Ages, Jawor is dominated by a castle that is a vestige of those times. Reconstruction has robbed the castle of much of its original splendour, but other buildings, which were painstakingly restored after World War II, enhance the town's historic atmosphere.

The most picturesque building is the large **Church of Peace** (Kościół Pokoju). It was one of three Protestant "peace churches" erected in Silesia after the Peace of Westphalia that marked the end of the Thirty Years' War (1618–48). It was built by Andreas Kempner, to a design by Albrecht von Säbisch, in 1654–6. With the church in Świdnica (see p185), it is among the world's largest timber-framed structures. Other notable buildings in Jawor are the 14th-century

Church of St Martin (Kościół św Marcina), and the late 15th-century Church of St Mary (Kościół Mariacki). The best place to finish a walk around the town is the Market Square, which is surrounded by arcaded Baroque houses.

🏛 **Gallery of Silesian Ecclesiastical Art**
ul. Klasztorna 6. **Tel** 076 870 30 86 or 870 23 21. ◯ Apr–Oct: 10am–5pm Wed–Sun; Nov–Mar: 10am–4pm Wed–Sun.

Złotoryja ❼

Road map B4. 👥 17,400. 🚉 🚌
ℹ️ Basztowa 15 (076 878 18 73).
🎪 World Gold-Panning Championships (May).

Derived from the Polish word złoto, meaning gold, the town's name reflects the fact that the gold-rich sands of the River Kaczawa, which flows through Złotoryja, have been exploited since the Early Middle Ages. Even today gold-seekers flock to contests organized by the local gold-panning association.

Features of interest in Złotoryja include the Gothic **Church of St Mary** (Kościół NMP), which has a 13th-century presbytery, and the remains of the town walls.

Environs
The volcanic **Wilcza Góra Geological Park**, also known as Wilkołak, lies 2 km (1¼ miles) south of Złotoryja. Unusual basalt formations known as "basalt roses" can be seen in the western part of the park.

Gothic doorway of the 15th-century Grodziec Castle

Grodziec ❽

Road map B4. 👥 500. 🚉
Złotoryja. 🚌 **Castle** ◯ daily.

An imposing fortification crowning a basalt hill, Grodziec Castle was built in the 15th century in the Gothic style as the seat of the dukes of Legnica. It was extended in 1522–4 and over the next four centuries it was destroyed several times, once during the Thirty Years' War (1618–48). It was rebuilt in the Romantic style in 1906–8.

The walls, which follow the contours of the hill, are irregular. The castle's tower and living quarters survive.

At the bottom of the hill is the magnificent, although neglected, palace built for the Frankenberg family by Johann Blasius Peintner in 1718–27. Its overgrown surroundings were once attractive gardens.

Lwówek Śląski ❾

Road map B4. 👥 9,300.
🚉 🚌 ℹ️ pl. Wolności 22 (076 647 79 12).
www.lwowekslaski.pl

Lwówek Śląski is a small town set on a precipice overlooking the River Bóbr, in the foothills of the Izerski Mountains. Remnants of the stone walls that once surrounded the settlement can be seen all around.

The centrepiece of the town is its Gothic-Renaissance **town hall**. Built in the 15th century, it was extended in

Gold-panning competition in Złotoryja

For hotels and restaurants in this region see pp303–5 and pp321–3

Gothic-Renaissance town hall in Lwówek Śląski

1522–5 and restored in 1902–5, when the delightful arcades around the building were added. Several town houses of historical interest stand in the Market Square.

The twin-towered **Church of the Assumption** (Kościół Wniebowzięcia) has an imposing Romanesque façade which dates from the 13th century. The tympanum over the portal depicts the Coronation of the Virgin. The main body of the church was not added until the turn of the 16th century. The Gothic chapel on the south side, which dates from 1496, has vaulting with beautiful 16th-century frescoes.

The ruins of another Gothic church also survive in Lwówek Śląski.

The church was built by Franciscan monks but fell into disuse in 1810.

Environs

The castle at **Płakowice**, 2 km (1¼ miles) south of Lwówek Śląski, is one of the finest Renaissance castles in Silesia. It was built in 1550–63 for the von Talkenberg family.

Czoch Castle ⓾

Road map A4. 🚌 Sucha. **Tel** 075 721 15 53. 🕐 10am–5:30pm daily. ℹ️ www.zamekczocha.com

Czoch Castle (Zamek Czocha) is one of Silesia's major tourist attractions. Standing in a picturesque location on the banks of Lake Leśniańskie, it can be seen for miles around.

The castle dates from the 14th century, and because it was destroyed and rebuilt several times over many centuries, incorporates a range of architectural styles. It was most recently renovated in the early part of the 20th century, when the Gütschoff family of Dresden had their dilapidated family seat rebuilt by Bodo Ebhardt in 1904–14. Ebhardt's Romantic vision restored Zamek Czocha to its former glory and the castle has since been used as the setting for several films. It is now an atmospheric hotel (see p304).

Lubomierz ⓫

Road map B4. 🏠 1,800. 🚉 🚌 ℹ️ ul. Wacława Kowalskiego 1 (075 783 35 73). 🎬 Review of Polish Comedy Films (Aug).

A sleepy little town in the foothills of the Izerskie Mountains, Lubomierz boasts a picturesque **market square** lined with large arcaded houses. The Baroque Benedictine church built by Johann Jakob Scheerhof in 1727–30 dominates the town.

Many Polish films have been shot in Lubomierz. The popular comedy film *Sami swoi* ("Just Our Own") brought it the greatest renown. The film follows the fortunes of displaced persons from Poland's eastern territories – which were lost to the Soviet Union after World War II – as they settle in the town, itself a former German territory ceded to Poland.

🏛 The Kargul and Pawlak Museum

ul. Wacława Kowalskiego 1. **Tel** 075 783 35 73. 🕐 10am–4pm Mon–Fri, 11am–3pm Sat & Sun. 📷 www.sami-swoi.com.pl

This museum is housed in Płóciennik House, built in the 16th century and reconstructed around 1700. Its collection includes items used during the making of Sylwester Chęciński's film *Sami swoi*.

The imposing outline of Czoch Castle in Sucha

The Foothills of the Karkonosze Mountains ⑫

The Karkonosze Mountains, the highest in the Sudeten (Sudety) chain, draw holidaymakers all year round. There are many footpaths and good facilities for hikers throughout the summer, while in winter skiers come to enjoy the exhilarating pistes. The upper parts of the Karkonosze Mountains are a national park, recognized by UNESCO as a World Biosphere Reserve.

In the lower parts of the mountains are several attractive small towns, such as Karpacz and Szklarska Poręba, as well as Cieplice and Sobieszów in Jelenia Góra district *(see p184)*.

Szklarka Waterfall ②
A forest of fir trees provides a scenic setting for the 15-m (45-ft) waterfall.

Cieplice ①
This popular spa town has a number of fine Baroque buildings, including Schaffgotsch Palace and its Cistercian and Protestant churches. There is also a natural history museum.

JAKUSZYCE E 65 ③ ②

Piechowice

Szklarska Poręba ③
This health resort is a good starting point for excursions into the Karkonosze Mountains. It is also famous for its glassworks – handmade crystal artifacts are available in local kiosks.

Jagniątków ④
A picturesque villa was built here by the Nobel Prize-winning author Gerhart Hauptmann for his second wife in 1900–02. It now houses a gallery of paintings illustrating scenes from Hauptmann's works.

Sobieszów: Chojnik Castle ⑤
Situated on a high escarpment, this 14th-century castle was built for Duke Bolko II. In the 15th and 16th centuries it was renovated by the Schaffgotsch family, but in 1675 was gutted by a fire after being struck by lightning.

Miłków ⑥
A Baroque palace and church surrounded by stone walls covered in penitentiary crosses are the main attractions of this village.

Mysłakowice ⑧

The village is noted for its Neo-Gothic palace, which once belonged to Kaiser Friedrich Wilhelm IV, for a church designed by Karl Friedrich Schinkel and for Tyrolean-style houses built by religious refugees fleeing persecution in the Tyrol.

TIPS FOR DRIVERS

Tour length: *About 70 km (46 miles).*
Stopping-off points: *Bars and restaurants can be found in Szklarska Poręba, Cieplice and Karpacz. The Spiż restaurant in Miłków is recommended.*
Other attractions: *Karpacz also has a chair lift to Kopa, which is one hour's walk from Mt Śnieżka. Another chair lift from Szklarska Poręba goes to Szrenica.*

KEY

■ Scenic route

■ Other road

☆ Viewpoint

0 km 5

0 miles 5

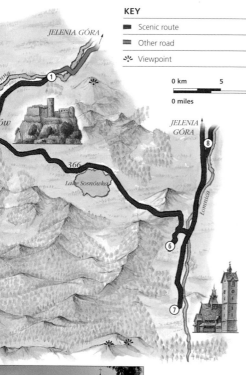

Karpacz ⑦

The buildings of this popular health resort are concentrated along a single street 7 km (4½ miles) long. The wooden Romanesque church here was brought from Vang, in Norway, in 1842–4.

Interior of the Cistercian Church of St Mary in Krzeszów

Krzeszów ⑬

Road map B5. 🏠 *1,300.* 🚆 *Kamienna Góra.* 🚌 **Church of St Mary, Church of St Joseph** *and* **Mausoleum of the Silesian Piasts** *Tel 075 742 33 80.* ⏰ *9am–6pm daily (Nov–Mar: to 4pm).* 📷 🚫

This tiny village in the Góry Kamienne Mountains has one of the most picturesque groups of historic buildings in Poland. Benedictine monks settled here in 1242, followed by Cistercian monks in 1292. They were responsible for building the Church of St Joseph (Kościół św Józefa), which has frescoes by Michael Willmann, in 1690–96. They also built the abbey **Church of St Mary** (Kościół NMP Łaskawej) in 1727–35. The interior is decorated with vertiginous trompe l'oeil paintings by Georg Wilhelm Neunhertz; sculptures by Anton Dorazil and Ferdinand Maximilian Brokoff make the pilasters, cornices and vaulting appear to float in mid-air. The figures of saints on the stalls in the chancel are of particular interest.

Behind the presbytery is the **Mausoleum of the Silesian Piasts** (Mauzoleum Piastów Śląskich), with the Gothic tombs of Bolko I (d. 1301) and Bolko II (d. 1368), dukes of Świdnica-Jawor. Figures of their wives, Agnieszka and Beatrycze, stand opposite the tombs. On the wall is an epitaph by the son of Bolko II, the last member of the Piast dynasty.

For hotels and restaurants in this region see pp303–5 and pp321–3

Arcaded houses around the Market Square in Jelenia Góra

Jelenia Góra ⑭

Road map B4. 🏛 *86,000.* 🚆 🚌
ℹ️ *pl. Piastowski 36 (075 755 88 44
or 755 88 45).* ⬤ *9am–5pm Mon–
Fri, 10am–2pm Sat.* ℹ️ *ul. Bankowa
27 (075 767 69 25).* ⬤ *9am–6pm
Mon–Fri, 10am–2pm Sat, Sun.* 🎭
*Cieplice Spring (May); International
Street Theatre Festival (Jul); Jelenia
Góra (Aug).* **www**.um.jeleniagora.pl

Situated at the foot of the
Karkonosze Mountains,
Jelenia Góra is a favourite
tourist destination and a
major starting point for
mountain hikers. The
town was granted city
status at the end of the
13th century. It was
once renowned for its
textiles – delicate batiste
and voile that were
exported as far as Africa
and America. It was
also one of the main
centres of engraved
glassware, examples
of which can be seen in
the **Regional Museum**.

Silesian glassware

The town's historic centre
is the Market Square, with
a Baroque town hall
surrounded by arcaded town
houses. In Ulica Maria
Konopnicka, east of the
Market Square, is the **Church
of Saints Erasmus and
Pancras** (Kościół św Erazma
i Pankracego), a Gothic
basilica of the late 14th to
early 15th centuries. The line
of the old defensive walls
here is marked by a chapel
that was once a keep.
In Ulica 1 Maja, on the
same axis, is the Church
of Our Lady, with two
penitentiary crosses *(see
p185)* set into the outer walls.
The street then leads to the
Baroque former Protestant
Church of the Holy Cross

(Kościół św Krzyża), known
also as the Church of Peace.
The town boundaries of
Jelenia Góra were expanded
in 1976 and now include
the spa of Cieplice, with its
Natural History Museum, and
the town of Sobieszów *(see
pp182–3)*, which includes the
**Karkonosze National Park
Natural History Museum**.

🔒 Church of Saints Erasmus
and Pancras
pl. Kościelny 1–2. **Tel** *075 752 21 60.*
This Gothic basilica of the
first half of the 14th century
features late Gothic
vaulting dating
from about 1550
and a Baroque
altar depicting the
Transfiguration.

🔒 Church of
the Holy Cross
ul. 1 Maja.
Tel *075 642 32 82.*
This church (Kościół
św Krzyża), built by Martin
Franze in 1709–18, is
modelled on St Catherine's
in Stockholm. A triple tier
of galleries lines the interior
and frescoes by Felix Anton
Scheffler and Jozef Franz
Hoffman cover the ceilings.
The altar, which is structurally
integrated with the organ loft,
is particularly striking.

🏛 Regional Museum
ul. Matejki 28. **Tel** *075 752 34 65.*
⬤ *9am–5pm Tue–Sun (Nov–Mar:
to 4pm).* 🎭 *(free on Sun).*
www.muzeumkarkonoskie.pl
Jelenia Góra's Regional
Museum contains the largest
collection of decorative
glassware in the whole
of Poland. A traditional
Karkonosze hut nearby
houses an ethnographical
exhibition.

🏛 Natural History
Museum
*Jelenia Góra – Cieplice, ul.
Wolności 268.* **Tel** *075 755 15 06.*
⬤ *Apr–Sep: 9am–6pm Tue–
Fri, 9am–5pm Sat, Sun; Oct–Mar:
9am–4pm Tue–Sun.* 🎭 *(free on
Sun).* **www**.muzeum-cieplice.pl

🏛 Karkanosze National Park
Natural History Museum
ul. Chałubińskiego 23. **Tel** *075 755
62 44.* ⬤ *10am–4pm Tue–Sun.*

Bolków ⑮

Road map B4. 🏛 *5,800.* 🚆 🚌

The great towering
**Castle of the Dukes of
Świdnica-Jawor** is the main
feature of this small town. It
was built in stages from the
mid-13th to the mid-14th
century. Sacked and destroyed
several times, in the 16th
century it was rebuilt in the
Renaissance style by Jakob
Paar. Today the castle is a
local history **museum**. The
Gothic Church of St Jadwiga
(Kościół św Jadwigi) is also
worth a visit. In the old town,
several fine houses survive.

🏛 Castle Museum
ul. Księcia Bolka. **Tel** *075 741 32 97.*
⬤ *May–Oct: 9am–4:30pm Tue–Fri,
9am–5:30pm Sat & Sun; Nov–Apr:
closes 1 hr earlier.* ⬤ *public hols*
🎭 *(free on Mon).*

Environs
In **Świny**, 2 km (1¼ miles) north
of Bolków, are the haunting
ruins of a castle. The upper part
was built in the 14th century.
The lower wing is a 17th-
century late Baroque palace.

**The crenellated tower of
Bolków Castle**

Książ ⑯

Road map B5. **Castle** Wałbrzych,
ul. Piastów Śl. *Tel 074 664 38 34.*
Apr–Sep: 10am–5pm daily (to 6pm
Sat & Sun); Oct–Mar: 10am–3pm Tue–
Fri, 10am–4pm Sat & Sun. **Palm**
House Wałbrzych-Lubiechowo, ul.
Wrocławska 158. *Apr: 10am–5pm*
Tue–Sun; May–Sep: 10am–5pm daily;
Oct: 10am–4pm Tue–Sun; Nov–Mar:
10am–3pm Tue–Fri, 10am–4pm Sat &
Sun. www.ksiaz-walbrzych.pl

Książ Castle, on the
outskirts of Wałbrzych, is the
largest residential building in
Silesia. This huge edifice was
built on a rocky hilltop overlooking the surrounding
wooded countryside. The late
13th-century Gothic **castle** of
Prince Bolko I was rebuilt in
the mid-16th century for the
Hochberg family of Meissen,
who remained its owners until
World War II. One of the most
powerful Silesian families, they
extended the building several
times, particularly in 1670–
1724 and 1909–23. The
Hochbergs' reputation was
coloured by several scandals.
The penultimate owner of the
castle was Hans Henry XV
von Pless. After divorcing his
wife, he married a much
younger Spanish woman.
She gave birth to a daughter,
but then left the elderly
prince for his son Bolko.

During World War II
attempts were made to
convert the castle into headquarters for the German
leader Adolf Hitler by drilling
tunnels into the rocky hill.
Today part of the castle
houses a museum, a hotel
and a restaurant. The grounds
are now the **Książ Nature**
Park. The stables and palm
house, still in use,
are open to
visitors.

**High altar in the Cathedral of
Saints Stanisław and Wenceslas**

Świdnica ⑰

Road map B5. 60,000.
www.swidnica.pl

For almost 100 years from
1292, Świdnica was the capital
of the independent duchy of
Świdnica-Jawor. It minted its
own coins and was renowned
for its beer, which was exported to many cities in central
Europe. The town's mercantile
traditions are well illustrated in
the **Museum of Silesian Trade**
that is housed in the town hall.

From the pretty market
square, with its fine Baroque
plague column *(see p177)*,
Ulica Długa, the main street,
leads to the 14th-century
Cathedral of Saints Stanisław
and Wenceslas (Katedra św
Stanisława i Wacława), a
Gothic building with the
highest tower in Silesia. The
interior is richly furnished and
decorated in styles ranging
from Gothic to Baroque. The
altar canopy was
made by Johann
Riedl in 1694.
The town's most
impressive build-
ing, however, is

the **Church of Peace** (Kościół
Pokoju). With that in Jawor
(see p180), it is one of two
surviving Protestant "peace
churches" built after the Peace
of Westphalia that ended the
Thirty Years' War (1618–48).
The timber-framed church,
designed by Albrecht von
Säbisch, was built in 1656–7.
Its undistinguished exterior
conceals an unusual interior,
with a two-tiered gallery, fine
paintings and furnishings.

Museum of Silesian Trade
Rynek 37. *Tel 074 852 12 91.*
10am–3pm Tue–Fri, 11am–
5pm Sat & Sun. *(free on Fri).*

Cathedral of Saints
Stanisław and Wenceslas
pl. Jana Pawła II. *Tel 074 852 27 29.*
daily.

Church of Peace
pl. Pokoju. *Tel 074 852 28 14.*
Apr–Oct: 9am–1pm and 3–6pm daily
(Sun: pm only); Nov–Mar: call first.

Environs
Jaworzyna, 10 km (6 miles)
northwest of Świdnica, has
Poland's largest museum of
steam locomotives.

**Penitentiary cross in Łaziska,
Upper Silesia**

PENITENTIARY
CROSSES

As a form of punishment,
criminals in the Middle
Ages sometimes had to
make a stone cross and
place it at the scene of
their crime or near a
church. Depictions of
the implement used to
carry out the deed (such
as a crossbow) or a part
of the victim's body
(such as the feet) were
engraved on the cross.

Książ Castle, set high above the River Pełcznica

Renaissance gate of Grodno Castle in Zagórze Śląskie

Zagórze Śląskie ⑱

Road map B5. 🏛 *430.*
🚌 🚉

The main attraction in this small village is **Grodno Castle**. Built by Bolko I at the end of the 13th century, it was altered by later owners and then fell into ruin, but was saved by major restoration work in 1907–29.

Today the castle houses a museum, whose more curious exhibits include the skeleton of a young woman. For the murder of her husband, she was condemned to death by starvation by her own father.

♣ Grodno Castle
Tel 074 845 33 60. ◯ *May–Oct: 9am–6pm daily (to 7pm Sat & Sun); Nov–Apr: 9am–5pm daily (to 6pm Sat & Sun).*

Environs
A few kilometres south of Zagórze Śląskie are underground **tunnels** dug secretly in the final year of World War II by prisoners of the Gross-Rosen (Rogoźnica) concentration camp.

🚇 Walim Tunnels (Sztolnie w Walimiu)
Tel 074 845 73 00. ◯ *May–Sep: 9am–6pm Mon–Fri, 9am–7pm Sat, Sun; Oct–Apr: 9am–4pm Mon–Fri, 9am–5pm Sat, Sun.* **www**.sztolnie.pl

🚇 Osowiec Tunnels (Sztolnie w Osówce)
Tel 074 845 62 20.
◯ *10am–6pm daily (Nov–Mar: to 4pm).* 🚫 *1 Nov, 24, 25, 31 Dec.* 🎦
📷 **www**.osowka.pl

Mt Ślęża ⑲

Road map B5.

Mt Ślęża is a conical peak visible from great distances all around. Used as a location for religious rituals during the Bronze Age (3500– 1500 BC), it is crowned with a stone circle, and mysterious statues of unknown origin stand beside the road leading to the summit. The best view of the surrounding country-side is from the terrace of the Neo-Romanesque **church** built on Mt Ślęża in 1851–2. The hill of neighbouring **Wieżyca** has at its summit a tower erected in honour of the German statesman Otto von Bismarck in 1906–7, and is also a good vantage point from which to view the entire area.

In Sobótka, at the foot of Mt Ślęża, a former hospital built by Augustinian monks houses the **Ślęża Museum**. The best place to stay, or stop for lunch, is the hotel Zamek Górka, located in a Gothic-Renaissance Augustinian presbytery that later became the palace of the von Kulmiz family.

🏛 Ślęża Museum
Sobótka, ul. św Jakuba 18. *Tel 071 316 26 22.* ◯ *9am–4pm Wed–Sun and last Tue in the month.*

Wojnowice ⑳

Road map B4. 🏛 *400.* 🚌
🚉 *Mrozów. Tel 071 317 07 26.*
www.zamekwojnowice.ig.pl/ang

Wojnowice presents a rare opportunity to see a genuine and well-preserved Silesian Renaissance **manor house**. It was built in the early 16th century for Nikolaus von Scheibitz and soon after was acquired by the Boner family, who converted it into a Renaissance castle with a small arcaded courtyard. Compact and moated, it is now a hotel, with an excellent restaurant. It is a superb place for a short break.

Moated Renaissance manor house in Wojnowice

Trzebnica ㉑

Road map C4. 🏛 *12,100.*
🚉 *Oborniki Śląskie.* 🚌
www.trzebnica.pl

In 1203 Jadwiga, wife of Henry I, brought an order of Cistercian monks from Bamberg, in southern Germany, to Trzebnica. Jadwiga was buried here and, after her canonization in 1267, the monastery became an important place of pilgrimage. The entire complex under-went major rebuilding in the second half of the 1600s, obliterating its Romanesque

Country track in Ślęża

architecture, although the tympanum of the main portal retains a fine relief of around 1230 representing the Old Testament figures David and Bathsheba. The Gothic chapel of St Jadwiga contains her Baroque-style tomb, dating from 1677–8. The figure of the saint was carved by Franz Josef Mangoldt in 1750.

Coronation of the Virgin in the portal of the Chapel of St Jadwiga

Oleśnica ②

Road map C4. 🏙 *38,000.* 🚉 🚌 www.olesnica.pl

The most impressive building in the town is the **Castle of the Dukes of Oleśnica**. While the Gothic interior is original, the exterior, with its circular corner tower, is the result of successive stages of rebuilding from 1542 to 1610 by the Italian architects Francesco Parr and Bernardo Niuron. The castle retains ornamental gables in the attic rooms in the wings and the unusual galleries supported on brackets overlooking the courtyard. Attached to the castle is the **palace** of Jan Podiebrad, built in 1559–63.

A pleasant way of rounding off a visit to Oleśnica is to walk through the old quarter to the Gothic **Church of St John the Evangelist** (Kościół św Jana Ewangelisty). Beside the presbytery is a chapel built in memory of the dukes of Wurtemberg, and containing the tombs of Jan and Jerzy Podiebrad. Other elements include the Mannerist pulpit and the Gothic stalls from the late 15th and early 16th centuries. Remnants of castle walls, with the tower of the Wrocławski Gate, and the Neo-Classical town hall, rebuilt after World War II, are other features of interest.

⚜ **Castle of the Dukes of Oleśnica**
Tel 605 356 193. ⬤ *daily.*

Wrocław ②

See pp188–197.

Brzeg ②

Road map C5. 🏙 *39,000.* 🚉 🚌 www.brzeg.pl

The attractive town of Brzeg, on the River Odra, has an illustrious history. It received its charter in 1245, and from 1311 to 1675 was the capital of the duchy of Legnica-Brzeg. The town's most

Renaissance sculpture on the gate tower of Brzeg Castle

impressive building is without doubt the **Castle of the Dukes of Legnica-Brzeg**. It was built originally in the Gothic style and a 14th-century Gothic chapel survives, in whose presbytery a mausoleum to the Silesian Piasts was built in 1567. The castle was transformed into a Renaissance palace in the second half of the 16th century. The three-winged complex features a circular courtyard and a tower over the entrance gate dating from 1554. The walls are decorated with busts of all the ancestors of Duke Jerzy II and his wife Barbara von Brandenburg. Today the castle houses the **Museum of the Silesian Piasts**.

Other buildings of interest are the **town hall**, erected in 1570–7, the 14th-century **Church of St Nicholas** (Kościół św Mikołaja) and the late Baroque Jesuit church, which was built in 1734–9.

🏛 **Museum of the Silesian Piasts**
pl. Zamkowy 1. *Tel 077 416 42 10.* ⬤ *10am–5pm Tue–Sun (last adm 4pm).* 🎫 *(free on Sat).*

Environs
A few kilometres from Brzeg is the small village of Małujowice, or Mollwitz, where on 10 April 1741 a major battle was fought in the Austro-Prussian war. The Gothic church there contains unusual 14th-century frescoes and Renaissance ceilings.

Courtyard of the Castle of the Dukes of Oleśnica

Wrocław

The city of Wrocław bears the stamp of several cultures. It was founded by a Czech duke in the 10th century and a Polish bishopric was established here in 1000. Later it became the capital of the duchy of Silesian Piasts, and then came under Czech rule in 1335. In 1526, with the whole Czech state, it was incorporated into the Habsburg Empire, and in 1741 was transferred to Prussian rule.

Emblem of the Golden Deer House in Market Square

The fierce defence that German forces put up here in the last months of World War II left almost three quarters of the city in ruins. However, reconstruction has largely healed the ravages of the past.

Baroque pietà in the Church of the Holy Name of Jesus

🏛 Wrocław University

pl. Uniwersytecki 1. **Aula Leopoldina**
***Tel** 071 375 26 18.* ☐ *10am–4pm Mon–Thu, 10am–5pm Fri–Sun.* 📷
www.uni.wroc.pl

Wrocław University was established as an academy by Emperor Leopold I in 1702 and in 1811 became a university. Many of its alumni have gained renown. They include nine Nobel laureates, among them the nuclear physicist Max Born (1882–1970). Since 1945 it has been a Polish centre of learning and university.

The centrepiece of this imposing Baroque building is the assembly hall, the Aula Leopoldina, of 1728–41. The decoration includes stucco-work, gilding and carvings by Franz Josef Mangoldt and paintings by Christoph Handke glorifying wisdom, knowledge and science, and the founders of the academy.

0 m — 200
0 yds — 200

The richly ornamented interior of the university assembly hall

For hotels and restaurants in this region see pp303–5 and pp321–3

CENTRAL WROCŁAW

🄰 Church of the Holy Name of Jesus

pl. Uniwersytecki 1.
Tel 071 344 94 23.

This church (Kościół Najświęt-szego Imienia Jezus), built for the Jesuits in 1689–98, is a good example of Silesian Baroque church architecture. The modest exterior conceals a breathtaking interior, built in 1722–34 by Krzysztof Tausch. The vaulting was decorated by the Viennese artist Johann Michael Rottmayer in 1704–6.

The Baroque Hochberg Chapel beside the Church of St Vincent

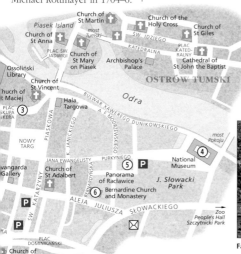

Key to Symbols *see back flap*

⚓ Plac Biskupa Nankera

The buildings in this square date from various periods. The Gothic **Church of St Vincent** (Kościół św Wincentego), at No. 5, was erected in the 13th to the 15th centuries. The late 17th-century Baroque monastery is now part of the University of Wrocław.

The group of Baroque monastic buildings at No. 16 encloses the small 13th-century **Church of St Clare** (Kościół św Klary). The church was used by the Piasts as a mausoleum, and it still contains Gothic ducal tombs. Next door, at No. 17, is the Gothic **Church of St Maciej** (Kościół św Macieja), which dates from the 14th and early 15th centuries and was once owned by the Knights Hospitallers of the Red Star. The pavilion of the gallery at No. 8, on the opposite side of the street, contains 13th-century walls of the **House of the Nuns of Trebnica**, the oldest surviving secular building in the city.

🏛 National Museum

pl. Powstańców Warszawy 5. *Tel 071 372 51 50.* ⬜ *Apr–Sep: 10am–5pm Wed–Sun (to 6pm Sat); Oct–Mar: 10am–4pm Wed–Sun (to 5pm Sat).* 🄰 *(free on Sat, limited availability).* www.mnwr.art.pl

The ground floor contains examples of Silesian and Gothic art, including the tombstone of Henry IV, the Good dating from 1300. The first floor has a collection of 16th- and 17th-century paintings, including works by the Silesian artist Michael Willmann (1630–1706) and wooden sculptures by Tho-mas Weissfeldt (1630–1712). The second floor is devoted to works by contemporary Polish artists.

Façade of the National Museum

🏛 Panorama of Racławice

ul. Purkyniego 11. *Tel 071 344 16 61.* ⬜ *9am–4pm Tue–Sun: to 5pm daily.* 🄰 *see the website for details.* 🄰 *(buy tickets online).* 🄰 www.panoramaraclawicka.pl

This painting depicts the Battle of Racławice of 4 April 1794, when the Poles defeated the Russians. It is 120 m (400 ft) long and 15 m (46 ft) high and took the artists Jan Styka and Wojciech Kossak nine months to paint. Unveiled in 1894 in Lviv, in Ukraine, it was brought to Poland in 1946 and put on display in Wrocław in 1985.

Rotunda containing the Panorama of Racławice

Wrocław Old Town

For those who enjoy exploring on foot, the old town of Wrocław is a delightful place. The restored buildings located around the large Main Market Square have been given over to an assortment of bars, restaurants and cafés with al fresco seating, while the churches nearby contain a wealth of religious art and ecclesiastical furnishings. The impressive Gothic town hall has a finely decorated interior.

On summer evenings the Main Market Square in the old town comes alive as local people and tourists alike gather there, some to gossip and exchange news, others to attend the concerts and many cultural events that are held in the square.

Modernist architecture, an office building of 1912–13 by an equally renowned architect, Hans Poelzig.

Detail of the ornamental façade of the House of the Seven Electors

Late Gothic portal of the Bernadine church

🔒 Bernadine Church and Monastery

ul. Bernardyńska 5. **Museum of Architecture** *Tel 071 344 82 79.*
🕐 *11am–5pm Tue & Fri–Sun, 10am–4pm Wed, noon–7pm Thu.*
🎫 *(free on Wed).* www.ma.wroc.pl

This impressive group of monastic buildings (Kościół i Klasztor pobernardyński) was constructed by Bernadine monks in 1463–1502. Having been rebuilt from their wartime ruins, they now house Poland's only Museum of Architecture. The monastery is of interest for its late Gothic cloisters and the Church of St Bernard of Siena, a towering Gothic basilica with a typically Baroque gable.

🔒 Cathedral of St Mary Magdalene

ul. Szewska 19. *Tel 071 344 19 04.*
🕐 *9am–noon, 4–6pm daily.*

The great Gothic Cathedral of St Mary Magdalene (Katedra św Marii Magdaleny) was erected between about 1330

and the mid-15th century, incorporating the walls of a 13th-century church that had previously stood on the site. Inside the basilica is a Renaissance pulpit of 1579–81 by Friedrich Gross, a Gothic stone tabernacle and tombstones of various periods. The portal on the north side is a fine example of late 12th-century Romanesque sculpture. It was taken from a demolished Benedictine monastery in Olbina and added in 1546 *(see p20).* The tympanum, depicting the Dormition of the Virgin, is now on display in the National Museum.

Detail of the Cathedral of St Mary Magdalene

🏛 Kameleon Store

ul. Szewska 6.

The Kameleon store (Dom Handlowy Kameleon) is an unusual building on the corner of Ulica Szewska and Ulica Oławska. Its semicircular bay, formed of rows of windows, juts out dramatically. It was built by the German architect Erich Mendelsohn as a retail store for Rudolf Petersdorf in 1927–8. Nearby, at the intersection of Ulica Łaciarskiej and Ofiar Oświęcimskich, is another interesting example of

🏛 Main Market Square

Rynek.

Wrocław's Main Market Square is the second-largest in Poland, after that in Cracow. In the centre stand the town hall and a group of buildings separated by alleys. The houses around the square date from the Renaissance to the 20th century. Some still have their original 14th and 15th-century Gothic vaults. The most attractive side of the square is the west, with the late Baroque **House of the Golden Sun**, at No. 6, built in 1727 by Johann Lucas von Hildebrandt, as well as the **House of the Seven Electors**, its paintwork dating from 1672. Also to the south is the Griffin House, at No. 2, built in 1587–9. It has a galleried interior courtyard. On the east side, at Nos. 31 and 32, is the Secessionist **Phoenix store** of 1904 and, at No. 41, the **Golden Hound**, a rebuilt town house of 1713. The north side was rebuilt after World War II.

Just off the corner of the market square, fronting the Church of St Elizabeth (Kościół św Elżbiety), are two small acolytes' houses, the Renaissance Jaś, of around 1564, and the 18th-century Baroque Małgosia.

🏛 Town Hall

ul. Sukiennice 14/15.
Historical Museum
ul. Kazimierza Wielkiego 35.
Tel 071 347 16 90. ⬜ *10am–5pm Tue–Fri, 10am–6pm Sat & Sun.* 🅿
Rynek Stary Ratusz Museum of Bourgeois Art
Tel 071 347 16 90.
⬜ *11am–5pm Wed–Sat, 10am–6pm Sun.* **www**.mmw.pl

The town hall in Wrocław is one of the most important examples of Gothic architecture in central and eastern Europe. Its present appearance is the result of an extensive period of rebuilding that took place between 1470 and 1510.

The town hall's southern façade was embellished with Neo-Gothic stone carvings in around 1871. Inside are impressive vaulted halls, the largest being the triple-aisled Grand Hall on the ground floor, and several late Gothic and Renaissance doorways.

Outside the entrance to the town hall is a plaque commemorating the prominent poet and comedy writer Aleksander Fredro (1793–1876), who acquired fame with his comedies about the Polish upper classes. The plaque was made in 1879 by Leonard Marconi and transferred to Wrocław from Lviv in 1956 *(see p25).*

Gothic gables of the east façade of the town hall

🔒 Church of St Elizabeth

ul. św Elżbiety. *Tel* 071 343 72 04.
The large tower dominating the market square is that of the Church of St Elizabeth (Kościół św Elżbiety), one of the largest churches in

Wrocław. The Gothic basilica was built in the 14th century on the site of an earlier church, although the tower was not completed until 1482. It became a Protestant church in 1525. Since 1946 it has been a garrison church.

The church has suffered damage from a succession of wars, fires and accidents. A fire in 1976 destroyed the roof and the splendid Baroque organ. Fortunately, more than 350 epitaphs and tombstones have survived, forming a remarkable exhibition of Silesian stone-carving from Gothic to Neo-Classical times.

Church of St Elizabeth with Jaś and Małgosia, acolytes' houses

⚓ Royal Palace

ul. Kazimierza Wielkiego 34/35.
Ethnographical Museum
ul. Traugutta 111/113.
Tel 071 344 33 13.
⬜ *10am–4pm Tue–Sun.*
🅿 *(free on Sat).* ♿
www.muzeumetnograficzne.pl
Archaeological Museum
ul. Cieszyńskiego 9.
Tel 071 347 16 96.
⬜ *11am–5pm Wed–Sat, 11am–6pm Sun.* 🅿

The Baroque palace, enclosed by a court of annexes, was built in 1719. After 1750, when Wrocław came under Prussian rule, it was a residence for the Prussian kings. On the side facing Plac Wolności, only a side gallery remains of the Neo-Renaissance palace built in 1843–6.

The Royal Palace contains two interesting collections: the Archaeological Museum and Ethnographical Museum, the latter illustrating Silesian folk history and art.

The Church of Saints Wenceslas, Stanisław and Dorothy

🔒 Church of Saints Wenceslas, Stanisław and Dorothy

Plac Wolności 3.
Tel 071 343 27 21.
Dedicated to three saints, the Czech St Wenceslas, the Polish St Stanisław and the German St Dorothy, this church (Kościół św Wacława, Stanisława i Doroty) was built in 1351 to cement relations between the three nationalities in Wrocław. The church's unusually narrow interior is Baroque. The Rococo tombstone of Gottfried von Spaetgen stands in the nave.

OSSOLINEUM

The National Ossoliński Institute was founded by Count Józef Maksymilian Ossoliński in Vienna in 1817. In 1827 it moved to Lwów (later Lviv), where it assembled collections of manuscripts, prints, etchings and drawings, promoted scientific research and engaged in publishing. After World War II most of the collections were transferred to the National Museum in Wrocław, while the manuscripts were housed in the Baroque monastery of the Knights Hospitallers of the Red Star.

The Baroque monastery that houses the Ossolineum

Ostrów Tumski and Piasek Island

Ostrów Tumski was once an island in the River Odra, and it is here that the history of Wrocław began. According to legend, the city was founded by Duke Vratislav of Bohemia. In the year 1000 a bishopric was established and the island grew into a centre of ducal power. After the city moved to the left bank of the Odra in 1292, the island remained the base of ecclesiastical authority. In the 19th century the northern arm of the Odra was filled in and Tumski ceased to be an island. Tumski Bridge connects it to Piasek Island, a small sandbank that since the first half of the 12th century has been the location of a monastery for canons regular.

Statue of St John Nepomuk

Church of the Holy Cross (Kościół św Krzyża)
This Gothic church is set on two levels. The upper church is reached via a portal enclosed by a double arch.

Church of St Martin

Tumski Bridge
The present bridge was built in 1888–92. The figures of St Jadwiga and St John the Baptist guarding it are by Gustav Grunenberg.

ŚW. MARCINA

MOST MŁYŃSKI

ŚW. JADWIGI

★ Church of St Mary on Piasek (Kościół NMP na Piasku)
The interior of the church was restored after World War II.

0 m   250
0 yds   250

STAR SIGHTS

- ★ Cathedral of St John the Baptist
- ★ Church of St Mary on Piasek

For hotels and restaurants in this region see pp303–5 and pp321–3

Church of St Giles
This tiny late Romanesque church, built in the 1230s, is the oldest surviving church in Wrocław.

Gate of the Church of St Giles
The gate of the Church of St Giles is decorated with a stone "dumpling" about which guides tell a variety of legends.

Arch-diocesan Museum

KANONIA

KARD. A. HLONDA

KARD. B. KOMINKA

PL. KATEDRALNY

KATEDRALNA

ument t John omuk

★ Cathedral of St John the Baptist
The cathedral presents a combination of styles from different periods. The spires on its towers were added in 1991.

Archbishop's Palace
The residence of the archbishops of Wrocław was once the chapterhouse. It was rebuilt in 1792 in the Neo-Classical style.

KEY

– – – Suggested route

Exploring Ostrów Tumski and Piasek Island

Wrocław's islands, bathed by the River Odra, are peaceful places for a stroll away from the bustle of the city. The cathedral, the islands' principal landmark, preserves its valuable interior despite having suffered the ravages of World War II. The Archdiocesan Museum is a rich repository of Gothic art. A walk through the islands' many narrow streets and alleys can be followed by a visit to the Botanical Gardens.

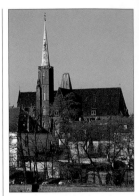

The Gothic Church of the Holy Cross, built on two levels

Gothic portal of the Church of St Mary on Piasek

🏛 Church of St Mary on Piasek

ul. Najświętszej Marii Panny 1.
The rather forbidding bulk of the Church of St Mary on Piasek (Kościół NMP na Piasku) dominates Piasek Island. The church was constructed for canons regular in the second half of the 14th century on the site of a 12th-century Romanesque building whose tympanum is built into the wall over the sacristy in the south aisle.

The Church of St Mary suffered extensive damage in World War II, but some impressive features survive. The asymmetrical tripartite rib vaulting over the aisles is unusual. The church also houses a fine collection of Gothic altars brought here from other churches in Silesia.

🏛 Church of St Martin

ul. św Marcina 7.
The first ecclesiastical building raised on the site now occupied by the Church of St Martin (Kościół św Marcina) was a stronghold chapel erected at the turn of

the 11th century. The present church dates from the late 13th century but was rebuilt after World War II because it had suffered major damage. The present building consists of an octagonal nave and an unfinished presbytery.

🏛 Church of the Holy Cross

pl. Kościelny. **Tel** *071 322 25 74.*
The two-tiered Church of the Holy Cross (Kościół św Krzyża) was established in 1288 by Henry IV, the Pious. Building continued in the 14th century, and the south tower was not completed until 1484. The lower church has been used by Uniates since 1956. The upper church, a narrow nave with a transept, was badly damaged during World War II, when most of its interior fittings were lost. The tombstone dedicated to the church's founder has been moved to the National Museum, but the original tympanum, depicting the ducal couple admiring the heavenly Throne of Grace, can be seen in the north aisle. The 15th-century triptych over the high altar comes from a church in Świny.

⛪ Archbishop's Palace

ul. Katedralna 11. ⬤ *to visitors.*
The present archbishop's residence, once the home of the canons of the cathedral, is a relatively plain building that was reconstructed from a more splendid Baroque edifice in 1792. The old bishop's palace, which stands at Ulica Katedralna 15 nearby, is a fine Neo-Classical building dating from the second half of the 18th century, although three 13th-century wings from the earlier palace remain.

🏛 Cathedral of St John the Baptist

pl. Katedralny. **Tel** *071 322 25 74.*
⬜ *daily.* **Tower** ⬜ *1 Apr–30 Sep: 10am–6pm Mon–Sat.*
The Cathedral of St John the Baptist (Archikatedra św Jana Chrzciciela) presents a combination of styles from different periods. The presbytery was built some time between 1244 and 1272;

Ulica Katedralna, with the Cathedral of St John the Baptist

Portal of the Cathedral of St John the Baptist on Ostrów Tumski

THE BRIDGES OF WROCŁAW

Situated on the River Odra, the city of Wrocław boasts more than 100 bridges crossing numerous streams, canals and inlets. The oldest is the Piasek Island bridge, dating from 1845. The best known is Grunwaldzki Suspension Bridge, dating from 1908–10, which under German rule was named the Kaiserbrücke.

Grunwaldzki Suspension Bridge

the basilica was built in the first half of the 14th century and the west tower was completed even later. Three quarters of the cathedral were destroyed in World War II, and most of the present building is the result of postwar reconstruction. The east end, with its interesting chapels accessible from the presbytery, survives in its original form. The Chapel of St Elizabeth in the south aisle was built in the Roman Baroque style by Giacomo Scianzi in 1680. The interior of the chapel is also the work of Italian artists: the tomb of Cardinal Frederyk, a Hessian landowner whose burial chapel this became, is by Domenico Guidi. The altar is by Ercole Ferrata.

The presbytery contains a late Gothic polyptych of 1522, which was brought from Lubin, and Baroque choir stalls from a church of the Premonstratensian order.

⛪ Archdiocesan Museum
ul. Kanonia 12.
Tel 071 322 17 55.
◯ *9am–3pm Tue–Sat.*
The Archdiocesan Museum (Muzeum Archidiecezjalne) stands among a group of buildings dating from three historical periods. The earliest is the Gothic-Renaissance chapterhouse built in 1519–27, which has fine portals and arcades. The later Baroque chapterhouse was completed in 1756. The purpose-built Neo-Gothic museum, libraries and archives of the archdiocese

were built in 1896. The museum contains an important and growing collection of Silesian religious art going back to the Gothic period. In addition to altars and sculptures, it has on display one of the earliest cabinets in the world, dating from 1455.

Archdiocesan Museum on Ostrów Tumski

✽ Botanical Gardens
ul. H. Sienkiewicza 23.
Tel 071 322 59 57.
◯ *Apr–Nov: 8am–6pm daily.* ◿
Wrocław boasts the most attractive botanical gardens in

Poland. They were established in 1811 by two professors from the University of Silesia in Katowice, and after being totally destroyed in World War II were reverently re-created. The gardens' central area contains ponds fashioned from what was an arm of the River Odra when Ostrów Tumski was still an island. The gardens contain palms, an alpine garden, cactuses and a 19th-century model of the geology of the Silesian town of Wałbrzych. On a walk through the gardens 7,000 plant species can be seen and a bust of the Swedish botanist Carolus Linnaeus (1708–78), dating from 1871, stands among the greenery. A branch of the gardens, with an extensive arboretum, has been established in Wojsławice, near Niemcza.

The Botanical Gardens on Ostrów Tumski

Around Central Wrocław

Many places of interest lie within walking distance of central Wrocław. A relaxing day can be spent at the zoo, the museums of natural history, geology and mineralogy and in Szczytnicki Park. The Jewish cemetery gives a fascinating insight into Poland's past. There are also several notable 20th-century buildings, such as the People's Hall and the 1920s Mieszkanie i Miejsce Pracy housing estate.

Some of the exhibits in the Mineralogy Museum

🏛 Geology and Mineralogy Museums

ul. Cybulskiego 30.
Geology Museum *Tel 071 375 93 27.* ◯ *9am–5pm Mon, Thu; 9am–3pm Tue, Wed, Fri; 10am–3pm Sat (Jul & Aug: 10am–3pm Mon–Sat).*
Mineralogy Museum *Tel 071 375 92 06.* ◯ *10am–3:30pm Mon–Fri; Jul & Aug: by appt (071 375 26 68).*
A vast building in a style typical of the German Third Reich houses two interesting museums run by the University of Wrocław. The Geology Museum contains a wealth of rocks and fossils from different geological eras, while the Mineralogy Museum delights visitors with colourful displays of minerals collected from all over the world.

🏛 Natural History Museum

ul. Sienkiewicza 21. *Tel 071 375 41 45.* ◯ *9am–3pm Tue–Fri, 10am–4pm Sat & Sun.*
This museum, which is very popular with children, has a substantial collection of animals and plants from all continents. The collections of tropical butterflies, shells and mammal skeletons are the largest in Poland. Some date back to the 18th century, and formed the beginnings of the University's Zoological Museum, which was set up

in 1820. Since 1904 the exhibits have been displayed in a purpose-built wing of this Art Nouveau building.

🦌 Zoo

ul. Wróblewskiego. *Tel 071 348 30 24.* ◯ *9am–5pm daily (summer: to 6pm, to 7pm Sat & Sun).* www.zoo.wroclaw.pl
Wrocław has one of the largest and best laid-out zoos in Poland, thanks to its long-standing directors Hanna and Antoni Gucwińscy, who for many years presented a TV programme on animal photography. The zoo, founded in 1865, is situated above the River Odra opposite Szczytnicki Park. While walking among the animal paddocks, it is worth taking a look at the old pavilions, which feature a variety of architectural styles.

🏛 People's Hall

ul. Wystawowa 1. *Tel 071 347 51 00.* ◯ *9am–4pm, except during trade fairs and sports events.* 📷
The People's Hall (Hala Ludowa), originally known as the Century Hall, was intended to be the centre-piece of an exhibition commemorating the centenary of the coalition's victory over Napoleon at Lipsk. It was designed by Max Berg and built in 1911–13. At the time of its construction, it was regarded as one of the finest modern buildings in Europe. The centre of the hall is covered by a reinforced concrete dome with a diameter of 65 m (200 ft). It is lit by a sophisticated method – the openwork design inside the stepped tambour consists of rows of windows that can be shaded or uncovered as required. The auditorium can accommodate up to 5,000 people. The hall has functioned as a concert hall and theatre, and today is used for sports events and trade fairs. Around the hall are some of the pavilions of the Historical Exhibition. It is also worth walking through the old exhibition grounds

Ostrich in a paddock at Wrocław Zoo

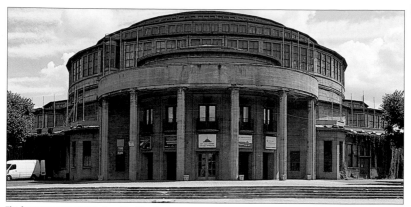

The former Century Hall designed by Max Berg

and seeing the oval pond, which is surrounded by shady pergolas. A steel needle 96 m (316 ft) in height made by Stanisław Hempel, stands outside the main entrance. It was erected here in 1948. The hall is a UNESCO World Heritage Site.

🍃 Szczytnicki Park

North of the exhibition area is an extensive park whose history dates back to the 18th century. It was originally the site of the residence of Duke Friedrich Ludwig von Hohenlohe-Ingelfingen, but that building was destroyed during the Napoleonic Wars (1799–1815), after which the area was remodelled as a landscaped park.

One of Szczytnicki Park's distinctive features is its delightful Japanese garden, which has been painstakingly restored with the help of Japanese gardening experts.

Japanese garden in Szczytnicki Park

The footbridges and pathways that run among the pavilions and plants make a charming setting for a leisurely walk. Look out for the rose garden and a small 12th-century wooden church that was brought over from Stare Koźle and reconstructed.

House designed by Hans Scharoun on the Mieszkanie i Miejsce Pracy housing estate

⛪ Mieszkanie i Miejsce Pracy Housing Estate

The Mieszkanie i Miejsce Pracy housing estate is a unique landmark in the development of residential architecture in the 1920s. The houses were examples of different residential buildings designed for the Exhibition of Living and Working Space organized by the Deutscher Werkbund movement in 1929. Many prominent German architects took part in the project. The most impressive building is an apartment block (at Ulica Kopernika 9) designed by Hans Scharoun, architect of several buildings in Berlin, including the National Library and the Berlin Philharmonic Orchestra's Concert Hall. Modern architecture enthusiasts should also visit Sępolno, which was built in 1924–8 and is a fine example of a garden city.

⛪ Jewish Cemetery

ul. Ślężna 37/39. **Tel** *071 791 59 03.*
⭕ *8am–dusk daily (to 6pm summer).*
🔲 *until noon.* ⚫ *Jewish holidays.*
This is one of the very few Jewish cemeteries in Poland that escaped destruction at the hands of the Nazis during World War II. Originally opened in 1856, it was the burial place of many celebrated citizens of Wrocław, including the socialist politician Ferdinand Lassalle, the painter Clara Sachs and the parents of Sister Theresa Benedicta of the Cross, who was born in Wrocław as Edith Stein.

Façade of the Cistercian church in Henryków

high altar, with *The Birth of Christ in the Vision of St Bernard of Clairvaux* by Michael Willmann, and the large, highly ornamented choir stalls. A plague column outside the church depicts the four archangels.

Other points of interest are the extensive monastery and the scenic park laid out at the rear of the monastery in the early 18th century. A summerhouse stands in the park.

towers and two internal piazzas, the castle has an ideal symmetry. Its magnificent ballroom has palm vaulting supported on a single central basalt column.

Unfortunately the palace's once superb art collection and library were destroyed just after World War II. Today the castle, while not yet wholly reconstructed, is open as a hotel. It stands in an attractive overgrown park.

Kłodzko Valley ㉗

See pp200–201.

Gothic town walls and tower in Paczków

Henryków ㉕

Road map C5. 🏘 *1,400.* 🚉 🚌
Cistercian Church pl. Cysterśow 1.
Tel *074 810 50 50.* ⬭ *Jul & Aug: daily; May, Jun, Sep: Sat & Sun.* 📷

The small town of Henryków is known for its **Cistercian church**, founded in 1227 by Henryk the Bearded. A series of allotments surrounding the abbey separate the church and monastery from the street, so that access to the church is by way of a series of gates. The church, originally in the Gothic style, was rebuilt in the early 14th century and remodelled in the Baroque style by Matthias Kirchberger in 1687–1702. Prominent features of the Baroque interior are the

Kamieniec Ząbkowicki ㉖

Road map B5. 🏘 *4,700.* 🚌 🚌

The small town of Kamieniec Ząbkowicki is dominated by the 14th-century Gothic church and Baroque monastery of its Cistercian abbey, which was founded in 1272.

There is also a Neo-Gothic **castle**, perched on a hill but well worth the effort of a climb to visit. It was commissioned by Marianna Orańska in the 1870s, and after her death was completed for her son, Duke Albrecht of Prussia. The architect was Karl Friedrich Schinkel. A massive residence with large circular external

Paczków ㉘

Road map B5. 🏘 *8,400.* 🚉 🚌
ℹ️ *Rynek 20 (077 431 67 90).*
www.paczkow.pl

Completely surrounded by a medieval wall set with towers and gates, Paczków has been dubbed the

Neo-Gothic castle in Kamieniec Ząbkowicki

"Carcassone of Silesia" after the medieval walled city in southwest France. Paczków was founded in 1254, and the old town retains its original street layout. It contains many distinctive town houses, a Neo-Classical town hall and the Church of St John (Kościół św Jana), an originally Gothic church that was rebuilt in the Renaissance style in 1529–36 and fortified for defensive purposes.

Otmuchów ㉙

Road map C5. 🏃 *5,400.* 🚊 🚌

Otmuchów has a picturesque setting between two lakes, Lake Głębinowskie and Lake Otmuchówskie. In spring and summer the town is filled with flowers, partly as the result of the spring flower festival that is held here.

From the 14th century until 1810, Otmuchów belonged to the bishops of Wrocław. Its historic buildings are all in close proximity around the sloping Market Square. On the lower side is the Renaissance town hall, built in 1538, with a later tower. On the upper side is the Baroque parish church of 1690–6, and the Palace of the Bishops of Wrocław. The adjacent palace, known as the Lower Castle, was the bishops' secondary residence.

The Beautiful Well in Nysa, with Baroque wrought ironwork

Nysa ㉚

Road map C5. 🏃 *48,000.* 🚊 🚌 ℹ️ *ul. Piastowska 19 (077 433 49 71).* **www**.nysa.pl

Nysa, founded in 1223, was once the capital of the dukes of Wrocław and the see of the duchy of Nysa (Niesse). In the 16th and 17th centuries it became the residence of the Catholic bishops of Wrocław, who were driven there from Ostrów Tumski during the Reformation. After 1742 the Prussians enclosed the town with ramparts. Despite suffering massive destruction during World War II, Nysa retains a number of interesting buildings. The town centre is dominated by the Gothic **Basilica of Saints James and Agnieszka** (Basilica św Jakuba i Agnieszki), with a separate belfry dating from the early 16th century. The well beside it, covered with unusual wrought ironwork, is known as the Beautiful Welland dates from 1686. Of

Renaissance town hall in Otmuchów

Nysa's many churches, the finest are the **Church of Saints Peter and Paul** (Św Piotra i Pawla) and the Jesuit **Church of the Assumption** (Wniebowzięcia NMP). Also of interest are the bishop's palace and manor, which stand beside a group of Jesuit buildings. The palace houses a local history museum.

🔒 Basilica of Saints James and Agnieszka
pl. Katedralny 7. **Tel** *077 433 25 05.*
A number of side chapels containing the tombs of bishops flank the lofty nave of this 14th–15th-century church (Kościół św Jakuba i św Agnieszki). The high altar only survived World War II because it was removed and hidden in the mountains.

🔒 Church of Saints Peter and Paul
ul. św Piotra. **Tel** *077 431 05 13.*
This late Baroque church (Kościół św Piotra i Pawła) was built by Michael Klein and Felix Anton Hammer-schmidt in 1719–27 for the Canons Regular of the Holy Sepulchre. Its original furnishings are intact. Entry is via the office of the seminary situated in the monastery.

🔒 Church of the Assumption
pl. Solny. ⬜ *daily.*
Jesuits were brought to Nysa by Bishop Karol Habsburg. This Baroque Jesuit church (Kościół Wniebowzięcia NMP), built in 1688–92, has a magnificent twin-towered façade. The interior features paintings by Karl Dankwart. It is one of a group of buildings known collectively as the Carolinum College.

🏛 Town Museum
pl. Bpa Jarosława 11. **Tel** *077 433 20 83.* ⬜ *9am–3pm Tue, Thu, Fri; 9am–5:30pm Wed; 10am–3pm Sat & Sun.* 📷 *(free Sat).* **www**.muzeum.nysa.pl
The Town Museum is located in the former bishop's palace, dating from 1660–80. It contains a fine collection of European painting, including pictures from the studios of Lucas Cranach the Elder (1472–1553) and Hugo van der Goes (c.1440–82).

Kłodzko Valley ⑳

The exceptionally beautiful Kłodzko Valley is renowned for its architecture and spas as well as for its scenery. A border region for many centuries, it is dotted with castles. Many dignitaries, attracted by its favourable climate and its mineral springs, built splendid residences here. The area has several well-equipped hiking trails, particularly on Góry Stołowe (Table Mountains), and a number of ski resorts.

Góry Stołowe ②
The Table Mountains are an unusual geological phenomenon – the strange shapes of the sandstone and marl hills were created by erosion. At Szczeliniec Wielki and Błędne Skały, fissures form natural mazes.

Wambierzyce ①
The village is an ancient place of pilgrimage. The Pilgrimage Church dates from 1695–1710, although its oval nave was built in 1715–20. In the village and nearby hills are more than 130 Stations of the Cross.

Kudowa Zdrój ③
The Chapel of Skulls (Kaplica czaszek) near Kudowa Zdrój was built in 1776. It contains 3,000 skulls and other bones of victims of the Thirty Years' War (1618–48) and ensuing plagues.

Duszniki Zdrój ④
Features of interest in this health spa are the Baroque pulpit in the Church of Saints Peter and Paul (Kościół św św Piotra i Pawła), by Michael Kössler, and the Museum of the Paper Industry.

Polanica Zdrój ⑤
Founded in the early 19th century, this spa is considered to be the most attractive in the whole Kłodzko Valley.

Kłodzko ⑪
The large 18th-century castle commands a panoramic view over the town. There is also a Gothic bridge with Baroque carving and an underground passage.

Kletno ⑨
Bear's Cave, the largest in the Sudeten range, has 3 km (2 miles) of subterranean passages on four different levels with stalactites and stalagmites in a variety of shapes.

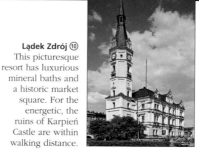

Lądek Zdrój ⑩
This picturesque resort has luxurious mineral baths and a historic market square. For the energetic, the ruins of Karpień Castle are within walking distance.

Międzygórze ⑧
This delightful resort at the foot of the Śnieżnik massif in the Wilczka River Valley is an ideal starting point for mountain hiking.

Bystrzyca Kłodzka ⑦
The town's Museum of Fire-Making is devoted to the manufacture of matches and cigarette lighters. The Gothic church that towers over the old town has an unusual double-nave interior.

WROCŁAW

Biała Lądecka

Stronie Ś

omaszków

0 km   5

0 miles   5

KEY

■ Hiking path

■ Other route

✵ Viewpoint

Gorzanów ⑥
The Renaissance-Baroque palace in Gorzanów dates from the 16th century. Its present form is the result of extensions carried out in the 17th century.

Opole 🔟

Road Map C5. 👥 126,000. 🚆 🚌
ℹ️ 077 441 25 22. 🎭 *Festival of Polish Song (Jun).* **www**.opole.pl

The origins of Opole, on the River Odra, go back to the 8th century. Once the seat of the Piast duchy, from 1327 it was ruled by Bohemia, from 1526 by Austria, and from 1742 by Prussia. Although it has been part of Poland only since 1945, it has always had a sizeable Polish population. The town hall was built in 1936 in imitation of the Palazzo Vecchio in Florence. Other notable buildings include the **Cathedral of the Holy Cross**, a Gothic church with a Baroque interior, and the late Gothic Franciscan church, containing the tombs of the dukes of Opole. On Piaseka Island, near the park's amphitheatre, stands the Piast Tower, all that remains of the Gothic ducal castle.

🏛 **Regional Museum**
ul. św Wojcecha 13. **Tel** 077 453 66 77. ☐ *9am–4pm Tue–Fri, 11am–5pm Sat & Sun (Jul–Sep: to 6pm Fri).* 🎫 *(free on Sat).* ♿

Góra Świętej Anny 🔟

Road Map C5. 🚌 *Leśnica.*
www.swanna.pl

Góra Świętej Anny is a place of pilgrimage for Catholics and a centre of commemoration of the Silesian uprisings of 1919–21. The great Pilgrimage Church of St Anne was built here by the Gaschin-Gaszyński family in the second half of the 1600s. The Stations of the Cross that make up the 18th-century Calvary are placed around the church and monastery. The Calvary draws large numbers of pilgrims.

During the Third Silesian Uprising in May and June 1921, two major battles were fought in the mountains near Góra Świętej Anny. They are commemorated by a commanding monument carved by Xawery Dunikowski in 1955 on the mountainside above a gigantic amphitheatre built in 1930–34. A **museum** contains records relating to the uprising.

🏛 **Museum of the Uprising**
Góra Świętej Anny. **Tel** 077 461 54 66. ☐ *9am–3pm Tue–Fri, 10am–4pm Sat, 11am–5pm Sun.* 🎫

Romanesque Rotunda of St Nicholas in Cieszyn

Cieszyn 🔟

Road Map D6. 👥 36,000. 🚆 🚌
ℹ️ 033 479 42 49. 🎭 *Viva il Canto Festival of Vocal Music (Jun); Cieszyńska Jazz Autumn Festival (Sep–Oct); Bez Granic Theatre Festival (Jun).* **www**.cieszyn.pl

This delightful town on the Czech-Polish border was founded in the 9th century. From the 13th to 17th centuries it was the capital of a Silesian duchy and in 1653 fell under Habsburg rule. On a hill where a castle once stood is the 11th-century Romanesque **Rotunda of St Nicholas** (Rotunda św Mikołaja), the Piast Tower, in the Gothic style, and a hunting palace built by Karol Habsburg in 1838.

The Market Square has some fine town houses and a Neo-Classical town hall. Cieszyn also has several churches, most importantly the Protestant **Church of Grace** (Kościół Łaski), of 1709.

The town is well kept, with a number of pedestrianized streets. Czech as well as Polish is heard in its homely pubs, bars and restaurants.

Pszczyna 🔟

Road Map D6. 👥 26,000. 🚆 🚌
ℹ️ *Brama Wybrańców (032 212 99 99).* **www**.pszczyna.info.pl

Pszczyna, on the edge of the ancient Pszczyna Forest, is named after a residence that was built within the walls of a Gothic castle in the area. The building, situated next to the forest and its wildlife, was used as a hunting lodge for many centuries.

The town hall in the Market Square in Opole

◁ **Góry Stołowe, the Table Mountains, overlooking Kłodzko Valley**

From 1846 Pszczyna was ruled by the Hochbergs of Książ (*see p185*). The **palace** was rebuilt for them in 1870–76 in the French Neo-Renaissance style.

Today the palace houses a **museum** with an interesting and well-stocked armoury, a collection of hunting trophies and a fine array of period furniture. The centrepiece of the palace is the extraordinary Hall of Mirrors, which contains two vast mirrors, each with a surface area of some 14 sq m (150 sq ft).

🏛 **Palace Museum**
ul. Brama Wybrańców 1. **Tel** *032 210 30 37.* ◯ *Jan–Mar & Nov–mid-Dec: Tue–Sun; Apr–Oct: daily. For opening hours, please consult the website.* ◉ *1 and 3 May, Easter, Corpus Christi, 1 and 11 Nov, 15–31 Dec.* 🏷 *(free on Mon Apr–Oct; Tue Nov–Mar).* **www**.zamek-pszczyna.pl

Portrait of Princess Daisy in the Palace Museum in Pszczyna

Upper Silesian Industrial Region ㉟

Road Map D5. 🚉 🚌

The vast conurbation of 14 towns that make up the Upper Silesian Industrial Region (Górnośląski Okręg Przemysłowy) was created by the coal-mining industry, which has been active in the area since the 18th century. The conurbation's hardworking inhabitants have their own unique dialect, which is spoken especially by the older generation.

Gliwice, one of 14 towns comprising the Upper Silesian Industrial Region

After World War I and following the three Silesian uprisings of 1919–21, almost the entire region was incorporated into Poland. Although the towns, with their mines, steelworks and power stations, seem unappealing, the region is of interest to tourists. Katowice, the capital, has particularly interesting buildings dating from the interwar years. In Kościusz Park stands a wooden church of 1510 that was moved here from Syryna, a Silesian village, as well as the **Archdiocesan Museum** and **Museum of Silesia**. The museum in Bytom has some interesting works of art. In Chorzów the main attraction is a park with a funfair. The **Upper Silesian Ethnographic Park** has a display of the traditional buildings of Upper Silesia.

🏛 **Archdiocesan Museum**
Katowice, ul. Jordana 39. **Tel** *519 546 023.* ◯ *2–6pm Tue & Thu; 2–5pm Sun.*
The museum has a collection of ecclesiastical art, the most outstanding piece being *Head of a Monk* by José de Ribera (1591–1652).

🏛 **Museum of Silesia**
Katowice, ul. Korfantego 3. **Tel** *032 779 93 00.* ◯ *10am–6pm Tue & Wed, 10am–7pm Thu, noon–4pm Fri, noon–6pm Sat; noon–5pm Sun.* **www**.muzeumslaskie.pl
Among the displays at the Silesian Museum is a collection of 19th and 20th-century Polish painting.

🏛 **Coal Museum**
Będzin, ul. Świerczewskiego 15. **Tel** *032 267 77 07.* **Castle and Palace** ◯ *9am–4pm Tue, Thu, Fri, 9am–5pm Wed (Nov–Mar: 8am–4pm), 9am–5pm Sat, 10am–3pm Sun (Jun–Sep: to 5pm).* **www**.zamek.bedzin.pl
Będzin Castle was founded by Kazimierz the Great. Constructed from roughly hewn boulders, it was erected in stages between 1250 and 1350. In 1834 it was restored in the romantic Neo-Gothic tradition by Franciszek Maria Lanci. The castle now houses the fascinating Coal Museum. Another branch of the museum is to be found in the Mieroszewski Palace.

Będzin Castle, now the home of the Coal Museum

For hotels and restaurants in this region see pp303–5 and pp321–3

WIELKOPOLSKA (GREATER POLAND)

Wielkopolska (Greater Poland) is the cradle of Polish statehood. It was here in the mid-10th century that the Polonians, the strongest of the Polish tribes, set up an enduring state structure. It was also in this region that the Piast dynasty, the first Polish dynasty, emerged to rule the country in the 10th century. The first two capitals of Poland, Gniezno and Poznań, lie in Wielkopolska.

During the Thirty Years' War of 1618–48, the region of Wielkopolska was settled by large numbers of dissenting Germans, particularly from neighbouring Silesia. The Protestant faith of the incomers set them apart from the existing inhabitants, who were Catholics.

During the Partitions of Poland, Wielkopolska was divided. Under the terms of the Congress of Vienna of 1815, the larger western part fell under Prussian rule, and the smaller eastern part came under Russian control. In the second half of the 19th century the Prussian part of Wielkopolska was subjected to repeated but unsuccessful campaigns of Germanization. Polish activists fought back in the courts and laid the economic foundations for the Polish section of the population. At the end of 1918, insurrection broke out in the western part of Wielkopolska and almost the entire region as it had been before the Partitions was reincorporated into the Polish state.

The inhabitants of Wielkopolska have a long-standing reputation for thrift and orderliness. The years of Soviet domination that followed World War II strained these qualities to the limit, although the local state-owned farms worked more efficiently than those in other parts of the country and many palaces and country mansions have survived in better condition than was the case elsewhere.

Poznań, the capital of Wielkopolska, abounds in historic buildings, as do other towns in the region. Almost every town, however small, contains something of interest. Wielkopolska maintains its identity: to this day the customs preserved in many of the region's towns and villages are distinct from those in other parts of Poland.

Old windmills in a typical Wielkopolska setting

◁ Anger, one of the vices depicted on the Romanesque columns of the Premonstratensian Church in Strzelno

Exploring Wielkopolska

Wielkopolska's extensive territory is mainly low-lying, but the landscape is far from monotonous. In the northern part of the region is a hilly area, with vast forests and lakes, that is ideal country for a walking or cycling holiday. Besides Poznań, the regional capital, other towns of interest include Gniezno, seat of an archbishopric and the first capital of Poland. In the area around Gniezno traces of the rise of Polish statehood can be seen on Ostrów Lednicki, in Strzelno, and in Kruszwica on Lake Gopło.

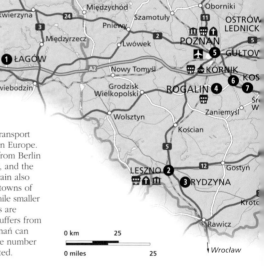

GETTING AROUND

Wielkopolska is situated on main transport routes between eastern and western Europe. The efficient express train service from Berlin to Poznań takes just under 3 hours, and the journey from Warsaw by express train also takes about 3 hours. All the larger towns of the region have rail connections, while smaller ones can be reached by bus. Roads are generally good, although Poznań suffers from almost permanent traffic jams. Poznań can also be reached by air, although the number of international connections is limited.

Skansen on Lake Lednicki

SIGHTS AT A GLANCE

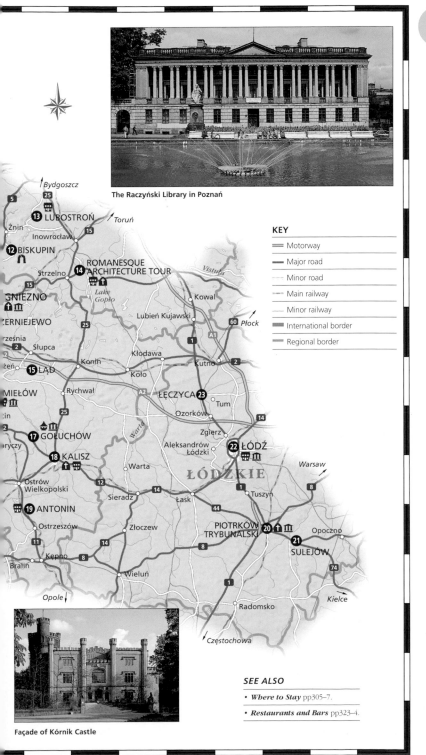

The Raczyński Library in Poznań

Bydgoszcz

5

25

13 LUBOSTROŃ

Toruń

Żnin

Inowrocław

15

12 BISKUPIN

Strzelno

14 ROMANESQUE ARCHITECTURE TOUR

15

Lake Gopło

Vistula

Kowal

GNIEZNO

Lubień Kujawski

60 Płock

ZERNIEJEWO

25

A1

rześnia

2

Słupca

Kłodawa

Kutno

żeń

Konin

Koło

2

15 LĄD

Rychwał

A2

ŁĘCZYCA **23**

Tum

MIEŁÓW

25

Ozorków

14

:in

Zgierz

2

17 GOŁUCHÓW

Aleksandrów Łódzki

22 ŁÓDŹ

ryczy

Warta

Warsaw

18 KALISZ

ŁÓDZKIE

Ostrów Wielkopolski

12

14

Sieradz

Łask

1

Tuszyn

8

19 ANTONIN

44

Ostrzeszów

Złoczew

PIOTRKÓW TRYBUNALSKI

20

Opoczno

11

14

8

21

Kępno

8

SULEJÓW

Braliń

Wieluń

74

1

Opole

Kielce

Radomsko

Częstochowa

KEY

▬▬ Motorway

▬ Major road

--- Minor road

-•- Main railway

— Minor railway

▬ International border

▬ Regional border

SEE ALSO

• *Where to Stay* pp305–7.

• *Restaurants and Bars* pp323–4.

Façade of Kórnik Castle

Łagów ❶

Road Map B3. 🏘 *1,600.* 🚉 🚌
🛈 *068 341 27 31.* 🎬 *Lubuskie Film Festival (Jun).* **www**.lagow.pl

Łagów, situated in woodland between lakes Łagów and Ciecz, is known for its film festival.

The tower of the 14th-century **castle** built by the Knights Hospitallers affords a magnificent view of the surrounding countryside, as does the 19th-century tower of the Neo-Classical Church of St John the Baptist (Kościoł św Jan Chrzciciela), dating from 1726. Around the town are also remains of the 15th-century town walls, with their gate towers, the Polish Gate and Marchian Gate.

Environs
Łagów Nature Park, near the town, contains protected areas of woodland and wild flowers.

About 16 km (10 miles) east of the town are the remains of a system of **fortifications** erected by the Germans just before World War II. Its surviving corridors and bunkers are now inhabited by thousands of bats.

Leszno ❷

Road Map B4. 🏘 *64,500.* 🚉 🚌
🛈 *ul. Słowiańska 24 (065 529 82 34).* 🎬 *Days of Leszno (May); Summer of Folklore (Aug).*
www.leszno.pl

In the 17th century Leszno gave asylum to religious dissidents fleeing the ravages of the Thirty Years' War (1618–48) in Silesia. Apart from Lutheran Protestants, they included a group known as the Bohemian Brethren, who founded the Arian Academy that gained renown across Europe. One of its members was Jan Amos Komeński (Commenius), a prominent philosopher of the Reformation.

The town was destroyed by fire in 1707, so that none

of its monumental buildings dates from earlier than the 18th century. The Baroque **town hall** was built just after the fire to a design by Pompeo Ferrari. Beside the market square is the distinctive Baroque **parish church**, built by Jan Catenaci at the turn of the 18th century. It has a delightful façade and interior with Baroque altars and tombs. Ferrari also designed the former Lutheran **Church of the Holy Cross** (Kościoł luterański św Krzyża), which was built after 1707.

The **Regional Museum's** finest collection is in the Polish Portrait Gallery, and features 18th-century coffin portraits of the Bohemian Brethren.

🏛 **Regional Museum**
pl. Metziga 17. **Tel** *065 529 61 40.* ◯ *9am–4:30pm Tue, 9am–2:30pm Wed–Fri, 10am–2pm Sat & Sun.* 🎟 *(free on Tue).*
Judaic section
ul. Narutowicza 31. **Tel** *065 529 61 43.* ◯ *9am–3pm Tue & Thu, 9am–2pm Wed & Fri, 10am–2pm first Sun of the month.* ● *Day after public holiday.* 🎟 *(free 1st Sun each month).*

Palace in Rydzyna, former seat of the Sułkowski family

Leszno's Baroque town hall

Rydzyna ❸

Road Map B4. 🏘 *2,700.* 🚌 🚉
www.rydzyna.pl

This small town is dominated by the **palace**, built in the 15th century. Its present late Baroque appearance dates from after 1737; further building work was carried out by Karl Martin Frantz in 1742, when paintings by Wilhelm Neunhertz were added to the ballroom ceiling. The ballroom was destroyed by fire in 1945.

The ceiling was painted in honour of the palace's owner, Prince Józef A. Sułkowski. A member of a noble family of relatively low rank, he was catapulted to success at the court of August III, but fell from the king's favour in 1738 and was replaced by Henryk Brühl. The palace remained in the possession of the Sułkowskis into the early 20th century, when it was sold to the Prussian rulers. It is now a hotel *(see p306).*

The Market Square is lined with Baroque houses, the **town hall** and two Baroque churches: the **Parish Church of St Stanisław** (Kościoł św Stanisława) designed by Karl Martin Frantz and Ignacy Graff in 1746–51, and the **Protestant church**, dating from 1779–83, also by Graff.

Rogalin ❹

See pp212–13.

Poznań ❺

See pp214–19.

A room with coffered ceiling and ornate floor in Kórnik Castle

Kórnik ❻

Road Map C3. 🏛 7,200. 🚉 🚌
www.kornik.pl

Set on an island and surrounded by a landscaped park, Kórnik Castle is one of the most picturesque castles in Poland. Its present appearance dates from the 19th century, when it was rebuilt in the English Neo-Gothic style by Karl Friedrich Schinkel. There have also been some subsequent alterations.

The castle's original interior survives: the Moorish Hall is decorated in the style of the Alhambra Palace in southern Spain and in the Dining Room the ceiling is covered with the coats of arms of all the Polish knights who fought at the Battle of Grunwald (1410). An inscription in Turkish on the ceiling of one hall is an expression of thanks to Turkey, which refused to recognize the partition of Poland. The castle also contains a collection of 18th- and 19th-century porcelain and other pieces.

The castle became the repository of the art treasures

Suit of armour, Kórnik Castle Museum

that were once kept at Czartoryski Palace in Puławy (*see p119*). In order to acquire the library at Puławy, Tytus Działyński persuaded his son Jan to marry Izabella, heiress to the Czartoryski fortune.

The castle has an extensive library and a museum. The museum's collections include a display of 16th to 19th century Polish and foreign paintings, as well as sculpture, drawings and an intriguing array of militaria, including a complete suit of armour. The **Kórnik Library** contains manuscripts of Polish poets' works and a substantial collection of prints and maps. There is also a

park that contains an arboretum with many rare species of trees, and a walk here is a relaxing way to round off a visit.

🏛 Kórnik Library
ul. Zamkowa 5. **Tel** 061 817 00 81 or 817 19 30. ☐ 8am–4pm Mon–Fri, 8am–1pm Sat. ● public hols, Easter, 1 Sep, Dec–Feb. **www**.bkpan.poznan.pl

Environs
There are several holiday villages scattered along the shores of lakes Kórnik and Bnin, to the south of Kórnik. The best known of them is **Zaniemyśl**, which boasts both a bathing beach and a holiday camp among its attractions. On Edward Island there is a 19th-century wooden pavilion built in the style of a Swiss chalet.

Koszuty ❼

Road Map C3. 🏛 400. 🚉 🚌

In an enchanting 18th-century country house, set in a landscaped garden, the interior of a Wielkopolska landowner's mansion has been reconstructed and is now the **Środa Land Museum**.

🏛 Środa Land Museum
Tel 061 285 10 23. ☐ 9am–3pm Tue–Fri, 10am–2pm Sat & Sun.

Environs
The town of **Środa Wielkopolska**, which is situated just 6 km (4 miles) east of Koszuty, has an interesting Gothic collegiate church dating from the 15th–16th centuries.

Country house in Koszuty dating from the 18th century

Raczyński Palace, Rogalin ❹

Rococo clock

Raczyński Palace, in the village of Rogalin, is one of the most magnificent buildings in Wielkopolska. It was begun in around 1770 for Kazimierz Raczyński, Palatine of Wielkopolska and Grand Marshal of the Crown. It was designed in the Baroque style, but during construction the architectural ornamentation was abandoned. The imposing main building, however, retains its late Baroque solidity. In 1782–3 curving colonnades were added and complemented by annexes in the classic Palladian style. A drawing room and grand staircase designed by Jan Chrystian Kamsetzer were added in 1788–9.

French Garden
The French garden at the palace's rear is elevated at one end to provide a view of the grounds.

★ Art Gallery
A pavilion built in 1909–12 contains a collection of European and Polish paintings dating from about 1850 to the early 20th century, including works by Jacek Malczewski and Jan Matejko.

The entrance courtyard is approached by a tree-lined drive and flanked by coach houses and stables. It also has riding stables on the northeast side.

0 m		100
0 yds		100

STAR FEATURES

★ Palace

★ Art Gallery

★ Palace
The main building of the late Baroque palace was given a more fashionable Neo-Classical character by the addition of curving colonnades.

Riding school

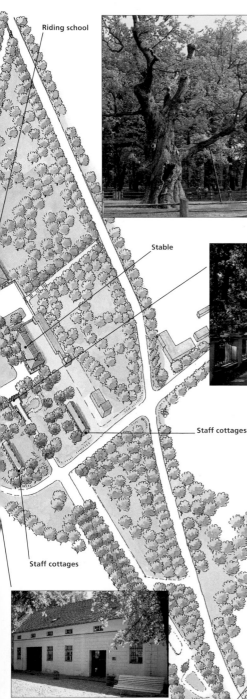

Stable

Staff cottages

Staff cottages

The Oaks of Rogalin
*Rogalin park contains one of the
largest protected oak woodlands
in Europe. The three largest trees
stand in the meadow off the
park's main avenue.*

Bridge and Gateway
*A three-arched bridge and a
wrought-iron gateway open
onto the entrance courtyard.*

Mausoleum Chapel
*Designed in the style of a
classical temple and built in
1817–20, the mausoleum
chapel contains the tombs of
prominent members of the
Raczyński family.*

The Coach House
*Built with the stables in around
1801, the coach house was
commissioned by Filip Raczyński.*

Poznań ❺

Poznań is the capital of Wielkopolska and its largest city. A stronghold by the name of Polan stood here in the 8th century, and in the 10th century it was the capital of the emerging Polish state. In 968 it became the seat of the first bishopric in Poland. Poznań has many historic buildings, the finest of which are the cathedral and those in the old town. A visit to the late 19th-century quarter is also rewarding. Today Poznań is Poland's second financial centre after Warsaw and a major centre of commerce. Annual trade fairs attended by producers and traders from all over the world have been held here since 1921.

Some of the houses in the Old Market Square were destroyed during the battles for Poznań in 1945, and were rebuilt after World War II, but others escaped serious damage. They include Mielżyński Palace, which dates from 1796–8, and **Działyński Palace**, both in the Neo-Classical style.

Interior of the former Dominican Church of the Heart of Jesus

🏛 Church of the Heart of Jesus

ul. Szewska 18.
Tel 061 852 50 76 or 853 33 59.
The Church of the Heart of Jesus (Kościół Serca Jezusowego), built in the 13th century, is the oldest church in the old town. It was a Dominican church until 1920, when it passed to the Jesuits. During the German occupation in World War II, a repository was set up here for Polish books removed from the libraries of Poznań.

🏛 Old Market Square

The **Old Market Square** (Stary Rynek) is the heart of the old town. It is surrounded by town houses with colourful façades, among which stands the Renaissance town hall. The ground floors of the buildings around the square are filled mainly by banks, cafés and restaurants, and the streets leading off the square contain elegant shops. From spring to autumn the square bustles with life, and the outdoor cafés with their tables and colourful sunshades are permanently busy. Local artists display their paintings, while children play on the steps of the town hall. The square is also a venue for cultural events.

🏛 Działyński Palace

Stary Rynek 78. *Tel 061 852 09 50.*
www.bkpan.poznan.pl
The palace was built in the late 18th century for Władysław Gurowski, Grand Marshal of Lithuania. The elegant Neo-Classical façade is crowned with a large eagle and set with figures of Roman soldiers made by Anton Höhne in 1785–7. It is worth going inside to see the columned Red Room upstairs. The building is now used as a library, theatre, exhibition and concert hall.

The Old Market Square in Poznań

The façade of Działyński Palace

CENTRAL POZNAŃ

🏛 Town Hall

Stary Rynek 1. **Museum of the History of Poznań Tel** 061 856 81 93. ☐ 9am–3pm Tue–Thu (Jun–Sep: 11am–5pm), noon–9pm Fri, 11am–6pm Sat & Sun. 🈯 (free on Sat). **www**.mnp.art.pl

Poznań's town hall is one of the finest municipal buildings in Europe. It was built in 1550–60 by the Italian architect Giovanni Battista di Quadro. The façade has three tiers of arcades, topped by a grand attic and a large tower and decorated with portraits of the kings of Poland.

The greatest tourist attraction is the clock tower, where at noon each day two clockwork goats emerge from doors 12 times to butt heads. The Great Hall, or Renaissance Hall, on the first floor was lavishly decorated to reflect the affluence of the city's municipal leaders. The coffered ceiling is covered with an intricate series of paintings. Other important collections can be seen in the Royal Hall and the Courtroom. The centrepiece of the Old Market Square is the Baroque **Proserpine Fountain** of 1766, depicting the abduction of the ancient Roman fertility goddess Proserpine by Pluto, ruler of the underworld. Nearby stands a copy of a stone **pillory** of 1535 and a 20th-century fountain with the figure of a Bamberka, a peasant woman from the Poznań area *(see p216)*. It commemorates the Catholic settlers who were sent to Poznań at the beginning of the 18th century from Bamberg, in southern Germany. Soon they became Polonized, although many of the city's inhabitants still claim to be descendants of the Bamberg settlers.

🔒 Church of Saints Mary Magdalene and Stanisław

ul. Gołębia 1.
Tel 061 852 69 50.

Construction work on this Baroque church, which was originally built for use as a Jesuit chapel, began in 1651 and continued for more than 50 years. Several architects, craftsmen and artists had a role in this extended project, among them Tomasso Poncino, Bartołomiej Wąsowski and Jan Catenaci.

The most impressive aspect of the church is probably its monolithic interior. Gigantic columns along the walls lead the eye towards the illuminated high altar, which was designed and constructed in 1727 by Pompeo Ferrari.

The Baroque buildings of a former Jesuit monastery and college stand close to the church. They were built for the brotherhood in 1701–33. Today, however, they are used for secular business by the members of Poznań's town council.

The Renaissance town hall, with its three tiers of loggias

Exploring Poznań

Bamberka statue in Poznań

Poznań holds much of interest beyond the old town. The Bernadine church in Plac Bernardyński has a remarkably narrow twin-towered façade built in the 18th century by Jan Steyner. It is matched by the former Lutheran Church of the Holy Cross (Kościół św Krzyża), dating from 1777–83. Walking towards the main railway station, you go through the town centre and across Plac Wolności, a square lined with shops and banks, then following Ulica św Marcina, where the old Kaiser's palace is located. The trade fair area can be seen on the other side of the railway.

♠ Przemysław Castle

Góra Przemysła 1. **Museum of Applied Art Tel** *061 856 81 83.* ◷ *9am–3pm Tue–Thu, noon–9pm Fri, 11am–6pm Sat & Sun.* 🎟 *(free on Sat).* www.mnp.art.pl
Little remains of the original castle built by Przemysław II in the 1200s. The reconstructed castle that now stands on the site houses the Museum of Applied Art, which holds a collection of everyday objects, decorative artifacts and religious items dating from the Middle Ages to the present. The Baroque **Franciscan church** on Ulica Góra Przemysła dates from the early 18th century. Frescoes by the Franciscan painter Adam Swach decorate the nave.

Statue of Hygeia, Greek goddess of health, outside the Raczyński Library

🏛 National Museum

al. Marcinkowskiego 9. **Tel** *061 856 80 00.* ◷ *9am–4pm Tue–Fri, 10am–5pm Sat & Sun.* 🎟 *(free on Sat).* www.mnp.art.pl
The National Museum is housed in what was originally the Prussian Friedrich Museum, a Neo-Renaissance building of 1900–1903. Its collections of Polish painting are among the best in Poland.

The Gallery of Polish Art includes medieval art of the 12th to 16th centuries and 17th to 18th-century coffin portraits *(see p29).* The best examples of painting of the Young Poland movement are the canvases of Jacek Malczewski (1854–1929). The Gallery of European Art, which is housed in its own wing of the museum, contains works from various collections, including that of Atanazy Raczyński, brother of the philanthropist Count Edward Raczyński *(see p212).* The most outstanding are by Dutch and Flemish painters including Joos van Cleve and Quentin Massys. Italian, French and Spanish painters are also represented.

🏛 Raczyński Library

pl. Wolności 19. **Tel** *061 852 94 42.* ◷ *9am–8pm Mon–Sat.* www.bracz.edu.pl
With its façade of columns, the Raczyński Library combines grandeur with elegance, and cannot be compared with any other building in Poznań. The idea for a library was initiated by Count Edward Raczyński in 1829. The aim of this visionary aristocrat was to turn Poznań into a "New Athens"; the library was to be a centre of culture and "a shrine of knowledge". Although the library's architect is unknown, it is thought to have been built by the French architects and designers Charles Percier and Pierre Fontaine. A seated **figure of Hygeia**, the ancient Greek goddess of health, with the features of Konstancja z Potockich, wife of Edward Raczyński, was installed in front of the library in 1906.

Another element of the "New Athens" of Poznań was to be a gallery (now non-existent) for the outstanding art collection owned by Edward Raczyński's brother, Atanazy *(see p212).*

🏛 Former Kaiser District

After the Second Partition of Poland in 1793, Poznań came under Prussian rule. In the second half of the 19th century, Prussia heightened its policy of Germanization in Wielkopolska. One of its instruments was the Deutscher Ostmarkenverein ("German Union of the Eastern Marches"), which the

The somewhat severe Neo-Renaissance façade of the National Museum

For hotels and restaurants in this region see pp305–7 and pp323–4

Poles called the "Hakata" colonization commission from the acronym of the initials of its founders. When the city's ring of 19th-century fortifications was demolished, a decision was made to use the space for government buildings. Designed by the German town planner Josef Stübben, they were built in 1903–14 and today stand amid gardens, squares and avenues, with a theatre, the colonization commission, a post office and the royal academy (now the university). Dominating the scene is the Kaiserhaus, designed by Franz Schwechten. The castle was rebuilt by the Germans, but little survives of its original splendour apart from a marble imperial throne and the décor of some of the rooms. The chairs from the Great Hall are now in the Sejm (parliament) in Warsaw. Today the Kaiserhaus accommodates the Kaiserhaus Cultural Centre.

Beside it, in Plac Mickiewicza, stands the Monument to the Victims of June 1956, which takes the form of two large crosses. The monument was unveiled in 1981 to commemorate the violent suppression of the workers' uprising in Poznań in 1956 *(see p52).*

The Opera, built in 1910, is flanked by statues of lions

churches face each other across a small square. One is the Discalced Carmelites' Church of St Joseph, built by Cristoforo Bonadura the Elder and Jan Catenaci in 1658–67. It contains the tomb of Mikołaj Jan Skrzetuski, who died in 1668 and on whom Henryk Sienkiewicz *(see p25)* based the hero of his historical saga *With Fire and Sword.*

The other is the small Gothic Church of St Adalbert, forming a pantheon with practically the same function as the Pauline Church on the Rock in Cracow *(see p143).* In the crypt are the remains of great figures in the history of Wielkopolska. They include Józef Wybicki (1747–1822), who wrote the Polish national anthem, and the Australian traveller and

scientist Paweł Edmund Strzelecki (1797–1873). A striking contrast to the rest of the building is the ultramodern glass, concrete and stainless steel entrance to the crypt, which was designed by Jerzy Gurawski in 1997.

The modern entrance to the crypt of the Church of St Adalbert

Monument to the Victims of June 1956

Hill of St Adalbert

The hill is said to be the spot where, 1,000 years ago, St Adalbert gave a sermon before setting off on his campaign to evangelize the Prussians. On the summit two

THE POZNAŃ TRADE FAIR

The trade fair area is in the city centre, the main entrance lying opposite Dworcowy Bridge. The Poznań International Trade Fair has been held here every year since 1921. It takes place in June, and for its duration the surrounding area is filled with an international throng of businessmen. If you visit at this time you will find that the local cafés and restaurants are often full and hotel accommodation can be extremely hard to come by.

The symbol of the Trade Fair is a steel needle erected over the lower part of the Upper Silesian Tower in 1955, the main part having been destroyed during World War II. When the tower was built in 1911, to a design by Hans Poelzig, it was considered by admiring critics to be a masterpiece of modern architecture in reinforced concrete.

The needle rising over the Poznań International Trade Fair

Poznań Cathedral

The first church, a pre-Romanesque basilica, was built in Poznań in 966, shortly after Poland adopted Christianity, and the first rulers of Poland were buried there. In 1034–8 the basilica was destroyed during pagan uprisings and the campaign of the Czech prince Brzetysław. It was then completely rebuilt in the Romanesque style. It was remodelled in the Gothic and Baroque periods, and after suffering war damage was restored to its earlier Gothic form. Vestiges of the pre-Romanesque and Romanesque churches can be seen in the crypt.

Coffin Portrait
The cathedral has a display of these portraits, which were used during funeral ceremonies in the 17th and 18th centuries.

Tomb of the Górka Family
The tomb of the Górkas, a prominent Wielkopolska family, was made in the Chapel of the Holy Cross by Girolamo Canavesi in 1574.

Main entrance

STAR FEATURES

★ Golden Chapel

★ Tomb of Bishop Benedykt Izdbieński

High Altar
The late Gothic polyptych on the high altar was probably carved in the workshop of Jacob Beinhart in Wrocław and painted in the Pasje studio of Upper Silesia. It was brought to the cathedral in 1952.

Gothic Church of St Mary, with the cathedral in the background

★ Tomb of Bishop Benedykt Izdbieński
The tomb was made by Jan Michałowicz of Urzędów, the most celebrated sculptor of the Polish Renaissance, in 1557–62.

★ Golden Chapel
The chapel, built in 1834–41, contains the tombs of two of Poland's first rulers, Mieszko I and Bolesław the Brave. Their statues were carved by Chrystian Rauch.

Ostrów Tumski Island
Ostrów Tumski Island is the oldest part of Poznań. In the 10th century it was the site of one of the first capital cities of the Polish state.

Today the island is dominated by the Gothic towers of the cathedral, which contains many fine works of art. Near the cathedral stands the small Gothic **Church of St Mary** (Kościół halowy NMP), which was built in the years 1431–48 for Bishop Andrzej Bniński by Hanusz Prusz, a pupil of the notable late medieval architect Heinrich Brunsberg.

Also of interest is the **Lubrański Academy**, the first institute of higher education to be established in Poznań. It was founded in 1518 by Bishop Jan Lubrański. Behind its inconspicuous façade lies a small arcaded Renaissance courtyard. The academy acquired its greatest renown in the early 16th century. One of its alumni was Jan Struś, a scientist and a prominent physician during the years of the Polish Renaissance.

In the gardens on the other side of Ulica ks. l. Posadzego stand a number of canons' and vicars' houses which are charming in appearance – if a little neglected. One of them contains the collections of the **Archdiocesan Museum**.

The late Gothic **Psalter**, which was built in around 1520 by Bishop Jan Lubrański, is another of Ostrów Tumski Island's notable buildings. Its fine stepped and recessed gables are enclosed by ogee arches.

Arcaded courtyard of Lubrański Academy

🏛 Archdiocesan Museum
ul. Lubrańskiego 1. **Tel** 061 852 61 95. ☐ 10am–5pm Tue–Fri, 9am–3pm Sat. ● public hols. 📷 📹
The superb collection of religious art on display in the Archdiocesan Museum includes examples of medieval painting and sculpture, pieces of Gothic embroidery and some fine *kontusz* sashes *(see pp28–9)*. The most important pieces in the museum are probably the *Madonna of Ołobok*, a Romanesque-Gothic statue dating from about 1310–29, and a fascinating group of coffin portraits *(see p29)*.

Façade of the Baroque and Neo-Classical palace in Gułtowy

Gułtowy ❽

Road Map C3. ⛰ 990. 🚉 🚌
Tel 061 852 61 56.
◯ by appointment only.

The pretty Baroque and Neo-Classical palace at Gułtowy was built in 1779–83 for Ignacy Bniński to a design by an unknown architect and subsequently altered by Ignacy Graff. The most striking feature of its interior is the two-tiered ballroom decorated with delicate trompe l'oeil paintings dating from about 1800.

Czerniejewo ❾

Road Map C3. ⛰ 2,600.
🚉 4.5 km (3 miles). 🚌
Palace Hotel Tel 061 427 30 30.
www.czerniejewo.pl

Czerniejewo has one of the finest Neo-Classical palaces in Wielkopolska. It was built for General Jan Lipski in 1771–80, and the monumental four-columned portico was added in 1789–91. Situated in a large park and connected to the town by a wide scenic avenue, it makes a grand impression. Within, the unusual circular ballroom is probably its finest feature. Today the palace is a hotel, a restaurant and a conference venue.

Ostrów Lednicki ❿

Road Map C3. 🚌 🚉
🚢 concides with opening hours for the Museum of the Firsts Piasts.
◯ 1 Nov–14 Apr.

The small island in Lake Lednickie has special significance as the place where Poland is believed to have adopted Christianity. In the 10th century a fortified town stood on the island, surrounded by earth ramparts enclosing the earliest known Christian buildings in Poland. Archaeologists have uncovered the foundations of a rotunda and a rectangular hall identified as a baptistery and palace. The remains of a church were also found.

The town is assumed to have been the seat of the Piasts (see pp38–9). The baptism of Poland, by which the country adopted Christianity, is believed to have taken place in this baptistery in 966.

🏛 **Museum of the First Piasts**
Lednogóra. **Tel** 061 427 50 10. ◯ 15 Feb–14 Apr: 9am–3pm Tue–Sun (from 10am Sun); 15–30 Apr & Jul– Oct: 9am–5pm Tue–Sun (from 10am Sun); May & Jun: 9am–6pm Tue–Sun (from 10am Sun). ● 1 Nov–14 Feb. 🖼
www.lednicamuzeum.pl

Gniezno ⓫

See pp222–3.

Biskupin ⓬

Road Map C3. 🚶 320. 🚌
ℹ 052 302 50 55. ◯ summer: 9am–6pm daily; winter: 9am–5pm daily. 🖼 🖼 Archaeology Gala (Sep).
www.biskupin.pl

The remains of a 2,500-year-old Iron Age fortified settlement can be seen on an island in Lake Biskupinskie. The settlement was built entirely of wood and was inhabited for about 150 years by people of the Lusatian culture. It was surrounded by a stockade and a wall of earth and wood 6 m (18 ft) high. Access was over a bridge and through a gateway. The wall enclosed more than 100 houses built in 13 terraces, and the streets were paved with wood. The population was about 1,000.

When the water level rose, the lake flooded the houses and covered the settlement with a layer of silt, so that the site was abandoned. It was rediscovered in 1934 by a local teacher, Walenty Szwajcer. It is the earliest known settlement in Poland and one of the most interesting prehistoric sites in the whole of Europe.

Some of the buildings have been reconstructed and there are pens with small ponies, goats and sheep similar to those that the inhabitants would have raised. The annual Archaeology Gala features exhibitions – of Iron Age hairstyles and archery, for example – and workshops where artifacts are made by prehistoric methods.

Reconstructed fortifications of the Iron Age lake settlement in Biskupin

Lubostroń ⑬

Road Map C3. 🚶 790. 🚌 **Tel** 052
384 46 23. **www**.palac-lubostron.pl

In 1795–1800 Fryderyk Józef Skórzewski, a landowner, commissioned Stanisław Zawadzki to build a palace in the Neo-Classical style here. It has a square floor plan with a central rotunda and columned porticos on all four sides, and is an outstanding imitation of the Villa Rotonda built in Vicenza, Italy, by the Italian Renaissance architect Andrea Palladio.

Lubostroń Palace has a rather severe and monumental appearance, but its interior is one of the finest surviving examples of Polish Neo-Classical architecture. It is decorated with a bas-relief depicting the history of the Wielkopolska region.

The palace is set in landscaped grounds which date from about 1800. Today it is used for conferences and also has guest rooms for hire.

Lubostroń Palace viewed from the courtyard

Romanesque Architecture Tour ⑭

See pp224–5.

Interior of the Baroque church in Ląd

Ląd ⑮

Road Map C3. 🚶 530. 🚌

Ląd was settled by Cistercian monks after 1193. The monastery retains a number of Romanesque and Gothic buildings, one of which contains a Gothic fresco of about 1372 commemorating the benefactors of the church. The Baroque church is considerably later. The twin-towered façade by Giuseppe Simone Belloti does not do justice to the ornately decorated nave, which was built in 1730–33. Commissioned by the abbot Mikołaj A. Łukomski, Pompeo Ferrari designed a single interior space covered by a large dome rising to a height of 36 m (119 ft); the paintings by Georg Wilhelm Neunhertz depict the Church Fathers during the land seizures and give visual expression to the methods by which the Counter-Reformation would triumph in Poland: by teaching and persuasion rather than by militancy.

Environs
In Ciążeń, 5 km (3 miles) west of Poznań, is a late Baroque bishop's palace, now owned by Poznań University Library. **Nadwarciański Nature Reserve** nearby is one of the world's most scenic refuges for wading and aquatic birds.

Śmiełów ⑯

Road Map C3. 🚌

The Neo-Classical palace in Śmiełów, built by Stanisław Zawadzki for Andrzej Ostroróg Gorzeński in 1797, is associated with the Romantic poet Adam Mickiewicz, who stayed here in 1831, hoping to cross into the annexed part of the country where the November Insurrection against Russian rule was taking place.

His plan failed, but the palace at Śmiełów, with its fine landscaped grounds, became the backdrop to Mickiewicz's love for Konstanta Łubieńska. Today, fittingly, the palace houses the **Adam Mickiewicz Museum**, dedicated to the poet's life and works and containing exhibits from the age of Romanticism.

🏛 **Adam Mickiewicz Museum**
Żerków.
Tel 062 740 31 64.
🕙 10am–4pm Tue–Sun.
🎟 (free on Sat).

Neo-Classical palace in Śmiełów, today the Adam Mickiewicz Museum

Gniezno ⑪

The 14th-century Gothic Cathedral of the Assumption (Archikatedra Wniebowzięcia NMP) stands on the site of two earlier churches. The first was a pre-Romanesque church built some time after 970, and the second a Romanesque church dating from the mid–11th century. When Princess Dąbrówka, wife of Mieszko I, was buried here in 977, Gniezno was the first capital of the Polonians. Its importance increased further when in 997 the relics of St Adalbert were laid in the church. From 1025 to the 14th century Poland's royal rulers were crowned in the cathedral.

Potocki Chapel
The chapel of Archbishop Teodor Potocki was built by Pompeo Ferrari in 1727–30. It is decorated with Baroque paintings by Mathias Johannes Mayer.

Baroque towers were reconstructed after the originals of 1779.

★ Tomb of Archbishop Zbigniew Oleśnicki
This tomb was carved in red marble by the late Gothic sculptor Veit Stoss in 1495.

★ Bronze Doors
The bronze doors of the cathedral, made in the late 12th century and depicting scenes from the life and martyrdom of St Adalbert, are among the finest examples of Romanesque art in Europe.

ST ADALBERT

St Adalbert (St Wojciech in Polish) was a bishop from Prague. In 977, at the suggestion of Bolesław the Brave, he left Poland for the heathen lands of Prussia, where he converted the inhabitants to Christianity but was martyred. Bolesław bought the saint's body from the Prussians, giving them in return its weight in gold, and laid the remains in Gniezno.

Pope Sylvester II acknowledged the bishop's martyrdom and canonized him.

In 1038, when the Czech prince Brzetysław invaded the city, the cathedral was sacked and the saint's relics taken to Prague.

Baptism of the Prussians, a scene from the cathedral doors

Exploring Gniezno

Besides its magnificent cathedral, Gniezno has many historic buildings and fine museums, making for a pleasant walk around the city. **Gniezno Archdiocesan Museum**, next to the cathedral, contains religious artifacts, including paintings, sculpture, textiles and coffin portraits (*see p29*). A smart street leads off the Market Square to the Gothic **Church of St John** (Kościół św Jana), which has 14th-century murals. It is hard to imagine that this small town was once the capital of the Polish nation. The history of the city is told in the **Museum of the Origins of the Polish State**, in Piast Park. In the park are the remains of a late medieval fortified town.

🏛 Gniezno Archdiocesan Museum

ul. Kolegiaty 2. **Tel** *061 426 37 78.*
◯ *May–Oct: 9am–5pm daily (to 4pm Sun); Nov–Apr: 9am–4pm Tue–Sat.* 🈳 *(free for clergy).*
This is an interesting museum containing various works of religious art, including a number of artifacts from the cathedral treasury.

🏛 Museum of the Origins of the Polish State

ul. Kostrzewskiego 1. **Tel** *061 426 46 41.* ◯ *9am–5pm Tue–Sun (Apr–Sep: to 6pm).* 🈳 *(free on Sun).* 🈳 🚻 www.mppp.pl
This interesting archaeological museum documents the early history of the town of Gniezno, as well as the period when it was the capital of Poland.

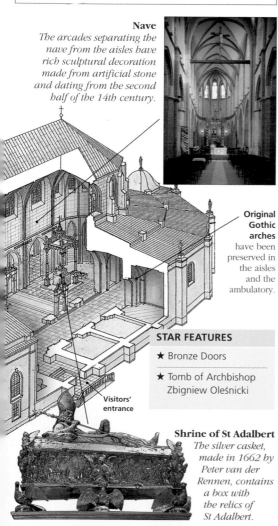

Nave

The arcades separating the nave from the aisles have rich sculptural decoration made from artificial stone and dating from the second half of the 14th century.

Original Gothic arches have been preserved in the aisles and the ambulatory.

STAR FEATURES

★ Bronze Doors

★ Tomb of Archbishop Zbigniew Oleśnicki

Visitors' entrance

Shrine of St Adalbert
The silver casket, made in 1662 by Peter van der Rennen, contains a box with the relics of St Adalbert.

Monument to Bolesław the Brave

Romanesque Architecture Tour ⑭

Sadly, few buildings survive in Wielkopolska from the earliest days of the Polish nation in the 10th century. For hundreds of years most building in Poland was in wood, and more durable brick or stone architecture was rare. A tour of pre-Romanesque and Romanesque buildings in Wielkopolska might start at Gniezno, then take in Trzemeszno and Mogilno. The finest Romanesque architecture in Poland is to be found in Strzelno – examples are the Rotunda of St Procopius and the Church of the Holy Trinity, with its remarkable Romanesque pillars. Another town of interest is Kruszwica, setting for the legend of King Popiel and home to the "Mouse Tower" of that tale.

Romanesque column in Strzelno

Gniezno ①
By the 14th century, Gniezno's Romanesque church had been replaced by a Gothic cathedral, but the bronze doors of the earlier building survive *(see pp222–3)*.

Trzemeszno ②
In the 12th century an order of Augustinian canons regular settled here on the site of a pre-Romanesque basilica and Benedictine monastery that had been demolished in 1038. In 1782–91 the church was rebuilt in the Baroque style.

POZNAŃ

Mogilno ③
The Benedictine church probably dates from the 11th century. After many phases of rebuilding it finally acquired a Baroque façade, although many Romanesque elements remain, in particular the crypt.

Strzelno ④
The Rotunda of St Procopius in Strzelno dates from the turn of the 13th century. In the Church of the Holy Trinity 12th-century carvings, discovered in 1946, depict personifications of the virtues and vices of Christian tradition.

Lake Gopło ⑦
This narrow lake is surrounded
mostly by marshy meadows.
It is home to many birds,
including bitterns, marsh
harriers, lapwings and
wild geese.

Kruszwica ⑥
Kruszwica was briefly the seat of a
bishopric and the mid-12th-century
Church of St Peter may well have been
its cathedral. The shell and the interior
of the church are built of granite
ashlars, which remarkably survive
almost in their original state.

KEY

■ Tour route

■ Other road

☀ Viewpoint

0 km   5

0 miles   5

Inowrocław ⑤
The most historic building in this health
resort is the Church of Our Lady, dating from
the turn of the 13th century, built in the time
of the dukes of Inowrocław.

THE LEGEND OF KING POPIEL

The legend of King Popiel was recorded
in the early 12th century by Gall Anonim,
the first Polish chronicler. According
to the legend, Siemowit Piast, founder
of the Piast dynasty, was a peasant
from Kruszwica. The
Polonians, terrified
by the atrocities
committed by their
king, Popiel, decided
to depose him and
chose Siemowit Piast
as his successor.
Popiel fled to his
tower but the rebels
turned into mice and
devoured him. The
Gothic tower
overlooking Lake

The Mouse Tower

Gopło in Kruszwica is called the "Mouse
Tower" but was in fact built in the 14th
century, a few hundred years after these
events were said to have taken place.

Castle in Gołuchów, home of the Działyński family

Gołuchów ⑰

Road Map C4. 🏯 1,500. 🚌
www.goluchow.pl

The castle at Gołuchów looks as if it belongs in the Loire Valley, in France, alongside the other Renaissance châteaux for which that region is celebrated. Although the castle at Gołuchów was built in the mid-16th to 17th centuries, its present exterior dates only from 1872–85, commissioned by the owners, Izabella Czartoryska and her husband, Jan Działyński. Izabella was the daughter of Adam Czartoryski, a Polish émigré leader in Paris, and was educated in France; her wish was to turn the residence into a "paradise on earth" according to her own tastes. She also built a museum that was open to the public. Initial plans for the renovation of the castle were made in around 1871 by the French architect Eugène Viollet-le-Duc. The rest of the castle was designed by his son-in-law, Maurice August Ouradou, after plans by Polish architects. Today the **castle museum** contains European and Oriental works

of art from the collection of the Działyński family.

🏛 Castle Museum
ul. Działyńskich 2. **Tel** 062 761 50 94. ⬜ 10am–4pm Tue–Sun (May–Sep: to 6pm Sun). 🎟 (free on Tue). 🖥 📷 www.mnp.art.pl

Environs
In **Dobryczy**, 23 km (14 miles) to the west of Gołuchów, is the Neo-Classical residence of Augustyn Gorzeński, a freemason, built in 1798–9.

Kalisz ⑱

Road Map C4. 🏯 106,000. 🚇 🚉 🛪 ul. Zamkowa (062 598 27 31). 🎭 Theatre Festival (May); International Jazz Festival (Nov–Dec). www.kalisz.pl

Kalisz, a settlement on the amber route between the Baltic Sea and Rome, has ancient origins. It is mentioned as Calisia by Ptolemy in his *Geography* of AD 142–7. However, a town did not grow up here until the 13th century, and it did not really develop until the 15th century, when Kalisz became a provincial capital. During the Partitions of Poland, Kalisz was the furthest outpost of the Russian empire. In 1914, just after the start of World War I, it was severely bombarded by Prussian artillery. Its rebuilding began in 1917, and the present city centre, with town houses surrounding the **Market Square**, the **town hall** and the Bogusławski Theatre, dates from that time. A substantial number of earlier buildings survive. These include the Gothic **Cathedral of St Nicholas** (Katedra św Mikołaja), the late Baroque collegiate **Church of the Assumption** (Kościół Wniebowzięcia NMP), and the neighbouring Mannerist **church**, formerly a Jesuit college. The group of Bernadine monasteries and

Bernadine church in Kalisz

the late Renaissance **Church of the Annunciation** (Kościół Nawiedzenia NMP) are also worth a visit.

🏛 **Cathedral of St Nicholas**
ul. Kanonicka 5.
Tel 062 757 39 19.

Antoni Radziwiłł's hunting lodge in Antonin

Antonin ⑲

Road Map C4. 🏠 *320.* 🚌 🚆
🎵 *Chopin Festival (Sep).*

When Duke Antoni Radziwiłł asked Karl Friedrich Schinkel to build him a hunting lodge, it was an unusual commission for the architect. The small larchwood building, dating from 1822–4, has a cruciform plan and an octagonal centre. The octagonal hall is surrounded by galleries supported by a large central pillar. It was here that, in 1827, Frédéric Chopin taught Wanda, Duke Radziwiłł's daughter, with whom he fell in love. Unfortunately, the piano on which the great composer played was chopped up for firewood by soldiers of the Red Army who were billeted in the lodge. It now houses a **Centre for Culture and Art**, and is the venue for concerts and festivals in honour of Chopin, as well as hunting balls.

🎭 **Centre for Culture and Art**
Pałac Myśliwski. *Tel* 062 734 83 00.
⊙ *7am–10pm daily.*

Environs
In the village of Bralin, 36 km (22 miles) north of Antonin, is a delightful wooden church called Na Pólku, dating from 1711.

Piotrków Trybunalski ⑳

Road Map D4. 🏠 *77,000.* 🚌 🚆
🚉 *Zamurowa 11 (044 732 60 51).*
www.piotrkow.pl

Before the partition of Poland, this was the town where sessions of the royal court and parliament were held, and after 1578 it was the seat of the Crown Tribunal. The town flourished and many magnificent churches bear witness to those times. Above **Tribunal Square** (Rynek Trybunalski) rises the brick tower and Baroque roof of the Gothic **Parish Church of St Jacob**. Synods and official ceremonies were conducted here. The large **Jesuit church**, dating from 1695–1727, contains remarkable *trompe l'oeil* paintings by Andrzej Ahorn, himself a Jesuit and a self-taught painter. The scheme includes a painting of a monk looking into the church through a painted grille. Other interesting churches include the **Piarist church and monastery**, now a Protestant church, a 17th-century **Dominican monastery complex** and the former **Dominican Church of Saints Jacek and Dorothy** (Kościół św Jacka i Doroty), with Rococo interior.

Detail from the castle in Piotrków Trybunalski

There is also a **Regional Museum** located in a Gothic-Renaissance castle that is essentially a large brick tower designed as a residence. The most interesting part of the museum is the exhibition of grand interiors of the 16th to 20th centuries.

🏛 **Regional Museum**
pl. Zamkowy 4. *Tel* 044 646 52 72.
⊙ *10am–3pm Tue–Sun (to 5pm Tue & Fri, to 4pm Sat).* ⊙ *pub hols & day after pub hols.* 🎫 *(free on Tue).* 🎥

🏛 **Church of St Jacob**
ul. Krakowskie Przedmieście 1.
Tel 044 646 51 40.

🏛 **Jesuit church**
ul. Pijarska 4. *Tel* 044 647 01 51.

Sulejów ㉑

Road Map D4. 🏠 *6,400.* 🚌
www.sulejow.pl

In 1177 a Cistercian abbey was founded here by Kazimierz the Just. The church was consecrated in 1232. It is in the Romanesque-Gothic style and has remained almost unaltered across the centuries, although the interior does contain Baroque altars and paintings in the same style.

The Romanesque portal in the west front bears what are said to be sword marks made by knights who in 1410 went to war with the Teutonic Knights. The monastery fell into ruin, although the remaining parts of it have been renovated and are now a hotel and **museum**. Near the abbey is a large artificial lake made in the 1970s on the River Pilica. It is a popular holiday spot.

🏛 **Regional Museum**
Tel 044 616 25 84.
⊙ *9am–6pm Mon–Sat.* 🎥

Cistercian abbey in Sulejów

Łódź ㉒

The centre of the Polish textile industry, Łódź developed at an astonishing rate as the industry thrived. Its population grew from just 15,000 in 1850 to more than half a million in 1914. It was a place of great contrasts, which were vividly documented in the novel *The Promised Land* (1899) by the Nobel Prize-winning author Władysław Reymont. The contrasts can still be seen in the architecture of the city, where vast fortunes and abject poverty existed side by side. Factories and opulent mansions sprang up in their hundreds, contrasting with the ramshackle homes of the factory workers.

VISITORS' CHECKLIST

Road map D4. 👥 *737,000.* 🚉
🚂 **Railway information** *Tel* 042 94 36. **Coach information** **PKS** *Tel* 042 631 97 06. ℹ *ul. Piotrkowska 87 (042 638 59 55).* 🎭 *International Ballet Festival (May).*

Exploring Łódź
The city's main thoroughfare is Ulica Piotrkowska, which is several kilometres long. Its most important section stretches from **Plac Wolności** to Aleje Piłudskiego. It is Poland's longest pedestrianized street and is lined with shops, cafés, restaurants and banks.

Behind the town houses, the brick factory buildings still stand, many of them now converted into stores. A noteworthy example is the one at **Piotrkowska 137/139**, built in 1907 for the cotton manufacturer Juliusz Kindermann by the architect Gustav Landau-Gutenteger, and featuring a gold mosaic frieze depicting an allegory of trade. In Plac Wolności is

Stained-glass window in Poznański Palace

a **Monument to Tadeusz Kościuszko** of 1930, rebuilt after its destruction in 1939 and a favourite meeting place for the city's youth. Beside it

stands the modest Neo-Classical **town hall**, which dates from 1827, when the foundations of industry were being laid in Łódź.

The city's **cemeteries** – the Catholic and Protestant cemeteries in Ulica Srebrzyńska and the Jewish cemetery in Ulica Bracka – contain some exceptionally interesting monuments that bear witness to the variety of cultures and nationalities that existed in Łódź before 1939, when it was a city with one of the largest Jewish populations in Europe. The grand mausoleums were built for local industrialists, who before 1914 were the wealthiest people in the Russian empire.

The **Leopold Kindermann Villa** at Ulica Wólczańska 31/33 is another Art Nouveau building designed by Gustav Landau-Gutenteger. It was built in 1902 and features fine

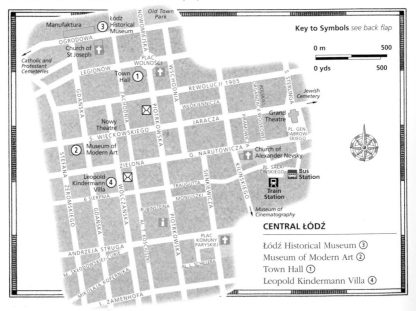

CENTRAL ŁÓDŹ

Key to Symbols *see back flap*

stained-glass windows. Today it houses an art gallery.

At the turn of the 20th century the townscape of Łódź was dominated by the industrialists' palaces. The finest surviving examples are the residences of the textile factory-owner Izrael Kalmano-wicz Poznański, at Ogrodowa 15 and Gdańska 36, and a remarkable palace at Plac Zwycięstwa 1 that rivals the one built by Karol Scheibler, the merchant celebrated as the "cotton king" of Poznań.

🏛 Łódź Historical Museum

ul. Ogrodowa 15. *Tel* 042 654 03 23. ⏰ 10am–2pm Mon, 10am–4pm Tue & Thu, 2–6pm Wed, 11am–6pm Sat & Sun. 📷 🎥 *(free on Sun)*. www.muzeum-lodz.pl

The museum is located in Poznański Palace, beside a large group of brick factory buildings. Alongside the palace stands a former spinning mill, a vast Neo-Renaissance edifice designed by Hilary Majewski in 1876. The eclectic palace, which has twin cupolas, was built in stages from 1888 onwards. Notable features of the interior are the grand staircase, the series of private apartments, the beautifully restored reception rooms, and the *belle époque* furniture.

Moorish stove in the Scheibler Palace, Łódź

Romanesque basilica at Tum, near Łęczyca

The museum contains exhibits associated with the pianists Władysław Kędra and Artur Rubinstein, who was born in Łódź.

🏛 Museum of Modern Art

ul. Więckowskiego 36. *Tel* 042 633 97 90. ⏰ noon–7pm Tue–Sun. 🎥 *(free on Thu)*. www.msl.org.pl

The Museum of Modern Art is housed in another of Izrael Poznański's palaces, this one built in imitation of a Florentine Renaissance palazzo.

Besides work by Poland's foremost modern painters, the museum also contains a collection of modern art, including works by Hans Arp, Piet Mondrian, Joseph Beuys and Max Ernst.

🏛 Museum of Cinematography

pl. Zwycięstwa 1. *Tel* 042 674 09 57. ⏰ 10am–5pm Tue, 9am–4pm Wed & Fri, 11am–6pm Thu, Sat & Sun. 📷 *(free on Tue)*. www.kinomuzeum.pl

Situated in the eclectic palace of Karol Scheibler, the muse-um contains a rich collection of films and film posters from the earliest days of cinema-tography to modern times. It also documents the works of Łódź's renowned film school, whose graduates include the directors Andrzej Wajda, Roman Polański, Krzysztof Kieślowski and Jerzy Skoli-mowski, and the much-praised cameraman Witold Sobociński.

Łęczyca ㉓

Road map D3. 🏛 15,100. 🚉 🚍

The royal castle at Łęczyca, built in 1357 by Kazimierz the Great, was the third fortified building to be raised in the town. Little is known about the first. The second was the seat of the rulers of another duchy.

The castle, with its brick tower, served as a jail for imprisoned aristocrats. The **Regional Museum** within it contains artifacts from prehistoric times to the present. The main attraction is the unusual exhibition dedicated to the devil Boruta, legendary guardian of the treasure hidden in the castle's cellar.

The devil Boruta at Łęczyca royal castle

🏛 Regional Museum

ul. Zamkowa 1. *Tel* 024 721 24 49 or 721 25 43. ⏰ May–Sep: 10am–5pm Tue–Sun (from 11am Sat & Sun); Oct–Apr: 10am–4pm Tue–Sun (to 5pm Tue, to 3pm Sat & Sun). 🚫 public hols. 📷 🎥

Environs

In **Tum**, 3 km (2 miles) from Łęczyca, is a splendidly pre-served Romanesque church. This granite building, conse-crated in 1161, was remodelled several times, but its current form is close to its original one. It consists of a triple-nave basilica with two circular and two square towers and an apse at the west and east ends. The west apse has a remarkable Romanesque fresco of *Christ in Glory*, painted in 1161.

For hotels and restaurants in this region see pp305–7 and pp323–4

GDAŃSK

*G*dańsk is among the finest cities of northern Europe, distinguished by beautiful buildings and a history that stretches back more than 1,000 years. For many centuries the wealthiest city in Poland, it was in 1939 the place where the first shots of World War II were fired. The end of the conflict brought destruction, but Gdańsk recovered as settlers moved in from other parts of Poland.

The earliest mention of Gdańsk occurs in 997. For more than 300 years it was the capital of a Slav duchy in Pomerania, and in 1308 it was taken over by the Teutonic Knights. Under their rule, the city grew.

In 1361 Gdańsk became a member of the Hanseatic League (a trade association of Baltic towns), further bolstering its economic development. From 1466 until the Second Partition in 1793, the city belonged to Poland; it was the country's largest Baltic port and an important centre of the grain and timber trade between Poland and the rest of Europe.

A wealthy city, Gdańsk played a pivotal role in the Polish Republic (see p42). It also became a major centre of the arts – goldsmiths fashioned fine jewellery for the royal courts of Europe, and the city's gemstone and amber workshops won great renown. From 1793 it was incorporated into Prussia, only becoming a free city under the Treaty of Versailles after World War I. It was almost totally destroyed during World War II, but a post-war rebuilding programme has restored many of the city's finest buildings and much of its historic atmosphere.

Today Gdańsk, attractively set between the coast and wooded hills, is renowned for its mercantile traditions and its openness to the world. Together with the coastal resort of Sopot and the port of Gdynia (see p263), it forms the conurbation known as Trójmiasto ("the Tri-City").

View of the main town of Gdańsk

◁ The Gdańsk Crane, the largest medieval port crane in Europe

Exploring Gdańsk

The most important buildings in terms of the history of Gdańsk are to be found in the city centre, which can be reached by taking a bus or tram to the Main Station (Dworzec Główny), the Highland Gate (Brama Wyżynna) or the Podwale Przedmiejskie, and continuing on foot from there. The bus, tram or urban railway (SKM) are all useful for travelling to outlying parts of the city. You can also take the SKM to reach Oliwa in the northwest, which has a fine group of cathedral buildings, one of which contains a famous organ, and a good park for walking.

View of Ulica Długie Pobrzeże on the River Motława

GETTING THERE

Gdańsk has good transport links. There are rail services to and from all the major cities in Poland – the express train from Warsaw takes just over 4 hours. There is an international airport at Rębiechowo, near Gdańsk. It is also easy to reach Gdańsk by car, whether from Warsaw (route E77), central Poland (route E75), Szczecin (route E28) or Berlin (route 22).

KEY

▮	Street-by-Street map *See pp234–5*
▮	Street-by-Street map *See pp240–41*
🅿	Parking
🛈	Tourist information
🚉	Railway station
⛴	Pier

0 m   300

0 yds   300

Church of St Catherine

LOCATOR MAP

SIGHTS AT A GLANCE

Museums and Galleries
National Museum p247 26
*Polish Maritime Museum
  p245* 23

Churches
Church of St Bridget 5
Church of St Catherine 4
Church of St Mary pp238–9 9
Church of the Holy Trinity 25
Oliwa Cathedral pp248–9 27

Historic Buildings
Arsenal 11
Artus Court 20
Gdańsk Crane 7
Golden Gate 14
Golden House 21
Great Mill 3
Green Gate 22
Highland Gate 12
Main Town Hall 18
Monument to the
  Shipyard Workers 1
Old Town Hall 2
Polish Post Office 6
Prison Tower 13
Royal Chapel 16
St George's Court 15
Uphagen House 17

Major Streets and Districts
Długi Targ 19
Spichlerze Island 24
Ulica Długa 16
Ulica Mariacka 8
Westerplatte 28
Wisłoujście Fortress 29

SEE ALSO

• **Where to Stay** p307.

• **Restaurants and Bars** pp324–5.

Street-by-Street: Along Raduna Canal

Despite wartime destruction, some fine buildings have survived on either side of the Raduna Canal. It was dug in about 1338, one of the greatest projects undertaken by the Teutonic Knights in Gdańsk, and for many centuries it was of great importance to the city's economy. The current in the canal was used to supply power for local mills, grindstones and a sawmill. Among the buildings look out for the Mannerist-style House of the Abbots of Pelplin, the Great Mill, which dates from the rule of the Teutonic Knights, and the enormous churches of St Catherine and St Bridget.

★ **Old Town Hall**
The Lord's Blessing in one of the rooms is from the ceiling of the house at Ulica Długa 39. It is ascribed to the workshop of 17th-century Pomeranian artist Hermann Hahn ❷

The Church of St Joseph is a former Carmelite church, built in 1482. After the devastation of World War II, it was rebuilt by the Church Fathers.

The Church of St Elizabeth was built in 1417 beside a *leprosorium*, or lepers' sanctuary.

Small Mill

RAJSKA

KORZENNA

ELŻBIETAŃSKA

NA PIASKACH

WIELKIE M

KOWALSKA

GARNCARSKA

House of the Abbots of Pelplin

★ **Great Mill**
Today this medieval brick mill houses a modern shopping centre ❸

STAR SIGHTS

★ Great Mill

★ Old Town Hall

★ St Catherine's Church

0 m   50

0 yds   50

LOCATOR MAP
See pp232–3

Church of St Bridget
This church was used as a place of worship by Solidarity members ❺

★ **St Catherine's Church**
The memorial to astronomer Johannes Hevelius (1611–87) was installed in 1780 by Daniel G. Davisson, his great grandson ❹

KEY
- - - Suggested route

Monument to the Shipyard Workers ❶

Plac Solidarności Robotniczej.
🚌 🚃 to Dworzec PKP.

The monument was built a few months after the famous Gdańsk Shipyard workers' strike of 1980 and the creation of the independent Solidarity trade union *(see p53)*. It was erected in honour of the shipyard workers who were killed during the strike and demonstrations of December 1970; it stands 30 m (100 ft) from the spot where the first three victims fell. Its three stainless steel crosses, 42 m (130 ft) high, were both a warning that such a tragedy might happen again and a symbol of remembrance and hope.

The monument was designed by the shipyard workers and a group of artists including Bogdan Pietruszka, Wiesław Szyślak, Robert Pepliński and Elżbieta Szczodrowska. It was built by a team of workers from the shipyard. In the 1980s, the cross was the rallying point for Solidarity demonstrations, which were suppressed by the police.

Monument to the Shipyard Workers

Old Town Hall ❷

Nadbałtyckie Centrum Kultury, ul. Korzenna 33/35. **Tel** 058 301 10 51.
♿ 📧 🍴 www.nck.org.pl

Built by Antonis van Opbergen in 1587–95, the Old Town Hall in Gdańsk is an outstanding example of Dutch Mannerist architecture. It is a compact, plain building with no distinctive ornamentation, and is equipped with a defence tower. The stone doorway was probably made by Willem van der Meer. Beneath each bracket are two distorted masks personifying vice, and two smiling, chubby masks, personifying virtue. Within the town hall, the painting, sculpture and furniture are very interesting, although little is left of the original decorative scheme of 1595. Of particular interest is the painted ceiling in one of the rooms which is by Hermann Hahn, a 17th-century Pomeranian artist. It was removed from a house at Ulica Długa 39 and transferred to the Old Town Hall some time after 1900. The theme of the ceiling paintings is allegorical: the central one depicts *The Lord's Blessing* and a figure of Zygmunt III Vasa also appears.

GDAŃSK SHIPYARD

The Gdańsk Shipyard is known throughout the world as the birthplace of Solidarity *(see p53)*. In December 1970, a shipyard workers' strike and protests in the city were crushed by the authorities. The next strike, in 1980, led to the establishment of the Independent Solidarity Trade Union. The strike leader was Lech Wałęsa, who was to become President of Poland (1990–5). Since 1989, in free market conditions, the shipyard has proved commercially unviable.

Main entrance to the Gdańsk Shipyard

The Great Mill from the Raduna Canal

Great Mill **❸**

ul. Wielkie Młyny 16. *Tel 058 305 24 05.* ☐ *10am–7pm Mon–Fri, 10am–4pm Sat.* ♿ 🚻 ⬆ 🎛

The Great Mill (Wielki Młyn) was one of the largest industrial buildings in medieval Europe. It was constructed during the rule of the Teutonic Knights, being completed in around 1350. It is built in brick and is crowned by a tall, steeply pitched roof.

At the front of the building stood a two-storey bakery with a chimney set against the gable of the mill which reached the height of its roof. Beside the mill stood 12, later 18, large poles to which millstones were attached for grinding various types of grain. The mill was destroyed by fire in 1945, but was restored after World War II. This remarkable old building now contains a modern shopping centre.

Church of St Catherine **❹**

ul. Profesorka 3. *Tel 058 301 15 95.*

The Church of St Catherine (Kościół św Katarzyny) is the oldest and also the most important parish church in the old town. It was built in 1227–39 by the dukes of Gdańsk-Pomerania and underwent major rebuilding in the 14th century.

Most of the Gothic, Mannerist and Baroque furnishings that the church once contained were pillaged

or destroyed in 1945. The most notable surviving pieces are the paintings by Anton Möller and Izaak van den Blocke, the Baroque memorials to various townspeople and the tombstone of the astronomer Johannes Hevelius, dating from 1659.

The tower, 76 m (250 ft) high, was first built in 1486. Demolished in 1944 and later rebuilt, it is once again a major landmark. It is well worth climbing to the top of the tower; the effort is rewarded by wonderful views of the city. The presbytery on the east side of the church has a fine late Gothic gable.

Gothic tower of the Church of St Catherine

Church of St Bridget **❺**

ul. Profesorska 17. *Tel 058 301 31 52.*

The Church of St Bridget (Kościół św Brygidy) was well known in Poland in the 1980s as a place of worship and sanctuary for members of Solidarity. It was built on the site of a 14th-century chapel dedicated to St Mary Magdalene, where

in 1374 the remains of the visionary St Bridget were displayed as they were being taken from Rome to Vadstena in Sweden. Soon afterwards a monastery for the Sisters of St Bridget was founded here. The church built beside it was completed in around 1514.

The brick shell of the Gothic church contrasts with the more recent belfry, built in 1653 by Peter Willer. The church's stark interior is an effective foil for the modern altars, tombstones and sculptures that it now contains. The most impressive of these are the high altar and the monument to Father Jerzy Popiełuszko, who was murdered in 1984 by Polish security service officials.

Polish Post Office **❻**

pl. Obrońców Poczty Polskiej 1/2. **Post Office Museum** *Tel 058 301 76 11.* ☐ *11am–3pm Mon, 10am–6pm Tue–Sun (from 11am Sun).* 📷 *(free on Mon).* **www**.mhmg.gda.pl

The Polish Post Office was the scene of some of the most dramatic events of the first days of World War II. At daybreak on 1 September 1939, German troops attacked the Polish Postal Administration that had its base here, in what was then the free city of Gdańsk. For 15 hours the postal workers resisted the onslaught, but they were finally overwhelmed. On 5 October more than 30 of them were executed by Nazi soldiers at the Zaspa Cemetery. Their heroism is commemorated in the Post Office Museum and by a monument depicting an injured postal worker atop scattered mail, handing over his rifle to Nike, Greek goddess of victory. It was designed by Wincenty Kućma in 1979 and bears an epitaph written by Maria and Zygfryd Korpalski in 1979.

Monument to Father Jerzy Popiełuszko in the Church of St Bridget

Ulica Mariacka, once the haunt of writers and artists

Gdańsk Crane ❼

ul. Szeroka 67/68. **Maritime Museum** *Tel 058 301 69 38.* ⬜ *Jul & Aug: 10am–6pm daily; Sep–Nov: 10am–4pm Tue–Sun; Dec–Jun: 10am–3pm Tue–Sun.* ⬤ *pub hols.* ▨ ✸ *www.*cmm.pl

The Gdańsk crane (Żuraw), icon of the city, is one of its finest buildings and a medieval structure almost unique in Europe. Built in the 14th century and renovated in 1442–4, when it acquired its present appearance, it combined the functions of a city gate and a port crane.

The crane, an entirely wooden structure, is set between two circular brick towers. It was operated by men working the huge treadmills within, and was capable of lifting weights of up to 2 tonnes to a height of 27 m (90 ft). The crane was used not only to load and unload goods but also in fitting masts to ships.

The crane was destroyed by fire in 1945. As part of the rebuilding programme after World War II it was repaired and reconstructed, together with its internal mechanism. It is now part of the collection of the Central Maritime Museum *(see p245).* The

Crane Tower looks out over Ulica Długie Pobrzeże, which runs alongside the River Motława. Once known as the Long Bridge, it was originally a wooden footbridge that functioned as a quay where ships from all over the world tied up. Today a fleet of yachts and small pleasure boats offering trips around the harbour in the Port of Gdańsk is moored here.

Ulica Mariacka ❽

Ulica Mariacka, regarded as Gdańsk's finest street, runs eastwards from the Church of St Mary to Długie Pobrzeże, terminating at the Mariacka Gate on the riverfront. Rebuilt from the ruins that resulted from World War II, the street contains outstanding examples of traditional Gdańsk architecture. Here, town houses that were once owned by wealthy merchants and goldsmiths have tall, richly ornamented façades; others are fronted by external raised terraces with ornamented parapets. It is small wonder that this picturesque street has for centuries inspired writers and artists.

The neighbourly porch gossip that once upon a time filled the evening air is sadly no more. Today, however, the street is a favourite haunt of lovers as well as tourists, most of whom are looking for picturesque subjects to photograph or browsing through the amber jewellery for which Ulica Mariacka is now celebrated. During the long summer evenings, a number of musicians provide free open-air concerts, and the welcoming street cafés stay open until late at night.

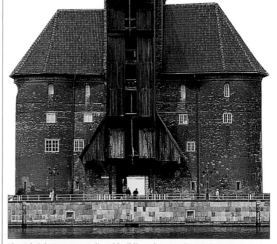

The Gdańsk Crane, a medieval building almost unique in Europe

Church of St Mary ➒

The Church of St Mary (Kościół Mariacki)
is the largest medieval brick-built church
in Europe. Building work began in 1343 and
took 150 years to complete. The final stage of
construction, involving the 100-m (325-ft) long
nave, was carried out by Henryk Hetzel. From
1529 to 1945, when it was destroyed, St Mary's
was a Protestant church. Like so many other
parts of Gdańsk, it was rebuilt
after World War II. The
interior contains furnishings
in the Gothic, Mannerist
and Baroque styles. Look
out for the memorial tablets
to prominent local families.

**★ Astronomical
Clock**
*The clock, made
by Hans
Dürunger in
1464–70, shows
the hour and also
the days, dates of
moveable feasts
and phases of the
moon. At noon
a procession
of figures
representing
Adam and Eve,
the Apostles, the
Three Kings and
Death appears.*

★ Tablet of Charity
*This ornate panel, made
by Anton Möller in
1607, once hung over
the church collection
box. Its purpose was
to encourage
churchgoers to
be generous.*

**★ Tablet of the
Ten Commandments**
*This panel of around
1480–90 depicts each of the
Ten Commandments in two
scenes, illustrating obedience
to and disregard of the laws.*

STAR FEATURES

★ Tablet of the Ten
  Commandments

★ Astronomical Clock

★ Tablet of Charity

The Beautiful Madonna of Gdańsk

The Chapel of St Anne contains this 15th-century figure of the Virgin and Child by an unknown artist.

Gothic Sacrarium

The sacrarium, in the shape of an open-work tower decorated with pinnacles, is over 8 m (26 ft) high.

Epitaph to Valentin von Karnitz

The memorial tablet to Valentyn von Karnitz, of around 1590, has many Dutch Mannerist features. The centre painting depicts the biblical tale of the Lamentation of Abel.

Royal Chapel ⑩

ul. św Ducha 58. *Tel 058 301 67 55.*

The Royal Chapel (Kaplica Królewska) was built by Jan III Sobieski as a place of worship for Catholics of the parish of St Mary's, which had become a Protestant church in 1529. The chapel was built in 1678–81 to designs by the great royal architect Tylman van Gameren.

The carving in the Kaplica Królewska is by Andreas Schlüter the Younger. The chapel itself is enclosed within a chamber and is situated on a raised floor. The interior is less ostentatious than the façade.

The Arsenal seen from Targ Węglowy

Arsenal ⑪

ul. Targ Węglowy 6. **Academy of Fine Arts** *Tel 058 301 28 01.* www.asp.gda.pl

The Arsenal is the finest example of the Dutch Mannerist style in Gdańsk. It was built, probably to plans by Antonis van Opbergen in collaboration with Jan Strakowski, in 1600–9.

Today the ground floor of the former weapons and ammunition store is filled with shops, while the Academy of Fine Arts occupies the upper storeys. The building has a finely decorated façade, with fascinatingly original carvings by Wilhelm Barth.

Street-by-Street: Długi Targ and Długa

Długi Targ and Ulica Długa, its continuation, are the most attractive streets in Gdańsk. Długi Targ leads westwards from the Green Gate on the River Motława to join Ulica Długa, which runs as far as the Golden Gate. These two pedestrianized streets are lined with old town houses that were once the residences of the city's wealthiest citizens. Most of the Main City's principal buildings, including the town hall and Artus Court, are on Długi Targ. Together the streets formed an avenue that was used for parades, ceremonies and sometimes public executions and from 1457 for the processions that accompanied royal visits – which is why the two streets were known as the Royal Way.

St George's Court
Built for the patricians of Gdańsk in 1487–98, the name derives from the exclusive Fraternity of St George, whose seat it was **15**

Highland Gate
The gate, built in 1574–5, has relief decoration with inscriptions and sculptures in the Italian Renaissance and northern Mannerist style **12**

Prison Tower
This was once used to hold prisoners sentenced to death. The tower currently houses the Amber Museum **13**

Golden Gate
This ceremonial gateway to the city, made in 1612–14 and surmounted by allegorical sculptures, embodies the spirit of Gdańsk's golden age **14**

STAR SIGHTS

★ Main Town Hall

★ Artus Court

★ Uphagen House

★ **Uphagen House**
The interior of this restored town house features 18th-century Rococo panelling, which survived wartime destruction **17**

For hotels and restaurants in this region see p307 and pp324–5

★ **Main Town Hall**
The Allegory of Justice *by Hans Vredeman de Vries decorates the main council chamber, also known as the Red Room* **18**

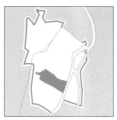

LOCATOR MAP
See pp232–3.

★ **Artus Court**
The bench of the Brotherhood of St Christopher, in this meeting house for dignitaries, is adorned with the story of Lot and his daughter by Laurentius Lauenstein **20**

Ulica Długa
Rebuilt after wartime destruction, this is the main street of old Gdańsk **16**

Golden House
The unusual façade of the house was once completely covered in gilt stone carvings **21**

Green Gate
This building in the Mannerist style was the official residence of the Polish kings when they came to Gdańsk on state visits **22**

Fountain of Neptune

| 0 m | 300 |
| 0 yds | 300 |

KEY

– – – Suggested route

Długi Targ
When the street was rebuilt after World War II, the houses and their stepped terraces were reconstructed **19**

The Highland Gate, part of the new fortifications of 1571–6

Highland Gate ⑫

ul. Wały Jagiellońskie.

The Highland Gate marks the beginning of the Royal Way that, following Ulica Długa and Długi Targ, descends eastwards to the Green Gate *(see p240)*. It was built by Hans Kramer of Saxony as part of the fortifications that were erected along the western limits of the city in 1571–6. Originally built in brick, the gate acquired its present appearance in 1588, when the Flemish architect Willem van den Blocke faced it with stone on its western side, making it look as if it were made of masonry blocks.

The upper level is decorated with cartouches containing coats of arms: that of Poland, held by two angels (on the breast of the eagle the coat of arms of Stanisław August, a bull calf, is visible) are flanked by the Prussian coat of arms, borne by unicorns, and those of Gdańsk, borne by lions.

Prison Tower ⑬

ul. Długa–Przedbramie. **Tel** 058 301 49 45. **Amber Museum** ☐ 10am–3pm Mon, 10am–6pm Tue–Sat, 11am–6pm Sun. 🎟 (free on Mon).

The mix of architectural styles in the Prison Tower is the result of several rebuildings. The tower was originally built as part of the now-destroyed Ulica Długa Gate that was erected in the second half of the 14th century as part of the medieval fortifications of the Main Town.

In the 15th and 16th centuries, the tower was heightened several times and the surrounding buildings altered accordingly. When the new fortifications were built in 1571–6 the entire complex lost its purpose. It began to be used as a prison, court and torture chamber.

It was remodelled for its new purpose in 1604 by Antonis van Opbergen, who gave it a northern Mannerist form, and by Willem van der Meer, who added decorative detail. The tower was the scene of many blood-curdling interrogations. There is a whipping post on the western wall, which was also the site of many executions. At the turn of the 20th century, in accordance with the new functions of the buildings, a stonecutter's workshop was installed in the courtyard.

The Prison Tower now houses the Amber Museum.

Golden Gate ⑭

ul. Długa.

The Golden Gate was built in 1612–14 on the site of the medieval Ulica Długa Gate. The architect, Abraham van den Blocke, devised the new construction in the style of a classical Roman triumphal arch through which the Royal Way would enter the city of Gdańsk.

The arches of the gate are framed by Ionic columns in the lower tier surmounted by composite columns in the upper tier. The gate is crowned with statues carved by Piotr Ringering in 1648 and reconstructed after the originals were damaged in World War II. The statues on the outer side of the gate, facing away from the city, depict peace, freedom, prosperity and glory, while those on the inner side, facing the city, represent prudence, piety, justice and harmony. The carved decoration is complemented by inscriptions in both Latin and German on the theme of civic virtue. The whole gate was designed and constructed in the Neo-Classical style but with Mannerist elements.

The Golden Gate, so called because of the gilding on its façade

St George's Court ⑮

ul. Targ Węglowy 27. 🌑 to visitors.

The fraternity of St George, an association of archers and the oldest of its kind in medieval Gdańsk, originally met in Artus Court. However, in 1487 the fraternity acquired its own premises, St George's Court, which was built under the direction of Hans Glothau in the Flemish style. It was completed in 1494.

The first floor contained an archery range and storerooms for archery equipment. Members of the fraternity met in the Great Hall on the first floor. The hall was also used for ceremonies, meetings and banquets and for the performance of plays.

In 1566 it was crowned by a figure of St George and the Dragon, which was removed and is now on display in the National Museum (the figure on the small tower is a copy). In the 19th century the building housed the School of Fine Art. Today Artus Court is the premises of the Gdańsk branch of the Association of Polish Architects.

The Red Room in the Main Town Hall

Looking down Ulica Długa from the Golden Gate to Długi Targ

Ulica Długa ⑯

Today, as in the past, Ulica Długa ("Long Street") is the Main Town's principal thoroughfare. The houses that line the street were once inhabited by the foremost burghers of Gdańsk, and virtually every one has its own colourful history. Although the oldest surviving houses on the street date from the Middle Ages, most were built during the heyday of the Hanseatic League.

With their narrow façades crowned by a variety of elements – from coats of arms and symbols to animals, allegorical figures and the heroes of classical mythology – the houses on Ulica Długa are typical of the architecture of Gdańsk. Unfortunately when they were modernized in the mid-19th century, all the stepped terraces that originally fronted the entrances to the houses were removed.

After the carnage of World War II, almost every building on Ulica Długa was left in ruins. Many of the houses were later reconstructed, but only the finest buildings were rebuilt in architectural detail.

Uphagen House ⑰

ul. Długa 12. *Tel 058 301 23 71.* **Part of the Museum of the History of Gdańsk** ◯ *11am–3pm Mon, 10am–6pm Tue–Sat, 11am–6pm Sun.* ▨ *(free Mon).* **www**.mhmg.gda.pl

The house that originally stood at Ulica Długa 12 was acquired by Johann Uphagen, a town councillor, in 1775. He had it demolished, and a new residence was built in its place. The architect, Johann Benjamin Dreyer, completed the project in 1787. The result was an attractive building combining Baroque, Rococo and early Neo-Classical features.

The sole ornamentation of the restrained façade is the Rococo decoration to the door, which is inscribed with the initial A, for Abigail, the owner's wife. The interiors, featuring Rococo and Neo-Classical elements, are splendid.

The Rococo doorway of Uphagen House

Main Town Hall ⑱

ul. Długa 47. **Museum of the History of Gdańsk** *Tel 058 767 91 00.* ◯ *11am–3pm Mon, 10am–6pm Tue–Sat, 11am–6pm Sun.* ▨ *(free Mon).* ▨ 🚹 **www**.mhmg.gda.pl

The city's first town hall was built after 1298 on the orders of Świętopełk II, Duke of Gdańsk-Pomerania. It functioned as an office of the Hanseatic League.

Work on the current building was begun in 1327. An elegant tower was added in 1486–8, during one of several phases of rebuilding. After a fire in 1556, this Gothic town hall was remodelled in the Mannerist style. The interior was lavishly decorated in 1593–1608 by the most prominent painters and craftsmen of the day, including Hans Vredeman de Vries, Izaak van den Blocke and Simon Herle. Their combined genius produced one of the finest town halls in all of northern Europe, proof of the city's wealth and power. It also served as a royal residence.

The highlight of the town hall is without doubt the Red Room, which was once the Great Council Chamber. The Renaissance fireplace is by Willem van der Meer and the centrepiece of the ceiling paintings is the *Apotheosis of Gdańsk* by Izaak van den Blocke. After being destroyed in 1945, the town hall was rebuilt and many of its furnishings reconstructed. It now houses the Museum of the History of Gdańsk.

Długi Targ ⑲

Długi Targ, a broad short street that runs on from Ulica Długa and terminates at the Green Gate on the River Motława, is the final part of the Royal Way leading from the Golden Gate through to the city centre. It also functioned as a marketplace as well as a site for the public execution of aristocratic prisoners. The townhouses on Długi Targ, like those elsewhere in the old town, were destroyed in 1945 but have been restored. Today the square is filled with souvenir shops. Its focal point is the Fountain of Neptune, which was installed outside Artus Court in 1633.

Fountain of Neptune in Długi Targ

St George killing the Dragon, a carving of 1485 in Artus Court

Artus Court ⑳

ul. Długi Targ 44. **Museum**
Tel 058 767 91 80. ☐ 11am–3pm
Mon, 10am–6pm Tue–Sat,
11am–6pm Sun. 🖳 (free on Mon).
🚫 🖾 🗋 👬

Artus Court was a meeting place for the wealthy burghers of Gdańsk, who were inspired by the chivalrous traditions of King Arthur and the Knights of the Round Table. Similar fraternities were set up throughout Europe, and they were particularly fashionable in the cities of the Hanseatic League. Visitors to the court came to discuss the issues of the day and to enjoy the fine beer that was served there in unlimited quantities. The first Artus Court in Gdańsk was established in the 14th century, but the original building was destroyed by fire in 1477. The present building opened in 1481. Its rear elevation preserves the building's original Gothic style, but the façade was twice rebuilt, first in 1552 and again in 1616–17 by Abraham van den Blocke. The interior furnishings were renewned several times, funded mainly by individual fraternities, who would gather for meetings seated on benches along the walls of the court. Despite wartime destruction, reconstruction has succeeded in recreating something of the court's historic atmosphere. A highlight of the interior is the intricately decorated 16th-century Renaissance tiled stove, 12 m (40 ft) high.

Golden House ㉑

ul. Długi Targ 41. ◉ to the public.

The Golden House, also known as Speimann House or Steffens House after its owners, was built in 1609–18 for Jan Speimann, mayor of Gdańsk and a wealthy merchant and patron of the arts, and his wife Maria Judyta.

The architect was Abraham van den Blocke, who also executed some of the stone carving. The most impressive feature of the house is its façade, which is covered in intricate gilt carvings, and which fortunately escaped the fires that ravaged the building in 1945.

Today the building houses the Maritime Institute. Local people claim that it is haunted; in one of the corridors the shining figure of the former lady of the house, Maria Judyta Speimann, is said to appear and can be heard whispering the words "A just deed fears no man".

Green Gate ㉒

ul. Długi Targ 24. ◉ to the public.

With its pinnacled roof and elaborate decorative stonework, the Green Gate hardly resembles the usual city gate – it is more like a mansion. There is good reason for this, because the gate was intended to serve as a residence for visiting royalty. In the event it was used in this way only once – when Maria Louisa Gonzaga arrived in Gdańsk from France in order to marry Władysław IV in 1646.

The gate was designed in the Mannerist style by the architect Johann Kramer from Dresden, and built in 1564–8 by Regnier from Amsterdam. Its windows provide a magnificent view of Ulica Długi Targ and the town hall in one direction, and the River Motława and Spichlerze Island in the other.

The Green Gate, not only a city gate but also a royal residence

Polish Maritime Museum ㉓

In the 17th century Poland strove to be "master of the Baltic Sea" and her seafarers were dedicated to maintaining Poland's maritime presence. The themes of the displays in the Maritime Museum are Gdańsk's seafaring traditions and navigation on the Vistula. Exhibits include a reconstruction of scenes from a sailor's life aboard the Swedish ship *Solen*, sunk at the Battle of Oliwa in 1627 and raised from the seabed in the Gulf of Gdańsk in 1970.

VISITORS' CHECKLIST

ul. Ołowianka 9–13. *Tel* 058 301 86 11. 🚌 106, 111, 138. ⏰ 10am–6pm daily (winter: 10am–4pm Tue–Sun). 🔴 pub hols. 📷 ♿ www.cmm.pl

Poles on the World's Seas
The Granaries contain waxwork exhibitions depicting the lives of Poles at sea.

Period Gdańsk
This reconstruction of a merchant's office is in the Harbour Town Life exhibition. It is part of the display in the Gdańsk Crane.

Maritime Culture Centre

Sołdek
The Sołdek, the first Polish oceangoing ship to be built after World War II, was built in the Gdańsk Shipyard in 1948. Its holds are now used for exhibitions.

MUSEUM GUIDE

The museum consists of several buildings either side of the River Motława, with the head office on Ołowianka Island. There is a Polish naval exhibition in the Gdańsk Crane. Skład Kolonialny hosts a collection of boats from distant parts of the world. The exhibition in the granaries is dedicated to Poland and Gdańsk at sea from the Middle Ages to the present.

Ferry
An easy way from one building to another is by ferry.

KEY

━ ━ ━ Suggested route

STAR FEATURE

★ Grain Warehouse

★ The Grain Warehouse
The naval weapons displayed here include 17th-century Polish and Ruthenic cannons, as well as cannons from the Swedish warship Solen.

Spichlerze Island ㉔

106, 111, 112, 138, 166, 178, 186. 🚋 *8, 13.*

Once joined to the mainland, Spichlerze Island was created when the New Motława Canal was dug in 1576. A centre of trade developed here at the end of the 13th century. What was then a relatively small number of granaries had grown to more than 300 by the 16th century. Each granary had a name and each façade was decorated with an individual emblem. The purpose of digging the canal, and thus of surrounding the district with water, was not only to protect the granaries against fire but also to safeguard their contents against thieves.

Everything was destroyed in 1945. Today a main road bisects the island, and the charred stumps that can still be seen in many places are all that remain of the granaries. The name signs on some ruins – such as Arche Noah ("Noah's Ark") on Ulica Żytnia ("Wheat Street") – remain legible. Reconstruction began several years ago. The first granaries to be rebuilt were those between the Motława and Ulica Chmielna ("Hop Street"). One of them is now the headquarters of ZUS, the Polish social security organization. Restoration of a group of buildings on Ulica Stągiewna was completed in 1999. Two 16th-century Gothic castle keeps, survivors of World War II, are in this street. They are known as the Stągwie Mleczne ("Milk Churns").

Chapel of St Anne, near the Church of the Holy Trinity

Church of the Holy Trinity ㉕

ul. św Trójcy 4. 🚋 *106, 111, 112, 138, 166, 178, 186.* 🚋 *8, 13.*

The imposing Church of the Holy Trinity (Kościół św Trójcy) was built by Franciscan monks in 1420–1514. In 1480, the Chapel of St Anne was constructed alongside the church. Protestantism quickly spread to Gdańsk, and one of its most ardent proponents in the region was the Franciscan friar Alexander Svenichen. When congregations declined because of Svenichen's activities, the Franciscans decided in 1556 to hand the monastery over to the city as

Monkey from the stalls of the Church of the Holy Trinity

a theological college. The head of the Franciscan order did not agree with the Gdańsk friars' decision to cede the monastery but the order's petitions to the Polish kings to have the property returned bore no result. As a result, the church was transferred to the Protestants. The grammar school that was established here later became the widely celebrated Academic Grammar School. It also came to house the first library in Gdańsk. However, centuries later in 1945 it was returned to the Catholics, after the violence of World War II had reduced it to a ruin.

The aisled church has a distinctive exterior with ornamental Gothic spires. They crown the elongated presbytery, the façade and the walls of the adjacent Chapel of St Anne. The presbytery, which was occupied by the friars, was separated from the aisles by a wall. Interesting features of the interior are the many tombstones that are set into the floor and the numerous works by Gdańsk artists. The very fine Gothic stalls were made by local craftsmen in 1510–11. Their carved decorations depict a wide variety of subjects, among them animals including a monkey, a lion fighting a dragon and several birds.

The church contains the oldest surviving pulpit in Gdańsk – it dates from 1541 and is another remarkable example of local wood carving. In the north aisle can be seen the marble tomb made by Abraham van den Blocke in 1597 for Giovanni Bernardo Bonifacio, Marquis d'Orii, a restless spirit and champion of the Reformation who founded the Gdańsk library. "Bones long since thrown ashore here finally rest from their earthly wanderings" reads the poetic Latin inscription.

Beside the church is a half-timbered galleried house dating from the 17th century.

The Milk Churns, two medieval keeps on Spichlerze Island

National Museum 26

The National Museum is laid out mainly in a former Gothic Franciscan monastery of 1422–1522. It contains a wealth of artifacts, from wrought-iron grilles to sculpture and painting. The museum's most prized piece is *The Last Judgement* by the Flemish painter Hans Memling (c.1430–94). In 1473, it was plundered by privateers from Gdańsk from a ship bound for Italy.

VISITORS' CHECKLIST

ul. Toruńska 1. **Tel** *058 301 68 04.*
106, 111, 112, 121, 138, 166, 178, 186. 8, 13. 10am–5pm Tue–Sun (Jun–Aug: noon–7pm Thu; Oct–Apr: 9am–4pm Tue–Fri, 10am–5pm Sat, Sun). (free Fri). www.mng.gda.pl

★ The Last Judgement
Hans Memling painted this monumental triptych in 1467–71. The left-hand side panel represents the Gates of Heaven, while the right-hand one shows the torments of Hell.

MUSEUM GUIDE
The exhibits on the ground floor include Gothic art and gold jewellery. The first floor has more recent paintings. The upper floor displays temporary exhibitions.

Longcase Clock
A Rococo clock made c.1750 is decorated with scenes from the biblical story of Tobias and the Raising of the Copper Snake.

"The Griffin's Talons"
This bison-horn cup was made in the 15th century and belonged to a sailing fraternity.

KEY

- Pomeranian medieval art
- Goldsmithery
- Metalwork
- Gdańsk and northern European furniture, 15th–18th centuries
- Ceramics
- Dutch and Flemish painting
- Gdańsk painting, 16th–18th centuries
- Polish painting, 19th and 20th centuries
- 19th-century Gdańsk artists (temporary exhibitions)
- Furniture-making in Gdańsk and eastern Pomerania in the 18th century
- The Last Judgement

STAR FEATURE
★ The Last Judgement

Oliwa Cathedral ㉗

Oliwa, a district to the northwest of Gdańsk, was once the base of wealthy Cistercians, who built a cathedral and monastery here. The present cathedral, built in the 14th century in the Gothic style, replaced the original 13th-century Romanesque church that was destroyed by fire in 1350. While the exterior has survived without major alteration, the interior has been redecorated in the Baroque style. Its famous organ can be heard in recitals.

The monastery buildings are now occupied by branches of the Diocesan, Ethnographical and Contemporary Art museums. Oliwa Park, with lakes and wooded hills, is a pleasant place for a walk.

Mannerist Stalls
The stalls in the chancel, decorated with bas-reliefs of the Apostles, were made in 1604.

The former high altar, built in 1604–6, has a depiction of the Holy Trinity.

Tomb of the Kos Family
The tomb was carved in around 1599, probably by the prominent Gdańsk sculptor Willem van den Blocke.

Main entrance

★ Organ Loft
The organ loft was made by local Cistercian monks in 1763–88. The organ, made by Jan Wulff and Fryderyk Rudolf Dalitz and completed in 1793, was the largest in Europe at the time.

STAR FEATURES

★ Organ Loft

★ High Altar

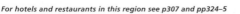

Portrait Gallery
*Portraits of Polish kings
and Pomeranian dukes,
the founders and
benefactors of the
cathedral, hang in
the presbytery.
They were
painted by
Hermann
Hahn in
1613.*

★ High Altar
*Thought to be by
Andreas Schlüter, it was
decorated by Andreas
Stech with images
of the Virgin and
St Bernard, patrons of
the monastery at Oliwa.*

The Monument to the Defenders
of Westerplatte

Westerplatte ㉘

🚋 106, 158, 606. Ferries in
summer season at Green Gate.
Guardhouse No 1 Museum ul. Mjr.
H. Sucharskiego. *Tel 058 343 69 72.*
◯ Apr–Nov: 9am–4pm daily
(Jun–Sep: to 7pm).

It was at Westerplatte that the
first shots of World War II
were fired, on 1 September
1939. The German battleship
Schleswig Holstein opened fire
on Polish ammunition dumps
in the Free City of Gdańsk.
The Germans expected the
capture of the Westerplatte to
take a matter of hours, but the
182-man garrison under Major
Henryk Sucharski resisted for
seven days, their heroism
becoming a symbol of Polish
resistance in the struggle
against the Nazi invasion.

Today ruined barracks and
concrete bunkers, together
with a huge Monument to the
Defenders of Westerplatte
unveiled in 1966, bear
witness to that struggle.

Wisłoujście Fortress ㉙

ul. Stara Twierdza 1.
Tel 058 531 22 44. 🚋 106, 606.
◯ 10am–7pm daily.

Fortifications were first built
on this strategic point at
the mouth of the River Vistula
in the time of the Teutonic
Knights. Work on the
construction of a brick tower
began in 1482. From here, a
duty was levied on passing
ships using a simple
enforcement method that was
impossible to avoid – a chain
was stretched across the river,
preventing the ship's passage,
and released only when the
captain had made the
required payment. Equipped
with a brazier in which a fire
was lit, the tower was also
used as a lighthouse.

In 1562–3 the tower was
surrounded by a system of
defences, and afterwards
was repeatedly fortified
and refortified as military
technology advanced. In
1586–7 the entire complex
was reinforced by four
bastions, designed by Antonis
van Opbergen and Jan
Strakowski, and an outer
moat was added. This was
followed by the addition of a
ditch in 1624–6. Also in the
17th century, 15 tall barrack
buildings were added around
the now-ageing tower.

Over the following years,
constant building, often
by prominent fortification
engineers of the time, steadily
enlarged the fortress. It
withstood several sieges
and was often used to
accommodate visiting royalty.

Wisłoujście Fortress, which once defended the mouth of the River Vistula

POMERANIA

Beautiful beaches and the resorts of the Baltic are Pomerania's main attractions, which every summer draw large numbers of holiday-makers in search of sand and sun. A less crowded but equally attractive aspect of the region are the Drawsko Lakes and the alpine scenery of Szwajcaria Kaszubska, west of Gdańsk.

Polish Pomerania is divided into the two regions of Western and Eastern Pomerania, each with an ethnically diverse population. The border between the two regions is in the districts of Bytów and Lębork.

Christianity was introduced to Western Pomerania by Bishop Otto of Bamberg, who founded a bishopric in Wolin in 1140. The Duchy of Pomerania, established in the 12th century, maintained its independence for several centuries and secured its economic development through the strength of its port cities, which were part of the Hanseatic League. The Thirty Years' War (1618–48) and the death of the last duke of the Gryfici dynasty brought this independence to an end. Most of Western Pomerania came under the rule of Brandenburg, while Szczecin and the surrounding area was engulfed by Sweden until 1713. In the 18th and 19th centuries, Western Pomerania became first Prussian, then German, territory. It was returned to Poland in 1945.

Eastern Pomerania was Christianized in the 10th century. Although it originally belonged to Poland, it became an independent duchy from the 12th century. Overrun by the Teutonic Knights in 1306, it then enjoyed strong economic development. In 1466, after the Second Peace of Toruń, areas of Eastern Pomerania, including Royal Prussia, were ceded to Poland. However, during the Partitions of Poland *(see p46)*, Eastern Pomerania became part of Prussia. It was finally returned to Poland in 1919. Gdańsk was given the status of a free city and only became part of Poland in 1945.

Pomerania's landscape was formed by the movement of glaciers. Its hilly countryside with small, clear lakes and its varied Baltic coastline make the region outstandingly beautiful.

Malbork Castle, the great fortress of the Teutonic Knights, on the River Nogat

◁ **Wild cliffs on Pomerania's Baltic coast**

Exploring Pomerania

Pomerania is one of Poland's most attractive regions, and in summer resorts such as Międzyzdroje, Kołobrzeg, Ustka, Łeba and Sopot teem with sunbathers and watersports enthusiasts. The most popular holiday spots are on the Hel Peninsula, where swimmers can choose between the open waters of the Baltic Sea or the calm of the Gulf of Gdańsk. For sightseeing at a slower pace there are the villages of Kashubia. The shady, tree-lined lanes in the region of Słupsk and Koszalin make for enjoyable cycle tours, while the clean rivers are attractive for canoeing. Those with an interest in history will not be disappointed with the great variety of historic buildings, from castles and cathedrals to small village churches and the stately houses of old seaside resorts.

A half-timbered house, typical of the Gdańsk region, in Różyny

GETTING AROUND

Szczecin and Gdańsk can be reached by air *(see pp352–3)*. The best way to tour Pomerania is by car. The E28 connects Gdańsk with Słupsk, Koszalin and Szczecin. Parallel to it but further to the south is route 22, which is part of the old German A1 from Berlin to Kaliningrad (Królewiec). The E75 goes south from Gdańsk to Gniew. All larger towns and cities have rail links. In the Gulf of Gdańsk there are also ferries to Sopot and Hel.

Fishermen's buoys on a Baltic beach

KEY

▬▬	Motorway
▬▬	Main road
▬▬	Minor road
┅┅	Main railway
──	Minor railway
▬▬	International border
▬▬	Regional border

For additional map symbols *see back flap*

SEE ALSO

- **Where to Stay** pp308–10.

- **Restaurants and Bars** pp325–6.

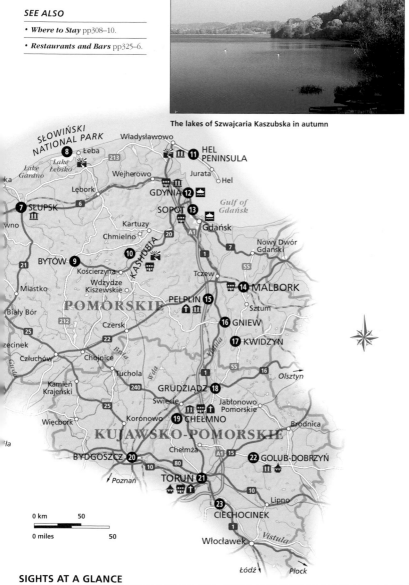

The lakes of Szwajcaria Kaszubska in autumn

SIGHTS AT A GLANCE

Szczecin ❶

Szczecin, on the river Odra, is a major port even though it is more than 65 km (40 miles) from the sea. It serves both ocean-going vessels and river traffic, and is linked with Berlin by the Odra and by canals. A castle and a fishing village existed here in the 9th century. Szczecin was granted a municipal charter in 1243 and soon after it joined the Hanseatic League. It became the capital of a Pomeranian duchy and in 1673–1713 was overrun by the Swedes. Under Prussian rule it became a major port. The city suffered severely during World War II; post-war restoration has been confined to its more important buildings.

The Gate of Prussian Homage, once known as the Royal Gate

The Castle of the Dukes of Pomerania, rebuilt in the Renaissance style

Exploring Szczecin

The old town of Szczecin is picturesquely laid out on a steep escarpment. The large **Castle of the Dukes of Pomerania** was founded in the mid-13th century and was rebuilt in the Renaissance style by Guglielmo di Zaccharia in 1575–7. It consists of five wings, with two interior courtyards and two towers. The east wing dates from the 17th century. After damage suffered during World War II, the castle was almost completely rebuilt and its once-magnificent interior re-created. The basement of the east wing houses the **Castle Museum**. In a Baroque building near the castle is the main section of the **National Museum**. From the

castle balcony overlooking the Odra, the **Tower of the Seven Cloaks**, the only remaining part of the city's medieval fortifications, can be seen. Across the road is the **Gate of Prussian Homage**, formerly the Royal Gate, one of a pair that was built under Swedish rule in 1726–8. The architect was Gerhard Cornelius de Wallrawe, and the sculptor Berhold Damart. North of the castle is the red-brick late Gothic **Church of Saints Peter and Paul** (Kościół św św Piotra i Pawła), while further along the banks of the Odra is **Ulica Wały Chrobrego**. This boulevard, an impressive municipal project of 1902–13, was known in German times as the Hakenterrasse

("Haken's Terrace") in honour of the mayor who initiated it. One of the buildings on the boulevard houses the **Maritime Museum**. From the terraces, with their decorative pavilions and a statue of *Hercules Fighting the Centaur* by Ludwig Manzel, there is a fine view of the harbour below.

North of the castle stands **Loitz House**, a sumptuous late Gothic town house built for the Loitz banking family in 1547. Further down, among the newly built townhouses in the old style, is the mainly 15th-century Baroque **town hall**. It houses the **Szczecin History Museum**. The **Cathedral of St James** (Katedra św Jakuba) was also rebuilt after almost complete wartime destruction; only the presbytery and west tower survived the bombing. It was originally erected in stages from the late 13th to the 15th centuries, with the involvement of the architect Heinrich Brunsberg. The cathedral has several Gothic altars origin-ating from other churches in Pomerania. From the cathedral it is possible to

View of Ulica Wały Chrobrego, with the Maritime Museum and local government offices in the distance

For hotels and restaurants in this region see pp308-10 and pp325-6

walk southwards towards the Gothic Church of St John (Kościoł św Jana), founded by the Franciscans, or to wander through the part of the city stretching out to the west that was built in the late 19th century. Many town houses and villas in a variety of styles have been preserved here, and the area has numerous bars and restaurants.

🏛 National Museum

ul. Staromłyńska 27. **Tel** *091 431 52 00.* ☐ *10am–6pm Tue–Fri, 10am–4pm Sat & Sun.* 🎫 *(free on Thu).*
www.muzeum.szczecin.pl
The museum's extensive collections comprise artifacts

Loitz House, once the home of a family of bankers

mainly from Western Pomerania. Among the many interesting exhibits are the displays of Gothic ecclesiastical art and jewellery and the ornate costumes of Pomeranian princes.

🏛 Maritime Museum

ul. Wały Chrobrego 3.
Tel *091 431 52 67.*
☐ *10am–6pm Tue–Fri, 10am–4pm Sat & Sun.* 🎫 *(free on Thu).*
www.muzeum.szczecin.pl
The museum's principal theme is the history of seafaring in the Baltic sea. The archaeological displays include amber and silver jewellery and a medieval boat. There are also models of ships, nautical instruments and an ethnographical section. Boats and fishing vessels are displayed in a *skansen* behind the museum.

🏛 Castle Museum

ul. Korsarzy 34. **Tel** *091 433 88 41.*
☐ *10am–6pm Tue–Sun.* 🎫
www.zamek.szczecin.pl
This museum is housed in the former crypt of the dukes of Pomerania. Among the exhibits are the tin coffins of the last of the Gryfici dynasty, and a special exhibition on the history and the restoration of the castle.

Portal of the Cathedral of St James

🏛 Szczecin History Museum

ul. Mściwoja 8. **Tel** *091 431 52 59.*
☐ *10am–6pm Tue–Fri, 10am–4pm Sat & Sun.* 🎫 *(free on Thu).*

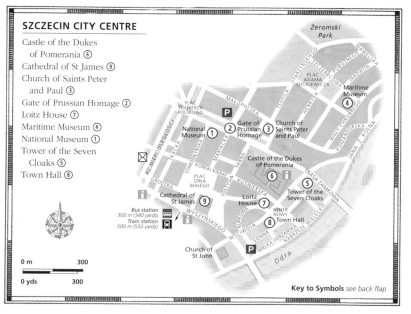

SZCZECIN CITY CENTRE

Castle of the Dukes
  of Pomerania ⑥
Cathedral of St James ⑨
Church of Saints Peter
  and Paul ③
Gate of Prussian Homage ②
Loitz House ⑦
Maritime Museum ④
National Museum ①
Tower of the Seven
  Cloaks ⑤
Town Hall ⑧

Żeromski Park

Bus station
300 m (340 yards)
Train station
500 m (550 yards)

0 m   300
0 yds   300

Key to Symbols *see back flap*

Around Wolin ❷

Wolin's forests, deserted sandy beaches and picturesque, sometimes dramatic, coastal cliffs delight walkers and inspire photographers. Wolin also has plenty to offer those with an interest in historic buildings – the cathedral in Kamień Pomorski is one of the finest in Poland.

Wolin National Park ④
Apart from its beaches and lakes, the park is known for its bison, which can be seen in a special reserve. The bird life includes the rare sea eagle.

Międzyzdroje ③
This renowned health resort was created in 1830. It has a seafront promenade and a pier from which the cliffs can be admired. It is also a good base for hiking in Wolin National Park.

Świnoujście ②
The town straddles Poland's two islands – Wolin and Uznam. The only way of moving between the two parts of the town is by ferry. It has a large port, wide beaches and the elegant buildings of a coastal resort.

Wolin ①
In the Early Middle Ages this small town was a major Baltic port. Today it is the venue for the Viking Festival that takes place every July as a reminder of the settlement's historic importance (see p33).

Stargard Szczeciński ❸

Road map B2. 🏠 71,000.
🚉 🚌 ℹ Rynek Staromiejski 4 (091 578 54 66). **www**.stargard.pl

With its own port in the Szczecin Lagoon at the mouth of the River Ina, Stargard Szczeciński once rivalled Szczecin as a merchant town of the Hanseatic League.

Almost three quarters of the old town was destroyed during World War II, although the Gothic defensive walls with their towers and gates survived. The town's finest building is the Gothic **Church of St Mary** (Kościół Mariacki), which was founded in the late 13th century but only given its present appearance by Heinrich Brunsberg in the mid-15th century. The rich decoration of glazed and moulded brick is quite striking. The magnificent town hall, built in the 16th century and then remodelled in 1638, has a gable with intricate tracery. A particularly pleasant way to round off a trip to Stargard Szczeciński is to visit the café in the former salt granary, a Gothic building overlooking a spur of the Ina.

The **Regional Museum** has some militaria and an archaeological and ethnographical display.

🏛 **Regional Museum**
Rynek Staromiejski 3. **Tel** 091 578 38 35. ☐ 10am–5pm Tue–Fri & Sun (Oct–Apr: to 4pm), 10am–2pm Sat. 🎫 (free on Sat).

Interior of the Gothic Church of St Mary in Stargard Szczeciński

Drawsko Lakes ❹

Road map B2.

The Drawsko Lakes are an oasis of quiet, unspoiled scenery. Their crystal-clear waters teem with fish and, in season, the forests are carpeted with mushrooms. The area is ideal for a canoeing or rowing holiday.

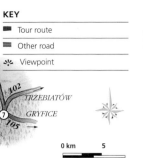

KEY

- ■ Tour route
- ■ Other road
- ☀ Viewpoint

TRZEBIATÓW

GRYFICE

0 km   5

0 miles   5

Kamień Pomorski ⑥
The town was the seat of a bishopric from 1176. Its widely admired cathedral contains a well-preserved collection of fine late Gothic murals as well as famous organs.

Dziwnów ⑤
A swing bridge across the River Dziwna links Wolin Island with the mainland.

GOLENIÓW

TIPS FOR DRIVERS

Tour length: 103 km (65 miles).
Stopping-off points: Plenty of good cafés and restaurants are to be found in Kamień Pomorski and Międzyzdroje.
Additional features: Golf course at Kołczewie. Bison reserve ☐ 1 Jun–15 Sep: 10am–6pm Tue–Sun; 16 Sep–31 May: 9am–3pm Mon, Fri.

Świerzno ⑦
The modest timber-frame palace here was built for the Fleming family in 1718–30. In the 17th century the family also founded the timber-framed church that stands nearby.

Lake Drawsko, the second-deepest lake in Poland

The largest of the lakes is Drawsko, on whose shores stands Stare Drawsko, with ruins of a once-impressive 14th-century Teutonic Knights' castle. In the delightful spa town of **Polczyn Zdrój** the mineral springs are surrounded by a park and there are some elegant early 20th-century sanatoria. **Złocieniec** has an outstanding example of Baroque architecture in the form of a palace that was built here in 1704–45.

Kołobrzeg ❺

Road map B1. 👥 *46,000.*
🚌 🚆 ℹ *ul. Dworcowa 1 (094 352 79 39).*
🎵 *Kołobrzeg Summer Music Festival.*
www.kolobrzeg.turystyka.pl

The fine sandy beaches of Kołobrzeg make it one of the most popular health resorts on the Baltic coast. It has a full complement of hotels, sanatoria, holiday homes and fried-fish stalls, but it is also a working fishing port. In the past it was a fortified coastal town of strategic significance. In summer the long promenade,

The sturdy brick-built lighthouse in Kołobrzeg harbour

leading to the **lighthouse**, is crowded with holiday-makers. The brick-built **Cathedral of the Virgin Mary** (Katedra NMP) was begun in 1255 and later altered and extended.

Among the remarkable objects it contains is a chandelier made by Johann Apengheter of Lübeck in 1327 depicting the Virgin and St John the Baptist. The Neo-Gothic **town hall** was built by the Berlin architect Karl Friedrich Schinkel in 1829–32. It is surrounded by alleys lined with old houses. The **fortress**, now in ruins, was unsuccessfully besieged by Napoleon's troops in 1807.

Darłowo ❻

Road map B1. 🏛 *15,300.* 🚌 🚇 ℹ️
*ul. Powstańców Warszawskich 54 (048
504 992 452).* **www**.darlowo.pl

Darłowo, set 2.5 km
(1½ miles) inland on the
banks of the River Wieprza,
is one of the most attractive
towns of coastal Pomerania.
In summer the waterfront
district swarms with tourists
and the fish stalls do a brisk
trade, but the town's real
charm lies in its old riverside
district, where there are many
historic buildings. The most
prominent of these is the
Gothic **Castle of the Dukes
of Pomerania**. Founded in the
14th century, it was rebuilt
several times and partially
demolished in the 19th
century; its surviving parts
now house a museum.

The castle is associated with
Erik of Pomerania, the war-
like Duke of Słupsk, whose
royal blood enabled him, in
1397, to hold the thrones of
Denmark, Sweden and
Norway. His turbulent rule
was marked by constant war-
fare. He was finally deposed
and returned to Darłowo,
where he established the
Duchy of Słupsk, crowning
himself and, as Erik I, retaining his rule over Gotland. He
was buried in the Church of
St Mary (Kościoł Mariacki),
and his sarcophagus, made in
1888, can be seen here in the
sepulchral chapel. Erik may
also have been the founder
of the late Gothic **Chapel of
St Gertrude** (Kaplica św Gertrudy) on Ulica Tynickiego,
an unusual 12-sided building.

Shifting dunes in Słowiński National Park

Słupsk ❼

Road map C1. 🏛 *99,000.* 🚌 🚇
ℹ️ *ul. Starzyńskiego 8
(059 842 43 26).* 🎵 *International
Festival of Organ Music (Jun–Aug).*
www.slupsk.pl

From 1368 to 1648, this town
on the River Słupia was the
capital of the Duchy of
Western Pomerania. The
Renaissance ducal castle was
built by Antonio Guglielmo
di Zaccharia in 1580–87.
Today it is the **Museum
of Central Pomerania**,
which, besides items of local
interest, has the country's
largest collection of portraits
by the painter and writer
Stanisław Ignacy Witkiewicz
(1885–1939), better known
as Witkacy.

The watermill opposite the
castle, dating from about
1310, is one of the oldest in
Poland. Now a branch of the
museum, it houses an ethnographical collection. In the
Dominican Church of St
Hyacinthus (Kościół św Jacka)
nearby are the black marble
and alabaster tombs of
Bogusław de Croy, the last of
the dukes of Pomerania, and
his mother, the Duchess Anna
de Croy. They were carved by

Kasper Gockhaller of Gdańsk
in 1682. The 14th-century
Church of St Mary (Kościół
Mariacki) is also of interest.

🏛 **Museum of Central
Pomerania**
ul. Dominikańska 5/9. **Tel** *059 842
40 81.* 🕐 *10am–5pm Tue–Fri,
10am–6pm Sat & Sun.* 📷 📷 📷
www.muzeum.slupsk.pl

**Effigy of Anna de Croy in the
Church of St Hyacinthus**

Słowiński
National Park ❽

Road map C1. 🚌 **Tel** *059 811 72
04.* **www**.slowinskipn.pl

Słowiński National Park is
renowned for its large,
shifting sand dunes, which
move at a rate of about 9 m
(30 ft) a year, leaving the
stumps of dead trees behind
them. The area was once a
gulf, of which the glacial
lakes Łebsko and Gardno are
vestiges. The park, a World
Biosphere Reserve, is a haven
for wild birds; more than 250
species, including the rare
sea eagle, are found here.

The park's highest point,
Rowokół, offers a fine view
of the dunescape. At its foot
is the village of Smołdzino,
with a small Baroque church
founded by Duchess Anna
de Croy in the 17th century.

In the hamlet of Kluki, on
Lake Łebsko, is a *skansen*
dedicated to the ancient local
Slovincian culture. Fishing
equipment and agricultural
implements are exhibited in

The castle of Erik of Pomerania, Duke of Słupsk, in Darłowo

For hotels and restaurants in this region see pp308–10 and pp325–6

the farmsteads. An electric train runs to the park from Rąbka, near the resort of Łeba. The town of Nowęcin, also near Łeba, has a Neo-Gothic palace built for the Wejher family in 1909. It now houses a hotel and restaurant.

Corner tower of the Gothic castle of the Teutonic Knights in Bytów

Bytów **9**

Road map C1. 🏘 *17,000.* 🚇 🚌
ℹ️ *ul. Zamkowa 2 (059 822 55 97).*
www.bytow.pl

Bytów, with nearby Lębork, was the westernmost outpost of the territory held by the Teutonic Knights. The town, which after its conquest in 1466 was established as a Polish fiefdom, was ruled by the dukes of Pomerania, and later by Brandenburg and Prussia. It has been part of Poland since 1945.

Few of Bytów's historic buildings survive. The most interesting is the **castle** of the Teutonic Knights, which was built in 1390–1405 and was one of the first castles in Europe to be adapted for the use of firearms. It has four circular corner towers and a

Timber-framed fishermen's cottages in Jastarnia, on the Hel Peninsula

residential wing was added in about 1570. It houses the **Museum of Western Kashubia**, which contains a collection of artifacts relating to the ancient Kashubian culture.

🏛 **Museum of Western Kashubia**
ul. Zamkowa 2. **Tel** *059 822 26 23.*
⬜ *16 Sep–30 Apr: 10am–4pm daily; 1 May–15 Sep: 10am–6pm daily (to 4pm Mon).* 🎟 *(free on Mon).* www.muzeumbytow.pl

Kashubia **10**

See p262.

Hel Peninsula **11**

Road map D1. 🚌 🚇 ℹ️ *Hel, ul. Wiejska 78 (058 675 10 10); Jastarnia, ul. ks. Pawła Stefańskiego 5 (058 675 23 40).* www.jastarnia.pl

The Hel Peninsula is about 34 km (22 miles) long and in width ranges from just 200 m (650 ft) to 3 km (2 miles). It is made up of sandbanks formed by sea currents; in the 1700s it was no more than a chain of islets. The peninsula is now the Nadmorski Park Krajobrazovy, an area of outstanding natural

beauty. When the railway line to Hel was completed in 1922, resorts began to appear on the peninsula. Their main attraction was the double beach – one part facing the sea, the other the Gulf of Gdańsk. At the base of the peninsula is the town of **Władysławowo**, named after Władysław IV, who founded a now-vanished fortress here. Today the town's boundaries embrace many resorts, such as Jastrzębia Góra, Cetniewo and Chałupy. **Jastarnia** is the most popular resort, as it still retains many of its original fishermen's cottages. The elegant resort of **Jurata** was established in 1928; modernist hotels dating from the 1930s can be seen here. At the very end of the peninsula is the fishing port and tourist resort of **Hel**, with its towering lighthouse and timber-framed fishermen's cottages. The former Protestant church, built in the 1400s, is now the **Fisheries Museum**. From Hel, passenger and tourist boats cross to Gdynia and Gdańsk.

🏛 **Fisheries Museum**
Hel, ul. Bulisar Nadmorski 2.
Tel *058 675 05 52.* ⬜ *10am–4pm Tue–Sun (Jul–Aug: to 6pm daily; Dec: to 3pm).* ⬤ *pub hols.*

The narrow Hel Peninsula, separating Puck Bay from the Baltic Sea

Kashubia ⑩

A trip to the part of Kashubia known as Szwajcaria Kaszubska ("Kashubian Switzerland") is a chance to experience the culture of a people who have inhabited this area for centuries. The Kashubian Museum in Kartuzy has a collection of original embroidery, toys and snuffboxes carved from horn, in Chmielno are working potteries and in Wdzydze Kiszewskie is a *skansen* with traditional Kashubian cottages.

Kartuzy ①
The town takes its name from the Carthusians, who founded a monastery here in the 1380s. The collegiate church still stands. The Kashubian Museum re-creates the daily life of the region.

Chmielno ②
This village has several workshops producing traditional Kashubian pottery. Potters can be seen at work, and their products are for sale.

Kashubian Park Krajobrazowy ③
The national park in Szwajcaria Kaszubska offers some breathtaking views from the summit of its moraine hills.

Wdzydze Kiszewskie ④
As well as traditional peasant farmsteads, this *skansen* has a windmill, an inn, a school and a small church.

Wieżyca ⑥
At 331 m (1,090 ft) above sea level, this is the highest point in Kashubia. Its slopes are popular for skiing in winter.

Kościerzyna ⑤
Although not in itself a scenic town, Kościerzyna is a good stopping place on a tour of Kashubia. A monument to Józef Wybicki, author of the Polish national anthem, stands in the town.

0 km   5
0 miles   5

TIPS FOR DRIVERS

Tour length: *120 km (75 miles).*
Stopping-off points: *There are bars and restaurants in Kartuzy, Chmielno and Kościerzyna.*
Places of interest: *Kashubian Museum, Kartuzy.* **Tel** *058 681 14 42.* ☐ *9am–4pm Mon–Fri, 9am–3pm Sat, 10am–2pm Sun.* ⬤ *Oct–Apr: Sun.* 🖼 🖥 *Kashubian Pottery Museum, Chmielno.* **Tel** *058 684 22 89.* ☐ *9am–5pm Mon–Sat (Oct–Apr: to 3pm).*

KEY

▬ Tour route
▭ Other road
☽ Viewpoint

Map labels:
WEJHEROWO
219   224
219
GDAŃSK
219
Lake Raduńskie Dolne
Radunia
Lake Ostrzyckie
238
Klukowska Huta
214
Lake Raduńskie Górny
Stężyca
20
6
BYTÓW
20
GDAŃSK
221
5
214
ZBLEWO
Wdzydze Tucholskie
Lake Wdzydze
4

◁ **Breakwaters along the Baltic Coast**

The three-masted training ship *Dar Młodzieży* moored in Gdynia

Gdynia ⑫

Road map D1. 🏙 250,000.
🚉 🚌 🛈 *ul. 10 Lutego 24 (058 622 37 66).* 🎭 *Days of the Sea (Jun); Festival of Polish Feature Films (Oct).* **www**.gdynia.pl

Gdynia, until 1918 a small fishing village, is one of the most recently developed towns in Poland. When, after World War I, Poland regained independence but did not control the port of Gdańsk, the authorities decided to build a major port at Gdynia. During World War II Gdynia and its shipyard were used by the German Kriegsmarine, and the town was renamed Gotenhafen by the Germans. A landmark in Gdynia's post-war history came in December 1970, when striking workers were fired on by the militia. In 1980 a monument in their honour was erected.

A walk along the Northern Pier offers an overview of the port at work and a sight of the town's most important landmarks. By the quay are two floating museums, the ships ***Błyskawica*** and ***Dar Pomorza***. The *Błyskawica* is a destroyer that saw action in World War II alongside Allied forces in Narvik, Dunkirk and during the Normandy landings. *Dar Pomorza* is a three-masted training vessel, built in 1909 and decommissioned in 1981. It was replaced by the *Dar Młodzieży*, which can sometimes also be seen moored in the port. At the end of the pier is a statue of the writer Joseph Conrad (1857–1924), who was born in Poland as Teodor Josef Konrad Korzeniowski. Beyond the pier stands the **Aquarium Gdyńskie**.

You can walk along Gdynia's seafront promenade all the way to the islet of Kępa Redłowska. A wander around the city's shopping area, with its boutiques and bars, is equally enjoyable.

Fish: street ornament in Gdynia

🏛 **Aquarium Gdyńskie**
al. Jana Pawła II 1.
Tel 058 732 66 01. 🕐 *Oct–Mar: 10am–5pm daily; Apr–Sep: 9am–7pm daily (Jun–Aug: to 8pm).* **www**.akwarium.gdynia.pl

⚓ **ORP *Błyskawica***
al. Jana Pawła II. **Tel** 058 626 37 27. 🕐 *May–Oct: 10am–1pm, 2–5pm Tue–Sun.* **www**.mw.mil.pl

⚓ **Dar *Pomorza***
al. Jana Pawła II. **Tel** 058 620 23 71. 🕐 *Sep–May: 10am–4pm Tue–Sun; Jun–Aug: 10am–6pm daily.*

Sopot ⑬

Road map D1. 🏙 43,000.
🚉 🚌 🛈 *ul. Dworcowa 4 (058 550 37 83).* 🕐 *9am–8pm daily (Oct–Apr: 10am–6pm).* 🎭 *International Festival of Song (Aug).* **www**.sopot.pl

Sopot is the most popular resort on the Baltic coast. It was established as a sea-bathing centre in 1824 by Jean Georges Haffner, a physician in the Napoleonic army who chose a spot on the coast that since the 17th century had been favoured by the wealthy burghers of Gdańsk for their mansions. Its heyday came in the interwar years, when it attracted some of the richest people in Europe. The pier is a continuation of the main street, Ulica Bohaterów Monte Cassino, colloquially known as Monciak. The pier is 512 m (1,680 ft long) and the bench running all the way around it is the longest in Europe. The pier is filled with bars, restaurants and cake shops as well as antique shops and boutiques selling amber. It is a pleasant place to enjoy a beer and the sea air. An alternative is coffee at the Grand Hotel, built in 1924–7, which overlooks the beach. This splendid Neo-Baroque building once housed a casino.

The town's narrow streets hide many delightful guesthouses. In the wooded hills behind the town is the Opera Leśna ("Opera in the Woods"), built in 1909 and the venue of the International Song Festival *(see p33).*

The Grand Hotel in Sopot, overlooking the beach and the Gulf of Gdańsk

For hotels and restaurants in this region see pp308–10 and pp325–6

Malbork ⑭

Malbork, the castle of the Teutonic Knights, was begun in the 13th century. In 1309 it was made capital of an independent state established by the order. The first major phase of building was the Assembly Castle, a fortified monastery later known as the Upper Castle. The Middle Castle was built some time after 1310, and the Palace of the Grand Master was begun in 1382–99 by Konrad Zöllner von Rotenstein. In 1457 the castle was taken by Poland and used as a fortress. It was restored in the 19th century, and again after World War II.

The well in the courtyard of the High Tower

Summer Refectory
It has double rows of windows and late Gothic palm vaulting supported on a granite central column. The Winter Refectory adjoins it on its eastern side.

★ **Palace of the Grand Master**
The grandeur of the four-storey palace was almost without equal in medieval Europe.

Upper Castle

★ **Golden Gate**
Built in the late 13th century, this is enclosed by a porch. The keystone in the vaulting is carved with the figure of Christ.

Church of St Mary is presently being restored but is open to visitors.

Cloistered Courtyard
The inner courtyard of the Upper Castle is surrounded by slender Gothic arches with triangular vaulting.

STAR SIGHTS

★ Palace of the Grand Master

★ Golden Gate

Lower Castle
These partly reconstructed farm buildings, abutting the former Chapel of St Lawrence, have been converted into a hotel.

VISITORS' CHECKLIST

Road map D1. 🏰 40,000. 🚌
🚉 ℹ *ul. Piastowska 15 (055 647 08 00) (summer).* **Castle Museum** *ul. Starościńska 1.* **Tel** *055 647 08 02.* ☐ *9am–7pm daily (mid-Sep–mid-Apr: 10am–3pm).* ● *1 Jan, 8 Apr, 1 Nov, 25 Dec.* **Courtyard** ☐ *1 hr longer.* 🚫 🚽 🍴 🏪 👪
Son et Lumière show *1 May–15 Sep.* www.zamek.malbork.pl

Battlements
A good view of the towers and walls surrounding the castle can be had from the east side.

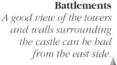

Teutonic Knight
The Teutonic Knights, or the Knights of the Teutonic Order of the Hospital of St Mary in Jerusalem, had a strict monastic code. In battle they were distinguished by the black crosses on their white cloaks.

Chapel of St Anne
Built in 1331–44 beneath the choir of the Church of St Mary, this contains the tombs of eleven Grand Masters.

The Altar of St Mary in the south aisle at Pelplin

Pelplin ⓯

Road map D2. 👥 *8,500.* 🚉 🚌
www.pelplin.pl

The beautiful Cistercian abbey at Pelplin is one of the finest examples of Gothic architecture in Poland. Work on the monastery began in 1276, when the Cistercians came to Pelplin.

The brick-built church, now a **cathedral**, dates largely from the 14th century, although its late Gothic vaulting was not completed until the late 15th and early 16th centuries. The imposing triple-naved basilica has no tower, and the west and east fronts are almost identical. The interior contains an outstanding collection of finely crafted furnishings, including

Gothic stalls with a rare carving of the Holy Trinity in which the Holy Ghost is depicted not as the customary dove but as a man. Other fine pieces include the 17th-century Mannerist and Baroque altar and a pulpit supported on a figure of Samson in combat with a lion. There are several paintings by Hermann Hahn, including a large *Coronation of the Virgin* on the high altar. The monastery was dissolved in 1823, and in 1824 the church became the **Cathedral of the Virgin Mary** (Katedra NMP). The monastery buildings now accommodate the **Diocesan Museum,** whose carved gallery contains a handsome collection of ecclesiastical art as well as illuminated manuscripts. The most highly prized exhibits are a Madonna cabinet from Kolonówka, a rare original Gutenberg Bible of 1435–55 and a 17th-century musical manuscript, the *Pelplin Tabulature for Organ.* A range of goldwork and liturgical objects are also displayed in the cathedral treasury.

Samson fighting a lion, Pelplin Cathedral

ⓘ **Cathedral of the Virgin Mary**
pl. Mariacki. **Tel** *058 536 15 64.*
⏰ *9am–4pm Mon–Sat (to 5pm in summer).* 📷

🏛 **Diocesan Museum**
ul. ks. Biskupa Dominika 11.
Tel *058 536 12 21.* ⏰ *10am–4pm Tue–Fri, 10am–5pm Sat, 11am–5pm Sun.* 📷 *on religious feast days.*

Gniew ⓰

Road map D2. 👥 *6,700.* 🚉 🚌
🎫 *Gniewniki (Jun); International Tournament for the Sword of Sobieski (Aug).* **www**.gniew.pl

This pretty little town on the River Vistula retains a medieval atmosphere. Founded by the Teutonic Knights in 1276, it was later the seat of a commander of the order and in 1466 became part of Poland. The town's narrow alleys lead into the **Market Square,** which is lined with arcaded buildings. While most date from the 18th century, some, like the town hall, have Gothic elements. Traces of the 14th to 15th-century fortifications that once protected Gniew from invaders still remain. The Gothic **Church of St Nicholas** (Kościół św Mikołaja) towers over the town. Probably built in the first half of the 14th century, it retains its magnificent interior,

Gniew seen from the River Vistula, framed by the Church of St Nicholas and the Castle of the Teutonic Knights

Kwidzyn Cathedral, seat of the bishops of Pomerania in the 13th century

🏛 **Castle Museum**
ul. Katedralna 1.
Tel 055 646 37 80 or 646 37 97.
◯ 9am–5pm Tue–Sun. 🖼

Grudziądz ⑱

Road map D2. 🏚 *101,000.* 🚆 🚌
ℹ 056 461 23 18. **www**.grudziadz.pl

which includes Gothic vaulting and Mannerist, Baroque and Neo-Gothic altars.

The town's most distinctive feature is the **castle** of the Teutonic Knights. This imposing fortress was begun in 1283 and completed in the mid-14th century. The castle has a regular plan, with four corner turrets and the remains of a mighty keep in the northeastern corner.

In summer the castle hosts festivals, jousting tournaments and reconstructions of medieval banquets.

🏛 **Castle Museum**
ul. Zamkowa 3. *Tel* 058 535 35 29.
◯ Apr–Nov: 9:30am–4:30pm Tue–Sun. 🖼 🔟 **www**.zamek-gniew.pl

🏰 **Church of St Nicholas**
ul. Okrzei 4. *Tel* 058 535 22 16.

Kwidzyn ⑰

Road map D2. 🏚 *37,000.* 🚆 🚌
www.kwidzyn.pl

From 1243 until 1525, the small town of Kwidzyn was the capital of the Pomezania bishopric, one of four to be established in the territory ruled by the Teutonic Knights. After the order was dissolved, the town passed in turn to Prussia, Germany and Poland.

The **cathedral** standing on a high escarpment and the **castle** attached to it are fine examples of Gothic architecture. The cathedral was built in the 14th century on the site of an earlier church, of which only the narthex (a portico or porch separated from the nave by a screen) remains. The porch dates from 1264–84.

In 1862–4 the cathedral was remodelled in the Neo-Gothic style by Friedrich August Stüler. The interior of this vast pseudo-basilica has Gothic murals, which unfortunately were excessively repainted in the 19th century. Many of the earlier furnishings are still in place, including a late Gothic bishop's throne of about 1510 and Baroque altars and tombs. The presbytery gives access to the tiny cell of the Blessed Dorothy of Mątowy, who ordered that she be immured there in 1393. By the north nave is the Baroque chapel of Otto Frederick von Groeben, which contains a tomb depicting the deceased accompanied in death by his three wives.

The castle resembles a knights' fortress, although it was in fact the seat of a chapter. It was built in 1322–47 and partially demolished in the 18th century. Among the interesting features of the castle are the well tower and the exceptionally tall latrine tower, which is connected to the castle by a gallery supported on large arches.

Grudziądz, situated on an escarpment overlooking the River Vistula, was once a major port. It was founded by the Teutonic Knights and became part of Poland in 1466. As a result of the Partitions of Poland, it became part of Prussia from 1772 and in 1918 was returned to Poland. Despite the damage it suffered during World War II, the town has some fine buildings. The Gothic **Church of St Nicholas** (Kościoł sw Mikołaja) was begun in the late 13th century and completed in the second half of the 15th. It contains a late Romanesque font from the 14th century. The former Benedictine abbey, including the Palace of the Abbesses of 1749–51, is also of interest. Part of the abbey now houses a museum and art gallery.

The huge complex of **harbour granaries**, 26 brick buildings built side by side along the waterfront, fulfilled a defensive function as well as being used for storage – seen from the river, the granaries appear to surround the entire hillside. They were built mostly in the 17th and 18th centuries, but some are significantly older.

🏛 **Grudziądz Museum**
ul. Wodna 3/5. *Tel* 056 465 90 63.
◯ from 10am Tue–Sun; closing times vary (see website). 🖼 (free on Tue). **www**.muzeum.grudziadz.pl

The granaries in Grudziądz

Chełmno ⑲

The lands of Chełmno that Konrad, Duke of Mazovia, presented to the Teutonic Knights in 1226 were the beginning of the vast state established by the order. The knights' first city, Chełmno, was founded in 1233 and was initially intended to be the capital of their state but this honour went to Malbork (*see p264*). The civic laws of Chełmno became a model for other cities.

VISITORS' CHECKLIST

Road Map D2. 🏘 *21,200.*
🚌 *ul. Dworcowa.* **Tel** 056 686
21 56. 🛈 *Rynek 28 (056 686
21 04).* **www**.chelmno.pl

Exploring Chełmno

Chełmno's medieval street plan and 13th to 15th-century fortifications survive virtually intact. The town walls are set with 23 towers and a fortified gate, the **Grudziądz Gate**, which was converted into a Mannerist chapel in 1620. The town's finest building is the **town hall**, a late Renaissance building of 1567–72 with traces of earlier Gothic elements. It houses the Chełmno Museum. At the rear of the town hall is an iron measuring stick equalling 4.35 m (just over 14 ft) and known as the Chełmno Measure, or *pręt*. The Baroque building on Ulica Franciszkańska, dating from the turn of the 18th

Baroque high altar in the Church of the Assumption, Chełmno

century, once housed the **Chełmno Academy**, which was founded in 1692.

Six Gothic churches have been preserved in Chełmno. The largest is the **Church of the Assumption** (Kościół Wniebowzięcia NMP) of 1280–1320, a fine aisled building containing early Gothic frescoes and stone carvings. Two monastery churches, the **Church of St James** (Kościół św Jakuba) and the **Church of Saints Peter and Paul** (Kościół św Piotra i Pawła), date from the same period. The Abbey of the Cistercian Nuns, established in the late 13th century, is an exceptional group of buildings. It was later transferred to Benedictine monks and then

The late Renaissance town hall in the Market Square

passed to the Catholic sisters who run a hospital here today. The entrance on Ulica Dominikańska leads to an internal courtyard, which in turn gives access to the **Church of St John the Baptist** (Kościół św Jana Chrzciciela), built in 1290–1340. It has two storeys, the lower one having

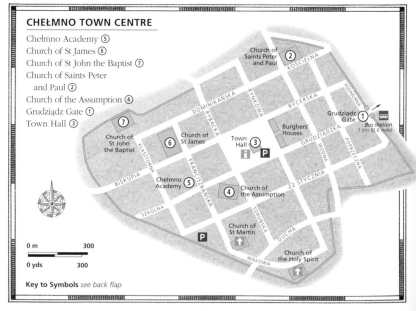

CHEŁMNO TOWN CENTRE

Chełmno Academy ⑤
Church of St James ⑥
Church of St John the Baptist ⑦
Church of Saints Peter
and Paul ②
Church of the Assumption ④
Grudziądz Gate ①
Town Hall ③

0 m   300
0 yds   300

Key to Symbols *see back flap*

two naves, and the upper a single nave that was reserved for the choir of the Order of Teutonic Knights.

🏛 Chełmno Museum
Rynek. *Tel 056 686 16 41.*
⭘ *10am–4pm Tue–Fri, 10am–3pm Sat, 11am–3pm Sun (Mar–Nov).* 📷

Environs
In Chełmża, 23 km (14 miles) north of Chełmno, stands the Gothic Cathedral of the Holy Trinity, built in 1251–1359 and rebuilt after 1422.

Bydgoszcz ⓴

Road Map C2. 👥 *363,000.* 🚃 🚌
ℹ *ul. Grodzka 7 (052 585 87 02).* 📷
Bydgoszcz Music Festival (Sep); Musica Antiqua Europae Orientalis (every 3 years, Sep). **www.**bydgoszcz.pl

Bydgoszcz lies at the confluence of the River Brda and the Bydgoszcz Canal, which then flow into the Vistula. The city was only briefly part of the state of the Teutonic Knights, after which its fate was linked with that of the rest of Poland. It was the scene of dramatic events on 3 September 1939, when the town's German minority attempted to stage a coup. The Nazis entered the town and massacred thousands of the Polish population.

The **old town** of Bydgoszcz is set on a bend of the Brda. It has several monumental town houses, the late Gothic church of Saints Nicholas and Martin (Kościół św Mikołaja i Marcina) and two monasteries: a Bernadine monastery with a church of 1545–52, and the Church and Convent of the Poor Clares (Kościół Klarysek), which today houses a **Regional**

Museum. The half-timbered **granaries** on the banks of the Brda, built in the 18th and 19th centuries, were used for the salt and wheat that the town traded and to store the beer for which it was renowned.

🏛 Regional Museum
ul. Gdańska 4. *Tel 052 585 99 66.*
⭘ *10am–5pm Tue, Wed, Fri (Oct–Mar: to 4pm); 10am–7pm Thu; 11am–5pm Sat & Sun (Oct–Mar: to 4pm).* 📷 *(free on Sat).* **www.** muzeum.bydgoszcz.pl

Toruń ㉑

See pp270–73.

Golub-Dobrzyń ㉒

Road Map D2. 👥 *12,800.* 🚃 🚌
ℹ *056 683 54 10.* 📷 *International Jousting Tournament (Jun).*
www.golub-dobrzyn.pl

This picturesque town was originally two separate settlements, one on either side of the River Drwęca. During the Partitions, Golub was part of Prussia and Dobrzyń part of Russia. Golub's main feature is the large **castle** built by the Teutonic Knights in 1293–1310. From 1466 Golub was part of Poland, and in the 17th century the castle became the residence of Queen Anna Vasa of Sweden, sister of Zygmunt III Vasa. The castle was rebuilt for her in 1616–23 in the Renaissance style. Highly educated and with an interest in botany and natural medicine, Anna Vasa was an unusual woman for her time. She remained a spinster, reputedly because of her ugly appearance.

The castle built by the Teutonic Knights in Golub-Dobrzyń

Today the castle hosts such events as jousting tournaments and oratory competitions, as well as New Year's balls, at which revellers say that the ghost of Queen Anna appears. By ironic coincidence, the Miss Poland beauty contests are also held here.

🏛 Castle Museum
ul. Zamkowa. *Tel 056 683 24 55.*
⭘ *Jun–Sep: 9am–7pm daily; Oct–May: 9am–3pm daily.* 🅱

Graduation tower for the production of salt in Ciechocinek

Ciechocinek ㉓

Road Map D3. 👥 *11,000.* 🚃 🚌
ℹ *ul. Zdrojowa 2 (054 416 01 60).* 📷 *Festival of Kujawy and Dobrzyń Folklore (Jul); International Festival of Gypsy Song and Culture (Jul).*
www.ciechocinek.pl

Ciechocinek is one of Poland's best-known spa towns, which grew and prospered thanks to its iodine-rich salt springs. It is not strictly part of Pomerania but of Kujawy, and has always been a Polish town. The town came into being in 1824, when Stanisław Staszic started to build saltworks and the first of three salt graduation towers. The "towers" are huge wooden frames filled with thorny brushwood which, washed with brine, accumulates salt crystals. Each "tower" is more than 1.7 km (1 mile) wide.

Other features of Ciechocinek are the group of baths built in a variety of styles between 1845 and 1913, a fine park with a flower clock, a pump room designed by Edward Cichocki, a bandstand and open-air theatre, and numerous elegant boarding houses, sanatoria and hotels dating from the start of the 20th century.

Toruń ㉑

Stained glass

Toruń's principal claim to fame is as the birthplace of the astronomer Nicolaus Copernicus *(see p273)*, but it is also renowned for its architecture. The city was founded by the Teutonic Knights in 1233 and quickly became a major centre of trade; in 1454, when its citizens rebelled against the knights' rule, it passed to the kings of Poland. The old town of Toruń, picturesquely situated on the banks of the River Vistula, retains its medieval street plan, and has a rare calm, since most of the streets are closed to traffic.

Star House, an early Baroque town house in the Old Market Square

The Wilam Horzyca Theatre

🎭 Wilam Horzyca Theatre

pl. Teatralny 1. *Tel 056 622 50 21.*
The delightful theatre, in the Art Nouveau style with Neo-Baroque elements, was built in 1904 by the Viennese architects Ferdinand Fellner and Hermann Helmer. The Kontakt Theatre Festival is held here each year in early summer, bringing together theatre performers from all over Europe and drawing large and enthusiastic audiences to its performances.

🏛 Church of the Virgin Mary

ul. Marii Panny. *Tel 056 622 26 03.*
The Gothic Church of the Virgin Mary (Kościół NMP) was built for Franciscan monks in 1270–1300. It has an unusually richly ornamented east gable. Late 14th-century wall paintings can be seen in the south aisle, while in the north aisle is a 16th-century Mannerist organ loft, the oldest in Poland. By the presbytery is the mausoleum of Anna Vasa *(see p269)*, sister of Zygmunt III, made in 1636. She was of royal blood but could not be buried at Wawel Castle because she was of the Protestant faith.

The elaborate east end of the Church of the Virgin Mary

🏛 Old Market Square

The Old Market Square is the city's finest open space and still the vibrant heart of its historic district. The centrepiece is the town hall, but on all four sides of the square there are fine buildings. On the south side, at No. 7, is the Meissner Palace, built in 1739 for Jakob Meissner, mayor of Toruń, and given a Neo-Classical façade in 1798. Many of the town houses retain their

Map labels:
Ethnographical Museum
PLAC TEATRALNY
WAŁY GEN. SIKORSKIEGO
① Wilam Horzyca Theatre
PODMURNA
WAŁY GENERAŁA SIKORSKIEGO
CHEŁMIŃSKA
SZEWSKA
FRANCISZKAŃSKA
FOSA
Church of the Virgin Mary ②
PIEKARY
PANNY MARII   OLD MARKET SQUARE ③
STAROMIEJSKA
Church of ⑤ the Holy Spirit
Museum of Far East
④ Town Hall
RÓŻANA
OLD TOWN
Cathedral of St John the Baptist & St John the Evang
AL. JANA PAWŁA II
PLAC RAPACKIEGO
DUCHA ŚWIĘTEGO
KOPERNIKA
MIKOŁAJA
KOPERNIKA ⑥ Copernicus House
ŻEGLARSKA
ⓠ
POD KRZYWĄ WIEŻĄ
PIEKARY
RABIAŃSKA
Palace of the Bishops of Kujawy ⑧
Crooked Tower ⑦
BANKOWA
Klasztorna Gate
Gołębnik Gate
Żeglar Gat
Train Station 1.6 km (1 mile)

original details, such as that at No. 17, with a portal made in 1630. The most attractive house in the square is Star House, at No. 35 on the east side, built in 1697. It has a richly ornamented façade, with stuccowork motifs of fruit and flowers. In the square stands a monument to Nicolaus Copernicus made by Friedrich Tiecek in 1853, and a fountain with the figure of a raftsman who, according to legend, rid the citizens of Toruń of a plague of frogs by playing his fiddle.

The town hall in the Old Market Square

VISITORS' CHECKLIST

Road Map D2. 🏙 *207,000.* 🚉 *Toruń Główny, ul. Kujawska 1 (056 699 930 44).* 🚌 *Toruń Miasto, pl. 18 Stycznia 4.* 🚏 🛈 *Rynek Staromiejski 25 (056 621 09 31 or 657 08 12).* 🎭 *Theatre Festival (May/Jun); Probaltica Baltic Arts and Music Festival (mid-May).* **www**.torun.pl

🏛 **Town Hall**
Rynek Staromiejski 1. **Regional Museum Tel** *056 660 56 12.* ◯ *10am–6pm (Oct–Apr: to 4pm) Tue–Sun.* ⬤ *see website for details.* 📷 *(ground floor free on Wed).* **Tower** ◯ *10am–8pm daily (Nov–Apr: to 4pm).* 📷 **www**.muzeum.torun.pl
The town hall, an imposing building with an internal courtyard, was erected in 1391–9 as a two-storey edifice. In 1602–5 the Gdańsk architect Antonis van Opbergen added the third floor and gave the building its current Mannerist appearance. The lower parts of the tower date from the 13th century. Standing 42 m (138 ft) high, it commands a fine view over the city of Toruń.

The town hall now houses a museum featuring Gothic art, 19th-century paintings and local crafts. The building's original interiors are also noteworthy, especially the vaulting of the former bakery and wool stalls on the ground floors of the east and west wings.

The town hall also features a restaurant and a popular pub, *Pod Aniołem*, in the basement.

Map

Bus station 180 m (200 yards)

LEONA SZUMANA
RÓŻYMUŻE
WYSOKA
SUKIENNICZA
PROSTA
PLAC ŚW. KATARZYNY
ŚW. KATARZYNY
Church of St Catherine ✝
JĘCZMIENNA
Children's Art Gallery ⊠
MAŁE GARBARY
SZPITALNA
⑪ NEW MARKET SQUARE
⑫ Church of St James
ŚW. JAKUBA
NEW TOWN
YKOWA
KRÓLOWEJ JADWIGI
MURAWA
BROWARNA
WIELKIE GARBARY
ROKA
FRYDAMEK
PODMURNA
WOLA ZAMKOWA
Ⓟ
MOSTOWA
Castle of the Teutonic Knights Ⓟ
SNA
⑩
BULWAR FILADELFIJSKI
Mostowa Gate
Wisła

0 m   100
0 yds   100

Key to Symbols *see back flap*

The Church of the Virgin Mary seen from the top of the town hall tower

Exploring Toruń

Toruń gingerbread

Toruń survived World War II relatively unscathed. It has well-preserved city walls and a series of gates that once opened onto the quayside. Granaries dating from the 15th to the 19th centuries still line the streets leading down to the river. The Cathedral of Saints John the Baptist and John Evangelist and the richly ornamented Palace of the Bishops of Kujawy are two of Toruń's finest buildings and the Copernicus Museum stands as a memorial to the city's most famous son.

🔒 Church of the Holy Spirit

ul. Piekary 24. *Tel 056 622 88 05.*
The Baroque Church of the Holy Spirit (Kościoł św Ducha) in the Old Market Square was built in the mid-18th century for the Protestant community of Toruń. It was begun by Andreas Adam Bähr, and completed by Ephraim Schroeger.

⊞ Copernicus House

ul. Kopernika 15/17. *Tel 056 622 67 48.* ◯ *Tue–Sun. Sep–mid-Apr: 10am–4pm; mid-Apr–Jun: 10am–6pm; Jul & Aug: 10am–6pm.*
🖳 www.muzeum.torun.pl
These two Gothic town houses from the 15th century are outstanding examples of Hanseatic merchants' houses. The painted façades and fine carving of the arched gables bear witness to the city's former wealth. The house at No. 17 was that of Mikołaj Kopernik, a merchant and the father of the boy who was to become the famous astronomer. The house, although it may not be the one in which the younger Mikołaj was born, is now a museum.

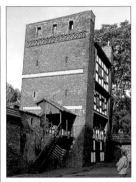

The Crooked Tower, part of the fortifications on the River Vistula

⊞ Crooked Tower

ul. Pod Krzywą Wieżą.
The Crooked Tower is one of Toruń's greatest attractions. It is part of the town's old fortifications system, and was probably built in the first half of the 14th century. Although it leans significantly from the perpendicular, the floors that were added later are perfectly level – so that beer glasses in the pub that it now houses can be set down

on the tables without danger of sliding off.

⊞ Gothic Granary

ul. Piekary 4.
The most remarkable of the many Gothic granaries still standing in Toruń is that on the corner of Ulica Piekary and Ulica Rabiańska. Although the granary was rebuilt in the 19th century, it retains its towering ornamental gable with fine pointed arches.

♣ Palace of the Bishops of Kujawy

ul. Żeglarska 8.
The palace was built by the Bishop Stanisław Dąmbski in 1693. In the 19th century it was converted into a hotel and then into a mess for military officers. Subsequent restoration work undid the damage inflicted by these conversions and returned the building to its former elegance. It is now the Academy of Fine Arts.

Cathedral of Saints John the Baptist and John the Evangelist

🔒 Cathedral of Saints John the Baptist and John the Evangelist

ul. Żeglarska 16. *Tel 056 657 14 80.*
The origins of the Cathedral of Saints John the Baptist and John the Evangelist (Kościoł śś Janów) go back to 1250. The oldest surviving part of the cathedral is the presbytery. The nave, with its numerous side chapels, was completed by Hans Gotland in about 1500, long after the tower had been finished in 1433. The interior is a treasury of art. The

A room in the Copernicus House

NICOLAUS COPERNICUS

Nicolaus Copernicus (Mikołaj Kopernik; 1473–1543), astronomer, mathematician, economist, doctor and clergyman, was born in Toruń. For most of his life he lived in Warmia. He wrote treatises on economics, but gained the greatest renown for his astronomical observations. His heliocentric theory of the universe, which he expounded in *De Revolutionibus Orbium Celestium* (1543), posited the fact that the planets rotate around the Sun.

Renaissance epitaph to Copernicus in Toruń

presbytery contains some fine 16th-century mural paintings. There are also altars, chandeliers, stained-glass windows, sculpture and many paintings. In one of the side chapels in the south aisle is the Gothic font where Nicolaus Copernicus was baptized and a memorial to him of about 1580. He was buried in Frombork Cathedral *(see p278)*.

⚓ Castle of the Teutonic Knights

ul. Przedzamcze. *Tel* 056 621 08 89. Little more than ruins remain of the castle that the Teutonic Knights built in Toruń. Before the castle at Malbork *(see pp264–5)* was built, Toruń was the knights' capital.

The castle was built in the 13th century and extended in the 14th. However, it was destroyed in 1454 when the people of Toruń rose up in rebellion against the knights. Only the latrine tower – a

tower overhanging a stream that acted as a sewer – were left standing, although part of the cellars and cloisters survive. The late Gothic house that was built on the site in 1489, probably with materials scavenged from the castle, was the meeting house of the Brotherhood of St George.

▦ New Market Square

The new town emerged as a separate civic entity in 1264. Although it does not have as many historic buildings as the old town, there is a good deal of interest here. In summer the square is filled with fruit and vegetable stalls.

In the centre, where the town hall once stood, is a former Protestant church, built in 1824, probably by the German architect Karl Friedrich Schinkel. It has been converted into a gallery of contemporary art. Fine houses, some with ornate façades like that of the Baroque house at No. 17, surround the square.

On the corner of Ulica Królowej Jadwigi and the

square is the Golden Lion pharmacy, a brick-built house originating in the 15th century.

🔒 Church of St James

ul. Rynek Nowomiejski 6. *Tel* 056 622 29 24. The Gothic Church of St James (Kościoł św Jakuba) was built in the first half of the 14th century as the new town's parish church. It was first used by Cistercian monks, and then by Benedictines. It contains wall paintings of the second half of the 14th century. In the south aisle is a late 14th-century Gothic Crucifix in the form of the Tree of Life, in which the figure of Christ is nailed to the branches of a tree containing the figures of the prophets. Above the rood beam is a rare depiction of the Passion of about 1480–90, consisting of 22 scenes of the Stations of the Cross.

Gothic tower of the Church of St James in the new town

🏛 Ethnographical Museum

ul. Wały gen. Sikorskiego 19. *Tel* 056 622 80 91. ⬜ mid-Apr–Jun: 9am–5pm Tue–Fri (to 4pm Wed & Fri), 10am–6pm Sat & Sun; Jul–Sep: 10am–6pm Tue, Thu, Sat & Sun, 9am–4pm Wed & Fri; Oct–mid-Apr: 9am–4pm Tue–Fri, 10am–4pm Sat & Sun. 🖼 The museum contains fishing tools and folk art. There is also a *skansen*, in which wooden houses from the region of Kujawy, Pomerania and Ziemia Dobrzyńska are displayed.

Latrine tower, the surviving part of the Castle of the Teutonic Knights

WARMIA, MAZURIA AND BIAŁYSTOK REGION

K *nown as the land of a thousand lakes, northeastern Poland is blessed with vast forests and undulating moraine hills as well as a large number of lakes and rivers. There are no major industrial areas. Its three regions, Warmia, Mazuria and Białostoc-czyzna, are ethnically diverse and have had very different histories.*

Warmia, the western part of the region, was once inhabited by the early Prussians, and in the 13th century was taken over by the Teutonic Knights, who established a bishopric here. Warmia became part of Poland in 1466. Under the Partitions it was transferred to Prussia, and was not returned to Poland until 1945. Warmia has many historic churches.

Mazuria and the Iława Lake District at its southern and eastern fringes were also once controlled by the Teutonic Knights. When the order was secularized in 1525, the region became known as ducal Prussia and was ruled by the Hohenzollern family, although until 1657 it was a Polish fiefdom. The area's subsequent history is linked to that of Germany, and it did not become part of Poland again until 1945. Many castles were built by the Knights and some Prussian mansions can be seen here today.

The Suwałki and Augustów lakelands and Białostocczyzna form the region's eastern part, which once belonged to the grand duchy of Lithuania. The area was covered in primeval forests, and three – the Augustów, Knyszyńska and Białowieża forests – remain today. The Biebrza valley contains Poland's largest stretches of marshland and peat swamps and offers plenty for naturalists. Those interested in religious culture are also well served: the Orthodox church in Grabarka, the old monastery of the Orthodox order of St Basil in Supraśl, the mosque in Kruszyniany and the synagogue in Tykocin represent a panoply of faiths.

View from the belfry of Frombork Cathedral

◁ **Sunset over the lakelands of northeast Poland**

Exploring Warmia, Mazuria and Białystok Region

Northeastern Poland is an ideal place for a
longer holiday. It is suitable for watersports
such as sailing trips on the Mazurian Lakes or
canoeing expeditions down the Czarna Hańcza
or Krutynia rivers, and there are also plenty of
opportunities for cycling tours. For unspoiled
primeval scenery, the Białowieża Forest National
Park with its bison reserve and the Biebrza
marshes, with their population of nesting birds,
are almost without equal.

Szczurkowo, a village where storks
outnumber people

SIGHTS AT A GLANCE

Baroque façade of the Jesuit
church in Święta Lipka

GETTING AROUND

The main road is Highway No. 16 from Grudziądz via Olsztyn to Augustów. Highway E77 goes from the south to Elbląg, highway 51 runs from Olsztyn to the border with the Russian Kaliningrad District, while highway 8 links Augustów with Białystok. Charter flights depart from Szymany, the region's only airport, near the town of Szczytno, and there are also connections with some airports in Germany. There are rail links with all major towns, and buses link other towns in the region.

The forests of Suwalszczyzna, carpeted with mushrooms

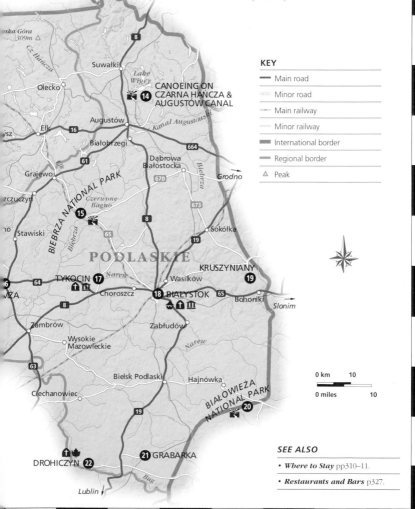

KEY

▬▬	Main road
▭▭	Minor road
⊷⊷	Main railway
──	Minor railway
▬▬	International border
▬▬	Regional border
△	Peak

SEE ALSO

Frombork ❶

The history of this fortified town goes back to the second half of the 13th century, when it became a Warmian chapter (diocesan capital). The Gothic cathedral, which was erected in 1342–88, has an unusual form, with no towers on its west end, giving it the appearance of a Cistercian monastery, and an eight-bay nave that allowed each member of the chapter to have a separate altar. There are also several canons' stalls in the chancel. The cathedral is surrounded by defensive walls set with towers and pierced by a large main gate in its south side. In the cathedral grounds are a bishop's palace and chapterhouse.

VISITORS' CHECKLIST

Road map D1. **Cathedral** ☐
9am–5pm Mon–Sat (8:30am–3pm winter). **Copernicus Tower** ☐
9:30am–5pm Tue–Sat (summer).
Museum *Tel 055 244 00 71.* ☐
9am–4pm Tue–Sun (4:30 summer).
Planetarium *Tel 055 244 00 83.*
☐ *9:30am–5pm daily.* 🎫 **Organ recitals** *noon, 3pm (summer).* 🎵

Altar of St Anne
The Altar of St Anne, in the north aisle, has as its focal point this subtle painting of 1639 by the Gdańsk artist Bartholomäus Strobel.

Former High Altar
Commissioned by Bishop Łukasz Watzenrode, uncle of Nicolaus Copernicus, the high altar was made in Toruń in 1504. It is in the form of a polyptych and is now in the south aisle. The central panel has a carving of the Virgin, depicted as a Maiden of the Apocalypse.

Bishop's Palace
The palace now houses the Copernicus Museum.

Organ
The instrument was made by Daniel Nitrowski of Gdańsk in 1683–4.

Main gate

Copernicus Tower

High Altar
Designed by Franciszek Placidi in 1742–52, the high altar is almost identical to that in the collegiate church at Dobre Miasto (see p280). The central panel is a painting of the Virgin by Stefan Torelli.

The Belfry
Also known as the Copernicus Tower, it houses a planetarium.

Braniewo ❷

Road map D1. 🏯 *17,100.*
🚌 🚉 www.braniewo.pl

The fortified town of Braniewo was founded by the Teutonic Knights in 1240. It was the seat of the bishops of Warmia and later became the diocesan capital of Warmia. A member of the Hanseatic League, the town was a busy port and grew prosperous through the linen trade. During the Counter-Reformation it played an important role as the first Jesuit centre in Poland: the Hosianum Jesuit College was founded here in 1565, and a papal college set up in 1578.

Just 8 km (5 miles) of the Russian border, Braniewo has become an important transit point for travellers crossing from one country into the other. Although it suffered severe damage during World War II, several fine buildings are still to be seen here.

🔒 Church of St Catherine
ul. Katedralna 3. **Tel** 055 243 24 29.
The nave of the Gothic Church of St Catherine (Kościół św Katarzyny) dates from 1343–81 and the vaulting and tower from the 15th century. War damage reduced the church to little more than ruins, but it has been extensively restored.

Church of St Catherine in Braniewo

🔒 Church of St Anthony
ul. Królewiecka 24.
Tel 055 243 23 61.
The Neo-Classical Church of St Anthony (Kościół św Antoniego) was built in 1830–38 by the German architect Karl Friedrich Schinkel. Originally Protestant, it is now a Catholic church.

🏰 Tower of the Bishop's Castle
ul. Gdańska. ⬤ *to the public.*
The tower, built in the 13th century as a town gate, led from the Castle of the Bishops of Warmia to a close linking it to the town walls.

Elbląg ❸

Road map D1. 🏯 *127,000.* 🚌 🚉
www.elblag.pl

Once a large port on a par with Gdańsk, Elbląg is today known for its large ABB engineering plant, its restored old town and for

Postmodern houses in the old town of Elbląg

producing the beer Specjal, which is popular in the Pomerania region. Founded in 1237 by the Teutonic Knights, the town was part of the Polish Republic from 1466 to 1772, when under the Partitions it passed to Prussian rule. After the devastation of World War II, only the most important old buildings of Elbląg were rebuilt. The Brama Targowa tower is all that remains of the former Gothic fortifications that surrounded the town.

In the old town, just a few town houses, on Ulica Wigilijna, survive. Today a programme of rebuilding is under way; houses in the style of the old Hanseatic merchants' houses, with stairways and their typical gables, are revitalizing the old town. The quarter is well provided with friendly bars and good restaurants.

🔒 Church of the Virgin Mary
ul. Kuśnierska 6. **Tel** 055 232 53 86.
⬤ *10am–6pm Tue–Sat, 10am–5pm Sun.* www.galeria-el.pl
This Gothic church with a double aisle was built for Dominican monks in the 14th century. After World War II it became the EL art gallery.

🔒 Church of St Nicholas
ul. Mostowa 18.
Tel 055 232 69 79 or 232 45 85.
The Church of St Nicholas (Kościół św Mikołaja) was begun in the 13th century and completed in 1510. The interior includes a font from 1387 by Bernhuser, a *Crucifixion* ascribed to Jan van der Matten and a late Gothic altar with the Adoration of the Magi.

The EL art gallery in the Church of the Virgin Mary

THE ELBLĄG CANAL

The Elbląg Canal is one of the most extraordinary feats of hydraulic engineering in Poland. A network of canals and locks connecting a number of lakes, it was built in 1848–72 by the Dutchman Georg Jacob Steenke. Including its branches, its total length is 212 km (133 miles). Ingenious slipways enable barges to be hauled overland from one lake to another where the difference in the water levels is too high for conventional locks to be built: there are five slipways along the 10-km (6-mile) section between

Buczyniec and Całuny, and from the canalside ships can be seen being hauled along them. You can book a boat trip along the canal that will take you through the Vistula valley and Iława Lake District.

Morąg

Road map D2. 🏘 14,900. 🚉 🚌
🛈 pl. Jana Pawła II 1 (089 757 38
26). **www**.morag.pl

Located in the lakelands of
Iławski Morąg, the town of
Morąg was founded by the
Teutonic Knights – like all
other towns in the region. It
received its municipal charter
in 1327. Despite joining the
Prussian Union, Morąg
remained part of the state of
the Teutonic Knights, and up
until 1945 its history was
linked to that of ducal Prussia.
In the town are the remains of
a 14th-century Teutonic castle,
a Gothic town hall that was
rebuilt after World War II, and
the Church of St Joseph
(Kościół św Józefa), built in
the 14th century and extended
in the late 15th, with Gothic
polychromes from that time.
Morąg is the birthplace
of the German philosopher
Gottfried von Herder *(see
below)*. A **museum** dedicated
to him is housed in a Baroque
palace that once belonged to
the Dohn family.

🏛 **Johann Gottfried von
Herder Museum**
ul. Dąbrowskiego 54. *Tel* 089 757
28 48. ⬜ 9am–5pm Tue–Sun (Oct–
May: to 4pm). 🖼

Dobre Miasto ❺

Road map E2. 🏘 11,000. 🚉 🚌
www.dobremiasto.com.pl

Founded in 1326, Dobre Miasto
owes its historical importance
to the fact that, in 1347, it
became the seat of a college
of canons of the diocese of

Interior of the Gothic collegiate
church in Dobre Miasto

Warmia. The vast Gothic
collegiate church that they
established was built in the
second half of the 1300s.
Its impressive interior
includes two Gothic side altars
as well as a Baroque high
altar almost identical in design
to that made by Franciszek
Placidi for Frombork Cathedral
(see p278). The church also
possesses richly decorated
Baroque stalls down each
side, which have remarkable
Gothic steps carved into
them in the shape of lions.

Lidzbark Warmiński ❻

Road map E1. 🏘 17,200. 🚉 🚌
www.lidzbarkwarminski.pl

From 1350 to 1795 Lidzbark
was the main residence of the
bishops of Warmia, and one
of the region's major towns.
Picturesquely set on a bend
of the River Łyna, the town is
dominated by the medieval
Bishops' Castle. The massive

edifice with corner towers was
built in the second half of the
14th century. Of special interest
are the Palace of Bishop
Grabowski and the Great
Refectory in the east wing, the
castle's Rococo chapel and
armoury in the south wing, the
Small Refectory in the west
wing and the bishops' private
apartments located in the north
wing. The cloistered courtyard
is decorated with murals.
The astronomer Nicolaus
Copernicus *(see p273)* lived
here as secretary and physician
to his uncle, Bishop Łukasz
von Wantzenrode, in 1503–10.
The castle now houses the
Warmia Museum and a bar
and art gallery in its cellars.
On the opposite bank of
the Łyna, in the historic town
centre, stands the fine **Gothic
Church of Saints Peter and Paul**
(Kościół św Piotra i Pawła).
There are also remnants of
the city walls, and the main
gate, the Brama Wysoka, still
stands. The former Protestant
church (now Orthodox)
nearby was built in 1821–3
by Karl Friedrich Schinkel.

🏛 **Regional Museum**
pl. Zamkowy 1. *Tel* 089 767 21 11.
⬜ 9am–4pm Tue–Sun (Jun–Aug: to
5pm). **www**.muzeum.olsztyn.pl
On display is a selection of
Warmian art and a unique
collection of icons from the
Convent of the Old Believers'
in Wojnowo *(see p284)*.

🛉 **Church of Saints Peter
and Paul**
ul. Kościelny 1. *Tel* 089 767 23 15.
⬜ 9am–5pm Tue–Sun (Sep–
19 May: to 4pm).

The Gothic cloisters of the Bishop's
Castle in Lidzbark

JOHANN GOTTFRIED VON HERDER (1744–1803)

The German writer and philosopher
Johann Gottfried von Herder, who was
born in Morąg, was one of the great
figures of the Enlightenment. He
studied theology in Königsberg
(Kaliningrad) before entering the priest-
hood. He saw the importance of nations
in the making of history and the role
of culture and language in
preserving national identity.
While living in Riga, he
recorded Latvian folk songs.

Olsztyn ❼

Road map E2. 🏯 *158,000.* 🚆 🚌
🛈 *ul. Staromiejska 1 (089 535 35 65).* ⭘ *8:30am–4pm Mon–Fri, 9am–noon Sat.* 🎭 *Olsztyn Blues Nights; Castle Poetry Readings (Jul).*
www.um.olsztyn.pl

Olsztyn is the largest city in Warmia and Mazuria and the main town of the two regions. It is a centre of both academic and cultural life as well as a major city. It is also associated with several sporting heroes, particularly in speedway and aerobatics. It hosts the various events that make up the Olsztyn Summer Arts festival *(see p33).*

The Gothic Castle of the Warmian Chapter, which was built in the 14th century, formed the beginning of the city. The castle was built on a hill on the banks of the Łyna. It was a four-sided fortress of modest proportions with residential quarters in the north wing and a service wing to the south. The palace in the east wing was added in 1756–8. The finest part of the building is the refectory, which has intricate crystalline vaulting. On the wall of the cloister is a remarkable diagram of an equinox probably drawn by Nicolaus Copernicus, who combined his duties as an administrator of the chapter in Olsztyn with his astronomical observations. The castle now houses the **Museum of Warmia and Mazuria**, which has a special

The High Gate, part of the defences of Olsztyn old town

section dedicated to Nicolaus Copernicus. The first floor contains an ethnographical and natural history collection.

The castle's fortifications were linked to the city walls, which were built after 1353 on the far side of the moat. The moat today has an open-air theatre that is used for concerts in summer.

In the picturesque old town of Olsztyn, set on a slope, are remnants of the walls and the High Gate. The quaint little Market Square surrounded by arcaded houses was built during the post-war reconstruction of the city, but the houses retain their original cellars, which today are given over to bars, restaurants and cafés. Standing in the middle of the square is a Baroque town hall, whose wings were added in 1927–9.

Another important building in the Market Square is the Gothic **Cathedral of St James** (Katedra św Jakuba), most

probably built between 1380 and 1445. The very fine crystalline vaulting was added in the early 16th century.

🏛 **Museum of Warmia and Mazuria**
ul. Zamkowa 2. **Tel** 089 527 95 96. ⭘ *Jun–Sep: 9am–5pm Tue–Sun (to 7pm Wed, free adm); Oct–May: 10am–4pm Tue–Sun.*
www.muzeum.olsztyn.pl

🔒 **Cathedral of St James**
ul. Staszica 12.
Tel 089 527 32 80.

Environs

Barczewo, 10 km (6 miles) east of Olsztyn, is the birthplace of Feliks Nowowiejski (1877–1946), composer of the *Rota*, a patriotic Polish anthem. His family home contains a small **museum**.

Halfway between Olsztyn and Nidzica, in the local Ethnography Park, lies the country's oldest **open air museum** of folk architecture, including traditional wooden windmills, arts and crafts.

🏛 **Feliks Nowowiejski Museum**
ul. Mickiewicza 13. **Tel** 089 674 04 79. ⭘ *9am–5pm Tue, Thu, Sat; 10am–6pm Wed, Fri. Sun by appt (660 017 208).*

🏛 **Budownictwa Ludowego Open Air Museum**
ul. Leszna 23. **Tel** 089 519 21 64. ⭘ *mid–end Apr, Sep, Oct: Tue–Sun; May–Aug: daily – hours vary.*

The Castle of the Warmian Chapter in Olsztyn

The monument to the Battle of Grunwald outside the town

Grunwald ❽

Road Map E2. 🕍 *420.* 🚌
🚩 *Battle of Grunwald (15 Jul).*

The fields between Grunwald and Stębark (Tannenberg in German) were the scene of one of the greatest battles of the Middle Ages. On 15 July 1410, the forces of the Teutonic Knights – some 14,000 cavalry plus infantry commanded by Ulrich von Jungingen, the Grand Master of the Teutonic Knights – faced 24,000 Polish-Lithuanian and Ruthenian cavalry and several thousand infantry led by Władysław II Jagiełło. The knights suffered a resounding defeat, and the Grand Master himself was killed. Historians believe that during World War I, in August 1914, the German Field Marshal

Hindenburg deliberately chose this site for his victorious battle against the Russians in order to negate the memory of that defeat. The monument to the medieval Battle of Grunwald that stands on the site was designed by Jerzy Bandura and Witold Cęckiewicz and unveiled in 1960. Nearby is a small **museum** with a collection of documents about the battle and archaeological finds from the site. For several years the battle's anniversary has been marked by re-enactments of the engagement as it is described in chronicles.

🏛 **Museum of the Battle of Grunwald in Stębark**
Stębark 1. *Tel* 089 647 22 15. ⬭
10 Apr–Sep: 9:30am–6:30pm daily.

Nidzica ❾

Road Map E2. 🕍 *15,200.* 🚃 🚌
🛈 *pl. Wolności 1 (089 625 03 70).*
🚩 *Nidzica Festival (May).*
www.nidzica.pl

The main feature of Nidzica is the Teutonic Castle, which overlooks the town from a hill. It was built in the late 1300s and altered in the 16th century. Reduced to ruins, it was rebuilt in the 1800s and again after World War II. Part of it is now a hotel. Some of the town's medieval fortifications also survive.

Environs
The **Tartars' Stone** lies 2 km (just over 1 mile) south of

Nidzica. This large rock, with a circumference of 19 m (63 ft), marks the spot where, according to legend, the leader of the Tartars was killed in 1656, thus sparing Nidzica from invasion in 1656.

Castle for the Bishops of Warmia, built to repulse Lithuanian attacks

Reszel ❿

Road Map E1. 🕍 *5,400.* 🚌
www.reszel.pl

This little town was once a major Warmian city. It was granted a municipal charter in 1337 and in the second half of the 14th century a Gothic **Castle for the Bishops of Warmia** was built here. The castle's tower commands a splendid view over the town. The castle is now a hotel and also houses a **gallery** of contemporary art.

There are two churches: the Gothic Church of Saints Peter and Paul, built in the 1300s with the addition of late 15th-century vaulting, and the former

The Gothic Castle of the Teutonic Knights in Nidzica

For hotels and restaurants in this region see pp301–11 and p327

Trompe l'oeil paintings in the pilgrimage church in Święta Lipka

Kętrzyn ⑫

Road Map E1. 🏘 28,300. 🚃 🚌
ℹ️ *pl. Piłsudskiego 10/1 (089 751 47
65).* www.ketrzyn.pl

From the 14th century, Kętrzyn
was the seat of the Prosecutor
of the Teutonic Knights, who
built the castle that can still be
seen today. Kętrzyn then
passed to Prussia and later
Germany, but retained a sizeable Polish population. The
original name for the town was
Rastembork; in 1946 it was
renamed in honour of Polish
national activist Wojciech
Kętrzyński. The old town was
almost entirely flattened during
World War II: only the town
walls and the Church of St
George (Kościół św Jerzego)
survived. Its exterior is modest,
but the interior is impressive –
its finest decoration is the crystalline vaulting of around 1515.

Environs
Ten km (6 miles) east of
Kętrzyn is **Gierłoż**, location
of the "Wolf's Lair", Adolf
Hitler's headquarters in 1940.
It consisted of dozens of
reinforced concrete bunkers
built in woodland. There was
also an airfield, railway lines
and a power station. Here,
on 20 July 1944, the German
officer Claus von Stauffenberg
made an unsuccessful attempt
on Hitler's life. The lair was
never discovered by the
Allies, and the bunkers were
blown up by the withdrawing
Germans in January 1945.

Church of St John the Baptist,
now an Orthodox church,
built in 1799–1800 in the
Baroque style.

🏛 Castle Gallery
ul. Podzamcze 4. **Tel** 089 625 03
70. ⬜ May–Sep: 9am–5pm daily;
Oct–Apr: 9am–4pm Tue–Sat.

Święta Lipka ⑪

Road Map E2. 🏘 190. 🚌
🎵 *Święta Lipka Music Evenings
(Jun–Aug).* www.swieta-lipka.pl

Święta Lipka has one of the
most important **shrines** of the
cult of the Virgin in Poland.
The name of the town means
"holy lime" (or linden tree),
and the legend that grew up
concerns a miraculous
sculpture of the Virgin that
was carved by a prisoner in
the 15th century and hung
from a roadside lime tree. A
chapel containing the statue
of the Virgin, destroyed during
the Reformation, was built
around it. The land was part
of ducal Prussia. In 1619 a

temporary chapel was built
here, followed in 1687–93 by
a proper church, which was
cared for by the Jesuits. In
1694–1708 cloisters and
outside chapels were added
and the façade and belfry
were completed in 1729.
    During the Counter-
Reformation Święta Lipka was
a Catholic stronghold within
Protestant ducal Prussia.
Large donations were made
for decorating the church,
resulting in one of the finest
and most intriguing examples
of Baroque art in Poland.
    The interior contains
frescoes, including trompe
l'oeil paintings in the dome
by Mathias Mayer, and the
high altar has an image of the
Virgin dating from about
1640. The figure organ built
in 1721 by Johann Mosengel
of Królewiec (Königsberg) is
a great attraction for both
tourists and pilgrims. In
summer, about eight organ
recitals are given every day,
and during some of them the
figures in the organ loft are
set in motion.

**Crystalline vaulting in the Church
of St George in Kętrzyn**

The Great Mazurian Lakes **⓭**

The Great Mazurian Lakes are the largest in Poland and
a popular holiday spot in summer. Despite this, the
countryside remains largely unspoiled, and many rare plants
and birds thrive here. The lakes are interlinked by rivers
and canals, and are suitable for yachting or canoeing trips.
Another way to see the region is to take a cruise aboard
a ship of the Mazurian Shipping Company or to drive
along the roads that wind among the lakeside trees.

    The district is a paradise for ramblers and for those who
delight in discovering secret spots. Its woods conceal
overgrown bunkers built by the Germans in World War II.

Sztynort, once the residence of
the Prussian Lehndorff family,
stands on a large peninsula.
Some of the oak trees in the
park surrounding the house
are three centuries old.

Ryn
*The castle that towers over
the town was built by
Konrad Wallenrod, Grand
Master of the Teutonic
Knights, for his brother
Frederick in 1394. It was
rebuilt in the English
Gothic style in 1853.*

Mikołajki
*The summer capital of the Mazurian Lake District is
the location of its main yachting marina. A variety
of vessels – from sailing dinghies, yachts and canoes
to motorboats – are available for hire.*

Wojnowo
*The church, cemetery
and convent at
Wojnowo were built by
the Old Believers, who
fled Russia in the 18th
and 19th centuries.*

**The Pranie Forester's
House Museum** honours
the poet Konstanty
Ildefons Gałczynski
(1905–53), who spent the
last days of his life here.

For hotels and restaurants in this region see pp310–11 and p327

Giżycko
In the woods beside the town, on an isthmus between the lakes, is the grim Prussian Boyen Castle, which was built in 1844.

VISITORS' CHECKLIST

Road map F1, F2, E2. 🚃 🚌
Giżycko, Pisz, Ruciane Nida.
ℹ️ *Mikołajki (087 421 68 50).*
Mazurian Shipping Company
Giżycko. **Tel** *087 428 53 32.*
Pisz Regional Museum
Tel *087 423 22 64.* 🕐 *1 Oct–30 Apr: 8am–3pm daily; 1 May–30 Sep: 8am–4pm daily.*

Lake Niegocin
Like most others in the region, the lake is popular with watersports enthusiasts and swimmers. Holiday resorts and campsites are scattered around the lakes.

Lake Śniardwy is not very deep but, covering an area of 114 sq km (44 sq miles), it is the largest in Poland.

Water Lilies
Several varieties of water lily can be seen in the region's lakes.

```
0 km            10
0 miles         10
```

KEY

▬ Major road

  Minor road

☆ Viewpoint

WILD SWANS

Lake Łuknajno, which is listed by UNESCO as a World Biosphere Reserve, has become one of Poland's finest nature reserves for wild swans. The fact that the lake is shallow – its average depth does not exceed 1.5 m (4 ft) – makes it easy for the birds to feed on the weed that grows on the lakebed. In 1922 eggs laid by the swans of Lake Łuknajno were used to regenerate Berlin's swan population. Lake Łuknajno attracts wildlife photographers from all over the world, lured by the chance of an unforgettable shot. To safeguard the natural habitat, boats are not allowed on the lake.

A swan on Lake Łuknajno

The local history museum in Pisz features a granite column with a human face known as the Prussian Woman.

Canoeing on the Czarna Hańcza and Augustów Canal ⓮

This is one of the most beautiful canoeing routes in Poland. In some places the narrow, winding River Czarna Hańcza is as swift as a mountain stream; in others its course slows as its banks widen. The route downstream passes swamps and lakes and goes through locks on the Augustów Canal that have remained almost unchanged since the time that they were built at the beginning of the 19th century. Canoe trips may be made individually or in organized groups.

Lake Wigry ①
Lake Wigry, in Wigry National Park, is the largest lake in the Suwałki region. Part of the "silent zone", it has numerous islands.

Camaldolite Monastery ②
This monastery stands on the peninsula in Lake Wigry. The monastery buildings have been converted into a hotel. Beyond, the Czarna Hańcza River flows from the lake.

The Czarna Hańcza River ③
The most beautiful stretch of the Czarna Hańcza, beyond the village of Wysoki Most, takes a meandering route. All around is the Augustów Forest.

Rygol ④
Here the river forks, its right arm joining the Augustów Canal. Canoeists may stray off the route and follow the canal leading to the border with Belarus, but they must turn back at the last lock before the border, which is closed.

Locks ⑤
The Augustów Canal connects the River Niemen with the River Biebrza and, further on, with the Vistula, passing through several locks on the way. Built in 1823–39, the canal was a great engineering achievement.

Typical landscape of the Augustów lake district

Augustów ⑥

Augustów is a major tourist town with many hotels, guesthouses and rest centres. There is a large yachting marina on the canal.

Białobrzegi ⑦

Canoeing trips usually end in Augustów, but canoeists may continue along the Augustów Canal through Białobrzegi southwards to the swamps on the River Biebrza.

| 0 km | 5 |
| 0 miles | 5 |

EY

- Canoeing route
- Main road
- Other road
- Viewpoint

Meadows covered by the floodwaters of the River Biebrza

Biebrza National Park ⑮

Road map F2. 🚌 🏠 *Osowiec National Park Management (085 738 30 35).* 🎫 *tickets available in the management office, foresters' lodges and gamekeepers' cottages.* www.biebrza.org.pl

Biebrza National Park is one of the wildest places in Europe, untouched by human activity. It stretches for 70 km (50 miles) along the banks of the River Biebrza and contains Poland's largest swamps, which are home to a wide variety of wildlife. A close encounter with a moose is a distinct possibility. The greatest attraction of the swamps, however, is their rich bird life; over 260 species live here, and bird-watchers from afar come to the swamps to observe them. The most interesting swamp for bird life is **Red Swamp** (Czerwone Bagno), part of a strictly protected nature reserve accessible only by means of a wooden walkway. Walkways have also been installed in other parts of the park. A walk along the red tourist trail holds a range of attractions – although you may have to wade through mud to reach them. Visitors may hire a guide and tour the swamps in a punt, or descend the River Biebrza in a canoe, for which a ticket and the permission of the park management are required.

In **Osowiec**, in the middle of the swamps, there is a beaver reserve. Nearby stand the partly blown-up walls of a Russian redoubt. Although it was impregnable, the Russians, fearful of the German offensive, abandoned it in 1915.

Łomża ⑯

Road map F2. 🏠 *62,000.* 🚉 🚌 🏠 *Woyska Polskiego 1 (086 216 47 18).* www.lomza.pl

Łomża is a large provincial town with many distinguished buildings. Its Gothic **cathedral**, built in the 16th century by the last dukes of Mazovia, has a number of notable features: in particular, the cellular and star vaulting of its interior, the silver reliefs on the high altar, and the tombs of Andrzej Modliszewski, mayor of Łomża, his wife and their son. The tombs are the work of Santi Gucci. The Capuchin church and regional museum are also of interest.

Environs

In **Nowogród**, on a high bank of the River Narew, 15 km (9 miles) northwest of Łomża, is a *skansen* in which the houses and other buildings of a typical Kurpie village are displayed. Opened in 1927, it is one of Poland's oldest *skansens*.

Star vaulting over the nave of Łomża Cathedral

For hotels and restaurants in this region see pp310–11 and p327

The synagogue in Tykocin, now a
Regional Museum

Tykocin ⓱

Road Map F2. 🚶 *1,800.* 🚌
ℹ️ *ul. Złota 2 (085 718 72 32).*

The town of Tykocin
was granted a
municipal charter
in 1425. In 1659 it
was given to Stefan
Czarnecki, hero of
the bitter wars with
Sweden, in recog-
nition of his service
to the king and to
Poland. It later
passed to the royal
field commander Jan
Klemens Branicki.
The town owes its
present appearance
to renovation –
financed by
Branicki – that
was carried out
after a fire in 1741.

In the centre of the
Market Square there stands
a Baroque monument to
Stefan Czarnecki that was
carved between 1761 and
1763 by the court sculptor
Pierre Coudray. The **parish
church** on the east side of
the square was built a little
earlier, in 1750. The Baroque
synagogue, which dates from
1642, is a relic of the town's
former Jewish population.
Inside, the walls are inscribed
with religious quotations in
Hebrew and Aramaic. The
synagogue now contains
the **Tykocin Museum**.

🏛 **Tykocin Museum**
ul. Kozia 2. **Tel** 085 718 16 26.
⏱ 10am–6pm Tue–Sun (Oct–Apr:
to 5pm). 🎫 (free on Sat.)

**Statue by
J.C. Redler at
Branicki Palace in
Białystok**

Białystok ⓲

Road Map F2. 🚶 *295,000.* 🚉 🚌
ℹ️ *ul. Malmeda 6 (085 732 68 31).*
🎉 *Białystok Days (around 20 Jun).*
www.bialystok.pl

Białystok is the largest town
in northeast Poland. Its
population is both Polish and
Belarussian, something that
can easily be read in the
cityscape: the domes of the
Orthodox church rise up next
to the towers of the Catholic
church, and there are many
Belarussian cultural institutions. Białystok was once
owned by the Branicki family;
indeed, the layout of the town
is dominated by their
former residence,
Branicki Palace.
The Baroque
palace was built by
Tylman van Gameren
in the 17th century
and extended by Jan
Zygmunt Deybel –
who gave it the
appearance of a royal
mansion – between
1728 and 1758. It was
modelled on the
Palace of Versailles,
and a formal park, with
terraces, canals, fountains,
summer houses and
numerous sculptures,
was laid out around it.
Like other members of
the high aristocracy,
Jan Klemens Branicki,
royal field commander
and an extremely
wealthy man in his
own right, maintained his
own private army. He was
also a connoisseur of art.

In political circles, however,
he was unpopular, opposing
reform and contributing to the
ruin of Poland. Parts of the
palace now house the town's
medical academy.

Another interesting building
is the **Church of St Roch**
(Kościół św Rocha), in
reinforced concrete, designed
by Oskar Sosnkowski, and
built between 1927 and 1946.
The Baroque town hall in the
Market Square houses a
Regional Museum.

⛪ **Branicki Palace**
ul. Kilińskiego 1. **Tel** 085 742 56 14.

🏛 **Church of St Roch**
ul. ks. Abramowicza 1. **Tel** 085 652
10 58 or 652 06 33.

🏛 **Regional Museum**
Rynek Kościuszki 10. **Tel** 085 742
14 73. ⏱ 10am–5pm Tue–Sun
(May–Sep: to 8pm Fri). 🎫 (free Sun).

Kruszyniany ⓳

Road Map G2. 🚶 *110.*

Kruszyniany and nearby
Bohoniki count among their
inhabitants the descendants of
the Tartars who settled here
in the 17th century. Although
they became fully integrated
into the community a long
time ago, their Muslim faith
and customs live on.
Descendants of the Tartars
also live in the Podlasie
villages of Nietupy, Łużyny
and Drahle. Kruszyniany has
a charming wooden **mosque**,
originating in the 18th century
and rebuilt in 1843. The
tombstones in the Muslim
graveyard face Mecca.

Wooden mosque in Kruszyniany, built by the descendants of the Tartars

Białowieża National Park ⓴

Road Map G3. 🚂 🚶 *Park Pałacowy 11 (085 681 29 01).*
www.bpn.com.pl

The Białowieża Forest, covering almost 1,500 sq km (580 sq miles), is Europe's largest natural forest. It lies partly in Poland and partly in Belarus. The larger – Belarussian – part is virtually inaccessible to tourists; the Polish part became a national park in 1932. Many parts of the park have preserved their natural character – that of a primeval forest. The areas of greatest interest may be visited only with a guide. Recently, the park's borders have been extended on the Polish side.

The forest has an impressive abundance of flora and fauna. There are several thousand species of plants and 11,000 species of animals, including many very rare birds, such as the capercaillie, black stork and golden eagle. Larger mammals include elk, deer, roe deer, wild boar, wolf, lynx and, most famously, the European bison.

On the road through the forest there is a bison-breeding centre and enclosures of bison, deer, wild boar and Polish ponies. The park also has a **forest museum**, whose exhibits were once housed in a brick hunting lodge used by the tsars. It was torched by German forces in 1944. Only an Orthodox church remains.

Białowieża National Park has been listed by UNESCO as a World Biosphere Reserve.

🏛 **Białowieża Forest Museum**
Palace Park Botanical Gardens. **Tel** 085 682 97 04. ◯ mid-Apr–mid-Oct: 9am–4:30pm Mon–Fri, 10am–6pm Sat & Sun; mid-Oct–mid-Apr: 9am–4pm Tue–Sun.

Grabarka ⓴

Road Map F3. 🏘 50. 🚂 Nurzec.
🚌 **Orthodox convent Tel** 085 655 00 10. **www**.grabarka.pl

For Poland's Orthodox Christians, there is no more important place of pilgrimage in the country than the Holy Mountain outside Grabarka. The story goes that in 1770, when the plague was ravaging the town, the inhabitants of Grabarka were directed by a heavenly sign to erect a cross on the hill. The

Part of the forest of crosses on the Holy Mountain outside Grabarka

Baroque façade of the Benedictine church in Drohiczyn

plague passed and the hill became a hallowed site.

To this day its slopes are covered with hundreds of votive crosses. The original wooden church, destroyed by an arsonist in 1990, was replaced by a brick-built church. The Orthodox convent next to it is the only one in Poland.

Drohiczyn ⓶

Road Map F3. 🏘 21,000. 🚌
🚶 ul. Kraszewskiego 13 (085 655 70 69). **www**.drohiczyn.pl

Drohiczyn, set on a high bank of the Bug River, is today a small, quiet town. As early as the 13th century, however, it was a major centre of trade, and in 1520 it became the provincial capital of Podlasie. In 1795, with the Third Partition of Poland, it was demoted to the status of an ordinary village.

The oldest surviving church in the town is the Baroque **Franciscan church**, dating from 1640–60. The cathedral, originally a Jesuit church, dates from 1696–1709. Nearby stands the former **Jesuit monastery**, later taken over by the Piarists. The striking **Benedictine church**, begun in 1744, has a typically Baroque undulating façade and elliptical interior. The **Orthodox church**, originally Greek Catholic, dates from 1792. To the east of the town, along the winding Bug River, lies a park, the **Podlasie Bug River Gorge**.

EUROPEAN BISON

The European bison *(Bison bonasus)* is the largest mammal native to Europe. The weight of an adult bull may reach 1,000 kg (2,200 lb). The largest population of bison ever recorded – 1,500 animals – was in Białowieża in 1860. Hunting these animals has always been restricted, but by World War I (1914–18) the species faced extinction. In 1929, several bison were brought to Poland from zoos in Sweden and Germany to be bred in their natural habitat. The first were set free in Białowieża National Park in 1952. Today bison can also be seen in the other great forests of Poland, including Borecka, Knyszyńska and Niepołomice *(see p162)*.

The European bison

TRAVELLERS'
NEEDS

WHERE TO STAY

The accommodation industry has come a long way since the late 20th century, when the standard of Polish hotels was much lower than that of their Western European counterparts. However, despite many luxury hotels being built and many existing hotels being modernized, there is still a dearth of good, affordable hotels. Many palaces and manor houses that would otherwise have fallen into ruin have been transformed into comfortable small hotels.

Porter at the Hotel Bristol in Warsaw

They are to be found all over Poland. While some offer luxurious suites, others provide rooms with period interiors at a moderate price. Cheap beds are also provided by PTTK hostels, mountain lodges and private guesthouses, and there are many campsites.

A list of selected hotels all over Poland, from the small and modest to the large and luxurious, including those run by international hotel chains, is to be found on pages 298–311.

Part of the elegant lobby of the Grand Hotel in Sopot *(see p310)*

HOTELS

At the upper end of the scale is a small number of luxury hotels with fine period interiors. These hotels were established in the 19th century or at the beginning of the 20th. The most elegant – and expensive – in this category is the Hotel Bristol in Warsaw. The Hotel Francuski in Cracow and Pod Orłem in Bydgoszcz may also be included in this group. The most common type of hotel is the architecturally mediocre modern building; against these, others such as the imposing Warsaw Sheraton, tend to stand out. Before 1989, the largest network of hotels in Poland was run by a state-owned company called Orbis. Today many Orbis hotels are part of well-known international chains, such as Novotel and Mercure.

For comfort at reasonable prices, try the small modern hotels with all conveniences and a pleasant family atmosphere. Recommended in this category are the Hanza, in the historic part of Gdańsk, and the Vivaldi in Poznań. Converted buildings are also recommended: among these are the Villa Hestia in Sopot, which has just a small number of rooms, and was once the eclectic home of a pre-war millionaire from Gdańsk, and the Jelonek in Jelenia Góra, a tastefully renovated Baroque tenement house.

MANOR HOUSES AND PALACES

Those who prefer staying in historic mansions can choose from a number of such establishments all over

The entrance to the Hotel Francuski in Cracow *(see p301)*

the country. Most – the former property of wealthy landlords or rich factory owners – were reduced to ruin in the communist era, so they are not filled with valuable paintings, fine antique furniture and the trappings of a comfortable lifestyle characteristic of old mansions. Some palaces have been thoroughly renovated,

One of the lounges in the luxurious Hotel Bristol in Warsaw *(see p298)*

◁ Outdoor cafés in the Market Square of the Old Town of Warsaw

The InterContinental hotel in Warsaw (see p298)

and their interiors refurbished with great attention paid to the needs and comfort of guests. They are usually quite expensive. Most of the grander hotels have a peaceful setting among trees in beautiful parks.

Others, at the cheaper end of the scale, tend to be furnished in a more basic manner, with functional rather than comfortable beds. This type of hotel will not have a swimming pool, lift or nightclub.

RESERVATIONS

When planning to visit a major town or city, a resort or a well-known tourist area, it is best to book a hotel in advance. Finding a room once you arrive can be difficult. In Warsaw, hotel accommodation is particularly scarce in June and July, from September to November and around public holidays. In Cracow, the tourist season lasts the whole year. In Poznań, accommodation is hard to find during the trade

The Hotel Neptun on the coast in Łeba (see p309)

fairs that take place here throughout the year. Rooms in resorts are hard to find during the holiday season. Accommodation in mountain resorts also tends to be scarce over Christmas and during the skiing season.

FACILITIES

Recent programmes of renovation and modernization mean that there has been a great improvement in the general standard of accommodation available in Poland. In many hotels, rooms have en suite toilets and showers or baths. Most have television and some have a video recorder. Generally, rooms tend not to be very large.

Some hotels offer an inexpensive laundry service; superior-standard hotels provide a 24-hour service and minibar. Guests should check out before noon. Those who wish to leave later may deposit their luggage in reception. Most hotel staff speak English.

PRICES AND REDUCED RATES

Hotel tariffs at the upper end of the scale are relatively high and change according to the season. The most expensive hotels are located in Warsaw and Poznań, closely followed by those in other major cities. During the trade fairs, accommodation prices in Poznań are usually much higher than at other times.

Hotels in small towns are generally cheaper, as are the

more out-of-the-way manor houses or palace hotels. Most hotels offer reduced rates at weekends and special rates for children.

Hotels belonging to international chains such as the Intercontinental offer a range of reduced rates. It is also acceptable to negotiate a reduction when booking. Budget accommodation is provided in the form of hotels that have been converted from hostels for workers, soldiers or students.

The restaurant of the Grand Hotel in Cracow (see p301)

HIDDEN EXTRAS

In most hotels, VAT (which currently varies from 7 to 22 per cent) and service are included in the price. As in other countries, international telephone calls made from hotel rooms can be quite expensive because the hotel charges a commission on top of the cost of the call. Breakfast is sometimes charged as an extra. Buffet breakfasts or pre-prepared breakfast sets are particularly popular. Tipping staff is not customary except in the more expensive hotels.

As a general rule there is no reduction for single travellers – the same price will be charged for a double room regardless of whether occupied by one or two guests. However, if there are many vacancies, some hotels may offer a double room for the same rate as they would charge for a single room.

The Hotel Amber in Międzyzdroje, located right on the beach

ROOMS AND FLATS TO LET

Rooms in private houses in towns and resorts are usually easy to find, even during the tourist season. In towns, the best way of obtaining information on private accommodation is from a tourist information centre. In a resort, it is better to explore and find a room on your own, comparing standards and prices. On the coast or at lakeside resorts, rooms may be hard to find outside the tourist season as many guesthouses only operate in summer. Accommodation agencies should provide a range of options from which to choose. When booking a room through an agency, payment must be made in cash. Cash is also the generally accepted form of payment in guesthouses.

AGRITOURISM

Agritourism, a type of ecological tourism connected with the countryside, has been developing since the beginning of the 1990s. As well as taking a room and enjoying home-cooked food and such things as fresh cow's milk, tourists may participate in daily farming tasks. At many farms, tourists can ride on horseback or in a horse-drawn carriage. Prices vary depending on the standard of accommodation and services

provided. Addresses of agritourist farms are available from tourist agencies. Such magazines as *Podróże, Voyage* and the tourist supplement issued with the Saturday edition of *Gazeta Wyborcza* may also be useful.

The Kadyny Palace Hotel

YOUTH HOSTELS

Poland has an excellent network of youth hostels. In most tourist areas they operate all year round. In summer, empty school buildings are converted into temporary hostels. Permanent hostels usually have shared rooms and a communal bathroom and kitchen. Due to their popularity, it is advisable

to book at least two or three days in advance.

On Fridays and Saturdays, as well as in spring and autumn, rooms in youth hostels are more difficult to find because they tend to be booked by school excursion groups. Hostels are usually closed from 10am to 4pm or 5pm, and again after 10pm.

The price per night is low, especially if you share a room with several other people. Holders of International Youth Hostel Federation cards are entitled to considerable reductions, even on these low rates.

MOUNTAIN LODGES

Hiking along marked mountain trails has long been popular in Poland and is one of the most important areas of tourism. The network of mountain lodges is very extensive; indeed, it is possible to walk the length and breadth of the Carpathian and Sudeten mountains staying only in mountain hostels.

Standards vary from modest to quite comfortable. It is advisable to book in advance, although after nightfall the staff cannot refuse to let you in, even if all the rooms are occupied. At worst you will end up sleeping on the floor. Mountain lodges usually have bathrooms, and buffets serving hot meals. It is also possible to hire equipment.

When hiking along Poland's southern border, hikers may stay in lodges on the Czech and Slovak side of the border and pay in Polish currency.

The Ornak alpine lodge in the Tatra Mountains

One of Poland's many campsites

CAMPSITES

While a few campsites are open all year round, most operate only from the beginning of May to the end of September. Standards do vary. Campsites can be found on the periphery of most large towns and cities as well as in some smaller towns, and at almost all tourist spots on the coast, beside lakes, rivers and in the mountains. In summer, some campsites are so crowded that tents almost touch one another, and it is usually quite noisy late into the night. All campsites are fenced in and have resident staff. Lighting, electricity (220 V), as well as running water, mobile toilets and showers are also provided. The large ones that operate throughout the year are better equipped and offer lounges, bungalows, playgrounds for children, and football pitches. At bivouacs, conditions are basic.

DISABLED TRAVELLERS

Newly built and renovated hotels and guesthouses usually have special facilities for disabled people, such as wheelchair access and chairlifts. Rooms with facilities for the disabled are also increasingly widely provided. However, provision for special needs is by no means universal, so it is advisable to contact the hotel beforehand to check what facilities for disabled people, if any, are provided.

TRAVELLING WITH CHILDREN

Children are welcome in most hotels and guesthouses; Polish culture is on the whole child-friendly. Extra beds in parents' rooms are usually provided on request. Many hotels offer special rates for children, and some make no charge for children up to the age of 3 or even, in some cases, 14. This cannot be assumed to be the case, however, so when booking it is definitely advisable to enquire.

Most hotel restaurants also serve special meals for children, although high chairs are rarely provided. Crèches and childcare facilities can be hard to find, so again, if childcare is required it is essential to check in advance.

Typical mountain lodge with rooms to let

DIRECTORY

ACCOMMODATION

Tourist Information Centre
Cracow,
ul. Pawia 8.
Tel 012 422 60 91.

Tourist Information Centre
Świnoujście,
Plac. Słowiański 6/1.
Tel 091 322 49 99.
www.swinoujscie.pl

Mazurian Tourism Promotion Agency
Giżycko,
ul. Warszawska 7.
Tel 087 428 52 65. .
www.gizycko.
turystyka.pl

Old Town Apartments
(Warsaw and Cracow)

www.warsawhotel.com
www.warsawtour.pl

Polish Hotels Chamber
Warsaw,
ul. Tarczyńska 8 lok. 17.
Tel 022 579 16 24.
www.ighp.pl

Polish Tourist Office (PTTK)
Warsaw,
ul. Senatorska 11.
Tel 022 826 22 51.
www.pttk.pl

Warsaw Private Accommodation Bureau
Warsaw,
ul. Miodowa 12 lok. 22.
Tel 022 636 86 99.
www.pando
apartments.com.pl

AGRITOURISM

Agritourist Information
Nowy Sącz, ul. Tarnowska
28. *Tel 018 441 41 55*
(7am–3pm) or
441 61 72 (7am–4pm).
www.stiazg.
agrowczasy.com

Polish Countryside Tourism Federation "Hospitable Farms"
Nałęczów,
ul. Kasztanowa 2.
Tel 081 501 43 11.
www.agroturystyka.pl

YOUTH HOSTELS

Polish Youth Hostels Association
Warsaw, ul. Chocimska 14.
Tel 022 849 81 28.
www.ptsm.org.pl

CAMPSITES

Polish Camping and Caravanning Federation
Warsaw, ul. Grochowska
331. *Tel 022 810 60 50.*
www.pfcc.eu

DISABLED TRAVELLERS

Office of the Government Plenipotentiary for the Disabled
Warsaw, ul. Nowogrodzka
11. *Tel 022 526 06 01.*
www.niepelnosprawni.
gov.pl

WEBSITES

www.polhotels.com
www.hotels.
inpoland.com
www.travelpoland.pl
www.orbis.pl

Choosing a Hotel

Hotels have been selected across a wide price range for facilities, good value and location. All rooms have private bath, TV and air conditioning, and they are wheelchair accessible unless otherwise indicated. The hotels are listed by area. For the street map of Warsaw, see pages 100–103. For the road map of Poland, see the back flap.

PRICE CATEGORIES
The following price ranges are for a standard double room and taxes per night during the high season. Breakfast is not included, unless specified.

ZL under 270 PLN
ZLZL 270–400 PLN
ZLZLZL 400–600 PLN
ZLZLZLZL 600–800 PLN
ZLZLZLZLZL over 800 PLN

WARSAW

ROYAL ROUTE Nathan's Villa Hostel

ul. Piękna 24-26, 00-549 **Tel** 022 622 29 46 **Fax** 022 622 29 46 **Rooms** 19   **Map** 3 B3

Warsaw's best-loved hostel boasts comfortable dormitories, modern fittings and a quiet courtyard location. Facilities on offer include fast Internet access, a fully equipped kitchen and daily laundry. A range of private rooms has been added for those who do not wish to share a dormitory. **www.nathansvilla.com**

ROYAL ROUTE (TRAKT KRÓLEWSKI) Le Royal Meridien-Bristol

ul. Krakowskie Przedmieście 42/44, 00-325 **Tel** 022 551 10 00 **Fax** 022 625 25 77 **Rooms** 205   **Map** 2 D4

A sumptuous Art Nouveau building and arguably the most famous hotel in Poland: the guest list runs from regents to rock stars. Rooms combine a pre-war aesthetic with 21st-century gadgetry, and the hotel has won countless awards for excellence. The Sunday brunches are renowned across the city. **www.lemeridien.pl**

CITY CENTRE Ibis Stare Miasto

ul. Muranowska 2, 00-209 **Tel** 022 310 10 00 **Fax** 022 310 10 10 **Rooms** 333   **Map** 1 C1

The typical Ibis standard, as replicated in their hundreds of hotels worldwide. Slightly anonymous rooms come with neutral colours and offer an atmosphere primed for travelling salesmen and tour groups. However, this remains one of the best deals in the city, and as such, it is often fully booked, so reserve in advance. **www.ibishotel.com**

CITY CENTRE Oki Doki

pl. Dąbrowskiego 3, 00-057 **Tel** 022 828 01 22 **Fax** 022 826 83 57 **Rooms** 37   **Map** 1 C5

Half-hostel, half-budget hotel. Rooms inside this Socialist-era building are decorated courtesy of local thrift stores and artists, and they come with names like Raspberry Thicket and House of the Cat. The bar promises to serve the cheapest beer in the city, and a fully kitted kitchen is available for independent-minded travellers. **www.okidoki.pl**

CITY CENTRE Holiday Inn

ul. Złota 48/54, 00-120 **Tel** 022 697 39 99 **Fax** 022 697 38 99 **Rooms** 336   **Map** 3 A1

This large modern hotel behind the main railway station is dwarfed by the skyscrapers around it. Rooms are worthy of the hotel's five stars and include games consoles, pay-per-view films and personally controlled air conditioning. The basement fitness club features a whirlpool tub and sauna. **www.holiday-inn.com/warsawpoland**

CITY CENTRE Residence St Andrews Palace

ul. Chmielna 30, 00-020 **Tel** 022 826 46 60 **Fax** 022 826 96 35 **Rooms** 24   **Map** 3 B1

Luxury apartments available for short- and long-term stays inside a building renovated to its pre-war 1900 glory. Accommodation overlooks a central courtyard, with fully kitted kitchens and separate living rooms, complete with mini-bar, sound system and cable TV. Housekeeping services are also provided. **www.residence.com.pl**

CITY CENTRE InterContinental

ul. Emilii Plater 49, 00-125 **Tel** 022 328 88 88 **Fax** 022 328 88 89 **Rooms** 326   **Map** 1 A5

A three-legged futuristic tower with a 40th-floor swimming pool that stares on to the Palace of Culture and Science. Immaculate rooms befit the hotel's ultra-modern style: they are colour-coordinated and offer Internet access and cable TV. Restaurants and bars can be found on the lower floors. **www.warsaw.intercontinental.com**

CITY CENTRE Marriott

al. Jerozolimskie 65/79, 00-697 **Tel** 022 630 63 06 **Fax** 022 830 00 41 **Rooms** 518   **Map** 3 A2

The Marriott ranks as a corporate favourite with a long line of celebrity guests. It is a *Dallas*-style city-centre skyscraper with countless amenities – from a top-floor bar to a casino and a collection of award-winning restaurants. The luxuriously appointed rooms have been magnificently renovated. **www.marriott.com**

CITY CENTRE Radisson SAS Centrum

ul. Grzybowska 24, 00-132 **Tel** 022 321 88 88 **Fax** 022 321 88 89 **Rooms** 311   **Map** 1 A4

Chic five-star lodgings in the heart of Warsaw's financial quarter. The hotel's modern front conceals rooms designed in three separate styles: maritime, Scandinavian and Italian. Amenities include swimming pool and gym, while those with less time on their hands will enjoy the addition of the "grab-and-run" breakfast. **www.radissonsas.com**

Key to Symbols *see back cover flap*

CITY CENTRE Sofitel Victoria

ul. Królewska 11, 00-065 Tel 022 657 80 11 Fax 022 657 80 57 Rooms 343 **Map** 1 C5

Located opposite the sprawling Saxon Gardens, the Sofitel Victoria was built in the 1970s in the Swedish style. It is a luxurious hotel with well-furnished rooms and comfortable beds. The two restaurants on site serve Polish and French cuisine. Cheaper rates are available for longer stays. **www.sofitel.com**

FURTHER AFIELD Campanile

ul. Towarowa 2, 00-811 Tel 022 582 72 00 Fax 022 582 72 01 Rooms 194

A pleasant mid-range hotel with well-appointed rooms and soothing colours. Standard trimmings such as air conditioning, bathtubs and cable TV can be expected, and the Campanile lies no more than a ten-minute walk from the main railway station. **www.campanile.com.pl**

FURTHER AFIELD Hotel MDM

pl. Konstytucji 1, 00-647 Tel 022 339 16 00 Fax 022 339 16 08 Rooms 132 **Map** 3 B4

This large hotel is in a prized location on one of Warsaw's best-known Socialist Realist housing developments, and many rooms offer superb views of the square outside. The renovated interior includes comfortable quarters equipped with mini-bars, cable TV and extra-thick curtains to guarantee a good night's sleep. **www.syrena.com.pl**

FURTHER AFIELD Premiere Classe

ul. Towarowa 2, 00-811 Tel 022 624 08 00 Fax 022 620 26 29 Rooms 126

Basic, box-style rooms come with TVs and adjoining modern bathrooms in this building, which also houses Premiere Classe's sister hotels: the Campanile and Kyriad Prestige. The best one-star choice in Warsaw, and recommended for budget travellers who count themselves too old for hostels. Advance booking essential. **www.premiereclasse.com.pl**

FURTHER AFIELD Karat

ul. Słoneczna 37, 00-789 Tel 022 849 84 54 Fax 022 849 52 94 Rooms 34

Tucked away in the expat enclave of Mokotów, the Karat features a reasonable three-star standard and affordable prices. Rooms follow a late 1980s aesthetic, though bathrooms have been fully updated. The Karat lacks the facilities of more modern competitors, but it does at least have a restaurant. **www.hotelkarat.pl**

FURTHER AFIELD Zajazd Napoleoński

ul. Płowiecka 83, 04-501 Tel 022 815 30 68 Fax 022 815 22 16 Rooms 24

This is the spot where Napoleon's troops camped on their disastrous march to Moscow, hence the name (Napoleon's Inn). Situated in a classic Polish manor house on Warsaw's right bank, it features rooms with a decidedly antique air, which is designed to evoke the Napoleonic era. **www.napoleon.waw.pl**

FURTHER AFIELD Golden Tulip Warsaw Centre

ul. Towarowa 2, 00-811 Tel 022 582 75 00 Fax 022 582 75 01 Rooms 144

One of the best three-star options in Warsaw, with well-soundproofed rooms that are each equipped with bathtub and cable TV. A gym and a sauna are also available for guests. The hotel is located inside a modern building with easy access to the train station. **www.goldentulipwarsawcentre.com**

FURTHER AFIELD Le Regina

ul. Kościelna 12, 00-218 Tel 022 531 60 00 Fax 022 531 60 01 Rooms 61 **Map** 2 D2

A quiet Nowe Miasto location proves the perfect position for this luxury retreat. Rooms are decorated in cream and caramel tones and feature furnishings imported from Italy and custom-made mosaics. Seemingly straight from the pages of a lifestyle magazine, Le Regina is one of the most memorable hotels you will visit. **www.leregina.com**

FURTHER AFIELD Radisson Blu Sobieski

pl. A. Zawiszy 1, 02-025 Tel 022 579 10 00 Fax 022 659 88 28 Rooms 435

A gaudy, multicovered façade shields a high-standard hotel with a marble lobby and glass-domed restaurant. Sitting directly on top of the restaurant is a courtyard garden that affords guests moments of solitude, while fitness facilities are available for more active residents. Past guests include Bill Clinton and Art Garfunkel. **www.sobieski.com.pl**

FURTHER AFIELD Rialto

ul. Wilcza 73, 00-670 Tel 022 584 87 00 Fax 022 584 87 01 Rooms 44

Poland's original boutique hotel features an Art Deco design and furnishings handpicked from the antiques stores of Paris. Rooms are individually decorated, with themes ranging from Colonial Africa to Jazz Age New York. The country's best-known chef, Kurt Scheller, plies his trade in the hotel's restaurant. **www.hotelrialto.com.pl**

FURTHER AFIELD Hyatt Regency

ul. Belwederska 23, 00-761 Tel 022 558 12 34 Fax 022 558 12 35 Rooms 246

Located in the embassy belt, a short walk from the historic Łazienki Park, the Hyatt has rooms that feature marble baths and stereo systems. Don one of the crested dressing gowns available to guests and relax. The 21st-century complex also boasts one of the top casinos and swimming pools in the city. **www.warsaw.regency.hyatt.com**

FURTHER AFIELD Westin

al. Jana Pawła II 21, 00-854 Tel 022 450 80 00 Fax 022 450 81 11 Rooms 361 **Map** 1 A5

A glass elevator spirits guests to deluxe rooms that feature specially designed "heavenly beds", Internet access and personally controlled air conditioning. A 24-hour health club, top-floor executive bar and Grade-A fusion restaurant are a few of the extras worth taking advantage of. **www.westin.com.pl**

MAZOVIA AND THE LUBLIN REGION

JABŁONNA Pałac Jabłonna   🚻 P   ⓩⓩ
ul. Modlińska 105, 05-110 **Tel** *022 782 54 89* **Fax** *022 774 48 62* **Rooms** *26*   **Road map** *E3*

An 18th-century palace with an English garden, Chinese pavilion and even a victory arch. Formerly the residence of Prince Poniatowski, this hotel has rooms filled with replica antiques, while the grand ballroom and restaurant evoke memories of Poland's golden age. A golf course and tennis courts are nearby. **www.palacjablonna.pl**

LUBLIN Mercure Lublin   🖥 🚻 🏄 📺 🗐 P   ⓩ
al. Racławickie 12, 20-037 **Tel** *081 533 20 61* **Fax** *081 533 30 21* **Rooms** *110*   **Road map** *F4*

A squat building that delivers far more than the blockish exterior would imply. Rooms feature a fresh, contemporary design and come complete with Internet access, air conditioning and cable TV. The restaurant, while unremarkable in style, is one of the better dining options in the city. **www.orbis.pl**

LUBLIN Grand Hotel Lublinianka   🖥 🚻 🏄 🗐 P   ⓩⓩⓩ
ul. Krakowskie Przedmieście 56, 20-002 **Tel** *081 446 61 00* **Fax** *081 446 62 00* **Rooms** *72*   **Road map** *F4*

Originally constructed in 1900, this majestic building was given a new lease of life in 2002, when it was renovated by the Von Der Heyden group and unveiled as Lublin's premier hotel. It is located on the border of the Old Town, and its rooms include marble bathrooms. **www.lublinianka.com**

PUŁTUSK Hotel Zamek   🚻 🏄 📺 P   ⓩⓩ
ul. Szkolna 11, 06-100 **Tel** *023 692 90 00* **Fax** *023 692 05 24* **Rooms** *92*   **Road map** *E3*

Situated in the castle of the bishops of Płock, this hotel is set on a hilltop beside the Narew River, where it towers over the town. Its three on-site restaurants specialize in large servings of traditional Polish food. The vast area of parkland around the hotel is good for walks and picnics. **www.zamekpultusk.pl**

RADZIEJOWICE Pałac w Radziejowicach   🚻 P   ⓩ
ul. Sienkiewicza 4, 96-325 **Tel** *046 857 71 75* **Fax** *046 857 71 13* **Rooms** *29*   **Road map** *E3*

Once the domain of Polish aristocracy, this 18th-century palace now houses the headquarters of the Creative Workshop of the Ministry of Culture and National Heritage, as well as providing accommodation both inside the palace and in the surrounding outbuildings. **www.palacradziejowice.pl**

ZAMOŚĆ Senator   🚻 🗐 P   ⓩ
ul. Rynek Solny 4, 22-400 **Tel** *084 638 76 10* **Fax** *084 638 76 13* **Rooms** *23*   **Road map** *G5*

A charming hotel situated within close reach of the town square. A defiantly Old World atmosphere reigns in the hotel lobby and restaurant, and while sleeping quarters are a little less atmospheric, the Senator still represents one of the best deals you'll find. Prices for large groups can be negotiated. **www.senatorhotel.pl**

ZAMOŚĆ Mercure   🚻 🏄 📺 🗐 P   ⓩⓩ
ul. Kołłataja 2/4/6, 22-400 **Tel** *084 639 25 16* **Fax** *084 639 28 86* **Rooms** *54*   **Road map** *G5*

A low-level hotel occupying a corner of Zamość's Renaissance Old Town. Rooms are generously sized, if a little bland, with the more expensive suites overlooking the town hall. A glass-covered atrium houses the reception, with other touches including a gymnasium and a commendable on-site restaurant. **www.accorhotels.com**

CRACOW

Abel   ⓩ
ul. Józefa 30, 31-056 **Tel** *012 411 87 36* **Fax** *012 411 94 90* **Rooms** *15*   **Road map** *D5*

While the rooms at this adorably eclectic hotel are not exactly large, what they lack in size they more than make up for in character. Each of the rooms is furnished individually and has an en-suite bathroom (sometimes just with a shower) and television. Not all are air conditioned, however. **www.hotelabel.pl**

Batory   🖥 🚻 🏄 P   ⓩ
ul. Sołtyka 19, 31-529 **Tel** *012 294 30 30* **Fax** *012 294 30 33* **Rooms** *29*   **Road map** *D5*

Not the most attractive hotel in Cracow, perhaps, but all doubts fade once you enter the bright lobby and are greeted by the friendly, helpful staff. Rooms are decorated in loud colours, are fairly large and come with televisions, en-suite bathrooms (some just with shower), safes and Internet connections. **www.hotelbatory.pl**

Dom Polonii   🚻   ⓩ
Rynek Główny 14, 31-008 **Tel** *012 428 04 60* **Fax** *012 422 43 55* **Rooms** *3*   **Road map** *D5*

On the third floor of a classic townhouse, this hotel may be the smallest in Cracow (it has just three double rooms), but the rooms themselves are enormous, with high, vaulted ceilings and a friendly member of staff always on hand to help out. The cheap prices make reservations here essential. **www.wspolnota-polska.krakow.pl**

Trecius   ㉑

ul. św. Tomasza 18, 31-020 **Tel** *012 421 25 21* **Fax** *012 426 87 30* **Rooms** *6*   **Road map** *D5*

Each room in this oft-renovated 13th-century house is decorated in a fabulous, unique way. They all feature showers (but not baths) and amenities such as satellite television. While prices are cheap for the location, note that breakfast is not included, and smoking is not allowed in any of the rooms. **www.trecius.krakow.pl**

Pollera   ㉒㉒

ul. Szpitalna 30, 31-024 **Tel** *012 422 10 44* **Fax** *012 422 13 89* **Rooms** *42*   **Road map** *D5*

An Art Nouveau gem in the heart of the Old Town, the Pollera was founded in 1834 by Kasper Poller and has welcomed its guests with flair and style ever since. During World War II, the Germans fell in love with the place and forbade anyone else (except staff) from entering. Today all are welcome, though you will need to book. **www.pollera.com.pl**

Pugetów   ㉑㉑

ul. Starowiślna 15a, 31-038 **Tel** *012 432 49 50* **Fax** *012 378 93 25* **Rooms** *7*   **Road map** *D5*

If money is no object, then this place takes some beating. Set in one of the loveliest houses in Cracow, this "art hotel" has original oil paintings lining the walls and Classical little porticos. Rooms are huge, and reservations should be made months in advance. **www.donimirski.com/hotel_pugetow**

Royal   ㉒㉒

ul. św. Gertrudy 26/29, 31-048 **Tel** *012 421 35 00* **Fax** *012 421 58 57* **Rooms** *101*   **Road map** *D5*

This elegant hotel is split into a one-star section and a two-star area. Both offer relatively basic amentities, but all have televisions and full en-suite facilities. The building that houses the hotel is a classic example of 19th-century Art Nouveau, and the setting, opposite a lovely park, is as grand as they come. **www.royal.com.pl**

Wit Stwosz   ㉑㉑

ul. Mikołajska 28, 31-027 **Tel** *012 429 60 26* **Fax** *012 429 61 39* **Rooms** *17*   **Road map** *D5*

This hotels offers generously sized but sparsely furnished rooms in a great location close to Market Square. All rooms have bathrooms with showers and televisions. The best rooms are those in the attic, with skylights and high, sloping ceilings. The restored façade and the ground-floor windows are sublime. **www.wit-stwosz.com.pl**

Fortuna   ㉒㉒㉒

ul. Czapskich 5, 31-110 **Tel** *012 422 31 43* **Fax** *012 411 08 06* **Rooms** *25*   **Road map** *D5*

A historical hotel where service always comes with a smile. Set in a charming building, it has rooms that are larger than usual for this type of building, and the bathrooms are also well sized. There is guarded parking on site, though reservations are needed for the handful of spaces. **www.hotel-fortuna.com.pl**

Hotel Francuski   ㉒㉒㉒

ul. Pijarska 13 **Tel** *012 627 37 77* **Fax** *012 627 37 00* **Rooms** *42*   **Road map** *D5*

Each and every room in this luxurious hotel is graced with antique furniture, and the hotel's location close to the Market Square makes it the perfect option for a relaxed and pampered stay in Cracow. The car park to the rear of the hotel is a rare luxury in the city. **www.orbis.pl**

Elektor   ㉒㉒㉒㉒

ul. Szpitalna 28, 31-024 **Tel** *012 423 23 17* **Fax** *012 423 23 27* **Rooms** *15*   **Road map** *D5*

Prince and Princess Takamodo of Japan, King Harald V of Norway and Grand Duke Jean of Luxembourg have all stayed at this outstanding hotel, widely regarded as the city's best. Nothing is beyond the staff here, who make it their mission to please all guests, royalty or otherwise. **www.hotelelektor.pl**

Grand Hotel Cracow   ㉒㉒㉒㉒㉒

ul. Sławkowska 5/7 **Tel** *012 424 08 00* **Fax** *012 421 83 60* **Rooms** *64*   **Road map** *D5*

For more than a century, this hotel has offered its guests the very best in comfort and service. The building itself is beautiful and could not be better located. The care taken to maintain the historic interior and the virtual guarantee of a relaxing stay make it well worth the expensive price. **www.grand.pl**

Sheraton   ㉒㉒㉒㉒㉒

ul. Powiśle 7, 31-101 **Tel** *012 662 10 00* **Fax** *012 662 11 00* **Rooms** *232*   **Road map** *D5*

The atrium at the Sheraton is one of the modern wonders of the city, all glass and marble, colonnades and fountains. Visitors can expect the best standards, with the biggest bathrooms in Cracow a major asset. Outstanding on-site dining and entertainment make this a refuge from which some never emerge. **www.sheraton.com/krakow**

MAŁOPOLSKA

BARANÓW SANDOMIERSKI Zamkowy   ㉑

ul. Zamkowa 20, 39-450 **Tel** *015 811 80 39* **Fax** *015 811 80 40* **Rooms** *46*   **Road map** *E5*

A magnificent Renaissance castle with luxurious, sympathetically furnished rooms. A fitness centre and nightclub are on site, while outdoor types should take advantage of the fishing and horse-riding opportunities. Both the museum and gallery are well worth exploring. **www.baranow.com.pl**

BIELSKO-BIAŁA Park Hotel Vienna

ul. Bystrzańska 48, 43-309 **Tel** *033 496 62 66* **Fax** *033 496 62 96* **Rooms** *113* **Road map** *D6*

An interesting building with a huge glass-fronted entrance attached to a curvy modern structure. Admire mountain views from the top-floor Panorama Café, or dance the night away in the glitzy nightclub. Modern rooms come with heated bathroom floors, Internet access and air conditioning. The best hotel in town. **www.vienna.pl**

BIELSKO-BIAŁA Prezydent

ul. 3 Maja 12, 43-300 **Tel** *033 822 72 11* **Fax** *033 815 02 73* **Rooms** *40* **Road map** *D6*

Known as the Kaiserhof Hotel when it opened for business back in 1892, the Prezydent casts an imposing shadow on Bielsko-Biała with its imposing Secessionist style. While some of the rooms appear a touch dated, all bathrooms have been refitted, and the hotel has an unmistakable historical air to it. **www.hotelprezydent.pl**

CZĘSTOCHOWA Mercure Patria

ul Popiełuszki 2, 42-200 **Tel** *034 360 31 00* **Fax** *034 360 32 00* **Rooms** *102* **Road map** *D5*

A reasonable hotel with comfortable rooms and a grand-looking glass-topped restaurant in which to eat your meals. The central location is another plus. Be aware that there is no air conditioning, so in summer keeping the windows open for ventilation might lead to unwelcome noise from the lively city centre. **www.orbis.pl**

GDÓW-WOLA ZRĘCZYCKA Dwór Bella Vita

near Podolany, 32-420 **Tel** *012 288 94 90* **Fax** *012 288 94 91* **Rooms** *11* **Road map** *E6*

A 19th-century manor house built from larchwood and positioned southeast of Cracow and the Wieliczka salt mine. The middle-of-the-road accommodation features timber-framed beds and oil paintings depicting country scenes. The surrounding gardens are frequently the site of impromptu barbecues. **www.noclegi.pl/bellavita**

JASIONKA Dwór Ostoya

near Rzeszów, 36-002 **Tel** *017 772 34 05* **Fax** *017 772 33 33* **Rooms** *32* **Road map** *F5*

An atmospheric manor house stuffed with antiques and gilt-edged furnishings. The restaurant also impresses, with its chandeliers, chamber music and classic Polish menu. Activities available to guests include clay-court tennis, horse riding, hunting and parachuting. **www.ostoya.rzeszow.pl**

KIELCE Kongresowy

ul. Solidarności 34, 25-323 **Tel** *041 332 63 93* **Fax** *041 332 64 40* **Rooms** *42* **Road map** *E5*

This modern high-rise hotel features parrots, tropical plants and even an artificial stream running through the hotel's patio restaurant. Rooms are a little more restrained, with comfortable modern furnishings and aquamarine-coloured bathrooms. Guarded parking is available. **www.hotelkongresowy.pl**

KOŚCIELISKO-ZAKOPANE Górska Hawira

ul. Pitoniówka 12 **Tel** *018 447 54 90* **Fax** *018 447 54 19* **Rooms** *10* **Road map** *D6*

A beautiful modern chalet with breathtaking mountain views. The pine-fitted rooms are basic but attractive and spotlessly clean. The downstairs lounge area boasts sturdy wooden furniture and a stone fireplace, ideal for winter evenings. There are also a billiard table and a sauna available for guests. **www.gorska-hawira.pl**

KRASICZYN Zamkowy

Krasiczyn 179, 37-741 **Tel** *016 671 83 21* **Fax** *016 671 83 16 ext. 510* **Rooms** *51* **Road map** *F6*

A superb hotel with rooms of varying price located inside a Renaissance castle, coach house and two separate pavilions. The Hunter's Pavilion features animal pelts and hand-woven rugs, while the castle wing has a gym and a billiard hall. Zamkowy is also home to an award-winning gallery. **www.krasiczyn.com.pl**

ŁAŃCUT Pałacyk

ul. Paderewskiego 18, 37-100 **Tel** *017 225 20 43* **Fax** *017 225 43 56* **Rooms** *7* **Road map** *F5*

This bijou inn was originally built at the beginning of the 20th century. Although it has only six bedrooms, the Pałacyk can boast guests of the calibre of Vaclav Havel and the former presidents of Poland and Ukraine in its visitors' book. Opt for one of the timber-beamed loft rooms. **www.palacyk-lancut.pl**

NIEDZICA Lokis

Zamek 76, 34-441 **Tel** *018 262 85 40* **Fax** *018 262 85 50* **Rooms** *22* **Road map** *E6*

A picture-book setting on the banks of Lake Czorsztyn with the Tatra Mountains rising in the background is one of the benefits here. From the outside, the hotel is redolent of an Alpine chalet, and though bedrooms are rather bare, some of the loft accommodation comes with warming timber touches. **www.lokis.com.pl**

NOWY SĄCZ Beskid

ul. Limanowskiego 1, 33-300 **Tel** *018 443 57 70* **Fax** *018 443 51 44* **Rooms** *72* **Road map** *E6*

Located within walking distance from the train station, this concrete monster of a hotel features a garish, 70s-style restaurant and unremarkable rooms that are nevertheless well kept and modern in appearance. Ask in advance if you are looking for a room with Internet access. **www.orbis.pl**

PASZKÓWKA Pałac w Paszkówce

Paszkówka 37, 34-113 **Tel** *033 872 38 00* **Fax** *033 879 32 61* **Rooms** *40* **Road map** *D6*

A Neo-Gothic palace with the appearance of something from the pages of Edgar Allan Poe. The hotel is full of 19th-century antiques, and rooms come replete with lurid oil paintings. While not as luxurious as the exterior suggests, this still presents a great alternative to a generic hotel chain. **www.paszkowka.pl**

Key to Price Guide *see p298* **Key to Symbols** *see back cover flap*

PRZEMYŚL Gromada

ul. Wybrzeże Marszałka Piłsudskiego 4, 37-700 **Tel** *016 676 11 11* **Rooms** *105*   **Road map** *F6*

Gromada is by far the best hotel in Przemyśl, in spite of the florid green-and-white exterior. Situated half a kilometre away from the town square, this is the most business-friendly hotel in the region, with high-speed Internet access inside smart rooms. Many command views of the Old Town. **www.gromada.pl**

RZESZÓW Hubertus

ul. Mickiewicza 5, 35-064 **Tel** *017 852 60 07* **Fax** *017 850 14 15* **Rooms** *13*   **Road map** *F5*

A fully renovated tenement building is the setting, and the hotel comes with a vaulted restaurant and sets of antlers and miscellaneous hunting trophies displayed in the corridors. The modern rooms come with blue-and-white-striped finishes, air conditioning, Internet access and immaculately clean bathrooms. **www.hubertus.rzeszow.pl**

SIENIAWA Pałac Sieniawa

ul. Kościuszki 32, 37-530 **Tel** *016 649 17 00* **Fax** *016 649 17 10* **Rooms** *59*   **Road map** *F5*

Painstaking renovation work has seen this Baroque residence restored to its pre-World War II glory, when it functioned as seat of the Czartoryski family. All rooms come with en-suite bathrooms and the stamp of aristocratic grandeur. The park is a popular location for wedding receptions. **www.sieniawa.net**

ZAKOPANE Mercure Kasprowy

ul. Szymaszkowa, 34-500 **Tel** *018 202 40 00* **Fax** *018 202 40 24* **Rooms** *288*   **Road map** *D6*

The 70s exterior of this vast hotel, built on the slopes of Mount Gubałówka, is at odds with the picturesque setting. Inside, the rooms are up to western standards, while amenities on offer include a swimming pool, bowling lanes and tennis courts. There are ski runs nearby. **www.orbis.pl**

ZAKOPANE Nosalowy Dwór

ul. Balzera 21d, 34-500 **Tel** *018 201 14 00* **Fax** *018 201 14 01* **Rooms** *29*   **Road map** *D6*

Rooms come in every shape and size – some are enormous – and all have satellite TV, heated bathroom floors and hairdryers. Run by a former Alpine skiing champion – as the trophies and memorabilia prove – the hotel also features sauna, Jacuzzi and a restaurant serving traditional mountain food. **www.nosalowydwor.zakopane.pl**

ZAKOPANE Litwor

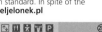

ul. Krupówki 40, 34-500 **Tel** *018 202 42 00* **Fax** *018 202 42 05* **Rooms** *53*   **Road map** *D6*

Situated on Zakopane's high street, this modern chalet-style building comes complete with turrets, a wood-roofed swimming pool and an underground car park. Deserving of each of its four stars, the Litwor offers rooms with balconies and mountain views, as well as heated bathroom floors and towel racks. **www.litwor.pl**

SILESIA

JELENIA GÓRA Jelonek

ul. 1 Maja 5, 58-500 **Tel** *075 764 65 41* **Fax** *075 764 752 37 94* **Rooms** *12*   **Road map** *B4*

Situated near the main pedestrian promenade, this miniature hotel can be found inside a Baroque structure dating from the 18th century. It features neat rooms decorated to an upper-range inn standard. In spite of the 20-seat conference room, this remains very much a tourist-oriented hotel. **www.hoteljelonek.pl**

JELENIA GÓRA Mercure Jelenia Góra

ul. Sudecka 63, 58-500 **Tel** *075 754 91 48* **Fax** *075 752 62 66* **Rooms** *188*   **Road map** *B4*

An upmarket modern hotel with many rooms looking on to the Karkonosze Mountains. A fitness centre houses a swimming pool and a solarium, and the restaurant is a safe choice. Ask at reception for details about rock climbing, hiking and similar outdoor activities. **www.orbis.pl**

KARPACZ Karkonosze

ul. Wolna 4, 58-540 **Tel** *075 761 82 77* **Fax** *075 761 80 33* **Rooms** *16*   **Road map** *B5*

This small mountain hotel has well-appointed rooms and an attractive exterior seemingly imported directly from the peaks of Switzerland. The suites, complete with communal lounge, kitchen and en-suite bathrooms, are a bargain. The hotel has its own piste, with artificial snow in case of heatwaves. **www.hotel-karkonosze.com.pl**

KARPACZ Rezydencja

ul. Parkowa 6, 58-540 **Tel** *075 761 80 20* **Fax** *075 761 95 13* **Rooms** *14*   **Road map** *B5*

A charming mountain hotel situated in the centre of the city. Built at the start of the 20th century, the hotel has tiers of balconies and crossed timber beams on the outside, as well as comfortably furnished modern rooms on the inside. Illustrious past guests include many Polish politicians. **www.hotelrezydencja.pl**

KATOWICE Qubus Hotel Prestige

ul. Uniwersytecka 13, 40-007 **Tel** *032 601 01 00* **Fax** *032 601 02 00* **Rooms** *150*   **Road map** *D5*

Soaring into the murky Katowice sky is this highly recommended modern hotel. Moments away from the flying saucer-style concert hall, rooms at the Prestige are equipped with air conditioning, a bathtub and disabled access. Enjoy views across the city from the bar on the 27th floor. **www.qubushotel.com**

KATOWICE Monopol
ul. Dworcowa 5, 40-012 **Tel** *032 782 82 82* **Fax** *032 782 82 83* **Rooms** *112*   **Road map** *D5*

In a city not known for its aesthetics, the Monopol is something of a treasure. The hotel lobby, furnished with potted palms and Art Deco columns, acts as a teaser to what lies ahead. An underground pool and a top-notch restaurant win bonus points for the hotel, while classy rooms complete the picture. **www.hotel.com.pl**

KOBIÓR Noma Residence
Near Tychy, 43-210 **Tel** *032 219 46 78* **Fax** *032 219 54 75* **Rooms** *13*   **Road map** *D5*

This former shooting lodge is the winner of countless accolades, both for its living quarters and restaurant. From the outside, Noma Residence looks like a fairytale residence, and guests will not be let down by the interiors. Stained glass and grand wooden fixtures add to the luxurious atmosphere of yesteryear. **www.promnice.com.pl**

KRASKÓW Pałac Krasków
Near Marcinowice, 58-124 **Tel** *074 858 51 01* **Fax** *074 858 52 52* **Rooms** *46*   **Road map** *B4*

Set inside the former residence of the Sedlitz family, this hotel features rooms furnished with expensive-looking antiques and paintings by artists past and present. If you are on a budget but want the thrill of staying at a palace address, opt for one of the rooms in the annexe and former millhouse. **www.kraskow.pl**

KROBIELOWICE Pałac Krobielowice
Near Kąty Wrocławskie, 55-080 **Tel** *071 316 66 48* **Fax** *071 316 61 14* **Rooms** *25*   **Road map** *B4*

A bewitching palace built in a Baroque-Renaissance style. Rooms are decorated with antiques; the restaurant, with stuffed birds and beasts. The mausoleum housing the former owner, Field Marshal Bucher, the Prussian who contributed to Napoleon's defeat at Waterloo, can be found inside the grounds. **www.palackrobielowice.com**

ŁOMNICA Pałac Łomnica
ul. Karpnicka 3, 58-500 **Tel** *075 713 04 60* **Fax** *075 713 05 33* **Rooms** *18*   **Road map** *B5*

Spend a few relaxing moments in the library after a day out in the nearby forests, then retire to the opulent bedrooms. This small, comfortable hotel is situated inside a Neo-Classical palace that rubs shoulders with a larger late Baroque palace. Queen Louisa of the Netherlands once owned property in the vicinity. **www.palac-lomnica.pl**

OPOLE Piast
ul. Piastowska 1, 45-081 **Tel** *077 454 97 10–16* **Fax** *077 454 97 17* **Rooms** *25*   **Road map** *C5*

A small hotel in a pre-war structure built on Piaseka Island, not far from the amphitheatre that hosts the annual Festival of Polish Song. The spacious rooms are light and breezy and decorated with a floral theme. The restaurant is a twee affair, ideal for romantic proposals. **www.hotelpiast.com.pl**

SOBÓTKA Zamek Górka
ul. Zamkowa 12 **Tel** *071 316 21 33* **Rooms** *24*   **Road map** *B4*

A pseudo-medieval castle, with a fairytale appearance and pretty, well-preserved interiors. The hotel itself is pleasant but modestly furnished, and the surrounding park is popular with tourists passing through on the way to the sacred Mount Sobótka. Guests should bear in mind that breakfast is not included in the price.

SUCHA Zamek Czocha
Near Leśna, 59-820 **Tel** *075 721 15 53* **Fax** *075 721 15 53* **Rooms** *38*   **Road map** *A4*

This magnificent castle, set on the lakeside, is reputedly haunted, a fact that is a source of great pride for the owners. The Harry Potter room comes with broomsticks and witches' capes pinned to the walls; others have bear pelts and ancient maps. Lodgings are basic but truly memorable. **www.zamekczocha.pl**

ŚWIERKLANIEC Pałac Kawalera
ul. Parkowa 30, 42-622 **Tel** *032 284 43 30* **Fax** *032 381 47 91* **Rooms** *20*   **Road map** *D5*

This comfortable hotel occupies the only part of the Neo-Baroque residence of the Donnersmarck dynasty to be preserved. A sweeping stairwell, complete with red carpet, spirits guests to slightly dowdy quarters. Cheer yourself up in the park grounds, which are dotted with dramatic monuments. **www.palackawalera.pl**

SZCZYRK Silveretta
ul. Myśliwska 44, 43-370 **Tel** *032 817 85 58* **Fax** *032 817 85 58* **Rooms** *7*   **Road map** *D6*

A small chalet-style pension with great mountain views. The budget-priced rooms, including a dormitory that sleeps six, are popular with outdoor types. Activities include paragliding, motorbiking, skiing, quad-biking and even ice-breaking sessions. Rock-bottom prices and a decent restaurant complete the picture. **www.silveretta.szczyrk.pl**

SZCZYRK Klimczok
ul. Poziomkowa 20, 43-370 **Tel** *033 826 01 00* **Fax** *033 826 01 10* **Rooms** *125*   **Road map** *D6*

A vast, modern mountain lodge with rooms in several different designs: choose from the likes of the Spanish Suite (sunny colours and whirlpool tub) and the Mountain Suite (wood furnishings and paintings depicting rural scenes). Tennis courts and thermal pools are also on site, as is a medley of restaurants, bars and clubs. **www.klimczok.pl**

SZKLARSKA PORĘBA Kryształ
ul. 1 Maja 19, 58-580 **Tel** *075 730 36 50* **Fax** *075 730 36 57* **Rooms** *33*   **Road map** *B5*

Five minutes from the ski lift, this three-floored wooden structure would not be out of place in the Alps. Rooms are modern and well looked after, if a little on the basic side. A two-lane bowling alley, a billiard table and a sauna are some of the attractions that keep guests busy. **www.hotelkrysztal.pl**

Key to Price Guide *see p298* **Key to Symbols** *see back cover flap*

WARSZOWICE Cyprianówka

ul. Stawowa 48, 43-254 **Tel** *032 472 99 03* **Rooms** *13*　　　　　**Road map** *D5*

An excellent choice for those looking to enjoy life in the slow lane. A country-cottage ambience dominates, with wagon wheels and farming equipment scattered in the fields outside. Inside, visitors can look forward to home-made local dishes, high-standard rooms and owners who will make a fuss over their guests. **www.cyprianowka.pl**

WROCŁAW Patio

ul. Kiełbaśnicza 24, 50-110 **Tel** *071 375 04 00* **Fax** *071 343 91 49* **Rooms** *50*　　　**Road map** *C4*

This small, modern hotel with a historic façade offers decent mid-range rooms grouped around a covered atrium that doubles as a shopping centre. Rooms are decorated in pleasant pale shades, with the occasional plastic plant and high-speed Internet access, while some boast original exposed brickwork. **www.hotelpatio.pl**

WROCŁAW Bugatti

ul. Kosmonautów 328, 54-041 **Tel** *071 349 35 23* **Fax** *071 349 14 26* **Rooms** *20*　　　**Road map** *C4*

Located on the edge of the city limits, this 100-year-old villa is ideal if you're willing to forego a central location in favour of character. You will be rewarded with with quirky decoration and a dining room stuffed with chandeliers and turn-of-the-century atmosphere. A golf course is located nearby. **www.hotelbugatti.pl**

WROCŁAW Dwór Polski

ul. Kiełbaśnicza 2, 50-108 **Tel** *071 372 34 15* **Fax** *071 372 58 29* **Rooms** *28*　　　**Road map** *C4*

A historic hotel with a central location and numerous legends attached to it; apparently, this is where Poland's King Sigismund once held covert meetings with his future wife. Gloomy corridors lead to decent rooms, many of which have been spruced up, though the hotel has been eclipsed by more modern rivals. **www.dworpolski.wroclaw.pl**

WROCŁAW Qubus Hotel

ul. św Marii Magdaleny 2, 50-103 **Tel** *071 797 98 00* **Fax** *071 341 09 20* **Rooms** *83*　　　**Road map** *C4*

This luxurious hotel occupies a spot in the shadow of the Maria Magdalena church. Take time out in the basement swimming pool, or enjoy high-quality meals in the hotel restaurant. Rooms feature all the modern amenities that one would expect at this level; the Presidential Suite is one of the finest splurges in town. **www.qubushotel.com**

WROCŁAW Radisson SAS

ul. Purkyniego 10, 50-156 **Tel** *071 375 00 00* **Fax** *071 375 00 10* **Rooms** *162*　　　**Road map** *C4*

This hotel features all the perks and class associated with the Radisson brand. Rooms come with a chic, modern edge, while the restaurant stands out as a top dining experience. Wrocław's biggest tourist attraction, the Racławicka Panorama, is just a few minutes' walk away. **www.radissonsas.com**

WROCŁAW Art Hotel

ul. Kiełbaśnicza 20, 50-110 **Tel** *071 787 71 00* **Fax** *071 342 39 29* **Rooms** *80*　　　**Road map** *C4*

A Neo-Gothic façade hides a modern hotel with luxury trimmings and rooms geared towards both business and pleasure. Found on one of Wrocław's most engaging streets, the Art Hotel is the closest the city comes to a boutique hotel, while the Wraclawia restaurant, in the vaulted cellars, promises a top class menu. **www.arthotel.pl**

WROCŁAW Park Plaza

ul. Drobnera 11/13, 50-257 **Tel** *071 320 84 00* **Fax** *071 320 84 59* **Rooms** *177*　　　**Road map** *C4*

A large hotel situated on the banks of the Odra River, the Park Plaza has rooms looking across on to Wrocław's Old Town. The modern rooms serve their purpose but are short on character; however, the hotel's popularity with the business community means that excellent discounts can be found at weekends. **www.parkplaza.pl**

WIELKOPOLSKA

ANTONIN Pałac Radziwiłłów

ul. Pałacowa 1, 63-421 **Tel** *062 734 83 00* **Fax** *062 734 83 01* **Rooms** *14*　　　**Road map** *C4*

This timber hunting lodge was the property of the Radziwiłł line of aristocrats. Rooms range from basic to reasonably salubrious, while occasional Chopin concerts keep guests entertained inside a banquet hall lined with the heads of hunted animals. Fishing, sleigh rides and walking trails are among the attractions.

CZERNIEJEWO Pałac Czerniejewo

ul. Generała Lipskiego 5, 62-250 **Tel** *061 427 30 30* **Fax** *061 429 12 30* **Rooms** *38*　　　**Road map** *C3*

A beautiful complex of Neo-Classical buildings, with accommodation ranging from exquisite suites to rooms suited to more modest means - those in the stable and coach house come without en-suite bathrooms, for example. Take advantage of the horse-carriage rides around the palace's parkland. **www.czerniejewo-palac.pl**

KOBYLNIKI Pałac Kobylniki

Near Obrzycko, 64-520 **Tel** *061 291 35 49* **Fax** *061 291 35 81* **Rooms** *14*　　　**Road map** *B3*

A brick palace with towers designed by Zygmunt Gorgolewski for the lord of the manor, Tadeusz Twardowski. Rooms are not as luxurious as the exterior would suggest, though this hotel does allow guests to enjoy aristocratic pursuits such as hunting, horse riding and archery. **www.palac-kobylniki.com.pl**

KRZEŚLICE Pałac w Krześlicach

near Pobiedziska, 62-010 **Tel** *061 661 966 813* **Fax** *061 817 75 38* **Rooms** *20*   **Road map** *C3*

A marvellous Neo-Gothic castle built in the second half of the 19th century. Luxurious rooms are decorated with period furnishings and offer an atmosphere primed for romantic weekends and honeymoon moments. Fishing, tennis courts and a gym are on offer for those wanting to enjoy active pursuits. **www.krzeslice.pl**

LESZNO Akwawit

ul. św. Józefa 5, 64-100 **Tel** *065 529 37 81* **Fax** *065 529 37 82* **Rooms** *63*   **Road map** *C3*

The most modern hotel in Leszno suffers from assuming the air of a teen holiday camp in the summer, due in part to the number of facilities that encourage kids to charge around, such as a water slide and tennis courts. Rooms are reasonably appointed with modern, if uninspiring, furnishings. **www.akwawit.pl**

ŁÓDŹ Daria   🄿   ㉑

ul. Studencka 2/4, 91-530 **Tel** *042 659 82 44* **Fax** *042 659 90 11* **Rooms** *10*   **Road map** *D5*

The family-run Daria is situated deep inside the Lagiewnicki nature reserve. An abandoned World War II artillery piece stands in the forecourt, while the inside of this ivy-covered establishment is stuffed with hunting trophies and plants. Rooms have creaky floorboards, Persian rugs and an air of history. **www.hoteldaria.oit.pl**

ŁÓDŹ Grand

ul. Piotrkowska 72, 90-102 **Tel** *042 633 99 20* **Fax** *042 633 78 76* **Rooms** *81*   **Road map** *D4*

Opened in 1888, this legendary Łódź hotel has had Himmler, Polański and Tito all walk through its revolving doors. Liveried bellboys guard the elevator, while at dinnertime the restaurant assumes the air of a 19th-century ballroom. A full renovation of all the rooms is on the cards for the near future. **www.grand.hotel.com.pl**

ŁÓDŹ Revelo

ul. Wigury 4/6, 90-301 **Tel** *042 636 86 86* **Fax** *042 636 70 83* **Rooms** *6*   **Road map** *D4*

Mimicking the domain of an eccentric aristocrat, Deja Vu boasts a decadent collection of drapes, rugs and black-and-white photography. The antique touches come paired with all the creature comforts of the 21st century in what rates Łódź's most successful attempt at boutique accommodation. **www.revelo.pl**

POZNAŃ Brovaria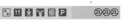

Stary Rynek 73, 74, 61-772 **Tel** *061 858 68 68* **Fax** *061 858 68 69* **Rooms** *21*   **Road map** *C3*

An Old Town location and a ground-floor microbrewery are not the only advantages of staying at Brovaria. Prim rooms are fitted with dark woods and soft-coloured fabrics, and some offer views straight on to the main square. A boutique atmosphere is complemented by modern facilities and a multilingual welcoming staff. **www.brovaria.pl**

POZNAŃ Don Prestige

ul. św. Marcina 2, 61-803 **Tel** *061 859 05 90* **Fax** *061 859 05 91* **Rooms** *53*   **Road map** *C3*

The best option in Poznań, Domina provides luxury serviced apartments on the border of the Old Town. Accommodation comes with fittings straight out of the pages of an interior-design magazine, and all apartments feature dressing gowns, sound systems, Internet access and a fully fitted kitchen. **www.donprestige.com**

POZNAŃ Vivaldi

ul. Winogrady 9, 61-663 **Tel** *061 858 81 00* **Fax** *061 852 29 77* **Rooms** *48*   **Road map** *C3*

An upmarket hotel with a wide range of rooms to pick from: from rattan-furnished doubles to luxury suites decorated with striped walls and cream leather seating. Though the swimming pool is little more than a very large bathtub, this hotel has charm aplenty, as well as friendly, dedicated staff. **www.vivaldi.pl**

POZNAŃ IBB Andersia

plac Andersia 3, 61-894 **Tel/Fax** *061 667 80 00* **Rooms** *171*   **Road map** *C3*

Situated in the highest skyscraper in Poznań, the sleek and elegant Andersia is close to all the major attractions in the city. Amenities include a swimming pool, a gym and a hairdresser. There are also two restaurants where, in addition to a large range of dishes, guests can enjoy live piano music. **www.andersiahotel.pl**

PRZYBYSZEWO Pałac w Przybyszewie

ul. Wiejska 12, 64-100 **Tel** *065 526 99 50* **Fax** *065 526 99 51* **Rooms** *11*   **Road map** *C3*

A small palace with elegant interiors filled with chandeliers, colonnades and flock wallpaper. There are cycle paths in the landscaped gardens, and guests can also enjoy one of the finest restaurants in the region. Top-range conference facilities make it popular for business weekends. Breakfast included. **www.palacprzybyszewo.com.pl**

ROKOSOWO Zamek Rokosowo

Near Łęka Mała, 63-805 **Tel** *065 573 11 56* **Fax** *065 573 33 04* **Rooms** *19*   **Road map** *C4*

Surrounded by a moat, this fairytale castle was completed in 1850 to serve as the seat of Count Józef Mycielski. The interiors feature vaulted ceilings, and important-looking oil paintings hang on the walls. Rooms are more modern in character, though some boast original stone hearths. Breakfast included. **www.rokosowo.pl**

RYDZYNA Zamek w Rydzynie

pl. Zamkowy 1, 64-130 **Tel** *065 529 50 40* **Fax** *065 529 50 26* **Rooms** *54*   **Road map** *B4*

Designed by Italian architects, this Baroque building has been used as a residence of King Stanisław Leszczyński, as well as a school for the Hitler Youth. Today the renovated interiors are perfect for luxury breaks. The majestic corridors are reputedly haunted by a "White Lady". Breakfast included. **www.zamek-rydzyna.com.pl**

SULEJÓW Hotel Podklasztorze

🍴 🏃 📺 🅿   ②

ul. Jagiełły 1, 97-330 **Tel** *044 616 24 00* **Fax** *044 616 20 02* **Rooms** *52* **Road map** *D4*

A modern hotel housed in what was once a Cistercian abbey. Wood-floored rooms that were once the private quarters of abbots and monks now house high-grade appealing lodgings. The hotel also boasts a large swimming pool, as well as several historical relics dating from the 13th century. **www.podklasztorze.pl**

UNIEJÓW Zamek Uniejów

🍴 🏃 🅿   ②

ul. Zamkowa 2, 99-210 **Tel** *063 288 89 50* **Fax** *063 288 80 71* **Rooms** *22* **Road map** *D3*

A Gothic-Renaissance castle with standard rooms and a suite decked out in scarlet and antique furniture. The restaurant is adorned with candelabra and coats of arms, while entertaining events on offer range from meetings with the resident ghost to re-enacted battles between medieval knights. Breakfast included. **www.zamekuniejow.pl**

ZGIERZ Stacja Nowa Gdynia

🖥 🍴 🏃 📺 🗐 🅿   ②②

ul. Sosnowa 1, 95-100 **Tel** *042 714 21 61* **Fax** *042 714 21 62* **Rooms** *19* **Road map** *D4*

A forest setting overlooking a lake is the backdrop for this masterpiece located a mere 20 minutes from central Łódź, and by far the best accommodation in the region. Gourmet cooking and a Western-style health club are further incentives to stay here. Very popular with visiting executives, so booking ahead is essential. **www.nowa-gdynia.pl**

ZIELONA GÓRA Qubus

🍴 🏃 🅿   ②

ul. Ceglana 14a, 65-211 **Tel** *068 329 31 00* **Fax** *068 329 32 00* **Rooms** *56* **Road map** *B3*

A modern hotel in the city centre, with an exterior that could easily be mistaken for a Japanese car factory. Rooms are furnished with crisp white and navy colours, and equipped with satellite TV, heated bathroom floors and fax machines. The restaurant is highly recommended. **www.qubushotel.com**

GDAŃSK

Wolne Miasto

🖥 🍴 🏃 🅿   ②②

ul. św. Ducha 2, 80-834 **Tel** *058 322 24 42* **Fax** *058 322 24 47* **Rooms** *43* **Road map** *D1*

A row of reconstructed tenement buildings hides this Old Town hotel. Rooms capture the spirit of pre-war Danzig, with sepia photographs of the city in its heyday, while also boasting 21st-century extras such as plasma screens and card keys. The restaurant is one of the most experimental in town. **www.hotelwm.pl**

Dwór Oliwski

🖥 🍴 🏃 📺 🗐 🅿   ②②②

ul. Bytowska 4, 80-328 **Tel** *058 554 70 00* **Fax** *058 554 70 10* **Rooms** *70* **Road map** *D1*

Hemmed in by carefully tended gardens, lodgings at this luxury hotel between Gdańsk and Sopot are located in a series of thatched buildings, as well as inside a fully renovated manor house. Plush rooms are furnished with a pink flourish, and the hotel also has an excellent indoor swimming pool. **www.dwor-oliwski.com.pl**

Hanza

🖥 🍴 🏃 🗐 🅿   ②②②

ul. Tokarska 6, 80-888 **Tel** *058 305 34 27* **Fax** *058 305 33 86* **Rooms** *60* **Road map** *D1*

In spite of Hanza's modern aesthetic, the façade of this riverfront hotel right in the heart of Gdańsk's historic quarter has been designed to fit seamlessly in with the surrounding burgher houses. Rooms have been thoughtfully designed with dark, polished woods and equipped with all the latest extras. **www.hotelhanza.pl**

Królewski

🖥 🍴 🏃 🅿   ②②②

ul. Ołowianka 1, 80-751 **Tel** *058 326 11 11* **Fax** *058 326 11 10* **Rooms** *30* **Road map** *D1*

A quayside hotel set inside a former granary building overlooking Gdańsk's historic crane. Smart rooms are decorated with muted colours and modern trappings, though for something a bit special consider booking one of the loft suites. The Central Maritime Museum is situated right next door. **www.hotelkrolewski.pl**

Szydłowski

🖥 🍴 📺 🗐   ②②②

ul. Grunwaldzka 114, 80-244 **Tel** *058 345 70 40* **Fax** *058 344 38 77* **Rooms** *35* **Road map** *D1*

Found in the suburb of Wrzeszcz, the Szydłowski is the best hotel you'll find within easy reach of Gdańsk's airport. Rooms are furnished and fitted to an unremarkable three-star standard, though the hotel is noted as being the lodging of choice for local-born German author Günther Grass. **www.szydlowski.pl**

Holiday Inn

🖥 🍴 🏃 📺 🗐 🅿   ②②②②

ul. Podwale Grodzkie 9, 80-895 **Tel** *058 300 60 00* **Fax** *058 300 60 03* **Rooms** *143* **Road map** *D1*

This squat modern building faces the train station, with the Old Town just minutes away on foot. The international Holiday Inn standard is impeccably observed here, with generous-sized rooms, well-trained staff and all the trappings associated with such a respected hotel chain. **www.gdansk.globalhotels.pl**

Podewils

🍴 🏃 📺 🗐 🅿   ②②②②

ul. Szafarnia 2, 80-755 **Tel** *058 300 95 60* **Fax** *058 300 95 70* **Rooms** *10* **Road map** *D1*

A Baroque-style mansion with views overlooking Gdańsk's small marina. A lobby filled with antiques and oil paintings generates the atmosphere of a private residence, while creature comforts in the upstairs rooms include DVD players and Jacuzzi tubs. The restaurant is rightfully regarded as an unmissable experience. **www.podewils.pl**

POMERANIA

BYDGOSZCZ City
ul. 3 Maja 6, 85-950 **Tel** 052 325 25 00 **Fax** 052 325 25 05 **Rooms** 168 **Road map** C2

A modern four-star hotel in the city centre, and a worthy member of the Polish Prestige Hotel group. Rooms have navy-blue tones, and the hotel's Chopin Restaurant is one of the better choices for dinner in Bydgoszcz. Live music keeps guests entertained. **www.cityhotel.bydgoszcz.pl**

BYDGOSZCZ Pod Orłem
ul. Gdańska 14, 85-006 **Tel** 052 583 05 30 **Fax** 052 584 02 24 **Rooms** 79 **Road map** C2

Serving as a hotel since 1899, Pod Orłem ("Under the Eagle") is a classy establishment with gold-plated balustrades and stained-glass windows. Music lovers should book the Rubinstein Suite, which features its own piano, among other luxuries. The hotel cake shop offers numerous temptations. **www.hotelpodorlem.pl**

BYTÓW Zamek w Bytowie
ul. Zamkowa 2, 77-100 **Tel** 059 822 20 94 **Fax** 059 822 20 95 **Rooms** 29 **Road map** C1

Atmospheric lodgings inside a red-brick Teutonic castle. Jousting tournaments, outdoor banquets and horse riding are a few of the activities that are held here, and the hotel also has a medieval-themed inn to while away the evenings. The timber-fitted rooms are pleasant, and some also have stone cladding. **www.hotelzamek.com.pl**

GDYNIA Hotel Gdynia
ul. Armii Krajowej 22, 81-372 **Tel** 058 666 30 40 **Fax** 058 620 86 51 **Rooms** 292 **Road map** D1

Located in an enormous skyscraper facing the Baltic Sea, Gdynia is run by the Orbis hotel chain. It is a medium-market affair the sheer size of which makes it particularly popular with visiting conferences and tour groups. There is a swimming pool on site. **www.orbis.pl**

GDYNIA Nadmorski
ul. Ejsmonda 2, 81-409 **Tel** 058 667 77 77 **Fax** 058 667 77 00 **Rooms** 90 **Road map** D1

A modern hotel with a discreet location overlooking the Bay of Gdańsk. Guests of note include the Ukrainian president Yuschenko and music celebrities such as Fatboy Slim and Snoop Dogg. Electronic card keys reveal immaculate rooms, while a range of restaurants and spa treatments make the Nadmorski a world unto itself. **www.nadmorski.pl**

GDYNIA Willa Lubicz
ul. Orłowska 43, 81-522 **Tel** 058 668 47 40 **Fax** 058 668 47 41 **Rooms** 16 **Road map** D1

A gorgeous hotel with interiors befitting of the building's classic 1936 design. Striking views and lots of smart wood panelling lend an impressive tone to this hotel, while the Captain's Suite is worth the outlay for those yearning for a swish maritime atmosphere. **www.willalubicz.pl**

JURATA Bryza
ul. Międzymorze 2, 84-141 **Tel** 058 675 51 00 **Fax** 058 675 54 80 **Rooms** 84 **Road map** D1

A low-level beachfront hotel whose many accolades include being named "the hotel of dreams" by *Sport & Tourism Weekly*. Each room has a sound system and satellite television, and many also offer views of the Baltic coast. Very much geared towards the active tourist, with indoor and outdoor pools and a modern spa. **www.bryza.pl**

KAMIEŃ POMORSKI Hotel Pod Muzami
ul. Gryfitów 1, 72-400 **Tel** 091 382 22 40 **Fax** 091 382 22 41 **Rooms** 12 **Road map** A1

Constructed in the 18th century, this historic residence has been operating as a hotel since a full renovation in 1995. Bedrooms have solid wooden fixtures, while the hotel boasts a beautiful exterior consisting of red-tile work and crossed timber beams. The traditional restaurant is highly recommended. **www.podmuzami.pl**

KOSZALIN Gromada
ul. Zwycięstwa 20-24, 75-035 **Tel** 094 342 79 11 **Fax** 094 342 79 11 **Rooms** 74 **Road map** B1

The lobby of this small three-star affair is festooned with a jungle of plants and fake-marble flooring, and the bedrooms are drab efforts with garish carpets, raising memories of Iron Curtain Poland. Still, the Gromada redeems itself with its central location. A casino and a nightclub can be found on site. **www.gromada.koszalin.pl**

KRĄG Podewils
near Polanów, 76-010 **Tel** 094 347 05 16 **Fax** 094 316 91 11 **Rooms** 50 **Road map** C1

Nearly demolished after World War II, this 15th-century castle built on water has since been subject to painstaking restoration and now offers a choice of well-designed double rooms and more opulent suites. Kayaks can be hired from reception, and the hotel also houses an exhibition detailing the castle's history. **www.podewils-hotel.pl**

KROKOWA Zamek
ul. Zamkowa 1, 84-110 **Tel** 058 774 21 11 **Fax** 058 774 21 10 **Rooms** 34 **Road map** C1

This renovated castle building was once the property of a Pomeranian aristocratic family, the von Krokows. The blue-painted rooms are at best mid-range in standards, but the hotel's public areas do come with impressive Dutch antiques and Baroque staircases. The grounds are home to the regional museum. **www.zamekkrokowa.pl**

Key to Price Guide see p298 **Key to Symbols** see back cover flap

ŁEBA Neptun

ul. Sosnowa 1, 84-360 **Tel** *059 866 14 32* **Fax** *059 866 23 57* **Rooms** *32* **Road map** *C1*

Completed in 1903, this beachside edifice includes a towering turret and a location right on the coastline. Rooms exude a plush, personalized style, with timber beams and views of the Baltic Sea. The restaurant, bar and nightclub are among the classiest in town, and the hotel also has a large outdoor pool. **www.neptunhotel.pl**

MACIEJEWO Pałac Maciejewo

near Maszewo, 72-130 **Tel** *091 418 12 85* **Fax** *091 418 11 30* **Rooms** *48* **Road map** *A2*

A Neo-Gothic 19th-century palace on the shores of Lake Lechickie, the lounge room comes with padded leather armchairs, chandeliers and a piano, but the rooms are furnished with usual taste, for example, the heart-shaped bed in the honeymoon suite. The restaurant suggests aristocratic grandeur. **www.palacmaciejewo.pl**

MALBORK Stary Malbork

ul. 17 Marca 26-27, 82-200 **Tel** *055 647 24 00* **Fax** *055 647 24 12* **Rooms** *31* **Road map** *D1*

Two townhouses dating from the 19th century have had a dividing wall smashed through, then been renovated and turned into this gem of a hotel. Rooms feature a homely style, and the hotel also boasts a small bar, a restaurant and a fireplace room - perfect for winter nights. **www.hotelstarymalbork.com.pl**

MIĘDZYZDROJE Nautilus

Promenada Gwiazd 8, 72-500 **Tel** *091 328 09 99* **Fax** *091 328 23 27* **Rooms** *17* **Road map** *A1*

The Nautilus has been occupying a spot next to the seaside promenade since 1906. Rooms feature wooden support beams and a cheerful maritime style, with vaguely arty paintings adding to the low-budget ambience. Larger studio rooms are available for groups. **www.hotel-nautilus.pl**

NOWĘCIN Soplica

ul. Jeziorna 2, 84-360 **Tel** *059 866 16 15* **Fax** *059 866 19 47* **Rooms** *30* **Road map** *C1*

Soplica was, apparently, an ancient palace, though the exterior does little to suggest this. Muted colours and contemporary bathrooms can be found in the bedrooms, while the manicured parkland outside features a pool, a playground and peacocks strolling around. The olde worlde restaurant is adorned with pretty birdcages. **www.soplica.com.pl**

PUCK Admirał

ul. Morska 5, 84-100 **Tel** *058 673 11 97* **Fax** *058 673 47 89* **Rooms** *6* **Road map** *D1*

Admirał is a small hotel in a 19th-century residence in the town centre, but its atmosphere is redolent of a country pension. The restaurant is the best in the area, the bar has a tiger's head nailed to a plinth, and the hotel corridors come with golf clubs attached to the walls. **www.golfhotel.pl**

RYNKÓWKA Grabowy Dwór

near Rychława **Tel** *052 332 84 29* **Fax** *052 332 84 29* **Rooms** *4* **Road map** *D2*

This fabulous hotel is housed in a 19th-century palace, but the building's history dates back even further, to the 15th century, when the Teutonic Knights built a castle here. The hotel can accommodate a maximum of 15 people at any one time, which creates a homely and intimate atmosphere in stylish surroundings. **www.zamekrynkowka.com**

RZUCEWO Zamek Jan III Sobieski

near Żelistrzewo, 84-100 **Tel/Fax** *058 673 88 05* **Rooms** *27* **Road map** *D1*

Situated on the Bay of Puck, this red-brick Neo-Gothic castle is accessed via a series of winding country roads. The hotel has period rooms, a two-floor library, a vaulted lobby and a well-stocked wine cellar. The Hunters Lodge is a perfect spot to retire after a day spent horse riding in and around the grounds. **www.zameksobieski.pl**

SOPOT Monte Cassino de Luxe

ul. Bohaterów Monte Cassino 50, 81-759 **Tel** *058 555 77 77* **Fax** *058 555 77 78* **Rooms** *5* **Road map** *D1*

As the name suggests, this is top-quality accommodation, at surprisingly low prices. Beautifully designed rooms boast amenities such as DVD players, flat-screen TVs and classical furnishings; Sony PlayStations are available from the reception. A stone's throw from Sopot's high street; advance bookings are recommended. **www.sopothotel.pl**

SOPOT Villa Baltica

ul Emilii Plater 1, 81-777 **Tel** *058 555 28 00* **Fax** *058 555 28 01* **Rooms** *33* **Road map** *D1*

A former orphanage that now boasts chic cream-coloured rooms (some with views of the sea) and sparkling bathrooms. The restaurant is in a class of its own, with a clean-cut ambience inside a hexagonal dining room attached to the hotel. The downstairs spa offers a full range of luxury beauty treatments. **www.villabaltica.com**

SOPOT Villa Sedan

ul. Pułaskiego 18/20, 81-762 **Tel** *058 555 09 80* **Fax** *058 551 06 17* **Rooms** *21* **Road map** *D1*

The best value you will find in Sopot, with rooms furnished with wrought-iron beds and wooden floors. Housed inside a rambling building, Villa Sedan has all the atmosphere of a boutique pension, with several personal touches. Book the loft suite to guarantee a memorable stay. **www.sedan.pl**

SOPOT Haffner

ul. Haffnera 59, 81-715 **Tel** *058 550 99 99* **Fax** *058 550 98 00* **Rooms** *106* **Road map** *D1*

This modern structure houses some of the finest lodgings in Sopot. All come with air conditioning and a crisp modern style, while suites boast two telephone lines, dressing gowns and plush lounge areas decorated with padded leather sofas. Wind down in the state-of-the-art spa and swimming pool. **www.hotelhaffner.pl**

SOPOT Sofitel Grand

ul. Powstancóv Warszawy 12/14, 81-718 **Tel** *058 520 60 00* **Fax** *058 520 60 99* **Rooms** *127*   **Road map** *D1*

The Grand is positioned right on the seashore, with Sopot's 19th-century pier flanking it to the side. The hotel's acquisition by the Sofitel group has seen a full renovation take place, with rooms following a splendid Art Deco style and evoking the interwar years, when Sopot was known as a millionaires' playground. **www.orbis.pl**

STRZĘKOCINO Bursztynowy Pałac

near Świeszyno, 76-024 **Tel** *094 316 12 27* **Fax** *094 316 14 42* **Rooms** *62*   **Road map** *B1*

Formerly the stamping ground of the Junker von Kamecke family, this hotel is split into the White and Amber Palaces, which are separated by a lake. Within the grounds lie an 18th-century ornamental park and ice house. The charming interiors feature antiques and an atmosphere primed for romantic getaways. **www.hotel-bursztynowy-palac.pl**

SZCZECIN Atrium

ul. Wojska Polskiego 75, 70-481 **Tel** *091 424 35 32* **Fax** *091 422 10 96* **Rooms** *30*   **Road map** *A2*

This town-centre hotel offers salmon pink, air-conditioned rooms paired with sparkling en-suite bathrooms. Guests have a choice of standard doubles, suites or apartments. On site are an Italian restaurant and a lounge room crowned by an open fireplace. **www.hotel-atrium.pl**

SZCZECIN Park

ul. Plantowa 1, 70-527 **Tel** *091 434 00 50* **Fax** *091 434 45 03* **Rooms** *32*   **Road map** *A2*

A small, quiet hotel in a restored building located in park grounds. A wood-panelled bar area features a fireplace and bookshelves, and the hotel also has a swimming pool filled with mosaics. The restaurant is ideal for romantic dinners, while rooms feature an elegantly modern design. **www.parkhotel.szczecin.pl**

SZCZECIN Radisson SAS

pl. Rodła 10, 70-419 **Tel** *091 359 55 95* **Fax** *091 359 45 94* **Rooms** *369*   **Road map** *A2*

At this Radisson, the most luxurious hotel in Western Pomerania, standard rooms are decorated with purple dashes, and equipped with broadband Internet and personally controlled air conditioning. Those investing in a suite can expect complimentary fruit baskets, bathrobes and a newspaper. City-centre location. **www.radissonsas.com.pl**

TORUŃ Mercure-Helios

ul. Kraszewskiego 1/3, 87-100 **Tel** *056 619 65 50* **Fax** *056 619 62 54* **Rooms** *110*   **Road map** *D2*

Originally built in the 1960s, the Mercure-Helios finds itself in the midst of a timely revamp, ridding itself of its reputation as a hotel stuck in a Communist-era time warp. The hotel is still unlikely to win awards for charm, though it does fill all the criteria for a pleasant stay. **www.orbis.pl**

WARMIA, MAZURIA AND BIAŁYSTOK REGION

AUGUSTÓW Delfin

u. Turystyczna 81, 16-300 **Tel** *087 644 31 12* **Fax** *087 643 85 23* **Rooms** *57*   **Road map** *F2*

A modern complex designed with the surrounding forest and lakes in mind. Above-average rooms feature plenty of pine, adding a vaguely Scandinavian atmosphere. The hotel pool features water slides, dolphin.murals and a space-age ceiling. Sailing and ballooning are just two of the activities on offer. **www.hotel-delfin.com.pl**

AUGUSTÓW Warszawa

ul. Zdrojowa 1, 16-300 **Tel** *087 643 85 00* **Fax** *087 643 85 04* **Rooms** *90*   **Road map** *F2*

This low-rise, modern hotel has bright, ordinary rooms and a classy restaurant with pristine linen arrangements. Sauna, Jacuzzi and solarium are all on offer, though the real reason for booking a room here is to enjoy the forest and lakes in the surrounding area. A member of the Polish Prestige Hotels group. **www.hotelwarszawa.pl**

BIAŁYSTOK Cristal

ul. Lipowa 3/5, 15-424 **Tel** *085 749 61 00* **Fax** *085 749 61 71* **Rooms** *89*   **Road map** *F2*

A three-star, city-centre hotel brought to you courtesy of the Best Western brand. The rooms come with high-grade fittings and a choice of pay-TV channels. Additionally, the on-site Club House Pub offers far more atmosphere than the hotel bars that you may be more accustomed to. **www.cristal.com.pl**

ELBLĄG Żuławy

ul. Królewiecka 126, 82-300 **Tel** *055 234 57 11* **Fax** *055 232 95 00* **Rooms** *27*   **Road map** *D1*

In spite of plastic plants and cheap watercolours, the Żuławy is a pleasant town-centre hotel with prim rooms equipped with en-suite bathrooms, direct-dial telephones and satellite TV. The restaurant serves perfectly acceptable local cuisine. Sauna, solarium and billiard table are also available. **www.hotel-zulawy.com.pl**

JACZNO Gościniec Jaczno

Near Jeleniewo, 16-404 **Tel** *087 568 35 90* **Fax** *087 568 35 91* **Rooms** *12*   **Road map** *F1*

A superb choice, Jaczno is a hillside wooden lodge with views over a lake and an atmosphere of complete isolation. Its interiors consist of scrubbed timber and stone walls, with a few choice antiques dotted around. Return visits are almost guaranteed, and the surrounding forests are a must-visit for nature lovers. **www.jaczno.pl**

Key to Price Guide *see p298* **Key to Symbols** *see back cover flap*

KADYNY Kadyny Country Club

Near Tolmicko, 82-340 **Tel** *055 231 61 20* **Fax** *055 231 62 00* **Rooms** *42* **Road map** *D1*

When a hotel can list Kaiser Wilhelm II and Tsar Nicholas II as its guests, it is only logical to expect excellence. Rooms come with solid oak beams, as well as modern-day comforts such as Internet access, cable TV and mini-bar. The hotel's restaurant was once used as the Kaiser's vodka distillery. **www.kadyny.com.pl**

KARNITY Zamek

near Miłomłyn, 14-140 **Tel** *089 647 34 65* **Fax** *089 647 34 64* **Rooms** *58* **Road map** *D2*

Formerly a Teutonic castle, the Zamek has preserved many of its original features, including several bits of carpentry, fireplaces and beamed ceilings. Accommodation is in the former stable buildings, and the plush decor is quite theatrical in style. Open-air concerts, folk festivals and knight re-enactments are held in summer. **www.karnity.pl**

KLEKOTKI Młyn Klekotki

near Godkowo, 14-407 **Tel** *055 249 00 00* **Fax** *055 249 00 00 ext.230* **Rooms** *42* **Road map** *D1*

Converted into an upmarket hotel in 1999, Klekotki offers boutique accommodation inside a mill originally dating from the 17th century. Rooms feature original beams, thick rugs and a country-cottage appeal. A private cinema, mini-golf and bar fitted with log-burning fireplace all add to the appeal. **www.hotelmlynklekotki.pl**

MIKOŁAJKI Gołebiewski

ul. Mrągowska 34, 11-730 **Tel** *087 429 07 00* **Fax** *087 429 07 44* **Rooms** *686* **Road map** *E2*

The largest hotel in the Mazurian Lakes, with a sprawling reception area, man-made lake and a plastic elephant beside the outdoor pool. A covered atrium houses a bar area and countless fake plants, and never-ending corridors lead to comfortably furnished, modern rooms. Kids will love the Water Park Tropikana. **www.golebiewski.pl**

MRĄGOWO Mrongovia

ul. Giżycka 6, 11-700 **Tel** *089 743 31 00* **Fax** *089 743 31 20* **Rooms** *215* **Road map** *E2*

Water slides, an all-year outdoor Jacuzzi, a bowling alley and a range of massage treatments are available for those who know what recreation is about. Rooms are more mundane, with smart chequered patterns and a range of bungalows available in the warmer season. Spend the evening in the chic bar. **www.mrongovia.hotel.pl**

OGONKI Stara Kuźnia

near Węgorzewo, 11-600 **Tel** *087 427 00 90* **Fax** *087 427 00 90* **Rooms** *9* **Road map** *F1*

A pension-style hotel with neon letters needlessly added to the roof of what is otherwise an attractive modern building. Loft rooms have been decorated with basic fittings that are not modern, but spotlessly maintained, and the hotel has a decent restaurant preparing dishes from traditional Polish recipes. **www.starakuznia.eu**

OLSZTYN Kopernik

ul. Warszwska 37, 10-081 **Tel** *089 522 99 29* **Fax** *089 527 93 92* **Rooms** *62* **Road map** *E2*

It comes as a surprise to find such a modern hotel in what is regarded as a far-flung corner of Poland. Rooms are bright affairs with yellow colours and a look not far removed from mid-range international brands. Sauna, massage and beauty parlour are some of the extras found within. **www.kopernik.olsztyn.pl**

OSIEKA Biały Książę

Near Bartoszyce, 11-200 **Tel** *089 762 62 66* **Fax** *089 762 12 16* **Rooms** *24* **Road map** *E1*

A renovated 19th-century palace with a stark white exterior. Rooms are spotlessly clean but could do with being updated. The restaurant features potted palms and a few antiques dotted around; it also boasts a strong menu of Polish dishes. The banquet hall is popular with conferences and wedding receptions. **www.bialyksiaze.pkt.pl**

RESZEL Zamek Reszel

ul. Podzamcze 3, 11-440 **Tel** *089 755 01 09* **Fax** *089 755 01 09* **Rooms** *21* **Road map** *E1*

Previous guests of this Teutonic castle include the father of modern astronomy, Nicolas Copernicus. Less is more at Zamek Reszel, with rooms featuring whitewashed walls, exposed brickwork and oak beams. Wrought-iron beds stand next to chunky furnishings. The hotel is a favourite with visiting artists. **www.zamek-reszel.com**

SORKWITY Pałac Sorkwity

ul. Zamkowa 15, 11-731 **Tel** *089 742 81 89* **Fax** *089 742 82 51* **Rooms** *37* **Road map** *E2*

A Neo-Gothic palace, and formerly the property of the noble Mirbach family, this hotel is situated in a park by the lake. It offers accommodation of a modest standard, with some rooms having to share bathrooms. The restaurant is a basic affair, offering the retro look of 1980s Poland and typical local cuisine. **www.palacsorkwity.pl**

STARE JABŁONKI Anders

Near Ostróda, ul. Spacerowa 2, 14-133 **Tel** *089 642 70 00* **Fax** *089 642 70 13* **Rooms** *119* **Road map** *E2*

A highly recommended hotel with accommodation split between salubrious quarters found inside a timber-framed modern building, and more basic digs inside a series of cottages. Squash courts, football pitches and a swimming centre attract keep-fit types, and the hotel also has a private harbour 100 metres away. **www.hotelanders.com.pl**

SUWAŁKI Hotel Holiday

Stary Folwark 106, 16-402 **Tel** *087 563 71 20* **Fax** *087 563 71 10* **Rooms** *32* **Road map** *F1*

One of the most modern hotels in northeastern Poland, the Holiday is the ideal place for both families and business-people. Its proximity to the Wigry National Park and the Suwałki Landscape Park means there is no shortage of activities for guests, from hiking and biking to water sports. **www.hotel-holiday.pl**

WHERE TO EAT

Polish food still suffers from a poor international image, but restaurants serving national dishes as well as delicacies from different parts of the world have been established in Poland. Generally, it is not difficult to find a good restaurant in a large town or city, although the prices are often exorbitant. In smaller

The sign of Cracow's Chimera restaurant

towns, on the other hand, a little exploration may be required, but will often reveal a restaurant serving good, inexpensive food.

The restaurants and bars listed on pages 316–27 have been selected on the basis of the quality of their cuisine and service. Many are hotel restaurants, because in Poland this is where the best cuisine is often to be found.

The Kubicki restaurant in Ulica Wartka, Gdańsk (see p324)

MEALS

The traditional Polish breakfast has a high calorie content. It consists of boiled or fried eggs, smoked meats, cheese and, in the winter, soup. Today, soup rarely appears at the breakfast table, although sausage and pâté are still normal sights. In town centres, tourists may have difficulty finding establishments serving breakfast. Only some bars and restaurants serve morning meals. Hotel restaurants, by contrast, customarily serve breakfast.

Traditionally, the evening meal – consisting of soup, a main course (usually a meat dish), and a dessert – is the most important meal of the day. Polish restaurants are gradually adopting a lighter cuisine, adding to traditional menus such dishes as salads, although this is not very common. Tourists may have problems finding good restaurants in small towns, where the choice is likely to be limited to soups, snacks and pork chops.

EATING OUT

Many tourists are surprised to find that, compared to other countries, Poland has a relatively small number of restaurants. This is because there is no great tradition of eating out, since most Polish people simply cannot afford to do it on a regular basis. Restaurant customers are therefore chiefly business people, commercial travellers and tourists.

In large towns and cities, particularly in Warsaw, there is a severe shortage of mid-price restaurants; nearly all restaurants are on the expensive side and the price of alcohol is exorbitant.

In Poland, lunch is served from noon and it is possible

to have your midday meal at any time in the afternoon. Restaurants then stay open until the late evening. In large towns and cities, they may keep their dining rooms open until the last guests are ready to leave, although the kitchens usually close at 10pm.

In more upmarket restaurants, be aware that customers are expected to be well dressed, although men are not usually required to wear a tie.

Most restaurants in large towns and cities accept credit cards. Elsewhere this is not the case and it is customary to pay in cash. Information on paying with credit cards is included in the list of restaurants on pages 316–27.

The Pod Aniołami restaurant in Cracow (see p319)

U Wnuka, an inn in Zakopane *(see p321)*

TYPES OF RESTAURANTS

Very good restaurants with gourmet menus can only be found in the largest cities, and even then they are not very numerous. In the countryside, the exceptions to the rule are restaurants in luxurious hotels, especially those located in castles or palaces. In most cities – and most especially in Warsaw – it is difficult to find a restaurant that serves good food at reasonable prices. In some cities it is possible to find bars serving so-called "home food", and it is often possible to have a good and inexpensive meal in a small town or village.

Cracow in particular is renowned for its good restaurants. Those in Poznań and Wrocław are also recommended, and Zakopane is famous for its regional cuisine.

CHEAP FOOD

There are some traditional establishments where it is possible to eat cheaply in Poland: bars. Unfortunately, few bars can be recommended, since most of them serve pre-prepared and often frozen food. In some places a "milk bar", a relic from Communist times, can be found and here a portion of pancakes or Russian ravioli *(pierogi)* costs very little.

There are also salad bars, where in addition to salads, which are sold by weight, sandwiches or soup are also served. Most pubs include one or two hot dishes on the menu. A traditional Polish café serves only drinks and desserts. Newly opened bars in large towns and cities go beyond this, offering a selection of additional light dishes, such as soups, spaghetti, salads and warm vegetable dishes, but this variety comes at a high price.

The Belvedere restaurant in Warsaw *(see p317)*

FAST FOOD

Poland has experienced a real invasion of fast-food outlets in the form of McDonald's, KFC and Pizza Hut. Many Polish fast-food establishments also offer takeaway hamburgers and portions of pizza. In coastal resorts and the Great Mazurian Lakes region, fish is served from seasonal fish stalls. Other options include open-air barbecues serving roast sausages, or stalls serving Vietnamese and Turkish dishes.

PRICES

Prices in Polish restaurants vary in the extreme. In a luxurious, renowned restaurant in a large town or city, especially in Warsaw, a three-course meal without wine may cost as much as 150–200 PLN. Elsewhere a comparable meal should cost not more than 70 PLN, and in smaller towns as little as 20–30 PLN.

Alcohol is relatively expensive in Poland, and the price of imported liquor is exorbitant.

The prices given on the menu include VAT and service. Beyond this, it is customary to leave a tip of 10 per cent. Very often, menu prices apply just to the main dish; an extra charge is made for potatoes, salads, and other side dishes, and they will appear on the bill as separate items. In the case of fish and meat dishes, such as a joint of pork, the price on the menu refers to a portion of 100 g (just under ¼ lb). When ordering, it is advisable to specify the weight of the portion, since the bill will show only the price of the whole meal.

Tables outside a restaurant in Wrocław in summer

The Flavours of Poland

Polish cuisine, like that of many central European countries, makes heavy use of meat, especially pork, which is often served quite plainly with potatoes or rice and cabbage. However, because of the long Baltic coastline in the north of the country, fish is also likely to feature on many menus. Carp, trout and herring are particular favourites. Around Cracow, in the south, the local forests yield a bounty of quality game, with duck being very popular. The legacy of former rule by Austria is also evident in the south, especially in some of the sophisticated cakes and pastries.

Pickled herring

Barbecuing meat at a street celebration on Palm Sunday

MEAT

Pork *(wieprzowina)* is the most popular meat by far in Poland. It usually comes as a steak *(kotlet schabowy)* or on the bone *(golonka wieprzowa)* and also appears in soups, sausages and as hams. Polish hams are generally cured and have a rich, sweet flavour. Ham is mainly served cold as an appetizer with cheese and pickles, though it may also be eaten for breakfast. Poland also produces high quality veal *(cielęcina)*, which is often dished up with a rich mushroom sauce *(cielęcina po staropolsku)* or with cabbage and raisins.

POULTRY AND GAME

Chicken *(kurczaka)* is a staple food in Poland and drumsticks *(podudzie)* are especially popular. Chicken livers *(wątróbka)*, served with a fruit sauce, are considered a delicacy.

A wide variety of game roams the forests of southern Poland. Pheasant *(bażant)*, duck *(kaczka)*, goose *(gęś)*, venison *(comber)*, rabbit *(królik)* and hare *(zając)* are found on many local menus. Availability varies with the season; autumn is the best time to enjoy game.

Parówka (pork frankfurters)
Gruba krakowska (smoked garlic sausage)
Chicken kabanos (air-cured sausage with caraway seeds)
Podwawelsi (smoked sausage)
Wiejska (garlic and herb sausage)
Smoked pork loin
Zagórska (smooth textured, smoked sausage)

Selection of typical Polish sausages and cured meat

LOCAL DISHES AND SPECIALITIES

Green cabbage

Many classic Polish dishes are offered at restaurants all over the country, but fish also features prominently on northern menus, while those of the the south offer a range of game. The most varied and cosmopolitan cuisine is found in large cities, such as Warsaw and Cracow, where top chefs run the kitchens of some of the grand hotels. The national dish, *bigos*, comes from eastern Poland. It is hearty and warming for the long, bleak winters found there, as is another dish from this chilly region, *pierogi* (pasta dumplings, stuffed with meat, cheese or fruit). Both are influenced by the food of neighbouring Russia. Polish cakes and desserts also tend to be heavy and rich, although most originate in the warmer south, once ruled by Austria.

Bigos *Chunks of meat and sausage are simmered with sauerkraut, cabbage, onion, potatoes, herbs and spices.*

A colourful display of locally grown vegetables at a city market stall

meat or fish. Cabbage soup (*kapuśniak*) and sauerkraut are on every menu. Potatoes are also a staple. They come boiled, baked and mashed, though rarely roasted. Peppers are popular too, often served stuffed with rice and minced meat or pickled in summer salads. Root vegetables such as carrots, parsnips, swede (rutabaga), turnips and beetroot make their way into a range of dishes. Mushrooms grow wild all over Poland and come both cooked and pickled as a tasty addition to many meals.

FISH

Fish features strongly on menus in northern Poland, where herring (*śledź*) is a central part of the diet. It comes pickled, in oil, with onions, with soured cream – in fact, with just about everything. *Rolmops po kaszubsku* (marinated herring wrapped around pickled onion, then spiked with cloves and dipped in soured cream) are widely enjoyed. Other popular fish are freshwater trout (*pstrag*) – served simply grilled with boiled potatoes; carp (*karpia*) – often accompanied by horseradish sauce; and salmon (*łosoś*). A treat in early summer is smoked salmon served with spears of fresh asparagus (*łosoś wędzony ze szparagami*), which is then in season.

VEGETABLES

Poland produces many fine quality vegetables. The hardy cabbage (*kapusta*) remains the country's top vegetable. It is used in so many ways, including raw in salads and simply boiled to partner

Polish pretzels on sale in a Cracow bread shop

SNACKS

Sausages A wide range of smoked and unsmoked varieties are on offer at the profusion of street stalls and snack bars that can be found on most city streets.

Precles (pretzels) Another favourite street snack, these are popular, freshly baked, at train and bus stations first thing in the morning.

Zapiekanki Often referred to as Polish-style pizzas, these are tasty, open-top baguettes, spread with cheese and tomato, then toasted and served piping hot. They are also a common item on street-stall menus.

Smalec This snack consists of fried lard, liberally sprinkled with sea salt, and eaten with chunks of crusty bread. It can be found as a bar snack in most pubs and makes a good accompaniment to beer.

Pierogi *These ravioli-style dumplings may be stuffed with meat, sauerkraut, mushrooms, cheese or fruit.*

Barszcz *This beetroot soup, flavoured with lemon and garlic, may be served clear or with beans or potatoes.*

Poppy seed roll *A rich yeasted dough is wrapped around a sweet poppy-seed filling and baked until lightly golden.*

Choosing a Restaurant

Restaurants have been selected for their good cuisine
and interesting location. They are listed by region, the
coloured tabs in the margins corresponding to those by
which the regions of Poland are identified throughout the
guide. For the street map of Warsaw, see pages 100-103.
For the road map of Poland, see the inside back cover.

PRICE CATEGORIES
The following price ranges are for a
three-course meal for one without
wine, including VAT.

ⓩ under 50 PLN
ⓩⓩ 50–70 PLN
ⓩⓩⓩ 70–90 PLN
ⓩⓩⓩⓩ 90–110 PLN
ⓩⓩⓩⓩⓩ over 110 PLN

WARSAW

OLD AND NEW TOWNS Kompania Piwna Podwale 25

ⓩ

ul. Podwale 25, 00-261 **Tel** 022 635 63 14

Map 2 D3

An Old Town gem with a courtyard designed to resemble a Central European town square and an interior filled with
wooden benches and drinking slogans on the walls. Heaps of meat and potatoes come served on wooden boards by
staff dressed in traditional attire. One of the few low-budget success stories in the Old Town.

OLD AND NEW TOWNS Sekret

ⓩⓩⓩⓩ

ul. Jezuicka 1/3, 00-272 **Tel** 022 635 74 74

Map 2 D3

This stylish and expensive restaurant is located next to the Old Town, close to the Royal Castle, in a maze of 16th-
century cellars. The menu includes a vast selection of traditional Polish meat and game courses, such as lamb shank
served with baked potato, and roast deer with juniper sauce and potato dumplings.

OLD AND NEW TOWNS U Fukiera

ⓩⓩⓩⓩⓩ

Rynek Starego Miasta 27, 00-275 **Tel** 022 831 10 13

Map 2 D3

A main-square location and a guest list that includes world leaders and royalty speak volumes for U Fukiera's
reputation – and prices. Set inside a beautiful network of chambers, the interiors alone are worth a visit, while the
menu focuses on Polish classics cooked with ingenuity. The summer courtyard represents starlit dining at its finest.

THE ROYAL ROUTE Adler

ⓩⓩⓩ

ul. Mokotowska 69, 00-530 **Tel** 022 628 73 84

Map 3 C3

Decked out with baskets of dried flowers and the odd *Pickelhaube* (spiked helmet), Adler embodies the atmosphere
of a Bavarian beer hall, with staff in ethnic costume rushing around delivering gigantic portions of pig's neck and
Schnitzel. Prices mean that it is mainly an older corporate crowd you will find hoisting tankards of beer, though.

THE ROYAL ROUTE India Curry

ⓩⓩⓩ

ul. Żurawia 22, 00-515 **Tel** 022 438 93 50

Map 2 C2

Indian food has not travelled well to Poland, with many chefs choosing to use inferior ingredients and cooking only
the mildest of curries. India Curry, however, gets everything right – from its menu, which goes beyond the mainstream
dishes, to the tasteful interiors, which include a bubbling fountain. Those on a budget will enjoy the lunch deals.

THE ROYAL ROUTE Papaya

ⓩⓩⓩ

ul. Foksal 16, 00-372 **Tel** 022 826 11 99

Map 4 D1

A great addition to Warsaw's booming fusion scene, Papaya features a tepanyaki grill and dishes like Kobe sirloin,
and tuna steak with Thai basil and shrimps. The white colour schemes generate a hip, urbane atmosphere that
attracts trendy young things in flashy sports cars. Expect a heavy bill at the end of your meal.

THE ROYAL ROUTE Sakana Sushi Bar

ⓩⓩⓩ

ul. Moliera 4/6, 00-07 **Tel** 022 826 59 58

Map 2 D4

Warsaw is sushi-crazy, and Sakana is the best out of the dozens of sushi restaurants to be found across town.
Food drifts by on paper boats, while a fashion-conscious crowd sits around the circular feeding area. The place
is definitely on the small side, so be prepared to wait for a seat if you turn up during the lunch rush.

CITY CENTRE Jajo

 ⓩⓩⓩ

ul. Zgoda 3, 00-018 **Tel** 022 826 44 93

Map 3 C1

A fashionable spot with hip lighting and a crowd consisting of "it-girls" and the men who adore them, the menu,
which specializes in spaghetti, has won fans across the city, but other continental bites are available too. This place
also doubles as a bar, and it is popular with a fun crowd.

CITY CENTRE Sunanta

 ⓩⓩⓩ

ul. Krucza 16/22, 00-526 **Tel** 022 434 22 16

Map 3 C2

Run by a native Thai, this small and cosy restaurant with a colourful interior is a real treat for those looking for an
interesting and exotic taste experience. All dishes are prepared with ingredients sourced from Thailand. Highlights
include green chicken curry and kung shrimps. Reservations recommended.

Key to Symbols *see back cover flap*

CITY CENTRE Galeria Bali & Buddha Club

ul. Jasna 22, 00-054 **Tel** *022 828 67 71*

Map *1 C5*

Fusion food at top-tier prices is served here, though the quality more than justifies the price tag. This restaurant brings Indonesia to your doorstep with choices such as stir-fried beef in oyster sauce and fried lobster in coconut crumbs. Everything is for sale here, from the cutlery to the gold-plated statue of Buddha that sits peacefully inside.

CITY CENTRE San Lorenzo

al. Jana Pawła II 36, 01-141 **Tel** *022 652 16 16*

Map *1 A3*

Reservations are advised at this elegant restaurant with frescoed walls and imported Italian furniture. San Lorenzo offers a wide range of dishes, but it is particularly renowned for its fish and seafood menu. Try the sea bass tartare with tuna flakes or the spaghetti with a lobster sauce.

FURTHER AFIELD Biosfeera

al. Niepodległości 80, 02-626 **Tel** *022 898 01 55*

Part of a growing trend towards healthy eating, Biosfeera is a modern space with paper lanterns and a hip atmosphere where you will find a sharply dressed young crowd feeding on salads and vegetarian tortillas and sipping non-alcoholic cocktails. The restaurant operates a strict no-smoking policy.

FURTHER AFIELD Radio Café

ul. Nowogrodzka 56, 00-695 **Tel** *022 625 27 84*

Map *3 B2*

Although Radio Café is comparatively inexpensive, its location in the shadow of the Marriott tends to ward off any cheapskates. A mixed group of Polish intellectuals and foreigners who appreciate the local food can be found enjoying their dinners here, and at night the restaurant assumes a smoky, alcohol-fuelled ambience. A local legend.

FURTHER AFIELD Banja Luka

ul. Puławska 101, 02-595 **Tel** *022 854 0782*

A Balkan menu that features Croat, Serbian and Bosnian specialities is served inside a warm interior reminiscent of a mountain lodge. Banja Luka is by no means central, so do expect to be travelling there and back by taxi, but the portions and prices make up for the trek. A superb summer garden, complete with pond, is the icing on the cake.

FURTHER AFIELD Le Cedre

al. Solidarności 61, 03-402 **Tel** *022 670 11 66*

Map *2 F3*

Across the river from the Old Town, Le Cedre must be one of few restaurants in Poland to tout views of a bear pit (belonging to the zoo opposite). Hookah pipes and the occasional belly dancer strive to create a Middle Eastern atmosphere, while the skewered meats are a pleasure. Its popularity with Lebanese diplomats speaks for itself.

FURTHER AFIELD Warsaw Tortilla Factory

ul. Wilcza 46, 00-679 **Tel** *022 621 86 22*

Map *3 B3*

This place offers by far the best Mexican food in Poland, with an array of salsas so hot they may lead to convulsions. Cheap by Warsaw's overpriced standards, Tortilla Factory is regularly crowded with locals and foreigners enjoying their burritos and quesadillas. The bar area is the source of some of the best margaritas in the city.

FURTHER AFIELD Dom Polski

ul. Francuska 11, 03-906 **Tel** *022 616 24 32*

Having dinner at Dom Polski has long been a vital rite of passage for holiday-makers and expats alike, and this stands out as one of the classiest treats in Warsaw. The menu changes with the seasons, but it always seems to include fantastic game dishes, while the interiors, set inside a detached pre-war villa, are redolent of a country manor.

FURTHER AFIELD Belvedere

ul. Agrykola 1 (on the grounds of Royal Łazienki Park), 00-460 **Tel** *022 558 67 00*

Map *3 C5*

A stalwart of Warsaw's dining scene, Belvedere enjoys an awesome location inside a conservatory in the heart of Łazienki Park. Watch peacocks amble outside while black-tie waiters deliver gourmet meals such as quail stuffed with liver to your table. Definitely on the expensive side but well worth the outlay if you are looking to impress.

MAZOVIA AND THE LUBLIN REGION

ADAMOWICE Karczma Sole

ul. Styropianowa 2, 96-320 **Tel** *046 857 30 74*

Road map *E3*

This pleasant, folksy lodge is far classier than one would imagine from first impressions. The menu is Polish, but it includes several international choices too; try the French-style duck served in cherry sauce. The lion's share of ingredients are imported from Italy, with the head chef also trained under Italian guidance.

GRÓJEC La Terrazza

ul. Graniczna 1b, 05-600 **Tel** *048 664 58 17*

Road map *E4*

This authentic Italian restaurant is run by cooks who hail from the southern Apennines. Wholesome, traditional cuisine and an extensive choice of dishes have earned La Terrazza its undeniable popularity. It is located on the A7 highway connecting Warsaw with Cracow.

KAZIMERZ DOLNY U Fryzjera

ul. Witkiewicza 2, 24-120 **Tel** *081 881 04 26* **Road map** F4

Located in a former barbershop, this charming restaurant serves Jewish delicacies such as stuffed goose neck, as well as numerous types of *pierogi* (stuffed pasta). The interior consists of creaky floorboards, barbershop equipment and sepia shots of bygone days. Live *klezmer* (Yiddish music) performances regularly have the crowds clapping in time.

KAZIMERZ DOLNY Zielona Tawerna

ul. Nadwiślańska 4, 24-120 **Tel** *081 881 03 08* **Road map** F4

This restaurant specializes in typical, traditional Polish cuisine, and the menu includes an excellent sirloin steak served in a pumpkin shell. The summer garden gets rather crowded on sunny days, while on the inside this white townhouse offers jazz music and a laid-back atmosphere.

LUBLIN Hades

ul. Peowiaków 12, 20-007 **Tel** *081 532 87 61* **Road map** F4

Housed in a former monastery, Hades is a fashionable restaurant with good cuisine specializing chiefly in Polish delicacies. The menu also includes several original dishes invented by famous guests, as well as a long line of tartar-steak specialities. Club nights and discos are held in a separate area of the restaurant.

LUBLIN Oberża Artystyczna Złoty Osioł

ul. Grodzka 5a, 20-112 **Tel** *081 532 90 42* **Road map** F4

This restaurant, positioned in the heart of the Old Town, has an intimate interior, bursting with wood and wicker fixtures, where local art exhibitions are frequently held. The dishes have intriguing names, such as "Donkey's Ear" and "Young Breasts", but the waiter will always be willing to offer clarification.

NAŁĘCZÓW Patataj

Kolonia Bochotnica 15, 24-150 **Tel** *081 501 47 01* **Road map** F4

Located on the road from Warsaw to Lublin, this family-run restaurant is housed in a typical 19th-century manor. In addition to spectacular views over the nearby forests, diners will be able to enjoy traditional Polish dishes. The *pierogi* dumplings stuffed with veal and sage butter are highly recommended. Closed Mon.

PUŁAWY Willa Cienista

ul. Zielona 23, 24-100 **Tel** *081 888 09 37* **Road map** F4

This charming modern villa constructed in Tyrolean style houses a plum-coloured bar supported by timber beams, as well as a nightclub. If your pleasures are less liquid, then the restaurant is a pretty affair with an atmosphere of muted elegance. The menu offers dishes from the Mediterranean and Polish traditions.

WIĄZOWNA Zajazd u Mikulskich – Mazowsze

ul. Parkingowa 18a, 05-462 **Tel** *022 780 43 77* **Road map** E3

Located in a mock country mansion, this elegant restaurant features a dining room with wood cabinets and pristine linen arrangements, where bow-tied staff deliver typically traditional Polish dishes to the tables. Those who are not impressed by refined atmospheres will be pleased to know that more basic dining rooms are also available.

ZAMOŚĆ Padwa

ul. Staszica 23, 22-400 **Tel** *084 638 62 56* **Road map** G5

The name reflects Zamość's former moniker, "Padua of the East", and this grand, brick-walled restaurant is lined with pictures of local celebrities. The main-square location guarantees plenty of tourist traffic, and the menu is a mix of both Polish and Hungarian dishes. Potato pancakes are the chef's speciality.

ZWIERZYNIEC Karczma Młyn

ul. Wachniewskiej 1a, 22-470 **Tel** *084 687 25 27* **Road map** F5

Although located in the town centre, this beautifully renovated mill has a sedate atmosphere thanks to its proximity to the lake and the many trees that surround it. The menu offers primarily regional food, but the locals claim that the home-made pizzas are the best in the area. Inexpensive accommodation is also available.

CRACOW

Green Way

ul. Mikołajska 14, 31-027 **Tel** *012 431 10 27* **Road map** D5

Part of a Poland-wide chain, this relatively expensive vegetarian fast-food bar has a few tables at the back where diners can enjoy their meat-free snacks in relative comfort. The food is less than adventurous, but with vegetarian options so thin on the ground in this city, the queues at lunchtime can be annoyingly long.

Pierogarnia

ul. Sławkowska 32, 31-014 **Tel** *012 422 74 95* **Road map** D5

No visitor to Cracow should leave the city without tasting the Polish speciality *pierogi* (stuffed pasta), and Pierogarnia is about the best place in town to enjoy that experience. Fillings are innumerable, and these tasty treats can be eaten as a snack or as part of a larger meal. The restaurant also serves other Polish delicacies.

Key to Price Guide *see p316* **Key to Symbols** *see back cover flap*

Rooster

ul. Szczepańska 4, 31-010 **Tel** *012 411 36 72*

Road map D5

At this excellent American diner-style restaurant, part of a Poland-wide chain, you can choose between grilled meat, pasta dishes and burgers which are Cracow's best. While prices are a little high for what you get, the friendliness of the waiting staff is legendary. The barman makes some fantastic cocktails.

Chimera

ul. św. Anny 3, 31-008 **Tel** *012 292 12 12*

Road map D5

Traditional Polish dishes, including roast pork and lamb, are served on the ground floor of this restaurant, while the salad bar in the basement serves light, healthy food and a wide selection of vegetarian options. Make sure you try one of the home-made fruit liqueurs, a speciality of the restaurant.

Klezmer Hois

ul. Szeroka 6, 31-053 **Tel** *012 411 12 45*

Road map D5

While Klezmer Hois is bold enough to admit that it has no rabbinical certificate of supervision (the Kashrut), it does keep strict standards, and all dishes are kosher, not to mention great value. Enjoy Sabbath soup, *shubaha* herring and Sephardic salads alongside meaty treats, such as stuffed goose neck.

Pod Wawelem

ul. St. Gertrude 26–29, 31-069 **Tel** *012 421 23 26*

Road map D5

Located at the foot of Wawel Hill, this restaurant serves large portions of Polish favourites at 1970s prices. Try the *pierogi* dumplings or the *golonka* (boiled and pickled ham hock), and wash your food down with Polish beer or home-made vodka. In summer, it is possible to dine alfresco, with a view of the castle.

Sukiennice

Rynek Główny 1/3, 31-042 **Tel** *012 422 24 68*

Road map D5

In summer, the terrace of this trendy venue on Market Square – set under the colonnades of a fantastic building – is packed out, with live bands performing impromptu sets to delighted diners. If the weather is inclement, head inside, where elegant tables, smooth lighting and simple fusion dishes make this a romantic place for a light meal.

Balaton

ul. Grodzka 37, 31-001 **Tel** *012 422 04 69*

Road map D5

The less-than-salubrious setting is redeemed by a delicious menu of specialities from Hungary. Try the Hungarian national dish, goulash, or spicy sausages. Paprika is used in most dishes on the menu, so if you would like your food on the mild side, mention it to your waiter. Reservations are often needed, since Balaton fills up early most evenings.

Farina

ul. św. Marka 16, 31-017 **Tel** *012 422 16 80*

Road map D5

In this simple, uncluttered restaurant, the bare, highly polished wooden floors and white-washed walls are geared towards focusing the diner's attention on the excellent menu. A successful mix of Polish and Italian dishes brings in crowds of locals and visitors. Reservations are necessary in the evenings.

Grill 15/16

Rynek Główny 16, 31-008 **Tel** *012 424 96 01*

Road map D5

Salads, grilled meats and well-mixed cocktails are served in the jungle-like surroundings of a leafy garden behind Market Square. During the summer there is live jazz almost every evening, which brings in a sophisticated crowd. Tables are hard to come by after 7pm, so be sure to make a reservation.

Pod Aniołami

ul. Grodzka 35, 31-001 **Tel** *012 421 39 99*

Road map D5

This restaurant is located in medieval cellars decorated with a selection of historical objects. The menu features traditional Polish dishes, in particular highlanders' delicacies. You can try *oszczypki* (a special kind of cheese prepared by Polish highlanders) or *żurek*, a rye flour-based soup.

Wentzl

Rynek Główny 19, 31-008 **Tel** *012 429 52 99*

Road map D5

Local merchant John Wentzl opened a restaurant here in 1792. Today that place is one of the best eateries in the city. The high ceilings, polished oak floors and outstanding service complement the menu, which is dominated by Czech, Slovak and Hungarian specialities. The wine list ranges from France, Austria and Spain to Chile and South Africa.

Cyrano de Bergerac

ul. Sławkowska 26, 31-014 **Tel** *012 411 72 88*

Road map D5

If prices here are high, the diners who reserve tables weeks in advance do not seem to mind. This is a world-class French restaurant spread over two elegant rooms, with a quiet patio used in the summer months. The food is exquisite, cooked under the auspices of masterchef Pierre Gallard. Try the *garbure soupe béarnaise*, made with goose.

La Fontaine

ul. Sławkowska 1, 31-014 **Tel** *012 422 65 64*

Road map D5

Located in a former warehouse in the heart of the Old City, close to Cracow's most important sights, this elegant French restaurant offers a sophisticated dining experience. Highlights on the menu include French onion soup, beef tournedos with a Roquefort sauce and a delicious bouillabaisse soup with garlic croutons and saffron sauce.

The Olive
ul. Powiśle 7, 31-101 **Tel** 012 662 16 60   **Road map** D5

As expensive as any restaurant in Cracow, the Sheraton's showpiece is an award-winning eaterie famed for its high-class Mediterranean cuisine. There is a particularly good selection of seafood and fish dishes, and the wine list is pitch-perfect. A glass roof makes dining here in winter a particularly pleasurable experience.

MAŁOPOLSKA

BIELSKO BIAŁA Patria
ul. Wzgórze 19, 43-300 **Tel** 033 812 24 08   **Road map** D6

The menu at this restaurant, with its interesting Secessionist interior, features predominantly Polish dishes, but it also offers delicacies from other European countries. The sumptuous and abundant *Danie Królewskie* (Royal Dish), which consists of three different types of meat served with rice and fruit, is particularly recommended.

BIELSKO BIAŁA Zajazd Klimczok
ul. Bystrzańska 94, 43-309 **Tel** 033 814 15 67   **Road map** D6

The decor at this wooden inn is enlivened by a fireplace, animal pelts and formal table arrangements. On the menu are traditional Polish and regional dishes, with Silesian fare dominating. Try the "Woodcutter's Food": potato pies filled with goulash and vegetables. Hotel accommodation is also available in the upstairs quarters.

BRENNA Skalny Dworek
ul. Wyzwolenia 45, 43-438 **Tel** 033 853 61 16   **Road map** D6

If you are here in the summer, ask to dine on the pretty terrace, since the restaurant itself offers little more than a droll interior of plastic plants and some timber fixtures. The menu is as you would expect in a chalet building: huge servings of meat and potatoes, cooked with a good degree of competence.

BRZESKO Pawilon
ul. Wesoła 4, 32-800 **Tel** 014 663 17 61   **Road map** E5

Located in a converted early 20th-century building, this inn is decorated with paintings from the village of Zalipie. Though no extraordinary gourmet experience, the food is wholesome, cheap and simple. There is a wide choice of Polish dishes, including generous servings of *pierogi* (stuffed pasta) and Zalipie-style *żurek* (sour-rye soup).

DWÓR Restauracja Nowina
near Głogoczów, 32-440 **Tel** 012 273 77 15   **Road map** D6

This award-winning traditional restaurant does more than enough to keep the nearby Chłopskie Jadło *(see below)* on its toes: for years Nowina was known as one of the top dining spots in the whole region. Owned by a suave, pipe-smoking aristocrat, this restaurant is famed for its great game dishes as well as its rum omelettes.

GŁOGOCZÓW Chłopskie Jadło
Głogoczów 196, 32-444 **Tel** 012 273 73 40   **Road map** D6

A popular restaurant chain serving traditional Polish recipes, with country dishes a speciality. As with all the Chłopskie Jadło ventures across Poland, the Głogoczów branch comes with hams and peppers hanging off turquoise walls, firewood stacked in the corner and bench seating. Their soups are highly recommended.

ŁANCUT Pensjonat Pałacyk
ul. Paderewskiego 18, 37-100 **Tel** 017 225 20 43   **Road map** F5

This restaurant is located in a late 19th-century villa and features period interiors and a medley of hunters' trophies. Traditional Polish and regional cuisine is prepared using home-grown produce, and there are even a few Oriental additions on the menu. To enjoy the scenery in all its glory visit in the summer months.

NOWY SĄCZ Panorama
ul. Romanowskiego 6, 33-300 **Tel** 018 443 75 15   **Road map** E6

While the interior of this restaurant is rather forgettable, Panorama (as the name suggests) enjoys panoramic views. The real reason for its popularity with the natives, however, is the food: the restaurant has been awarded the prestigious Silver Frying Pan award no fewer than three times.

NOWY SĄCZ Kupiecka
Rynek 10, 33-300 **Tel** 018 442 08 31   **Road map** E6

Located in picturesque vaulted cellars, this is a lovely spot to bask by the fireplace and dine by candlelight. Ten out of ten for interiors, and equally high marks for the European and Polish cuisine found on the menu. The *golonka* (knuckle of pork) in honey is particularly recommended, and this is the perfect spot for dinner for two.

OGRODZIENIEC Zamkowy Ogródek
On castle grounds, 42-440 **Tel** 506 174 038   **Road map** D5

Regional dishes are served in the grounds that surround the ruins of the castle of Ogrodzieniec. The house favourite is the "Breasts of the Castle's Chickens", while at weekends diners can choose from an array of smoked and grilled meats. This is the ideal place for an unusual, scenic summer dinner.

Key to Price Guide see p316 **Key to Symbols** see back cover flap

OJCÓW Zajazd Zazamcze

Ojców 1b, 32-047 **Tel** *012 389 20 83* **Road map** *D5*

A chalet-style building with beautifully tended gardens and a dining room with shiny floors that is decorated with promotional brewery signs and a token animal head. The house speciality is "Flaming Trout", though carnivores will be more interested in the "Pig Slaughter Feast", which involves a selection of pork cuts.

RABKA ZDRÓJ Siwy Dym

ul. Kilińskiego, 34-700 **Tel** *018 267 66 74* **Road map** *D6*

The interior of this mountain-style wooden lodge consists of timber tables and the obligatory animal hides, with the staff dressed in traditional local costume. The live music is often excellent, and the owners themselves are known for taking to the stage. The menu revolves mostly around meat, though there are a few options for vegetarians.

SIENIAWA Winiarnia

ul. Kościuszki 32, 37-530 **Tel** *016 649 17 00* **Road map** *F5*

The Baroque former home of the Sieniawski family houses a small hotel and an excellent restaurant. In the elegant dining room, featuring chandeliers and shining floors, the discreet waiting staff ferry plates of Central European food to the tables. There is also a large list of wines available for diners to enjoy.

SUCHA BESKIDZKA Karczma Rzym

Rynek 1, 34-200 **Tel** *033 874 27 97* **Road map** *D6*

Head to this traditional inn specializing in hearty local dishes when you are in the mood for a winter warmer. The name derives from the legend of Pan Twardowski, who allegedly crossed the path of the devil at Karczma Rzym; as a tribute to this character, all the dishes on this menu bear devilish names.

TARNÓW Pasaż

Pasaż Tertila, 33-100 **Tel** *014 627 82 78* **Road map** *E5*

From the outside, Pasaż looks like a slightly shady place, a great shame considering the 18th-century tenement location. Interiors are more classy, with an atmosphere that brings to mind the days of the Habsburg dynasty. Polish recipes like pork with apples and pikeperch San Domingo contribute to making this the best restaurant in town.

ZAKOPANE Czarny Staw

ul. Krupówki 2, 34-500 **Tel** *512 351 733* **Road map** *D6*

Meat is cooked on a noisy open grill in the middle of the room, though it is the fish dishes that this place is renowned for; the fish soup is served from a small kettle, and the trout on a fish-shaped wooden board. A *górale* band plays live music here every day.

ZAKOPANE U Wnuka

ul. Kościeliska 8, 34-500 **Tel** *018 206 41 67* **Road map** *D6*

Excellent highlanders' dishes are served in small rooms in this 150-year-old wooden house. The *kwaśnica* (a sour soup typical of the region), the lamb with fried cabbage and the spare ribs are particularly delicious – and reasonably priced, too. A highlanders' band provides live music at weekends.

ZAKOPANE Bąkowo Zohylina

ul. Piłsudskiego 6, 34-500 **Tel** *018 206 62 16* **Road map** *D6*

Set in a converted barn surrounded by fir trees off the road to the ski jump, this traditional restaurant boasts a great atmosphere. Dance to traditional music under the cauldron dangling from the ceiling in the middle of the room, and enjoy the excellent goulash, venison filet and fresh trout. Most evenings feature yodelling mountain bands.

ZAKOPANE Dworek Bawarski

ul. Bogdańskiego 5, 34-500 **Tel** *018 206 65 11* **Road map** *D6*

This restaurant, housed in a beautiful lodge on the edge of the forest on the Giewont trail, serves classic Bavarian dishes, including *Strüdel*, along with foaming *Steins* of German beer. The dining hall features a stone fireplace with a bear's head glowering down from above. A great atmosphere is guaranteed.

SILESIA

CZECHOWICE-DZIEDZICE Rist

ul. Brzeziny 4, 43-502 **Tel** *032 214 26 48* **Road map** *D6*

Rist's elegant dining room features chandeliers and painstaking linen arrangements. You will pay far more than in most other local restaurants, but the high-end offerings, such as New Zealand lamb and roe deer, are worth the splurge. The restaurant also specializes in Silesian dishes, including dumplings stuffed with cabbage leaves.

CZELADŹ Calvados

ul. Bytomska 30, 41-254 **Tel** *032 763 60 17* **Road map** *D5*

Head to Calvados for a Mediterranean menu with several seafood options. The maritime interior is designed to look like a galleon, and the place is regularly packed to the rafters with locals, who seem to enjoy dining amid the rigging and lanterns, while the busy staff rush around keeping control of the crowds.

GLIWICE Spichlerz
ul. Wiejska 16b, 44-121 **Tel** *032 305 24 52*   **Road map** *D5*

Located inside a converted granary building, this gorgeous restaurant features original details like brick walls and exposed beams. In spite of offering top-class meals, the atmosphere is far from formal. Start with the mushroom soup, served inside a loaf of bread, before moving on to generous plates of wild boar and deer.

KATOWICE A Dong
ul. Matejki 3, 40-077 **Tel** *032 258 66 62*   **Road map** *D5*

Decorated with the requisite paper lanterns, A Dong offers diners a thick menu with an extensive choice of Chinese and Vietnamese dishes. Meals range from eel Saigon-style to stuffed chicken wings in a sweet and sour sauce. A take-away service is also available, and the restaurant has sister branches in Gliwice and Sosnowiec.

MIĘDZYGÓRZE Willa Millenium
ul. Wojska Polskiego 9, 57-514 **Tel** *074 813 52 87*   **Road map** *B5*

A charming white building, not unlike a Swiss chalet, is the setting for this restaurant. The interiors are slightly disappointing, with crass additions such as plastic sunflowers, paper napkins and a calendar featuring women in suggestive poses by the bar area. Fortunately, the menu boasts good local food, especially the Galician-style trout.

PSZCZYNA Frykówka
Rynek, 43-200 **Tel** *032 449 00 20*   **Road map** *D6*

Housed inside an 18th-century tenement building, Frykówka is an attractive space. Diners consume their meals under vaulted ceilings and the watchful eye of the nobility pictured in the paintings on the wall. The wine list is extensive and the menu combines traditional Polish fare, local Silesian dishes and a number of Italian options.

WISŁA Niby Nic
ul. 1 Maja 61, 43-460 **Tel** *033 855 22 38*   **Road map** *D6*

A pleasant restaurant with a scarlet colour scheme and framed photos, Niby Nic is situated on the town's main promenade. The menu features Polish and European dishes – all cooked, apparently, to old, traditional recipes. This restaurant is the ideal gathering place for ski-jumping fans.

WROCŁAW Abrams' Tower
ul. Kraińskiego 14, 50-153 **Tel** *071 725 66 52*   **Road map** *C4*

In the past you had to travel to Warsaw to enjoy decent Mexican food, but Abrams' Tower means that this is no longer the case. Indeed, this restaurant looks set on changing the conservative dining habits of the locals. The owners stress that this is Mexican food prepared Californian-style, all done inside the trendy interior of a medieval tower.

WROCŁAW Le Bistrot Parisien
ul. Nożownicza 1d, 50-119 **Tel** *071 341 05 65*   **Road map** *C4*

A foggy atmosphere and walls decorated with a collection of artistic photos and clippings taken from the French press create a convincingly Parisian atmosphere. This is a superb spot to while away a lazy evening. The menu includes a recommended range of pancakes, as well as more filling options. All are worth considering.

WROCŁAW Art Restauracja i Kawiarnia
ul. Kiełbaśnicza 20, 50-110 **Tel** *071 787 71 02*   **Road map** *C4*

The Art Hotel is one of the best hotels in town, so it comes as no surprise to hear that that quality extends to the kitchen. Descend to the basement to find a vaulted brick cellar decorated with murals of town scenes. The menu changes with the seasons and sees the chef experimenting with recipes from a wide range of European countries.

WROCŁAW Czwartkowa and Królewska
Rynek 5, 50-106 **Tel** *071 372 48 96*   **Road map** *C4*

No expense has been spared on the interiors, which consist of three vaulted halls designed to evoke the glory days of the Habsburg Empire. Decorated with swish drapes and oil paintings, this classy restaurant offers a menu that includes high-brow interpretations of Polish and Central European dishes; the game offerings are especially recommended.

WROCŁAW Karczma Lwowska
Rynek 4, 50-106 **Tel** *071 343 98 87*   **Road map** *C4*

Found inside a historical building on the market square, Karczma Lwowska is all dark, gloomy woods paired with luridly yellow tablecloths and black-and-white pictures of Wrocław's twin town, Lwów. The food, however, is surprisingly good – and liberally priced, considering the location – with several notable grill dishes to choose from.

WROCŁAW Piano Bar Casablanca
ul. Włodkowica 8a, 50-072 **Tel** *603 877 777*   **Road map** *C4*

One of the most revered restaurants in town (and one popular with local celebrities) is inside a building decorated with North African rugs, shrubbery and framed pictures of Humphrey Bogart. The garden outside feels a world away from the frantic flutter of central Wrocław, and the menu offers a blend of local and Mediterranean dishes.

WROCŁAW Sakana
ul. Odrzańska 17/1a, 50-113 **Tel** *071 344 61 05*   **Road map** *C4*

This restaurant is owned by the same team behind the best sushi stop in the capital. Wrocław's version of Sakana is equally good, the only difference being that this venture is actually larger that the Warsaw branch. Once more, the food floats around a circular bar on paper boats, eagerly consumed by a young and fashionable crowd.

WROCŁAW Spiż

Rynek Ratusz 2, 50-106 **Tel** *071 344 72 25* **Road map** *C4*

This venture is split into two rooms: a microbrewery with huge copper vats and a formal dining room. The service is not fast, but you will be treated to outstanding home-brewed beer, as well as a menu that features Argentinian beef and saddle of lamb among Polish choices. The restaurant section is popular with an older crowd.

WROCŁAW Splendido

ul. Świdnicka 53, 50-030 **Tel** *071 344 77 77* **Road map** *C3*

One of Wrocław's best choices, provided you're willing to part with cash. Interiors are cluttered with exposed beams, vases of flowers and lampshades, and the menu is a collection of Mediterranean dishes. The seafood is especially noteworthy, with a superb sea bass prepared in balsamic sauce. The exclusive Vulevu Club is found in the basement.

WIELKOPOLSKA

GRABOWNO Dworek Koper

Near Miasteczko Krajeńskie, 89-350 **Tel** *067 287 41 28* **Road map** *C2*

This rambling manor house is home to an excellent restaurant decorated with antiques that also doubles as an art gallery. The menu contains a vast selection of Polish and Lithuanian delights, as well as a number of vegetarian options. The *kołduny* (dumplings stuffed with meat) are highly recommended.

IWNO Zajazd Podbipięta

ul. Gnieźnieńska 2, near Kostrzyń Wielkopolski, 62-025 **Tel** *051 669 23 70* **Road map** *C3*

Proving that not all Polish 1970s architecture is bad, this is a picturesque roadhouse serving good, inexpensive meals. Foodies from Poznań and elsewhere come here to enjoy the "family joint of pork", which feeds up to four people. For starters, try the house speciality, *żurek* soup served inside a large bun.

JAROCIN Gościniec Walcerek

ul. Poznańska 73, 63-200 **Tel** *062 747 28 18* **Road map** *C3*

A chalet-style guesthouse with a curious mix of classy touches, such as chandeliers and a piano, and cheap-looking fittings, like stone cladding. The alcohol selection is vast and paired well with the rich meat offerings. Gościniec Walcerek offers cheap and cheerful Polish cuisine at its finest, with a quiet outdoor terrace to retire to afterwards.

ŁÓDŹ Ciągoty i Tęsknoty

ul. Wojska Polskiego 144a, 91-711 **Tel** *042 650 87 94* **Road map** *D4*

One of the few restaurants in Łódź that could survive in a more competitive environment. Tracking it down may lead to adventure, but intrepid diners will be rewarded with a superb ambience, not too different from a French country kitchen. Multilingual waiters take the orders and deliver high-quality meals, such as chicken in lemon sauce.

ŁÓDŹ Anatewka

ul. 6 Sierpnia 2/4, 90-422 **Tel** *042 630 36 35* **Road map** *D4*

A restaurant that harks back to the day when Łódź was known for its large Jewish population. The decor includes menorahs, framed pictures of old Łódź and even a couple of mannequins sporting prayer shawls and Hassidic locks. Superb staff deliver dishes like duck served in cherry sauce while *klezmer* (Yiddish) music plays in the background.

POZNAŃ Jazz Sarp

Stary Rynek 56, 61-772 **Tel** *061 853 24 64* **Road map** *C3*

A hyper-modern space that comes with a sushi bar, a non-smoking policy and some of the best jazz performances in the city. Poznań's movers and shakers love this place, and it is not surprising. Images of Poznań in its pre-war golden glory are projected on to the walls, while expert bar staff are adept at mixing beautiful and tasty cocktails.

POZNAŃ Bee Jay's

Stary Rynek 87, 61-772 **Tel** *061 853 11 15* **Road map** *C3*

Bee Jay's boasts a main-square location and a menu that surprises with each turn of the page. You will find burgers on one page, Mexican on the next, and Indian on the following. Perhaps even more surprising is that the ethnic food is pretty good, a real bonus in such a gastronomically conservative town. Big-screen live sports spice things up.

POZNAŃ Brovaria

Stary Rynek 73/74, 61-772 **Tel** *061 858 68 68* **Road map** *C3*

Brovaria consists of a hotel, a restaurant and a microbrewery – all under one roof and each winning praise for excellence. The chic restaurant offers beautifully presented dishes served on square plates. Try the veal stuffed with chicken and veal mousse, before finishing off with cocktails at the impressive steel-and-glass bar.

POZNAŃ Zagroda Bamberska

ul. Kościelna 43, 60-534 **Tel** *061 842 77 90* **Road map** *C3*

Traditional regional specialities such as duck on cabbage with cranberries are on offer at this restaurant, housed in a 19th-century farm-style building with flower baskets hanging from wooden beams. It is half an hour on foot from Market Square, but there are rooms upstairs for those who don't fancy the walk back into town after a big meal.

POZNAŃ Delicja

pl. Wolności 5, 61-738 **Tel** *061 852 11 28*   **Road map** *C3*

Twice named Poland's restaurant of the year by *American Express* magazine, this is one of the most famous dining rooms in Poznań, with elegant interiors containing marble columns and ticking clocks. The menu is a mix of Polish, Italian and French delicacies, cooked by a team of award-winning chefs. In summer don't miss a visit to the garden.

POZNAŃ Le Palais du Jardin

Stary Rynek 37, 61-772 **Tel** *061 665 85 85*   **Road map** *C3*

Another excellent dining experience, this one with a main-square location directly across from the town hall. The Palais has won numerous awards for excellence, and the menu is little less than nouvelle cuisine at its finest. The owner is a self-confessed wine buff, a fact reflected in the extensive wine list.

POZNAŃ Sioux Classic

Stary Rynek 93, 61-773 **Tel** *061 851 62 86*   **Road map** *C3*

Styled after a 19th-century Wild West saloon (and featuring serving staff in costume), Sioux Classic has a typical Tex-Mex menu, with the occasional European dish thrown in for good measure. Despite the prices being quite high for the food on offer (steaks, burgers, wings), the restaurant is very popular and usually packed in the summer months.

POZNAŃ Nowa Bażanciarnia

Stary Rynek 94, 61-773 **Tel** *061 855 33 58*   **Road map** *C3*

The property of celebrity restaurateur Magda Gessler, Nowa Bażanciarnia boasts a dining room that has been designed to look like the banquet hall of an eccentric aristocrat: flowers and fruit stand on the shelves, while paintings of pheasants adorn the walls. The game dishes are superb and regarded as some of the best in the city.

GDAŃSK

Chata Chłopska

ul. Gielguda 4, 80-207 **Tel** *058 524 00 95*   **Road map** *D1*

Local diners flock to this thatched lodge located just outside the fringes of the Old Town to eat vast portions of meat dishes and hoist their beers in the air. The rustic interiors prove a great escape from downtown Gdańsk's more formal eateries, and the menu provides a great whistle-stop tour of traditional Polish food.

Kubicki

ul. Wartka 5, 80-841 **Tel** *058 301 00 50*   **Road map** *D1*

Founded in 1919, this legendary restaurant is still in the hands of the same family. The interiors are full of interesting old furniture, while the food is typical of traditional Polish port cities, with a good selection of starters and an excellently prepared fried trout. Make sure you leave some room for the delicious cheesecake.

Pizzeria Margherita

ul. Cystersów 11, 80-330 **Tel** *058 552 37 16*   **Road map** *D1*

Do not be put off by the suburban location: this pleasant restaurant serves 28 types of pizza – allegedly the best in Gdańsk – at competitive prices. This is a good stop if you find yourself touring around the district of Oliwa; if not, you will be pleased to hear that they also deliver across the city. Ideal for those on a tight budget.

Kresowa

ul. Ogarna 12, 80-826 **Tel** *058 301 66 53*   **Road map** *D1*

Highly recommended, this restaurant is located in the Old Town, next to the shipyard where the anti-Communist party Solidarność was born. The excellent menu borrows liberally from the culinary traditions of Poland, Russia, Lithuania and Armenia, and dishes are served by waiters dressed in traditional costumes.

Pierogarnia u Dzika

ul. Piwna 59/60, 80-831 **Tel** *058 305 26 76*   **Road map** *D1*

Boar pelts and animal heads cheer up a peach-coloured interior, but design issues should be overlooked by anyone who appreciates good, inexpensive food. As the name suggests, *pierogi* (stuffed pasta) are the speciality here, and there is a vast collection of fillings to choose from: from meat and cabbage to seasonal offerings such as fresh fruit.

Tawerna Mestwin

ul. Straganiarska 20/23, 80-837 **Tel** *058 301 78 82*   **Road map** *D1*

Time stands still in Tawerna Mestwin, a restaurant serving traditional Kashubian cuisine, which amounts to tasty offerings of hunks of meat. Staffed by a friendly team of golden oldies, this spot is crammed with enough local arts and crafts to make you think you are visiting an ethnographic museum. Excellent fare at low prices.

Metamorfoza

ul. Szeroka 22/23–24/26, 80-835 **Tel** *058 320 30 30*   **Road map** *D1*

With its modern, minimalist decor, this restaurant in the city centre is very different from other eateries in Gdańsk. The fusion cuisine on offer combines Polish and Mediterranean elements in dishes such as traditional sour rye soup (*żurek*) and lasagna with spinach. Open from 7am Mon–Fri; from noon Sat & Sun.

Key to Price Guide *see p316*   **Key to Symbols** *see back cover flap*

Restauracja w Pałacu Opatów

ul. Cystersów 18, 80-333 **Tel** 058 524 56 99 **Road map** D1

This wonderful restaurant in the shadow of the Oliwa cathedral offers fine dining at its best. A maître d' escorts diners to the tables, which are spread out over three rooms elegantly decorated in the style of an aristocrat's retreat. The menu changes with each season, and the blini with caviar are perfect for small appetites.

Turbot

ul. Korzenna 33/35, 80-851 **Tel** 058 307 51 48 **Road map** D1

A highly lauded restaurant situated in the basement of a town-council building. The attractive interiors are filled with flowers and theatrical touches, while the menu features all the dishes ever committed to paper by the local-born German author Günther Grass. The wine list is one of the best and most extensive in the region.

VNS

al. Grunwaldzka 82 (4th floor, Manhattan Shopping Centre), 80-244 **Tel** 058 767 79 00 **Road map** D1

Shopping-mall dining has been completely reinvented. Forget about stopping for a fast-food burger, VNS is a class act with a designer look generated by skylights, a piano stage and a clean-cut interior. The menu is like any other you would find in an international restaurant, though dishes like duck in honey prove to be divine.

Pod Łososiem

ul. Szeroka 52/54, 80-835 **Tel** 058 301 76 52 **Road map** D1

Luminaries such as George Bush Sr and Pope John Paul II have dined in this opulent setting. The name means "under the salmon", and grilled salmon is, indeed, the house speciality here, though guests should also keep an eye on the game dishes. This historic building originally housed the first Goldwasser vodka distillery in the city.

POMERANIA

BOROWO Checz Rybacka

ul. Jeziorna 2, 83-332 **Tel** 058 685 34 04 **Road map** D1

This restaurant serves the best fish in Poland, and it has won several awards to support this claim. Located in a modern detached home, Checz Rybacka features a pleasant green interior, while the menu boasts a carp-based speciality that attracts foodies from far and wide.

BYTÓW Zamek

ul. Zamkowa 2, 77-100 **Tel** 059 822 20 94 **Road map** C1

Set inside a 14th-century castle, Zamek invites diners to feast on dishes such as the "Knight's Platter of Meat" or the "Knight's Cauldron", a spicy goulash that is perfect for winter days. The *rutabega* soup is a great starter based on goose broth. The awesome surroundings are best viewed in summer, when the restaurant garden is open.

GDYNIA Hollywood Diner

ul. 3 Maja 21, 81-363 **Tel** 058 621 09 23 **Road map** D1

This US-style diner is decorated with motorbikes and palm trees. On the menu you will find a variety of dishes from all over the world, from Hungarian soup to Italian pizza to the classic American hamburger. A highlight of the list is a dish called "Fantazja", consisting of pork loin served with potato, pineapple, sliced bacon, tomato and cheese.

GDYNIA Pueblo

ul. Abrahama 56, 80-387 **Tel** 058 621 60 07 **Road map** D1

A charming restaurant designed to resemble a Mexican adobe dwelling. Sombreros and ethnic rugs hang from the walls, and cheerful staff do well to keep track of the orders from the crowds that congregate. One of the few Mexican restaurants in Poland that actually gets the food right, and definitely worthy of repeat visits.

HEL Maszoperia

ul. Wiejska 110, 84-150 **Tel** 058 675 02 97 **Road map** D1

Primarily a fish bar, Maszoperia also has a range of Kashubian specialities on offer. The salmon is the pride of the proprietor and is served with a variety of sauces to choose from. Within easy access of the sea, this restaurant is housed in a low-ceilinged fisherman's cottage typical of the early 19th century.

JASTRZĘBIA GÓRA Kredens

ul. Kaszubska 1, 84-104 **Tel** 058 674 95 81 **Road map** D1

If you have visited Warsaw, you may already be familiar with the Kredens chain. If not, expect a vast menu composed of typical bar food, high-end Polish recipes and well-prepared European foods. The interior is designed to recreate a fisherman's cabin, and it is decorated with fishing nets, ship lanterns and an antique globe.

MALBORK Zamkowa

ul. Starościńska 14 **Tel** 055 272 27 38 **Road map** D1

This large restaurant with a knightly theme is located in the rebuilt wings of the castle outbuildings. The menu serves up traditional Polish cuisine, including a dish called "Castle Soup" – in reality, this is more of a beef goulash, accompanied with olives and capers. A good stop to regenerate the spirits after a day spent touring Malbork castle.

MIĘDZYZDROJE Marina

ul. Gryfa Pomorskiego 1, 72-500 **Tel** *091 328 04 49*   **Road map** *A1*

A small, attractive hotel with a restaurant serving a combination of Polish and Mediterranean cuisine. The elegant interiors are decorated with velvet drapes and strings of sausages and hams hanging from behind the bar. The pikeperch baked in brandy and wine and served with garlic and parsley is the house speciality.

MIELNO Meduza

ul. Nadbrzeżna 2, 76-032 **Tel** *094 348 08 90*   **Road map** *B1*

Rebuilt in 1904 according to extant etchings of the original structure, this beachside dining room enjoys a beautifully central location, on Mielno's main promenade. Typical French cuisine is prepared and served with panache in this very popular seasonal spot.

SASINO Ewa Zaprasza

ul. Morska 49, 84-212 **Tel** *058 676 33 39*   **Road map** *C1*

Considered one of the best restaurants in the country, Ewa Zaprasza touts a homely atmosphere with bookshelves and typewriters dotted around the dining area. The duck with apples is the signature dish, and one that cannot be recommended highly enough. Visit the place at its seasonal best, when the summer garden is open. Closed Dec.

SŁUPSK Zamkowa

ul. Dominikańska 4, 84-101 **Tel** *059 842 04 79*   **Road map** *C1*

This restaurant is considered the best in and around Słupsk, even though the interior is rather severe. On the menu are typical Kashubian dishes, including nut soup with meatballs. There is also a distinct emphasis on fish, with the "Głębia Wód" (Depth of the Waters), a platter of three fish from the Baltic, coming particularly recommended.

SMOŁDZINO Gościniec pod Rowokolem

ul. Bohaterów Warszawy 26, 76-214 **Tel** *059 811 73 64*   **Road map** *C1*

A picturesque inn serving simple renditions of regional and traditional Polish dishes, with house specialities including *pierogi* (stuffed pasta) and *golonka* (knuckle of pork). The restaurant is decorated with garish local handicrafts that sometimes push the realm of good taste, but the food and warm welcome act as a counterbalance. Closed Oct–Mar.

SOPOT Rucola

ul. Poniatowskiego 8, 81-777 **Tel** *058 555 53 55*   **Road map** *D1*

Occupying a spot in the basement of the Museum of Sopot, this restaurant is an attractive space with black-and-white tiling and linen-covered seating. The menu offers a small selection of Polish dishes, but the restaurant is especially renowned for its Mediterranean dishes. Try the lemon soup.

SOPOT Image

ul. Grunwaldzka 8, 81-759 **Tel** *058 550 75 76*   **Road map** *D1*

The eccentric interior of this restaurant in Sopot's city centre is decorated with scenes from the *Kama Sutra*. Diners come here to enjoy Mediterranean dishes such as beef carpaccio with capers, as well as traditional Polish specialities, such as sour rye soup with mushrooms. The wine list covers all of the world's main wine-producing regions.

SOPOT Klub Wieloryb

ul. Podjazd 2, 81-805 **Tel** *058 551 57 22*   **Road map** *D1*

Ring the doorbell to gain entrance and then take your time to admire the grotto-like interior. Submarine engines, grotesque sculptures and other decorative oddities will leave your mind spinning. The menu is French-influenced, with offerings like pork in curry sauce. A meal here will prove to be one of the best in the region.

SOPOT Rozmaryn

ul. Grunwaldzka 12/16, 81-759 **Tel** *058 551 11 04*   **Road map** *D1*

A charming cottage-style building hides a disappointingly dull interior, but that should not act as a deterrent to visit Rozmaryn. This is lauded as the best Italian restaurant in the Tri-City region, and rightly so. The menu changes each month, but the seafood, especially the fish soup, is renowned across the city.

SOPOT Villa Baltica

ul. Emilii Plater 1, 81-777 **Tel** *058 555 28 00*   **Road map** *D1*

This stand-out restaurant located a short walk from the beach is attached to the luxurious hotel of the same name. It comes with a clean cream colour scheme, interesting pieces of modern art and soft music playing in the background. The menu ranges from light snack options to more substantial dishes, such as boar.

STRZYŻAWA Jermir

Near Bydgoszcz **Tel** *052 343 92 19*   **Road map** *C2*

This motel restaurant has a rather stale design but is worth visiting for the outstanding food. The menu offers Polish and European meals, and diners should order the *jermierski pieróg* (a rolled loin of pork stuffed with rice, raisins and dried prunes). If the interior is too depressing, check out the huge garden in good weather.

TORUŃ Gromada

ul. Żeglarska 10/14, 87-100 **Tel** *056 622 60 60*   **Road map** *D2*

A hotel restaurant with a rather outdated design but some very good food to quell any original misconceptions. The menu revolves around typical Old Polish cuisine, including tripe and *żurek* soup. The potato dumplings served in *czernina* (soup made with duck blood and chicken broth) is a particularly impressive dish.

Key to Price Guide *see p316* **Key to Symbols** *see back cover flap*

WARMIA, MAZURIA AND BIAŁYSTOK REGION

AUGUSTÓW Hetman

ul. Sportowa 1, 16-303 **Tel** *087 643 42 89*   **Road map** *F2*

Situated right on the banks of Lake Necko is this stone building originally dating from 1939, it is the Polish dishes on the menu that really draw diners here. The *kotlet Hetmański* is this restaurant's secret weapon: a delicious combination of sirloin steak and chicken fillet served as one. Hetman also doubles as a hotel.

BIAŁOWIEŻA Żubrówka

ul. O. Gabiec 6, 17-230 **Tel** *085 681 23 03*   **Road map** *G3*

This hotel restaurant specializes in game dishes, and what is on the menu on a particular day depends entirely on the results of the hunt. If it is available, try the saddle of deer in cherry sauce, layered with pears and served on a crisp potato pancake. As expected, a hunting theme dominates, with stuffed animals at every turn.

BIAŁYSTOK Cristal

ul. Lipowa 3 **Tel** *085 749 61 59*   **Road map** *F2*

This long-established popular restaurant is famous for its Polish cuisine, although the menu also features food from several other countries – France, in particular. The pork sirloin stuffed with nuts and cheese is a well-known crowd-pleaser. The Old Town location adds to the appeal of this local legend.

IŁAWA Kormoran

ul. Chodkiewicza 3, 14-200 **Tel** *089 648 59 63*   **Road map** *D2*

Kormoran is situated by the lake, overlooking a beautiful landscape, which compensates for the severity of the decor. The fish dishes deserve special attention, and much of the menu rests on the results of the daily catch. The fried pikeperch always seems to be available, though, and is highly recommended. A European menu is also popular.

KĘTRZYN Zajazd Pod Zamkiem

ul. Struga 3a, 11-400 **Tel** *089 752 31 17*   **Road map** *E1*

This charismatic restaurant is situated next to the walls of a Teutonic castle, making garden dining an attractive proposition in warm weather. The menu is an unusual but successful combination of traditional Polish grilled meats and Chinese dishes. A pleasant inn can be found in the same building.

KRUTYŃ Krutynianka

Near Pieckich, 11-710 **Tel** *089 742 12 19*   **Road map** *E2*

Krutynianka is the first restaurant in the Mazuria region to serve traditional, local dishes, so this is just the place to head for if you have never tried nettle soup. The terrace is situated just metres from the river, and not surprisingly, the menu also features a wide range of freshwater fish.

MIKOŁAJKI Malaj Kino

Plac Wolności 10, 11-730 **Tel** *087 421 61 60*   **Road map** *E2*

Polish cooking is served in the atrium of an old cinema co-owned by actor Wojciech Malajkat. Specialities include breaded pikeperch and superb hot apple pie served with whipped cream and ice-cream. Moderate prices and a market-square location keep business brisk in this popular local haunt.

MŁYN IDZBARSKI Młyn Pod Mariaszkiem

Near Ostróda, 14-100 **Tel** *089 646 03 55*   **Road map** *E2*

At this beautifully renovated 19th-century mill on the Gdańsk-Warsaw highway, the ceiling is supported with huge wooden beams. Local artwork, colourful tablecloths and a piano add to the cluttered charm. The menu has excellent *pierogi* (stuffed pasta), as well as home-made bread and cakes. Wash it down with a glass of birch juice.

OLSZTYN Przystań

ul. Żeglarska 2, 10-160 **Tel** *089 523 77 79*   **Road map** *E2*

With a beautiful location on the banks of Lake Krzywe and outside tables in the summer, Przystań specializes in fish- and wild mushroom-based dishes. Of particular note are the sturgeon fillets in crab sauce or in fresh dill and cream sauce. The menu also offers several vegetarian choices.

RYN Karczma u Wallenroda

pl. Wolności 3a, 11-520 **Tel** *087 421 86 75*   **Road map** *E2*

In this plain brick building with dark furnishings and a gloomy atmosphere, a log fire brightens up proceedings. The kitchen is the source of a variety of grilled meats and other such carnivorous offerings. The bar area houses a billiard table, and accommodation can be found upstairs.

TOLKMICKO Stara Gorzelnia

Near Kadyny, 82-340 **Tel** *055 231 61 20*   **Road map** *D1*

Stara Gorzelnia is situated in what was once Kaiser Wilhelm's personal vodka distillery, with the surrounding grounds featuring what is reputed to be the oldest oak tree in Poland. The restaurant is a large, upmarket affair, and the menu has everything from roast beef with Yorkshire pudding to fondue sets. Completely recommended.

SHOPPING IN POLAND

Poland is known first and foremost for its handicraft goods. Polish silver and amber jewellery are especially renowned, but hand-embroidered tablecloths, cut glass from Silesia, porcelain from Ćmielów and ceramics from Bolesławiec are also very popular. Thick, hand-knitted woollen sweaters and ornamented

leather slippers are produced by the highlanders of Zakopane and its environs. CDs of Polish classical and contemporary music are available all over the country. Large-format, lavishly illustrated books of the Polish landscape and on art, some of which are published in English, French or German, are other tempting souvenirs of a visit to Poland.

Ceramics from Bolesławiec

Amber jewellery and other goods displayed in a shop window

WHERE TO SHOP

Although there are retail shops everywhere, it often makes more sense to purchase goods from factory and established licensed shops. The most competitively priced handicraft goods can be bought direct from the manufacturers in the markets. Duty-free goods are also available at Warsaw airport.

SHOPPING IN WARSAW

Most shops are located in the city centre. There are many elegant boutiques in the Old Town, along Ulica Krakowskie Przedmieście and Ulica Nowy Świat. There are many clothes shops in Ulica Chmielna, Aleje Jerozolimskie and Ulica Marszałkowska. If you are interested in antiques visit the Sunday morning market in the Koło district on the western side of Warsaw.

Popular department stores are **Galeria Centrum**, **Galeria**

Mokotów, **Arkadia**, **Wola Park** and **Złote Tarasy**. Large shopping centres such as **Reduta** and **Promenada** are located away from the main tourist areas, while **Klif** is smaller and close to the centre. Browsing for bargains is an attraction of large markets, for example those held in Plac Defilad, or Jarmark Saski bazaar in the east of Warsaw.

OPENING HOURS

Shops are open from 10am to 6pm Monday to Friday and, in the main, from 10am to 2pm on Saturdays. In the larger cities, shops usually close at 7pm, with most of the department stores staying open for an extra hour and closing at 8pm.

In the run-up to Christmas, the majority of shops are open much longer hours, and shopping centres open

Klif, one of Warsaw's main shopping centres

on the last Sunday before Christmas. Normal Sunday opening times are restricted to a few food shops and major shopping centres, although in summer souvenir shops in popular tourist resorts open as well.

On public holidays all shops are closed, with the exception of some pharmacies and food shops (those that are open at night). As a last resort, a 24-hour petrol station may fulfil any particularly pressing needs.

PAYING

Although cash (in złote, of course) is always welcomed by Polish traders of all kinds, credit cards are nonetheless accepted in most shops in the big cities (this should be indicated by stickers on the door – if not, ask before making a purchase). However, small shops sometimes prefer to give a small discount for payment in cash rather than take a card, so there may be a little margin for haggling. Polish shops do not usually accept travellers' cheques, but it is perfectly easy to change them in banks (see pp348–9). There is VAT on the price of Polish goods, but a range of goods is tax free to foreign nationals, and on such goods (minimum value 200 PLN) a VAT refund can be obtained.

An antiques market in Cracow's Main Market Square

BOOKS AND RECORDS

Well-stocked bookshops can be found in most towns and cities. The **EMPiK** chain of bookshops, with outlets in all big cities, offers the widest choice, and not only of books; there are music and CD-ROM sections as well. Guidebooks in foreign languages and glossy coffee-table books aimed at the tourist market are available from tourist information centres. Many secondhand bookshops, to be found in the old parts of big cities, often stock an interesting selection of old books.

Highlanders' sweaters and other local goods at a Zakopane market

HANDICRAFTS

Traditional handicraft products such as hand-woven tapestries, embroidered tablecloths and doilies, leather goods, decorative cut-outs, ceramics and even furniture are sold in **Cepelia** shops, which are to be found in all big cities. In Cracow, most of these shops are located in the Sukiennice in Main Market Square. In Gdańsk, the retail outlet Sklep Kaszubski specializes in artifacts made by folk artists from Kashubia. Local markets are also worth visiting. For example, one of the best

places to buy highlanders' sweaters is at the market in Zakopane; embroidered tablecloths are on sale at stalls in Święta Lipka and Kashubian ceramics in pottery workshops in Chmielno.

A shop showroom with ceramics and other Polish handicraft goods

AMBER GOODS

Amber is a fossilized tree resin that ranges in colour from cream through translucent yellow and orange to rich brown. Most Polish amber comes from the Gulf of Gdańsk, and Polish amber goods are largely made in Gdańsk and its environs. Amber jewellery is extremely popular in Poland. It is sold at a range of outlets, but to avoid the risk of buying a fake it is best to go to an established shop. In Gdańsk

there are several such shops, located chiefly in the Old City, particularly in Ulica Mariacka and Ulica Długie Pobrzeże – for example in **Bursztynowa Komnata**, the **Nord Amber Gallery** and the **Wydra Gallery**. The town of Mikołajki in the Great Mazurian Lakes region also offers a wide choice of amber artifacts.

MODERN ART

Some of the greatest attractions for tourists in Poland are contemporary paintings, prints and posters, which are available at very reasonable prices in galleries. Art galleries also sell original glass, ceramics and designer jewellery. Silver, in the form of sophisticated jewellery and various other artifacts, is relatively cheap.

Painting on glass also has a strong tradition in Poland, and small pieces, with traditional or modern designs, are offered for sale in many galleries around the country.

In Wrocław, the former meat market in Kiełbaśnicza has been taken over by artists. In Cracow, there are many galleries in the historic city centre – for example, **Kocioł Artystyczny**. In Warsaw there is **Zapiecek** and **Art Gallery ZPAP** (Union of Polish Artists and Designers). There are small private galleries in many towns, even the smaller ones, and prices there are, as one might expect, usually lower than in Warsaw. All in all, the Polish arts and crafts scene is a thriving one, providing the visitor with a wide range of work at attractive prices.

Baskets for sale at the market in Sokółka

ANTIQUES

In most towns throughout Poland, antiques and collectables are sold in **Desa** shops. Second-hand goods, however, are sold in privately run shops that are to be found in both large and small towns and also in tourist spots. Visitors should bear in mind that there are special provisions pertaining to the export of objects made before 1945; under Polish customs regulations, such objects may not be exported, unless a special permit is obtained.

POTTERY AND PORCELAIN

Poland has a long tradition of porcelain manufacture, and there are a few factories that still produce porcelain in both traditional and modern designs. The most renowned type is Ćmielów porcelain, which is available all over Poland. Just as attractive is the porcelain produced by the factory in Wałbrzych, which has its own retail shop situated in **Książ Castle** *(see p185)*. Popular also are traditional ceramics such as those made in Bolesławiec, especially the white and navy-blue crockery decorated with spots, circles and small stylized flowers.

GLASS AND CRYSTAL

High-quality glass, in both modern and traditional designs, is another Polish speciality, as is traditional cut glass, known as crystal. Designer glassware is also popular and in great demand. The most beautiful cut glass

Gdański Bówka, a shop in Gdańsk selling all sorts of souvenirs

comes from Silesia, where glass production dates back to the 14th century. The Julia glass factory in Szklarska Poręba, which was established in 1841 as Josephinenhütte, is also renowned.

Wedel, one of Warsaw's smartest sweet shops

CLOTHES AND ACCESSORIES

Poland has never been synonymous with high-quality clothing, but the quality of clothes made in Poland has greatly improved, and many factories can now compete with Western European clothing manufacturers. Shirts from Wólczanka, suits from Bytom and coats from

Próchnik are in demand. They are available in department stores and from shops in big cities. Many Polish designers also have their own boutiques, which stock unique collections of suits and dresses.

Poland is well known for its high-quality leather goods, such as bags, belts and wallets. In Warsaw, Andrzej Kłoda's shop at the end of Krakowskie Przedmieście and Maciej Batycki's shop on Ulica Złota, are well worth a visit.

FOOD AND DRINK

Polish liquor is internationally renowned, especially the pure vodkas, which – much like Scotch whisky – are available in a bewildering range of varieties. The most popular brands are *Premium* and *Chopin,* the latter sold in elegant, slender bottles decorated with a picture of the famous composer.

Another popular spirit is *żubrówka*, a vodka with a distinctive, slightly herbal flavour; it is obtained from hierchloe grass, which grows only in the Białowieska Forest. Another alcoholic drink is mead. Made with honey according to traditional recipes, it is the perfect accompaniment to desserts.

Many distilleries have their own retail outlets, where private buyers can taste the different specialities on offer. Such an establishment is **Polmos**, in Cracow.

Polish sweets are of a high quality. Chocolates made by the Warsaw firm **Wedel** and the Cracow firm **Wawel** are particularly esteemed.

A tasty present from Poland could be, for instance, a jar of dried ceps (porcini mushrooms, honey, smoked eel or dried sausage. The best places to buy such items are bazaars and markets. There are good markets in Warsaw in Hala Mirowska near Plac Mirowski, in Cracow in Stary Kleparz, in Poznań in Plac Wielkopolski, and in the market halls of Wrocław and Gdańsk.

If travelling to the UK, avoid fish or meat products as they are subject to an import ban.

A flower stall in Cracow's Main Market Square

DIRECTORY

DEPARTMENT STORES AND SHOPPING CENTRES

Arkadia
Warsaw,
ul. Jana Pawła II 82.
Tel 022 323 67 67.

Galeria Centrum
Warsaw,
ul. Marszałkowska 104.
Tel 022 551 46 00.

Galeria Mokotów
Warsaw,
ul. Wołoska 12.
Tel 022 541 41 41.

Klif
Warsaw,
ul. Okopowa 58/72.
Tel 022 531 45 00.

Promenada
Warsaw,
ul. Ostrobramska 75c.
Tel 022 611 39 52.

Reduta
Warsaw,
al. Jerozolimskie 148.
Tel 022 823 94 00.

Traffic Club
Warsaw,
ul. Bracka 25.
Tel 022 692 18 88.

Wola Park
Warsaw, ul. Górczewska
124. *Tel 022 533 40 00.*

Złote Tarasy
Warsaw,
ul. Złota 59.
Tel 022 222 22 00.

BOOKS

EMPiK Megastore
Warsaw,
ul. Nowy Świat 15/17.
Tel 022 627 06 50.

Gdańsk, ul. Podwale
Grodzkie 8.
Tel 058 301 62 88.

**EMPiK Salon
Megastore "Junior"**
Warsaw, ul.
Marszałkowska 116/122.
Tel 022 551 44 42.

Hetmańska
Cracow,
Rynek Główny 17.
Tel 012 430 24 53.

**Wydawnictwo
Baran i Suszczyński**
Cracow, ul. Pijarska 5.

HANDICRAFTS

Cepelia
Gdańsk,
ul. Długa 47/49.
Tel 058 301 27 08.
www.cepelia.com.pl

Bydgoszcz,
ul. Gdańska 17.
Tel 052 322 17 28.

Warsaw,
Marszałkowska 99/101.
Tel 022 628 77 57.

Cracow,
Sukiennice.
Tel 012 422 55 04.

Olsztyn,
ul. Prosta 1/2.
Tel 089 527 25 97.

AMBER GOODS

**Bursztynowa
Komnata**
Gdańsk, ul. Długie
Pobrzeże 1.
Tel 058 346 27 17.

Nord Amber Gallery
Gdańsk,
ul. Mariacka 44.
Tel 058 301 41 31.

MODERN ART

Art Gallery ZPAP
Warsaw, ul. Krakowskie
Przedmieście 17.
Tel 022 828 51 70.

Galeria Art
Lublin, ul. Krakowskie
Przedmieście 62.
Tel 081 532 68 57.

Galeria Miejska
Wrocław,
ul. Kiełbaśnicza 28.
Tel 071 344 67 20.

Galeria Piekary
Poznań,
ul. Piekary 5.
Tel 061 663 61 48.

**Galeria Sztuki
Współczesnej**
Wałbrzych,
Zamek Książ,
ul. Piastów Śląskich 1.

Łódź,
ul. Piotrkowska 113.
Tel 042 632 58 96.

Galeria Top–Art
Toruń,
ul. Kopernika 21.
Tel 056 621 08 46.

Galeria ZPAP
Cracow,
Łobzowska 3.
Tel 012 632 46 22.

**Kocioł
Artystyczny**
Cracow, ul. Sławkowska
14, 1st Floor.
Tel 012 429 17 97.

Wydra Gallery
Gdańsk,
ul. Mariacka 45 & 49.
Tel 058 301 77 79.

Yam
Zakopane,
ul. Krupówki 63.
Tel 018 206 69 84.

Zapiecek
Warsaw,
ul. Zapiecek 1.
Tel 022 831 99 18.

ANTIQUES

Antyki
Katowice,
ul. Mariacka 5.
Tel 032 253 99 22.
www.desakatowice.com

Antykwariat Daes
Wrocław,
pl. Kościuszki 15.
Tel 071 343 72 80.

Desa
Warsaw,
ul. Nowy Świat 48.
Tel 022 826 44 66.

Warsaw,
Rynek Starego Miasta 4/6.
Tel 022 831 16 81.

Bydgoszcz,
ul. Gdańska 20. *Tel 052
339 30 50.* **www**.
galeriabwa.bydgoszcz.pl

**Galeria Sztuki
Współczesnej
Parter**
Łódź,
ul. Piotrkowska 82.
Tel 042 633 25 33.

Koneser
Lublin,
ul. Lubartowska 3.
Tel 081 534 41 60.

**Salon Dzieł Sztuki
i Antyków "Paga"**
Kielce,
ul. Piotrkowska 2.
Tel 041 368 13 14.

CERAMICS AND GLASS

Krosno
Krosno,
ul. Tysiąclecia 13.
Tel 013 432 87 55.

Salon Czasu
Przemyśl,
ul. Franciszkańska 31.
Tel 016 678 53 59.

CLOTHES

Elux
Warsaw,
al. Solidarności 92.
Tel 022 636 90 65.

Vistula
Warsaw,
al. Jana Pawła II 82.

CONFECTIONERY

E. Wedel
Warsaw,
ul. Szpitalna 8.
Tel 022 827 29 16.

Wawel
Cracow,
Rynek Główny 33.
Tel 012 423 12 47.

What to Buy in Poland

Folk carvings

The range of folk art and handicrafts in Poland is truly impressive. Almost every region has its own speciality. The production of Christmas tree ornaments, painted Easter eggs and Christmas crib figures is a distinctive folk industry. The work of Polish artists, in the form of paintings, prints, posters and sculpture, is also highly esteemed and can be found in commercial galleries. Designer jewellery, another high-profile Polish craft, and amber products, which are reasonably priced, are also attractive. Vodka, the national drink, is available in various flavours.

Dolls in Traditional Costume
Small dolls dressed in the traditional costume of the Cracow or Zakopane region make ideal gifts or souvenirs.

HIGHLANDERS' PRODUCTS

The Podhale region is famous for its original folk products. The hand-knitted socks and sweaters and the traditional leather *kierpce* (soft shoes with pointed toes) are very popular.

***Oscypek*, sheep's milk cheese**

Woollen socks

Patterned leather *kierpce*

Embroidered *serdak*

Hand-carved Christmas crib

Christmas Cribs
Christmas cribs are extremely popular, especially in southern Poland. The finest are hand-carved in wood. As well as a whole crib, it is possible to purchase individual figures.

Hand-painted Christmas decoration

Wooden angel

Easter Decorations
Easter eggs and lambs are essential on the Easter table. Not only are the eggs painted, but patterns are also created by scratching into the shell and applying paper and ribbons.

Sugar lamb

Decorated eggs

Jug made out of a hollow eggshell

Christmas Decorations
Traditional Polish Christmas decorations range from painted glass balls to ornaments made of wood, straw, paper or coloured ribbons.

Gingercake
Gingercake, a traditional delicacy from Toruń, is made using old moulds and is sometimes decorated with colourful frosting.

Toruń gingercake

FOLK ART
Folk art is deeply rooted in Polish tradition. It takes many forms – from painting, carving and embroidery to other skilled handicrafts. Painting on glass is a particularly vibrant aspect of the genre.

Wicker baskets from Kurpie

Colourful bas-relief

Silver rings

Jewellery
Silver jewellery is a speciality of Polish craftsmen. It is relatively cheap and comes in a variety of sophisticated modern designs.

Nativity scene painted on glass

Paper cut-out

Amber
Amber artifacts epitomize Polish craftsmanship. The translucent material is turned into original jewellery and ornaments and is also used for lampshades and such intricate pieces as model ships.

Amber ship

Art Nouveau-style lamp

Embroidered Doilies
Embroidered tablecloths, doilies and clothes are part of the folk art of many regions of Poland. The finest embroidery is that of Kashubia and Małopolska.

ALCOHOL
Pure vodka is a Polish speciality. High-grade vodkas, those with a mixture of herbal and other extracts – *żubrówka*, for example – and liqueurs such as Goldwasser are also very popular.

Pure vodkas: Cracovia   **Wyborowa**   **Goldwasser**

Cut Glass
Cut glass is made in many Silesian factories. The delicate hand-cut patterns on perfectly transparent glass are appreciated the world over.

ENTERTAINMENT IN POLAND

Poland has a vibrant cultural life. In all the big cities there is an abundance of things to do: nightclubs, jazz clubs, casinos, theatres, opera, cinemas and concert halls. In summer, even the smaller tourist resorts have much to offer, and it is possible to chance upon many interesting and unusual events, such as a jousting tournament or a music festival. For those travellers who enjoy

A bill-post

taking part in more strenuous pastimes, there is much to satisfy, with trekking, rock-climbing, cycling, windsurfing, canoeing, ice sailing and many other sports (see pp338–9) on offer. There are also various spectator sports such as boxing, soccer, speedboat racing and dirt-track motorcycle racing. For animal lovers the country boasts a number of zoos.

José Carreras and Edyta Górniak singing at a charity concert

INFORMATION

For information on Poland's cultural events it is best to consult the local tourist information centres. In larger cities, information bulletins are also issued. In Warsaw, for example, there is *Informator Kulturalny Stolicy* and in Cracow, *Karnet*. The local supplement that is folded into the main copy of Friday's *Gazeta Wyborcza,* is another useful source of information. Details of cultural events are also published in the local press.

Bulletins printed in English are available in most large hotels and from tourist information centres. These are entitled *What, Where, When* and *Welcome to…* and form a series issued for Warsaw, Cracow, Poznań, Gdańsk, Wrocław and Upper Silesia. *The Warsaw Voice*, published in English, has a comprehensive guide to cultural events in and outside Warsaw.

TICKET RESERVATIONS

In Warsaw, advance booking for plays, concerts and other cultural events in the capital is dealt with by the **ZASP box office**. In Cracow, tickets can be bought in advance at the

A giraffe in one of Poland's several zoos

Cultural Information Centre

(see p337). Theatre, cinema and concert hall box offices will also reserve tickets for their own performances, and these may be collected just before the performance begins. The larger hotels will book tickets for guests on request. Surcharges may be applied for agency bookings.

VENUES

Many cultural events, apart from theatrical performances and classical concerts, take place in large public halls. In Warsaw, many spectacles are organized in the Sala Kongresowa in the Pałac Kultury. In Katowice, a hall called Spodek (The Flying Saucer) is the venue for both concerts and sports events. Wrocław has the Hala Ludowa (People's Hall) and Gdańsk the Hala Olivia. In summer, concerts and festivals are often organized in amphi-theatres, for example in the famous Opera Leśna (Forest Opera) in Sopot, the amphitheatre in Opole or in Mrągowo in the Great Mazurian Lakes region. In Szczecin and Olsztyn, artistic shows take place in the castle courtyard. Castles, palaces and churches all over Poland also host various cultural events.

THEATRES

In Poland, almost all big cities have their own theatres – the country has, in total, over 80. Although theatrical companies move out of town for the summer holiday season, their

A theatrical production at the Teatr Wielki in Warsaw

premises are often used for festivals or theatre reviews. In Warsaw, the most popular theatres include **Ateneum**, Studio, Polski, **Współczesny, Powszechny, Narodowy** and Kwadrat, which specializes in comedy shows. The **Teatr Żydowski** (Jewish Theatre) presents spectacles in Yiddish; it is the only such place in Poland and attracts an international audience. In Cracow, the best theatres are considered to be **Teatr Stary** and **Teatr im. Słowackiego**. The major theatres in Wrocław are Teatr Polski and Współczesny (Contemporary Theatre).

Poland has enjoyed considerable fame for its avant-garde theatre. The productions of the Cracovian theatre company **Cricot 2** have become world classics; unfortunately, since the death of Tadeusz Kantor, its founder, performances by the company have seldom taken place. The experimental theatre of Jerzy Grotowski and his company, the Laboratorium, was also renowned. The Jerzy Grotowski (Theatrical-Cultural) Research Centre operates in Wrocław. The Pantomime Theatre, founded by Henry Tomaszewski and presenting Polish shows, is still active. Poznań has its famous **Teatr Ósmego Dnia**.

MUSICALS, OPERA AND BALLET

For those who do not understand the Polish language, musicals, opera and ballet can provide the best form of entertainment, and there is certainly much to choose from in these genres. Poland has many operetta companies. The **Teatr Muzyczny** in Gdynia puts on very popular shows. **Operettas** are performed in Cracow and Gliwice and at **Roma** in Warsaw, which also presents musicals. For opera lovers, the productions of the **Teatr Wielki** in Warsaw are recommended. There are also opera houses in Gdańsk, Wrocław, Bydgoszcz, Łódź, Poznań and Bytom, and operas are staged at the Teatr im. Słowackiego in Cracow. The **Warsaw Chamber Opera**, which specializes in Mozart operas, has won international recognition but performs only a few times a month. Poland's two best ballet companies can be seen in the **Teatr Wielki** (Great Theatre) in Warsaw and Poznań.

A concert in Warsaw's Concert Studio S1

CLASSICAL MUSIC

There are over 20 classical orchestras in Poland and they perform in almost all the country's big cities. Particularly renowned are the **Filharmonia Narodowa** (National Philharmonic Orchestra) in Warsaw, **WOSPR** (Great Symphony Orchestra of Polish Radio) in Katowice and the Poznań Orchestra, which gives concerts in the University Hall. In Poznań there are performances by Poland's most famous choir, Poznańskie Słowiki (The Poznań Nightingales), founded by Stefan Stuligrosz.

Classical music is performed in museums, churches and palaces throughout the year. In the summer, concerts are given in the open air. Concerts of Chopin's music are given on Sundays in Żelazowa Wola and Łazienki Park in Warsaw.

FOLK MUSIC

In Poland there are many bands that perform the traditional folk music of individual regions, although it can be difficult to track down their concerts. The most likely occasions are the festivals and reviews that mostly take place in summer *(see p336)*. Regional groups sometimes give concerts on public holidays or harvest festivals. Many singing and dancing groups perform especially for tourists in concerts organized by hotels or tourist agencies, but in most cases their shows have little in common with genuine folk traditions. Polish folk music and dance have been popularized outside Poland by such high-profile groups as *Śląsk* and *Mazowsze*. Their shows are professional spectacles based on folk traditions, rather than authentic performances.

The folk dance group *Mazowsze* in Cracovian folk costume

Musical performance at the Dominican Street Market in Gdańsk

ROCK, JAZZ AND COUNTRY MUSIC

Student clubs and music pubs are the best places to go to hear rock, jazz and country music in Poland. In most big cities it is quite easy to obtain information on current shows. Polish rock bands are on tour throughout the year, and in summer they usually perform in tourist resorts. There are many festivals for particular kinds of music, so whatever the visitor's taste it will very likely be catered for.

FESTIVALS, CONCERTS AND REVIEWS

Poland hosts many festivals, both local and international. Two of the major drama festivals are **Malta International Drama Festival**, held from late June to early July in the streets and theatres of Poznań, and **Kontakt**, which takes place in Toruń from May to June. In Warsaw, there is also the **Garden Theatres Competition** (Konkurs Teatrów Ogródkowych), which lasts all summer, and the **International Festival of Street Theatre** (Międzynarodowy Festiwal Teatrów Ulicznych) in Jelenia Góra in late September. **Warsaw Theatre Meetings** (Warszawskie Spotkania Teatralne) are also among the most exciting theatrical events.

Opera festivals, such as the **Mozart Festival** in Warsaw, and ballet festivals, for example in Poznań are also popular. The most famous classical music festivals are the **Chamber Music Days**, organized in May in Łańcut Palace, the **Chopin Music Festival** in Duszniki Zdrój and the **Moniuszko Music Festival** in Kudowa Zdrój. Events of international renown include **Warsaw Autumn**, the great modern music festival, and the excellent **Wratislavia Cantans**, a religious song festival that takes place in Wrocław in September.

Lovers of church music gather in Hajnówka in June for the **Festival of Orthodox Church Music**. In summer, churches and cathedrals with especially fine organs host festivals of organ music; these take place in Gdańsk-Oliwa, Kamień Pomorski, Koszalin, Słupsk, Święta Lipka, Pasym, Warsaw, Cracow and other towns. Music lovers also enjoy such major international competitions as the Chopin Piano Competition, which takes place every five years in Warsaw in October, and the Wieniawski Violin Competition, which is held in Poznań every four years.

Song is celebrated at the **Polish Music Festival** in Opole in June and at the International Festival of Song in Sopot in August. **Country Picnic**, taking place in Mrągowo in July, is a country music festival. Jazz festivals are also very popular.

Major jazz events include the Warsaw **Jazz Jamboree** in late October, **Jazz on the Oder** in Wrocław in May, and **Jazz All Souls' Day** in Cracow in early November. The **International Festival of Mountain Folklore** in Zakopane and the **Festival of Folk Bands and Singers** in Kazimierz Dolny at the end of June are major showcases for folk music.

TOURNAMENTS AND STREET MARKETS

Many of the tournaments and street festivals that take place in Poland are colourful events and are popular with tourists. Medieval **jousting tournaments** are organized in medieval castles, some of which – Bytów, Gniew and Golub-Dobrzyń – have witnessed dramatic though bloodless skirmishes. As well as the jousting tournaments and displays of archery, feasts of meat roasted on open-air fires may be enjoyed.

Church fairs, festivals, picnics and street markets also take place in towns and villages throughout Poland. The best-known include the **Dominican Street Market** held in Gdańsk at the beginning of August and **St John's Street Market**, which is held in Poznań. As well as the numerous stalls selling an extraordinary range of goods, there are concerts, games and other events to suit every taste.

A knight at a tournament at the castle in Gniew

DIRECTORY

INFORMATION AND TICKET SALES

Cultural Information Centre
Cracow, ul. św Jana 2.
Tel 012 421 77 87.
www.karnet.krakow.pl
www.pogodzinach.pl

Kasy ZASP (Central Box Office)
Warsaw, al. Jerozolimskie 25. *Tel 022 621 94 54.*

THEATRES

Ateneum
Warsaw, ul. Jaracza 2.
Tel 022 625 24 21.
www.teatrateneum.pl

Narodowy (National Theatre)
Warsaw, Plac Teatralny.
Tel 022 690 26 09.
www.narodowy.pl

Powszechny
Warsaw, ul. Zamoyskiego 20. *Tel 022 818 00 01.*
www.powszechny.art.pl

Teatr im. J. Słowackiego
Cracow,
pl. Świętego Ducha 1.
Tel 012 424 45 00.

Teatr im. St. Witkiewicza
Zakopane, Chramcówki 15.
Tel 018 206 82 97.

Teatr Ósmego Dnia
Poznań, ul. Ratajczaka 44.
Tel 061 855 20 86.
www.osmego.art.pl

Teatr Stary
Cracow, pl. Szczepański 1.
Tel 012 422 40 40.

Teatr Żydowski
Warsaw,
pl. Grzybowski 12/16.
Tel 022 620 62 81.

Wrocławski Teatr Pantomimy
Wrocław, al. Dębowa 16.
Tel 071 337 21 04.

Współczesny (Contemporary Theatre)
Warsaw,
ul. Mokotowska 13.
Tel 022 825 07 25.
www.wspolczesny.pl

MUSICALS, OPERA AND BALLET

Opera
Wrocław, ul. Świdnicka 35.
Tel 071 370 88 50.
www.opera.wroclaw.pl

Opera i operetka
Cracow, ul. Lubicz 48.
Tel 012 296 61 00.
www.opera.krakow.pl

Opera Leśna
Sopot, ul. Moniuszki 12.
Tel 058 555 84 00.

Opera Śląska
Bytom, ul. Moniuszki 21.
Tel 032 396 68 00.
www.opera-slaska.pl

Polski Teatr Tańca
Poznań, ul. Kozia 4.
Tel 061 852 42 42.

Roma (Musical Theatre)
Warsaw,
ul. Nowogrodzka 49.
Tel 022 628 03 60.

Śląski Teatr Tańca
Bytom, ul. Żeromskiego 27.
Tel 032 281 82 53.

Studio-Buffo
Warsaw, Konopnickiej 6.
Tel 022 622 63 93.
www.studiobuffo.com.pl

Teatr Muzyczny
Poznań, ul. Niezłomnych 1a.
Tel 061 852 17 86.

Teatr Muzyczny w Gliwicach
Gliwice, ul. Nowy Świat 55.
Tel 032 230 67 18.
www.teatr.gliwice.pl

Teatr Wielki
Łódź, pl. Dąbrowskiego 1.
Tel 042 633 99 60.

Teatr Wielki-Opera Narodowa
Warsaw, pl. Teatralny 1.
Tel 022 692 02 00.
www.teatrwielki.pl

CLASSICAL MUSIC

Filharmonia
Cracow, ul. Zwierzyniecka 1.
Tel 012 619 87 21.

Filharmonia Bałtycka
Gdańsk, ul. Ołowianka 1.
Tel 058 320 62 62.

Filharmonia Częstochowska
Częstochowa,
ul. Wilsona 16.
Tel 034 324 42 30.

Filharmonia im. M. Karłowicza
Szczecin, pl. Armii Krajowej 1.
Tel 091 422 12 52.

Filharmonia im. Witolda Lutosławskiego
Wrocław,
ul. Piłsudskiego 19.
Tel 071 342 20 01.

Filharmonia Łódzka im. A. Rubinsteina
Łódź, Narutowicza 20/22.
Tel 042 664 79 10.
www.filharmonia.lodz.pl

Filharmonia Narodowa
Warsaw, ul. Sienkiewicza 10.
Tel 022 551 71 11.
www.filharmonia.pl

Filharmonia Poznańska
Poznań, ul. św Marcin 81.
Tel 061 852 47 08.

NOSPR
Katowice,
ul. Sejmu Śląskiego 2.
Tel 032 251 89 03.
www.nospr.org.pl

Opera Bałtycka
Gdańsk, al. Zwycięstwa 15. *Tel 058 763 49 12.*

Studio Koncertowe S1 im. W. Lutosławskiego
Warsaw, ul. Woronicza 17.
Tel 022 645 52 52.

Teatr Muzyczny
Gdynia, pl. Grunwaldzki 1.
Tel 058 661 60 02.
www.muzyczny.org

ROCK, JAZZ AND COUNTRY

Jazz Club Tygmont
Warsaw, ul. Mazowiecka 6/8. *Tel 022 828 34 09.*
www.tygmont.com.pl

Jazz Club u Muniaka
Cracow, ul. Floriańska 3.
Tel 012 423 12 05.

Pod Jaszczurami
Cracow, Rynek Główny 8.
Tel 012 429 45 38.
www.podjaszczurami.pl

Regeneracja
Warsaw,
ul. Puławska 61.
Tel 022 646 38 08.

Swingo
Warsaw, al. Jana Pawła II 52. *Tel 022 831 08 43.*

NIGHTCLUBS

Blue Note Club
Poznań, C.K. Zamek,
ul. Kościuszki.
Tel 061 657 07 77.
www.bluenote.poznan.pl

Hybrydy
Warsaw, ul. Złota 7/9.
Tel 022 822 30 03.
www.hybrydy.com.pl

Park
Warsaw, al. Niepodległości 196. *Tel 022 825 91 65.*

Parlament
Gdańsk,
ul. św Ducha 2.
Tel 058 320 13 65.

Platinum
Warsaw, ul. Fredry 6.
Tel 022 596 46 66.

Remont
Warsaw,
ul. Waryńskiego 12. *Tel 022 234 91 11.*

Stodoła
Warsaw, ul. Batorego 10.
Tel 022 825 60 31.
www.stodola.pl

Sport and Leisure

Tourists in Poland – those, at least, who are interested in such things – are fortunate in the enormous range of open-air activities available to them. The possibilities – which range from strenuous rock climbing and exhilarating skiing at one end of the scale to serene sailing or peaceful mountain trekking at the other – are almost endless. Horse riding is very popular as Poland has a centuries-old reputation for its excellent stud farms. There are also lakeside fishing and long canoeing trips *(see pp288–9)*. Winter attractions include skiing and ice sailing on the frozen Mazurian Lakes.

A tourist information signpost

The caves in the Jurassic rocks of the Cracow-Częstochowa Upland

Rock climbing – a sport for the fit and courageous

ROCK CLIMBING

The most difficult and dangerous climbing routes are in the Tatra Mountains. Climbing equipment is available in specialist shops. Although a licence is needed for climbing in the Tatra National Park, climbers have free access to the *skałki* (rocks) of the Karkonosze Mountains and of the Cracow-Częstochowa Upland.

In areas where there is a dearth of mountains, climbers can practise on concrete walls; early 20th-century fortifications have found a new use.

HORSE RIDING

Polish studs have long enjoyed high esteem for the quality of their horses. Even when they were nationalized under Communist rule, they were highly regarded. Horse riding is once again popular, attracting increasing numbers of enthusiasts. In addition to stables with long-standing traditions, more riding stables, both large and small have been established. While some of these are open to all, others are quite exclusive.

HIKING

Hiking is very popular in Poland. The most attractive areas with beautiful landscapes usually have specially marked hiking routes. Hiking maps are available both in specialist bookshops and in local stores and newsagents. Hikers can rest or stay overnight in tourist hostels, which are numerous in the mountains.

When hiking in the mountains, it is forbidden to stray off the marked track. Hiking can be done independently.

Alternatively, it is possible to join a hiking camp. Such camps are organized by travel agencies, usually student ones.

CYCLING

It is possible to travel the length and breadth of Poland on a bicycle. However, tourist cycling tracks are not marked, so it is definitely advisable to buy one of the guidebooks for cyclists in Poland before setting out. Narrow, busy roads should be avoided. It is also difficult to cycle safely in big cities, as there are few cycle lanes.

HANG-GLIDING

There are numerous hang-gliding schools in Poland. While some operate throughout the year, others are open only in the tourist season. All

Hiking in the foothills of the Tatra Mountains *(see pp164–5)*

the schools have up-to-date, officially approved equipment. There are courses for individuals or small groups. Although hang-gliding is associated with mountains, it is also popular in lowland areas, on the coast or around the lakes.

SAILING AND WINDSURFING

The lakes and rivers of northern Poland offer endless scope for sailing. Yachts and other boats can be hired from lakeside hostels. A stay in a sailing camp is a popular holiday. The longest and most attractive sailing routes are those on the Great Mazurian Lakes, the estuary of the Vistula and Szczecin Bay. Windsurfing – on the lakes, the coastal bays and the Baltic Sea – is an increasingly popular sport.

A windsurfing competition in the Gulf of Gdańsk

CANOEING

The most attractive routes for canoeing trips are in the north of Poland, in the region of the Augustów Canal *(see pp288–9)*, and in the Great Mazurian Lakes district. The most beautiful trips are those along the River Krutynia and on the Western Pomeranian Lakes. Most canoeing trips last from a few days to a fortnight, and travellers usually make overnight stops at campsites. Canoes can be hired at riverside hostels. Route maps are available in specialist bookshops or local stores. For the fit, this is a wonderful way to see the country.

Sailing is a popular summer sport

ICE SAILING

The best place in all of Poland for ice sailing is Lake Mamry, one of the Great Mazurian Lakes *(see pp284–5)*. Lake Mamry happens to be one of the coldest lakes in Poland, and in winter, when it is frozen over, it is perfect for ice sailing. International ice-sailing competitions have been held here since the inter-war years.

SKIING

Zakopane *(see pp164–5)*, situated at the foot of the Tatra Mountains, is the winter capital of Poland. There are pistes both for beginners and experienced skiers. The longest and most difficult descents are on Mount Kasprowy, and include the Gąsienicowa run, 9.7 km (6 miles) long, and the Goryczkowa run, 5.25 km (3 miles) long. The skiing season runs from November to March. Pistes on Mount Nosal, 590 m (over 1,900 ft) high, are the most popular. Those on Mount Gubałówka, 1,600 m (5,250 ft) high, are less demanding. Beginners will find many easy pistes in the vicinity of Białka and Bukowina Tatrzańska. There are also many long, perfectly prepared ski runs in Szczyrk Brenna, Wisła and Ustroń in the Beskid Mountains of Silesia, and also in Szklarska Poręba in the Karkonosze Mountains and on the slopes of Mount Śnieżnik. The ski routes down Mount Jaworzyna near Krynica Górska are among the longest in Poland.

GOLF

Golf did not become popular in Poland until the late 1980s. It is a novel and exclusive sport. Most famous politicians, businessmen and those with a high profile in the arts frequent the 18-hole golf course at Rajszewo, near Warsaw. The best golf courses are in Pomerania and Warmia.

DIRECTORY

SPORTING ORGANIZATIONS

Mountain Climbing
Warsaw, ul. Noakowskiego 10/12.
Tel 022 875 85 05.
www.pza.org.pl

Horse Riding
Warsaw, ul. Lektykarska 29.
Tel 022 639 32 40.
www.pzj.pl

Sailing
Warsaw, ul. Ludwiki 4.
Tel 022 541 63 56.
www.pya.org.pl

Yachting
Warsaw, Wał Miedzeszyński 377.
Tel 022 617 63 11.
www.warszawa.ykp.pl

Rowing
Warsaw, ul. Kopernika 30.
Tel 022 826 43 64 or 827 11 30.

Skiing
Cracow, ul. Mieszczańska 18/3.
Tel 012 260 99 70.
www.pzn.pl

Hang-Gliding
Warsaw,
ul. Krakowskie Przedmieście 55.
Tel 022 826 20 21.

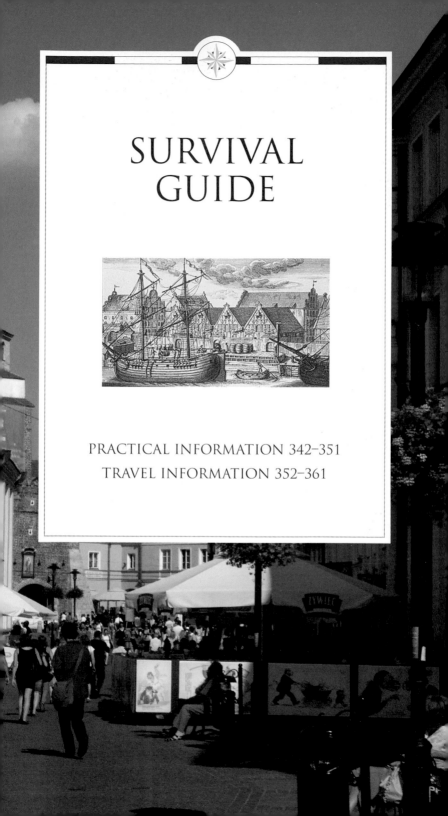

SURVIVAL
GUIDE

PRACTICAL INFORMATION

Logo for a tourist
information office

Poland's popularity with visitors has been growing steadily since the mid-1990s, and the country's infrastructure has undergone major changes as a result. Tourist information centres are easy to find, and tourist-friendly signs help visitors find their way around the major towns and cities. Credit and debit cards are widely accepted, and Wi-Fi Internet is a common feature of hotels, restaurants and bars.

Railway stations in big cities have been modernized, although those in smaller towns offer only limited facilities. Poland's road network has also undergone a significant overhaul, and there are now a number of motorways linking the major cities. Elsewhere, roads are frequently busy with traffic and quite often poorly surfaced, so travelling around the country by road can be time-consuming.

Relaxing at a café in the Cloth Hall, on Cracow's Main Market Square

WHEN TO GO

Poland enjoys warm summers; mild springs and autumns; and cold, dry winters. Spring and summer are frequently hit by rain, so it is wise for visitors to pack waterproof clothing regardless of the season.

Spring and summer draw big crowds to much-visited cities such as Warsaw and Cracow, as well as to the country's coastal, lakeside and mountain resorts. Many cultural institutions, such as theatres and concert halls, tend to close in the summer; however, big museums and galleries are at their busiest at this time. The skiing season runs from the end of November until mid-March.

If you are travelling in peak season, it is a good idea to book accommodation in advance. In spring and autumn, many guesthouses, hotels, clubs and restaurants in popular coastal resorts and lakeside spots are closed.

VISAS AND PASSPORTS

Citizens of countries in the European Union, the USA, Australia, Canada and New Zealand can enter Poland without a visa, on production of a valid passport. Visitors from other countries should check the latest visa regulations with their local Polish embassy. Poland is a member of the Schengen group of European Union countries, which means that there are unlikely to be any border controls when entering Poland from another Schengen-zone country.

Foreign embassies are located in Warsaw, although a few countries also maintain consulates outside the capital

(the USA and UK have one in Cracow, for example). Be aware that consulates can help only with minor problems; if you lose your passport, you will be referred to the embassy in Warsaw.

CUSTOMS INFORMATION

If you are travelling to or from another EU country, there are few restrictions on items that can be brought into and taken out of Poland, for personal use.

Visitors from outside the EU should check the customs regulations of their home country – there are likely to be limits on the amount of cigarettes, alcoholic beverages, toiletries and gifts that can be taken home. The maximum value of currency that can be brought into or taken out of Poland is €10, 000 (or equivalent). Sums in excess of this must be declared to the customs authority.

You will need a licence to export any item that is more than 100 years old or any

The tourist information centre in Zakopane

◁ Promenade Krakowskie Przedmiescie, Lublin

Strolling on ulica Floriańska by the Florian Gate, Cracow

artwork that is more than 50 years old and exceeding 16,000zł in value. For more information contact the Ministry of Culture and National Heritage (www. mkidn.gov.pl).

TOURIST INFORMATION

Most major towns and cities in Poland have a tourist information centre on or near the main square, although they will vary in size and usefulness. Most tourist centres have well-informed staff who speak English or one other major language and can provide free leaflets about attractions in the area. Very often they will be able to supply a free map or offer a range of local maps for sale. The telephone numbers and addresses of tourist information centres are listed in the relevant parts of this guidebook.

The **Polish National Tourist Office** has a good multilingual website; several regional tourist office websites also have useful content.

OPENING HOURS AND ADMISSION PRICES

Generally, Polish museums are open from Tuesday to Sunday, usually from 9 or 10am to 4 or 5pm. Entrance charges for major museums and big art exhibitions are similar to those in Western Europe, although ticket prices in smaller towns are often quite low. In many

institutions, admission is free on one day of the week. Churches in big cities are open from dawn till dusk, although visitors are discouraged from sightseeing during religious services. In small towns and villages, churches are frequently closed during the day, so try to arrive just before or just after Mass; Mass times are usually advertised on the church door. Admission to churches tends to be free.

Sign indicating a church

LANGUAGE

In terms of nationality, Poland is a very uniform country, and Polish is spoken everywhere. Polish belongs to the same Slavonic family of languages as Czech, Russian, Ukrainian and others; however, these languages are not always mutually intelligible. Younger Poles are likely to understand English, and as a rule, people who work in the tourist industry speak English very well. German is also widely spoken in the north of the country. Older Poles and staff in banks, post offices and railway stations are less likely to speak English.

It is useful – as well as courteous – for visitors to master at least a few basic words and phrases in Polish (see pp382–4).

ETIQUETTE AND SMOKING

Poland is one of the most devout Roman Catholic countries in Europe, with most citizens trying to attend Mass at least once a week. Religious holidays are solemnly observed, and the cult of the Virgin Mary is particularly strong. Eastern Poland has a large Orthodox minority, and Poland's Tatar population maintains mosques in a handful of eastern villages and in the city of Gdańsk.

Sightseeing is allowed in churches, but visitors should refrain from making noise and use cameras discreetly. In addition, visitors should dress modestly (no bare arms for women; no summer shorts for men).

Before 1939, there was a Polish Jewish population of over 3 million. The vast majority were murdered during the Holocaust. Today, there are working synagogues in a handful of big cities, while many synagogues in small-town Poland are preserved as museums. Some require visitors to wear a black skullcap; these are available at the entrance.

Smoking is banned from most public places. Almost all restaurants and cafés are totally smoke-free indoors, although smoking is still permitted at the outdoor tables in those establishments that have a pavement terrace or garden. Only a handful of bars and clubs have retained a self-contained indoor area where smoking is allowed.

ACCESS TO PUBLIC CONVENIENCES

Public conveniences are rare in Poland, although most shopping centres, museum attractions and petrol stations have free toilets. Bus and railway stations have pay-to-use toilets in varying states of cleanliness (usually the bigger the station, the better). Facilities in restaurants and bars are free for guests, except in old-fashioned establishments, where everyone must pay.

Crowds celebrating the annual Gay Pride parade in Warsaw

TRAVELLERS WITH SPECIAL NEEDS

Facilities for the disabled in Poland are improving. All renovated and modern public buildings have ramps or lifts for the convenience of disabled people. An increasing number of trams and buses have low-floor entrances for easy wheelchair access, and special wheelchair-friendly taxis are also available. Some pedestrian crossings have low kerbs, and the number of those equipped with an audio message for the blind is on the rise. However, moving around in a wheelchair is not always easy on account of the cars parked on pavements. Most shops in cities have wheelchair access.

Parking sign for disabled people

TRAVELLING WITH CHILDREN

The Polish are a family-oriented people, and they quickly warm to travellers with small children. Many public parks feature play areas, and facilities for kids are improving in all of Poland's major tourist attractions.

In Warsaw, the **Copernicus Centre** is largely devoted to children, with hands-on science experiments for all ages and interactive displays for teenagers. Also in the capital, the Chopin Museum

(see p78), has a kids' corner with educational toys and a touch-screen jukebox. In Cracow, the **Stanislaw Lem Garden of Experiences** is an outdoor science park involving lots of opportunities for play.

GAY AND LESBIAN TRAVELLERS

Poland is a conservative-minded country in which gay and lesbian communities have not yet met with across-the-board public acceptance. There is a Gay Pride march in Warsaw in June, and a Tolerance march in Cracow in April/May; however, both events are frequently met with counter-demonstrations organized by religious groups opposed to gay rights.

Warsaw is the most liberal of Poland's cities, with a handful of gay-friendly hotels and plenty of bars and clubs that have a pronounced gay or lesbian clientele. In Cracow there is a handful of dedicated gay and lesbian nightlife venues and many more bohemian bars and clubs that are tolerant of people of all persuasions.

TRAVELLING ON A BUDGET

Young visitors and students travelling to Poland can enjoy great benefits by applying for international youth and student cards prior to their trip. The **ISIC** (International Student Identity Card) and the **European Youth Card**, for example, entitle holders to reduced rates in museums, tourist attractions and inter-city buses, as well as to discounts at a wide range of businesses throughout Poland, from hostels and car hire firms to restaurants and entertainment venues. The businesses offering discounts display the logos of the cards in their windows.

An ISIC card is available to anyone who is either a full-time student or under the age of 26. It can be purchased in your home country or through youth tourism specialist **Almatur**, which has offices in most major Polish cities, providing you have documentary evidence of your status. The European Youth Card is available to anyone under the age of 30 and can be bought from numerous outlets throughout Europe or online via the European Youth Card website.

The colourful reception of a budget hostel, Cracow

TIME

Poland is in the Central European Time zone, which is 1 hour ahead of Greenwich Mean Time, 6 hours ahead of US Eastern Standard Time and 11 hours ahead of Australian Eastern Standard Time. Summer time, 2 hours ahead of Greenwich Mean Time, applies from late March to late October.

ELECTRICAL APPLIANCES

In Poland, the electric voltage is 220 V. Plugs are of the two-pin type, as is the case in most continental European countries. It is wise to purchase a European travel adaptor in your own country before you leave for Poland.

RESPONSIBLE TOURISM

Green issues have made little impact on Poland as a whole. A handful of hostels advertise themselves as eco-friendly, and there are moves to promote rural B&B tourism under the "ecotourism"

banner, but green policies are still in their infancy here.

Travelling responsibly is largely a matter of common sense. Eating in chain restaurants or fast-food outlets increases the likelihood that you will be consuming cheaply supplied products that have not come from ecologically sound sources. When shopping for food, head for an outdoor market. Stall-holders at Cracow's **Stary Kleparz** market (held Mon–Sat) or Warsaw's **Hala**

Mirowska market (held daily) are far more likely to sell seasonal produce of local provenance than large supermarkets. **BioBazar** is an organic farmers' market held in Warsaw every Saturday.

Instead of relying on the plastic bags offered by Polish shops, take your own multiple-use bag. When disposing of rubbish, ask locals to direct you to the nearest recycling points. These usually offer bins for paper, glass and plastics.

Fresh produce on sale at the Stary Kleparz market, Cracow

DIRECTORY

EMBASSIES AND CONSULATES

Australia
ul. Nowogrodzka 11, Warsaw.
Tel 022 521 34 44.
www.australia.pl

Canada
ul. Matejki 1/5, Warsaw.
Tel 022 584 31 00.
www.canada.pl

Ireland
ul. Mysia 5, Warsaw.
Tel 022 849 66 33.
www.embassyofireland.pl

New Zealand
al. Ujazdowskie 51, Warsaw.
Tel 022 521 05 00.
www.nzembassy.com/poland

United Kingdom
Św. Anny 9, Cracow.
Tel 012 421 70 30.
www.ukinpoland.fco.gov.uk

United States
Stolarska 9, Cracow.
Tel 012 424 51 00.
http://krakow.usconsulate.gov

TOURIST INFORMATION

Polish National Tourist Office
www.poland.travel

Cracow
Cloth Hall, Rynek Główny.
Tel 012 433 73 10.
www.krakow-info.com

Gdańsk
Długi Targ 28/29.
Tel 058 683 54 85.
www.gdansk4u.pl

Poznań
Stary Rynek 59/60.
Tel 061 852 61 56.
www.poznan.pl

Warsaw
PKiN (Palace of Culture & Science), pl. Defilad 1.

Map 3 A1/B1.
Tel 022 19431.
www.warsawtour.pl

Wrocław
Rynek 14.
Tel 071 344 31 11.
www.wroclaw-info.pl

TRAVELLING WITH CHILDREN

Copernicus Centre
Wybrzeże Kościuskowskie 20, Warsaw.
Tel 022 596 41 00.
www.kopernik.org.pl

Stanisław Garden of Experiences
Aleja pokoju, Cracow.
Tel 12 346 1285.
www.ogroddoswiadczen.pl

TRAVELLING ON A BUDGET

Almatur
Warsaw: ul. Kopernika 23.
Tel 022 826 26 39.

Cracow: Rynek Główny 27.
Tel 012 422 46 68.

Gdańsk: ul. Długi Targ 11.
Tel 058 301 24 03.

Poznań: ul. Ratajczaka 8.
Tel 061 855 76 33.

Wrocław: al. Armii Krajowej 12a.
Tel 071 343 41 35.
www.almatur.pl

European Youth Card
www.europeanyouth card.org

ISIC
www.isic.org

RESPONSIBLE TRAVEL

BioBazar
ul. Żelazna 51/53, Warsaw.

Hala Mirowska
pl. Mirowski 1, Warsaw.

Stary Kleparz
ul. Krowoderska, Cracow.

Personal Security and Health

City guard sign in Warsaw

Poland is a relatively problem-free country in which to travel, and visitors are unlikely to encounter any trouble providing they take the usual precautions against petty crime. Pharmacies are stocked with well-known remedies, so minor cases of ill health are easily dealt with. Polish hospitals are not as well equipped as their Western European counterparts, but staff are just as highly trained. Basic hospital care is free for citizens of EU countries, although specialized or private treatment can be expensive. Visitors are advised to take out travel insurance before embarking on their trip.

A typical Polish police car, silver with a navy-blue band

POLICE

Security in Poland is provided by several different forces. The state police are armed and have the right to arrest suspects. Policemen patrol streets on foot or in navy-blue-and-silver cars. In many Polish cities the regular police force is augmented by the Municipal Watch (*Straż Miejska*), who are unarmed, and have no power of arrest but still perform an important street-patrolling function. There are also private security agencies, which are generally responsible for security in large shops and public buildings, as well as during public events. They are usually uniformed and should always carry identification badges.

Traffic wardens are mainly concerned with the enforcement of parking and traffic regulations. They wear different uniforms from town to town, and their cars carry plates bearing the town emblem.

The highway police are responsible for traffic offences. Anyone found driving a car, motorcycle or bicycle with over 0.02% of alcohol (equivalent to half a glass of wine) in their blood will be subjected to a spot fine or arrested. In the event of a serious road accident, you are required by law to call an ambulance and the fire brigade. You are also required to contact the traffic police.

Police sign

WHAT TO BE AWARE OF

Poland is largely a law-abiding country, but visitors should exercise a common-sense level of caution when in big cities and busy areas. Crowded bars, public transport, major

Two policemen patrolling the streets of Cracow

railway stations and busy markets are the places where pickpockets are most active. Keep an eye on your bag or rucksack, and carry it in a safe way. Do not put your passport, wallet and other valuables in a back pocket or the external pockets of a rucksack. Pickpockets frequently operate in gangs, and a sudden push or other distraction caused by them is hardly ever accidental. If possible, leave your valuables in the safe of your hotel.

Car break-ins are common, and valuables should never be left unattended in the car. You may save your windows from being smashed by removing the radio and taking it with you. A number of guarded car parks are available in city centres, and it might be wise to use them.

Few Polish cities have no-go areas, although visitors are advised to avoid badly lit neighbourhoods of suburban Warsaw and to take taxis home from outlying nightlife destinations rather than walking.

Polish cities that are popular with young weekend tourists (notably Cracow) are prone to overcharging, so avoid the tourist-trap bars and clubs. Male visitors travelling solo or in small groups should be wary of overfriendly young females suggesting a drink in a nearby bar – a hugely inflated bill will probably be the result. Late-night noisy behaviour in Cracow and other party cities is frequent, but outright public disorder is actually very rare.

Many Polish soccer teams have a racist skinhead following, and although violence sometimes flares up at matches, outsiders are unlikely to be involved.

IN AN EMERGENCY

Call 112 for emergencies requiring medical, police or fire services. Ambulance services are on call day and night. Minor health problems can often be dealt with in a pharmacy; for more serious injury or illness, head for the casualty department of one of the big city hospitals. The main pharmacies and hospitals are listed in the Directory.

LOST AND STOLEN PROPERTY

If you lose something in a café, restaurant or museum in Poland, there is a good chance that the staff will keep it for a day or two in the expectation that you will return. It is a good idea to write your phone number inside bags and wallets – in the event of loss, a good citizen or a policeman may well call to inform you that it has been found.

If you lose property on the Warsaw public transport system, call 022 663 32 97 (for trams), 022 655 42 42 (metro) or 022 699 72 35 (suburban trains). Items left on planes, inter-city trains or buses will be kept at lost property offices at the airport, railway station and bus station respectively. There are two lost property offices in Cracow – one for items lost on public transport (MPK Transport Office, ul. Brożka 3, Tel 012 254 11 50), and one for items misplaced elsewhere in the city (Biuro Rzeczy Znalezionych, ul. Wielicka 28, Tel 012 616 57 13).

For any stolen items, contact the police *(see Directory)*.

HOSPITALS AND PHARMACIES

Both state and private health care are available in Poland. Staff are highly trained and professional in both sectors, though private hospitals are more likely to have up-to-date equipment. In the state sector, first aid is provided free of charge, but other

The old-fashioned façade of a pharmacy in Cracow

treatment may be subject to a fee, which is often required in advance, along with a passport for identification.

Treatment for minor cases is available at pharmacies, where helpful trained staff can provide advice on remedies. Polish pharmacies stock all kinds of international over-the-counter medicines.

TRAVEL AND HEALTH INSURANCE

Travel insurance that includes provision for health care is highly recommended. The longer you stay abroad, the more important it is to ensure that you have substantial health cover. Many airlines and travel agents offer insurance when you book your holiday. **World Nomads** is a reputable service that offers travel insurance to citizens of 150 countries.

EU nationals are entitled to state health care in Poland on production of a valid **European Health Insurance Card** (EHIC). In the UK, this can be obtained from a post office or online. A booklet details what health care you

are entitled to, and where and how to claim. You still may have to pay in advance to obtain treatment and claim the money back later. As not all treatments are covered, it is advisable to take out additional health insurance; you must keep official medical reports and receipts in order to recoup the costs of treatment.

Make sure you travel with all relevant insurance documents. Keep a copy in your hotel room or with a reliable family member back home.

DIRECTORY

IN AN EMERGENCY

Ambulance, Police and Fire
Tel 112.

HOSPITALS AND 24-HOUR PHARMACIES

Cracow
Szpital im. Gabriela Narutowicza
ul. Prądnicka 35.
Tel 012 416 22 66.

Apteka Pod Opatrznością
Karmelicka 23.
Tel 012 631 19 80.

Gdańsk
Apteka Dyżurna
Wały Jagiellońskie 28/30.
Tel 058 320 78 37.

Warsaw
Apteka Beata
al. Solidarności 149.
Tel 022 620 08 18.
Also:
Warszawa Centralna train station
Medicover
al. Jana Pawła II 27.
Tel 500 900 500.
www.medicover.pl

TRAVEL AND HEALTH INSURANCE

European Health Insurance Card
For UK residents:
www.ehic.org.uk
For Irish residents:
www.ehic.ie

World Nomads
www.worldnomads.com

An ambulance with flashing blue lights

Banking and Currency

**Logo of
PKO Bank**

Financial transactions are easy in Poland. ATMs taking all major cards can be found in cities and towns throughout the country. Bureaux de change frequently offer more favourable exchange rates than the banks, and they can be found near railway stations, in city centres and at most tourist destinations. Credit and debit cards are accepted by an increasing number of shops and restaurants, especially in the main cities. Signs displayed by the entrance to the establishment indicate which cards are accepted.

Automated teller machine (ATM) for cash withdrawal

BANKS AND BUREAUX DE CHANGE

Banks are located in most Polish town centres. In the bigger cities, they can also be found in outlying residential areas. Banks generally open at 9 or 10am and close at 5 or 6pm. Banks are busy, and you should expect queues. At some branches, you have to take a numbered ticket at the entrance and wait until the number is displayed on a screen before approaching the counter. Most banks have their own exchange service, but better rates are offered by independent bureaux de change (*kantor*), which do not charge commission. Most banks cash travellers' cheques, but the process can be time-consuming. Foreign currency can also be changed at hotels (some have a 24-hour service), but rates are usually poor.

Big Polish banks with numerous branches around the country include **PKO Bank** (Bank Polski) and **Bank Pekao**. International banks with branches in Poland include ING, HSBC and Raiffeisen.

The entrance to a branch of PKO Bank (Bank Polski) in Warsaw

ATMS

ATMs (*bankomat*) can be found outside most banks, as well as in shopping centres, airports, and railway and bus stations. Instructions are usually available in Polish and English plus two or three other major languages. Symbols indicating which cards can be used will be displayed on the machine. Check these carefully – the vast majority of ATMs accept all cards belonging to the VISA and Maestro/MasterCard families, but a small number do not.

ATM withdrawals will be marginally more expensive than changing cash, the exchange rate is fractionally less advantageous, and a small fee will be added by your bank for each ATM transaction carried out when abroad. The maximum amount of cash you can withdraw in one day will be fixed by your bank at home; check this before you travel.

Be aware of your surroundings when using an ATM. Make sure you shield your PIN and be careful when removing your card.

CREDIT AND DEBIT CARDS

Credit and debit cards are accepted in hotels, car rental outlets, larger railway stations, big museums, most city centre shops, most restaurants and many cafés and bars. Cards are unlikely to be accepted in markets, suburban railway stations and in smaller establishments in suburban areas or country villages so it is a good idea to carry a small amount of Polish cash with you. Owners of rural B&Bs frequently take cash only. Establishments usually indicate which cards they accept by displaying the appropriate stickers in their windows.

It is advisable to notify your bank before you travel so that they expect your card to be used in Poland.

DIRECTORY

BANKS

Bank Pekao

Cracow: Rynek Główny 31.

Gdańsk: Garncarska 23.

Poznań: ul. Święty Marcin 52/56.

Warsaw: al. Jerozolimskie 44.

PKO Bank

Cracow: Wielopole 19.

Cracow: Rynek Główny 21.

Warsaw: Nowogrodzka 35/41.

Wrocław: Wita Stwosza 33/35.

BUREAUX DE CHANGE

777

al. Jerozolimskie 65/7,

Warsaw.

Tel 022 630 51 07.

www.777.com.pl

Dukat

Starowiślna 12, Cracow.

Tel 012 421 12 03.

Euro-Kantor

Szewska 21, Cracow.

Tel 012 421 55 65.

Kantor Dime

Krakowskie Przedmieście 41,

Warsaw.

Tel 022 826 16 85.

www.dime.com.pl

CURRENCY

The Polish unit of currency is the złoty, a term that literally means "golden" and that dates back to the Middle Ages, when gold pieces were used. Złoty is most commonly abbreviated to zł, although you will see the abbreviation PLN in banks and on your credit card statement. One złoty is made up of 100 groszy (gr). Polish coins come in denominations of 1, 2, 5, 10, 20 and 50 gr and 1, 2 and 5 zł. Bank notes come in denominations of 10, 20, 50, 100 and 200 zł. Each bank note bears the portrait of a Polish king.

10 złote

20 złote

50 złote

100 złote

Bank notes
Polish bank notes are issued in denominations of 10, 20, 50, 100 and 200 zł. All bear the portrait of Polish rulers and are embossed to make them recognizable to blind people. In addition to standard protection against fraud, the 100- and 200-zł notes are also marked with holograms.

200 złote

5 złote

2 złote

1 złoty

50 groszy

20 groszy

Coins
Polish coins are issued in denominations of 1, 2, 5, 10, 20 and 50 groszy, and 1, 2 and 5 złote. The reverse bears the Polish eagle wearing a crown. The smallest coins – the 1-, 2- and 5-grosz pieces – are made of copper alloy. The 10-, 20- and 50-grosz coins and the 1-złoty piece are made of nickel alloy. The 2- and 5-złoty pieces are gold- and silver-coloured.

10 groszy

5 groszy

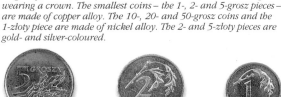

2 groszy

1 grosz

Communications and Media

Post office logo

The main telephone service is provided by Telekomunikacja Polska (TP), although there are several mobile phone operators such as Plus, Orange and T-Mobile. Card-operated public telephones can be found in town centres but are increasingly rare elsewhere. Some phone booths are wheelchair-accessible. Many hotels and cafés offer free Wi-Fi access to their guests. International newspapers and magazines are widely available, and most hotel rooms have cable TV. There is no shortage of post offices, which are run by Poczta Polska.

INTERNATIONAL AND LOCAL TELEPHONE CALLS

To make a telephone call in Poland, you may choose to use a public telephone or go through the operator service at the post office. Note that calling from your hotel room will work out much more expensive, so it is better to find a public telephone at the hotel or in its vicinity.

The vast majority of public phones are card-operated. Telephone cards *(karty telefoniczne)* can be bought from newsagents and post offices. It is possible to find 15-, 30- and 60-unit cards. A local call will only use up a few units of a phone card, but for long-distance calls the highest-value card is a much better option.

MOBILE PHONES

Most European mobile phones will function perfectly well in Poland. However, mobile phones supplied by providers in the US may have only limited global coverage. Contact your service provider prior to your trip for details.

To use your mobile phone abroad, you will need to check with your provider that roaming has been enabled. Remember that you will be charged for the calls you receive as well as for the calls you make, and that you may have to pay a substantial premium for the international leg of the call.

To limit the cost of using a mobile phone while in Poland, you could purchase a SIM card that uses a local

Public telephone

mobile network and top it up as you go. You can do this only if your handset is unlocked – ask your network provider for advice.

If you are using a smart phone, be aware that charges for data roaming can be high. If you want to make and receive calls while abroad but do not wish to be charged for use of the Internet or other data, it is possible to switch off the data roaming setting for the duration of your stay and continue using the telephone functions as normal.

PUBLIC TELEPHONES

With so many Poles now using mobile phones, public telephones are less commonplace than they used to be. However, they can still be found around town centres and near railway and bus stations.

To make a telephone call, lift the receiver and wait for a continuous dialling tone. Insert a telephone card when the words *włóż kartę* ("insert card") are displayed. The screen will indicate the amount of credit *(kredyt)* available. Dial the number you wish to reach, and await connection. Note that a short, rapidly repeating tone indicates that the number is engaged. When you have finished the call, simply replace the receiver and remove the ejected card.

INTERNET ACCESS

If you are travelling to Poland with a laptop or a smart phone, there are numerous opportunities to log on to the Internet for little or no cost. Several hotels, cafés and bars provide Wi-Fi access to their guests. Some places charge for Wi-Fi use, but in most cases it is free. Establishments that offer Wi-Fi access will display a Wi-Fi sticker in the window. Free Wi-Fi zones can be found in many Polish cities, frequently in the main square.

Wi-Fi sign

For those who are travelling without a Wi-Fi-enabled device, most hotels and hostels have a computer terminal in the lobby that can be used by guests. In addition, most Polish towns have at least one Internet café *(kafejka*

USEFUL DIALLING CODES AND NUMBERS

- For national (Polish) directory enquiries, dial 118 913.
- For international directory enquiries, dial 118 912.
- To book a long-distance or international call, dial 900.
- To call overseas, dial 0 and wait for the tone; dial 0 again, followed by the country code and the area code (omitting the initial 0) and the subscriber's number.
- Country codes: UK 44; Canada and USA 1; Eire 353; Australia 61; South Africa 27; New Zealand 64.

People using the Internet at a Cracow bar

Internetowa), offering reasonable rates (around 10zł/hour) for Internet use. See the Directory for the main ones.

POSTAL SERVICES

Post offices are usually prominently located in city centres and town squares. In the bigger cities, there are also branches throughout the suburbs. Post office opening hours are usually 8am–6pm Monday to Friday. In major cities there is often a main post office that keeps slightly longer hours (including Saturday mornings). There are also 24-hour branches in Warsaw *(see Directory)* and Cracow (ul. Lubicz 4).

Post box

At post offices you can buy stamps, send telegrams and parcels, and arrange international money transfers. A *poste restante* (mail holding) service is also available. Stamps can also be purchased from selected newsagents.

Inland letters are delivered within 2 to 3 days, but international mail takes about a week. Letters and cards sent by express service will arrive sooner. Courier services – available from the larger post office branches, as well as from **DHL** and other courier companies – are the fastest but are very expensive.

NEWSPAPERS AND MAGAZINES

Foreign newspapers and magazines are available from the larger newsagents and bookshops in Poland's major cities. The biggest choice is

available from the **Empik** chain of multimedia stores. Most branches of Empik will stock international fashion and lifestyle magazines, as well as a full range of Polish-language publications.

The most important locally produced English-language titles are the travel and lifestyle monthly *Warsaw Insider*, the weekly news-oriented *Warsaw Voice*, and the economics and finance-related *Warsaw Business Journal*. In Cracow, the monthly *Krakow Post* is a good source of local news and views and can be picked up from many hotels and restaurants free of charge. The *New Poland Express* is a very useful Internet-only resource in English.

A newspaper stand in Gdańsk

TELEVISION

Most hotel rooms will have a TV offering a handful of Polish-language stations and a choice of German-, English-, Italian- and French-language stations. News channels like CNN or BBC are more

common than entertainment or film channels. Polish TV stations broadcast a lot of English-language films and drama, although these are usually dubbed into Polish or read by just one person.

TRAVEL INFORMATION

Most main Polish cities have international airports, and every region in the country can be reached by air. The flexibility offered by budget airlines makes it easy to enter the country at one airport and leave it from another, enabling visitors to travel around more. Coaches from the UK and Western Europe run to virtually every Polish city;

Plane from LOT's fleet

car ferries are a good way of approaching from Scandinavia and northern Germany. Poland's rail network is extensive, but station infrastructure and train carriages are in various states of modernization. Polish roads are of mixed quality; modern highways link several cities, but slow, traffic-clogged roads are more common.

ARRIVING BY AIR

Poland is well connected with the rest of the world. As well as major airports, such as Warsaw's **Chopin Airport** and Cracow's **John Paul II Airport**, there are international airports at Katowice, Gdańsk, Poznań, Łódź, Wrocław, Szczecin, Bydgoszcz and Rzeszów. Many of these are served by budget airlines from the UK and Western Europe.

The national carrier **LOT** operates direct flights to Warsaw and Cracow from the UK and North America. **British Airways**, **Lufthansa**, **Air France** and **Austrian Airlines** also fly to Warsaw from their home countries, providing useful connections for travellers starting out in South Africa, Australasia or the Far East. Low-cost airlines – **easyJet**, **Wizz Air**, **Ryanair**, **Jet2**, **OLT Express**, **Eurolot** and **Germanwings** – offer a wide choice of flights to Poland's international airports from the UK and many Western European cities.

Domestic flights linking Warsaw with provincial Polish cities are operated by LOT; both Eurolot and OLT Express offer internal flights linking the main cities – and without the need to change planes in Warsaw.

WARSAW AIRPORT

Warsaw Chopin Airport, at Okęcie, 6 km (4 miles) north of the city centre, has just one terminal, Terminal A, which handles both domestic and international flights. Confusingly, the check-in areas within the terminal are also designated by letter: A, B, C, D and E. Terminal A offers ATMs, a restaurant, cafés, car hire desks and a tourist information office.

A railway station beneath Terminal A links the airport to Warsaw city centre. Local trains run by Koleje Mazowieckie travel to Warsaw Central Station (20 minutes). Municipal train company SKM operates two services: S2 to Warszawa

Logo of LOT, the Polish national airline

Zachodnia (Warsaw West) and S3 to Warszawa Śródmieście (next to Warsaw Central Station) and Warszawa Wschodnia (Warsaw East). Both companies accept all public transport tickets, including single fare, short-term and unlimited ride. Tickets can be purchased from newsstands and ticket machines at the station.

There are also bus services between the airport and the city centre. Route 175 runs past Warsaw Central Station and then along Krakowskie Przedmescie to the Old Town, while route 188 goes to Praga Południe, on the eastern side of the Vistula River. Tickets can be bought at newsagents in town and at the airport, or from the bus driver – although in this case the exact fare, plus a handling charge, is required.

Taxi services also run to and from the airport and cost about 80zł.

CRACOW AIRPORT

Situated 15 km (9 miles) west of the city centre, Cracow-Balice John Paul II Airport is modern and easy to get around. ATMs and car hire desks are in the arrivals hall.

The airport is connected to Cracow's main railway station (Kraków Głowny) by train every half hour between about 5am and 11pm. The journey takes 20 minutes. Tickets (10zł) can be bought from the conductor on board. The airport railway station is 200 m (220 yards) from the international

The modern exterior of Chopin Airport, Warsaw

The check-in area at Cracow's John Paul II Airport

terminal. Follow the signs, or wait for the shuttle bus that departs every 10–15 minutes. Two daytime bus routes (nos. 208 and 292) link the airport to the main railway station (a journey time of 40 minutes), running through parts of western Cracow, where several hotels are situated. Between 11pm and 5am, night bus no. 902 makes the same journey.

The taxi journey into town takes 20–30 minutes and costs about 50zł (expect to pay more at night and weekends).

OTHER AIRPORTS

Airports at Bydgoszcz, Gdańsk, Katowice, Łódź, Poznań, Szczecin, Rzeszów and Wrocław all receive flights from the UK and Western Europe, mostly run by budget airlines.

Gdańsk, Łódź, Poznań and Wrocław are popular city-break destinations; Bydgoszcz is close to the medieval city of Toruń; and Katowice is a convenient gateway to south-central Poland. Szczecin is a good entry point for the Baltic coast, and Rzeszów is a great springboard to the mountains of the rural southeast.

Gdańsk, Poznań and Wrocław airports are close to their respective cities and have good bus links. Szczecin, Katowice and Rzeszów are a bit further out, and connecting buses are less frequent.

TICKETS AND FARES

Prices vary greatly depending on the time of year and how far in advance you book. The peak periods are Easter, June–August, and the winter festive season. Tickets booked direct from the airline's website a

month or more in advance are generally cheaper than tickets booked through travel agents or tickets booked near to your date of travel.

Low-cost airlines should be your first port of call if you are looking for inexpensive deals. Be aware, however, that these airlines usually charge extra for each item of hold luggage and add booking fees dependent on what kind of credit or debit card you use, driving up costs considerably.

Some airlines offer reductions for children under 12. Children under 2 years old usually travel free, providing they occupy the same seat as the accompanying parent.

ARRIVING BY SEA

The ports of **Świnoujście** and **Gdynia** have connections with northern Germany and Scandinavia. **Stena Line** operates a service to Gdynia from Karlskrona in Denmark; **Finnlines** serves Gdynia from Rostock and Helsinki. **Polferries** links **Gdańsk** with Nynäshamn, near Sweden's capital Stockholm, while Świnoujście has a regular **Unity Line** connection with Ystadt, in southern Sweden.

For information on fares, visit the relevant website.

A POL ferry approaching the port of Gdańsk

DIRECTORY

ARRIVING BY AIR

Air France
www.airfrance.co.uk

Austrian Airlines
http://uk.austrian.com

British Airways
www.britishairways.com

easyJet
www.easyjet.com

Eurolot
www.eurolot.com

Germanwings
www.germanwings.com

Jet2
www.jet2.com

LOT
www.lot.com

Lufthansa
www.lufthansa.com

OLT Express
www.oltexpress.com

Ryanair
www.ryanair.com

Wizz Air
www.wizzair.com

AIRPORTS

Cracow-Balice John Paul II Airport
Tel 012 295 58 00 or 801 055 000.
www.krakowairport.pl

Warsaw Chopin Airport
Tel 022 650 42 20.
www.lotnisko-chopina.pl

ARRIVING BY SEA

Finnlines
www.finnlines.com

Polferries
www.polferries.com.pl

Stena Line
www.stenaline.nl

Unity Line
www.unityline.pl

FERRY PORTS

Gdańsk
Tel 058 343 18 87/69 78.

Gdynia
Tel 058 660 92 00.

Świnoujście
Tel 091 321 61 12.

Travelling by Train

Logo for PKP's InterCity trains

Poland's rail network is comprehensive and links all major towns and cities. Many big-city railway stations are fully modernized and feature clear, traveller-friendly signage. A lot of stations in provincial Poland, however, lack modern facilities and information displays. Trains are run by a confusing number of different operators, but the process of buying tickets is simple once you know where and when you want to go. Despite some sections of high-speed track between Warsaw and Gdańsk and Warsaw and Cracow, train travel is generally slow.

An InterCity train travelling through the Polish countryside

ARRIVING BY TRAIN

Train services run between all major European and Polish cities. It is possible to travel from London to Warsaw with Eurostar (changing at Brussels and Cologne) in 18 hours, and from Paris (changing in Cologne) in about 16. From Berlin there are fast trains to Poznań, Warsaw, Wrocław and Cracow. Prague offers direct services to Katowice and Cracow, and there are overnight trains from Budapest to both Warsaw and Cracow. From the east, there are frequent overnight trains from Moscow to Warsaw and from Kiev to Cracow.

TRAINS

Most express inter-city trains, including InterCity and TLK services, are run by **PKP**. A number of other express and fast trains, such as InterRegio, RegioExpress and RegioPlus, are operated by **Przewozy Regionalne**. This company also runs the Regio trains, slow services that stop at every station.

Suburban trains in the Warsaw region are run by Koleje Mazowieckie, while fast city trains in Warsaw (SKM) are operated by the municipal transport authority (ZTM). The SKM suburban train is the main link between the coastal settlements of the Tri-City (Gdańsk, Sopot and Gdynia).

PKP's InterCity trains provide the fastest and most comfortable way to travel, with first- and second-class seating. Seat reservations are obligatory and can be made at the time of purchasing the ticket. TLK, InterRegio, RegioExpress and RegioPlus trains are not as fast as the InterCity (and InterRegio only offers second-class seating), but they are cheaper and allow the transport of bicycles.

PKP InterCity services offer a complimentary hot drink and a snack, and they also have a buffet car and trolley service. Other trains do not always provide a buffet car, so you are advised to buy refreshments before boarding.

PKP InterCity trains are modern and comfortable, but carriage quality gets worse the further down the scale you go. Toilets on all but express trains are usually in bad shape.

TICKETS

Ticket counters in Polish railway stations sell tickets for all trains, regardless of the operator. However, tickets for one operator will not be valid on another operator's train; always state clearly which service you want.

Fares on TLK, InterRegio, RegioPlus and Regio trains are reasonable, while the PKP InterCity is much more expensive due to the extra speed and comfort provided. A one-way ticket on the Warsaw–Cracow PKP InterCity (a trip of just under three hours) costs 120zł; the same trip on an InterRegio train takes 3 hours 15 minutes and costs 60zł. Teenagers and students up to the age of 26 who hold valid student cards are entitled to reduced fares (see p344).

Queues for tickets are often long, so arrive early or book your tickets the day before.

Credit and debit cards can be used to pay for tickets in big-city stations but not in small towns and villages. If you are unable to buy a ticket in the station, report to the conductor upon boarding the train and buy one from him. An additional handling fee will be charged.

SLEEPERS AND COUCHETTES

Couchettes and sleeping cars are provided on trains that travel overnight between the extreme north of Poland and the far south. A sleeping car has two or four beds in each compartment. A couchette usually has six beds that can be folded down during the day to form benches. Tickets for domestic sleepers and couchettes can be bought from all mainline stations. It is wise to book them a few days in advance. Sleepers and couchettes on international trains can be booked from the international ticket counter at railway stations.

Kraków Główny, Cracow's historic main railway station

RAILWAY STATIONS

In the larger cities, stations feature easy-to-read displays with information and train times, and lifts for the disabled. Elsewhere in Poland, unmodernized stations can often be disorienting, with confusing signage and electronic display boards that don't work.

Train stations are badly lit at night and signs may be illegible, so be extra careful not to miss your stop.

TRAIN INFORMATION

Arrivals *(przyjazdy)* and departures *(odjazdy)* are clearly listed in the ticket hall of each station – arrivals on a white background, departures on yellow. The type of train and the train operator are also clearly marked. Trains marked with the letter R require seat reservations. Online timetables provided by **Dworzec Polski** and **Deutsche Bahn** are excellent sources of information.

LEFT LUGGAGE

There is a charge for the left luggage service – often a kind of insurance, the price being dependent on the declared value of the luggage. Travellers should, of course, make sure that their luggage is fully insured before travelling to Poland.

The larger stations have a system of coin-operated luggage lockers.

DIRECTORY

TRAINS

PKP
http://intercity.pl/en

Przewozy Regionalne
http://rozklad-pkp.pl

TRAIN INFORMATION

Deutsche Bahn
www.bahn.de

Dworzec Polski
www.rozklad-pkp-pl

THE POLISH RAILWAY NETWORK

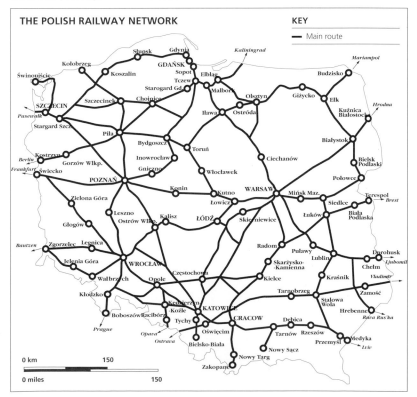

Travelling by Coach or Bus

Dworzec PKS

An information board for travellers

Poland's coach and bus network offers comprehensive coverage of the country, and it is particularly useful in rural areas not reached by the railways. Inter-city coaches run between major centres on good roads, and they are a viable alternative to express trains. Comfort in buses varies enormously, with modern, air-conditioned coaches increasingly common on the inter-city routes, and old vehicles with sagging seats operating in rural areas.

Buses parked outside Warsaw's bus station

The modern interior of the bus station in Cracow

ARRIVING BY COACH

Most European countries have coach connections with Poland's major towns and cities. Often (especially if travelling from the UK or Western Europe), coach travel involves an overnight journey, which can be uncomfortable. Regular stops ensure that you can stretch your legs, but a good night's sleep is probably out of the question. Poland itself is a big country, and if you are aiming for a city in central or eastern Poland, the journey from Western Europe can be gruelling indeed. However, travelling by coach is usually much cheaper than travelling by air or rail.

Eurolines offers routes from all major European cities. International coach tickets can also be bought from Polish agencies **Jordan** and **Sindbad**.

COACH STATIONS

Coach stations in Poland vary widely – Cracow, for instance, has a modern, well-signposted terminal, while many other cities have old-fashioned, badly lit stations.

Some have good websites providing departure information; others have barely decipherable timetable boards that may not even be properly updated.

The central bus station in Warsaw, linked via a pedestrian tunnel to the Warszawa Zachodnia (Warsaw West) railway station, can be difficult to navigate, since the train platforms that take you into central Warsaw are badly signposted. Other bus stations are nearer their respective city centres, which may be only a walk or a short bus or tram ride away. Many are next door to a railway station, allowing easy onward travel. Cracow bus station is linked to the main railway station's platforms by underground tunnel, and it is only a ten-minute walk from the main square.

Most city coach stations have pay-to-use toilets, a left-luggage office, newsagents, simple cafés and an ATM. The smaller the town, the less likely it is that these facilities will be available. The central bus station in Warsaw is poorly equipped with

traveller facilities and has limited eating and drinking opportunities, so buy food and drinks before setting out.

Bus timetables are extraordinarily complicated, with a huge array of symbols denoting when the bus runs (such as weekends or holidays). Fast *(pospieszny)* buses, which carry a small supplement, are marked in red; the slow ones are in black.

Tickets should be bought in advance from the ticket counter. Ticket clerks in Cracow and other cities popular with tourists are likely to speak English, but staff outside these areas do not always speak foreign languages; write down your required destination and departure time on a piece of paper to avoid misunderstandings. Bus station ticket counters are unlikely to accept debit or credit cards.

A coach parked outside the bus station at Szczecin

The vibrant livery of PolskiBus

COACHES

Coach travel in Poland used to be run by the state-owned PKS organization. This has now been fragmented into regional companies, many of which still use the initials PKS in their name. There are also many private coach companies running a multitude of both inter-city and rural services. The bigger firms running popular routes are likely to have modern, air-conditioned coaches, although coach quality can be unpredictable whatever route you are travelling on. Some companies (such as PKS Poznań and PKS Białystok) are introducing fast luxury coaches with free Wi-Fi on their much-patronized Warsaw-bound routes.

   PolskiBus, the coach equivalent of a budget airline, sells inter-city tickets cheaply over the Internet. PolskiBus coaches have steward/stewardess service and free Wi-Fi, but they pick up and drop off in suburban parking lots rather than main bus stations. **Dworzec Autobusowy w Krakowie (RDA)** provides coach timetable information in Cracow.

LOCAL BUSES

Buses are frequently the only means of travelling to small towns and villages not included on the Polish railway network. Rural bus services are very reliable and punctual, but the buses themselves are often old and uncomfortable. Tickets are available from the driver. Be aware that before 8am and in the afternoon, local buses may be crowded. When planning to visit a small town or village, it is best to check local bus connections in advance, since timetables at more remote bus stops are often vandalized and unreadable. Tourist information offices are frequently the best sources of timetable information in small towns.

MINIBUSES

Minibus services providing both long- and short-distance connections run in many towns and tourist spots in Poland, and provide an extremely cheap and convenient way of getting about locally.

   Minibuses are particularly useful in the tourist areas of the Tatra Mountains, where regular services from Zakopane *(see p164)* and Szczawnica *(see p167)* take hikers to beauty spots and trail heads. Minibuses are also well organized in Cracow, where services depart from the main railway station (or nearby) and serve most neighbouring villages, including Wieliczka and Niepołomice *(see p162)*. Tickets, which cost approximately twice the fare of a standard public transport

DIRECTORY

ARRIVING BY COACH

Eurolines
www.eurolines.com

Jordan
Tel 012 421 21 25.
www.jordan.pl

Sindbad
Tel 012 429 69 11.
www.sindbad.krakow.pl

COACHES

Dworzec Autobusowy w Krakowie (RDA)
Tel 700 300 150 (from a landline) or *720 80 50* (from a mobile; note that the star symbol is part of the number and has to be dialled).
www.rda.krakow.pl

PolskiBus
www.polskibus.com/en

ticket, can be purchased directly from the driver.

   Minibuses are also used on long-distance inter-city routes as a faster alternative to coaches. Due to the limited number of seats, minibuses fill up quickly, and it is not always possible to get a seat in the service of your choice. If the minibus is departing from a main bus station, it will be possible to buy tickets in advance – otherwise, it is advisable to arrive early and hope for the best. Minibuses are speedy little vehicles, and they will not suit travellers who are claustrophobic or prone to travel sickness.

A typical bus stop in Gdańsk

Travelling by Car

Road sign for city of Gdańsk

Poland is a big country involving large distances, and roads still vary widely in terms of quality. The number of fast inter-city highways is increasing, and travel times between the major centres are getting shorter. Away from the main highways, however, progress can be slow, with columns of traffic building up on popular routes. Road surfaces in general are improving, although rural routes may be bumpy. Car crime is a worry but can be easily guarded against by parking in secure garages and removing your valuables from the vehicle.

A road leading into the city of Cracow

ARRIVING BY CAR

The big cities of western Poland – plus Warsaw and Cracow – are easily reached via Germany thanks to the German Autobahn network and Poland's own stretches of fast motorway. There is also a good fast road from Prague to Katowice and Cracow. If you enter Poland from the south or the east, though, travel is on single-lane roads and progress is slow.

WHAT YOU NEED

Drivers in Poland need to have the following items: a current driving licence, a sticker denoting the country in which the car is registered, the original certificate of insurance, and a red warning triangle in the boot. UK drivers should also affix headlamp converters.

Foreign drivers from outside the EU are also required to carry a green card.

ROADS

Poland's main inter-city highways (*autostrady*; denoted by the letter A) provide fast travel along the country's main east–west and north–

Signpost indicating traffic diversion

south corridors, with the city of Łódź at the centre of the network. Not all of the highways are complete, so travel from one major city to another may involve long stretches of highway interspersed with sections of single-lane road. The most complete stretches of highway run from the German border through Wrocław and Katowice to Cracow, and from the German border to Poznań then Warsaw.

Most other main cross-country routes are classified as expressways (*drogi ekspresowe*; denoted by the letter S); these are largely single-lane affairs. Road surfaces on expressways are good, but traffic can build up. Poland's regional trunk roads (*drogi krajowe*) are numbered

from 1 to 94 and labelled red on maps. Regional roads running between major centres can be busy, while those in rural areas are often pleasant and relaxing to drive on. Minor roads are not numbered and are much more unpredictable in terms of quality.

REGULATIONS

The wearing of seat belts is compulsory. Children under the age of 12 are not allowed to travel in the front of the car, and small children must be strapped into special child seats. Headlights must be on, day and night, regardless of the weather conditions.

The national speed limit in built-up areas is 50 km/h (30 mph) between 5am and 11pm, and 60 km/h (35 mph) between 11pm and 5am; on roads it is 90 km/h (55 mph), and on motorways it is 110 km/h (68 mph). Radar speed controls are frequent, and offenders will be given an on-the-spot fine.

The use of mobile phones while driving is banned unless the phone is a hands-free model. The permitted alcohol content in blood is so low in Poland that drinking and driving should be avoided altogether (*see p346*).

PARKING

Parking regulations vary from city to city. There is an increasing number of parking

Parking meter in Cracow

A breakdown van at a garage in Gdańsk

garages, especially in or near shopping mall developments just outside city centres.

In central Warsaw there are parking meters in operation, as well as many car parks where you pay a fee to an attendant, although the car park is unguarded.

In the main streets of Gdańsk and Gdynia, coin-operated parking meters have been installed.

Central Wrocław and Poznań have a system of parking cards, which are available from newsagents; the driver circles the date and time of parking and places the card in the windscreen.

In Cracow, most of the Old Town is a no-parking zone for non-residents, although there is usually a limited amount of spaces available for hotel guests. Elsewhere in Cracow, a system of parking cards similar to that in place in Wrocław and Poznań applies.

Illegally parked cars are prone to clamping. Details of where to pay the fine and get the clamp removed will be posted on the windscreen.

PETROL

In big cities and on major roads, finding a 24-hour petrol station is not a problem. In addition to selling fuel and car accessories, petrol stations usually have shops. Those outside towns also have bars where travellers can have a coffee or a hot meal.

Drivers planning journeys to rural areas, however,

should fill up in advance because most petrol stations in the countryside might close at 6pm or for the weekend.

BREAKDOWN SERVICES

If your car breaks down, the **National Emergency Road Service** will send help to the scene – usually within 1 hour of your call, but quicker if you are near a major urban area. Fees for their services depend on where you are and what the fault is, so it is recommended that you take out full breakdown insurance. The website www.pomoc-drogowa.pl has contact telephone numbers for car mechanics in each region of the country.

Warsaw town sign

CAR HIRE

All major international car rental companies – including **Avis**, **Europcar** and **Hertz** – operate in Poland, as well as the Polish firm **Joka**. It is best to book a particular make of car before your arrival. Key conditions are a valid full driving licence and a minimum age of 21 (or 25, depending on the company). Before signing the rental agreement, it is also advisable to check the level of insurance cover provided. Travellers would be wise to take out adequate insurance independently.

GREAT DRIVES

Poland is a largely rural country and driving away from the main cities can be a

DIRECTORY

BREAKDOWN SERVICES

National Emergency Road Service
Tel 96 37.

CAR HIRE

Avis
Cracow, ul. Lubicz 23.
Tel 601 200 702.
Warsaw Airport.
Tel 022 572 65 65.
www.avis.pl

Europcar
Cracow Airport.
Tel 012 257 79 00.
Gdańsk Airport.
Tel 058 348 12 22.
Warsaw Airport.
Tel 022 650 25 64.
www.europcar.pl

Hertz
Cracow, al. Focha 1.
Tel 012 429 62 62.
Warsaw Airport.
Tel 022 500 16 20.
www.hertz.com.pl

Joka
Cracow, ul. Zacisze 7.
Tel 601 545 368.
Gdańsk Airport.
Tel 058 320 56 45.
Warsaw, ul. Okopowa 47.
Tel 022 636 63 93.
Wrocław Airport.
Tel 071 781 81 88.
www.joka.com.pl

great pleasure. The rolling lake-speckled countryside east of Olsztyn, taking in waterside settlements such as Mikołajki, Giżycko and Węgorzewo, is an ideal introduction to northeastern Poland – although take note that this area can be busy on summer weekends. A highlight of the southeast of the country is the Bieszczady Mountains Tour *(see pp168–9)*, which takes in bucolic villages and wooded valleys. South of Cracow, the Pieniny mountain trail *(see pp166–7)*, taking in Sczawnica, Krościenko, Czorsztyn and Niedzica, involves castles, subalpine meadows and lakes.

Travelling within Cities

Taxi sign

On account of its size, Warsaw is the one city in Poland where exploring everything on foot is not an option. Luckily, the capital has a well-integrated metro, tram, bus and suburban train network. Other Polish cities are compact and easy to walk around, with the occasional tram or bus ride helping you to reach outlying sights. Cycling is a popular way of getting around; facilities for cyclists are improving, and bike hire establishments are more and more widespread. Taxis are widely available and inexpensive.

GREEN TRAVEL

Polish cities suffer from traffic congestion and a shortage of parking spaces. If possible, refrain from adding to this pressure on the local infrastructure. Electric-powered trams and municipal trains are the cleanest forms of public transport. Cracow, Gdańsk and other Polish cities are increasingly bike-friendly, and local authorities throughout the country are trying to extend the number of cycle lanes in busy areas. In Cracow, the electric-powered *meleks* vehicles available for hire on the Market Square provide an emissions-free alternative to hiring a taxi; rickshaw drivers in Łódź provide a similar service.

WALKING

Most Polish cities can be easily explored on foot. Warsaw, Cracow, Gdańsk and Poznań boast pedestrianized Old Towns with clearly displayed tourist signage. Parks are a major feature of the urban scene: the Saxon Gardens in Warsaw and the Planty Park in Cracow provide a relaxing way of strolling from one part of the city to another. The streets in most Polish cities are in good order, though visitors might come across the occasional uneven paving stone and crumbling kerb.

TRAMS AND BUSES

In most Polish cities, public transport consists of an integrated network of trams and buses. In major conurbations such as Warsaw, Cracow, Katowice and Łódź, trams represent the best way of covering long cross-town distances. The PST in Poznań is a super-fast tram line that speeds its way across the city. Cracow and other cities are investing in similarly fast tram lines. Some of the smaller cities (such as Lublin, Olsztyn and Białystok) do not have trams, and the municipal bus system is much more prominent.

Daytime services usually run from just before 5am until 11pm. Night buses, which run in big cities, operate between 11pm and 5am. Tram and bus stops are clearly marked by signs bearing tram or bus pictograms. Route and timetable information is usually displayed at each stop. Trams always stop at every stop, although you may have to press a button to open the doors. Most municipal buses stop at every stop, although there are some express routes (often marked with a red route number) that stop at key points only.

METRO

The Warsaw metro, the only urban underground rail network in Poland, consists of two lines: Line 1 (north–south) and Line 2 (east–west). The latter is only partially open and will be extended in future. Line 2 is a particularly handy way of getting from the city centre to the Praga district, on the east bank of the river.

The metro is safe, clean and punctual. Entrances are marked by a stylized red M on a yellow background. Stations have lifts for disabled people.

The clean interior of a Warsaw metro station

TICKETS

Each city has an integrated ticketing system of its own, in which tickets valid for trams are also valid for buses (and, in the case of Warsaw, the metro too). Although in some cases tickets can be bought from a tram or bus driver, it is far better to buy them in advance. Tickets are available from newspaper kiosks and coin-operated machines placed beside tram stops; in Warsaw, they can also be bought at metro stations. The tickets are then validated by punching them in a machine located just inside the entrance of the bus or tramcar. On the Warsaw metro, tickets should be punched before crossing the yellow line that divides the ticket hall from the platforms.

Colourful trams in Cracow

An official taxi waiting for a fare in Gdańsk

Random checks are carried out by ticket inspectors – plain-clothes officials wearing a conspicuous badge. Passengers travelling without a valid punched ticket are often fined on the spot. Fines are usually several times the price of a normal single fare.

Most cities price their tickets according to a zonal system; tickets for zone one (the city centre) tend to be adequate for most sightseeing visitors. Single-journey tickets cost 3.60zł in Warsaw, less in other cities. In Warsaw, Cracow and some other cities, cheaper single tickets for journeys that only last 15–20 minutes are also available. Most cities offer 24-hour, 2-day and 3-day tickets that offer very good value for money if you plan on using public transport for the majority of your stay. Family tickets, offering a day's travel for two adults and two children, are also available. Children under the age of four and senior citizens over 70 usually travel free of charge.

TAXIS

Taxi ranks can be found at railway and bus stations, as well as at the main entrances to pedestrianized zones in city centres. Flagging down taxis on the street is rarely possible, and it's best to go to a rank or order a taxi by phone.

Most taxi journeys are metered, although you may be able to negotiate a fee if you are going a particularly short or long distance.

Private taxis, which do not display a company name and phone number, should be avoided. Similarly, taxi touts in airports or railway stations should be ignored, since their charges may be several times the official rate.

DRIVING

Driving in city traffic is by its nature stressful and it is wise to use alternative ways of getting around. In addition, it can be difficult to find a parking space in big cities, although hotels sometimes have parking spaces for guests.

CYCLING

Polish cities are increasingly bike-friendly, with a growing number of cycle lanes and signed cycle routes in Warsaw, Cracow and many other cities. Green spaces around Cracow and coastal cycle paths near Gdańsk are perfect for easy cycling. In urban zones, cycling on the pavement is permissible in areas where bike lanes do not exist, which means that cyclists don't have to dodge traffic. However, cyclists on pavements should always give way to pedestrians. Bike rental outlets are easy to find in Cracow and are becoming popular in other cities as well.

BikeOne
Bike One sign

Visitors on rental bikes in Cracow

Index

Acknowledgments

Dorling Kinderlsley would like to thank the following people whose contributions and assistance have made the preparation of this book possible.

Publishing Manager
Helen Townsend

Managing Art Editor
Kate Poole

Art Director
Gillian Allan

DTP Designer
Jason Little

Production Controller
Marie Ingledew

Design and Editorial Assistance
Ben Barkow, Sonal Bhatt, Arwen Burnett, Carlos Canal, Lucinda Cooke, Jo Cowen, Caroline Elliker, Rhiannon Furbear, Lydia Halliday, Marcus Hardy, Victoria Heyworth-Dunne, Laura Jones, Piotr Kozłowski, Wojciech Kozłowski, Priya Kukadia, Maite Lantaron, Catherine Palmi, Marisa Renzullo, Emma Rose, Simon Ryder, Sands Publishing Solutions, Richard Schofield, Sadie Smith, Leah Tether, Conrad Van Dyk, Karen Villabona, Stewart Wild.

Project Manager
Tamiko Rex

Additional Photography
Jamie Howard, Krzysztof Kotowski, Piotr Kozlowski, Rough Guides/Chris Christoforou, Tomasz Wylamowski.

Additional Contributors
Beatrice Waller, Lucilla Watson, Chris Barstow, Alison Bravington, Matheusz Jozwiak, Joanna Hanson.

Special Assistance
Dorling Kindersley would like to thank the staff at the featured museums, shops, hotels, restaurants and other organizations in Poland for their invaluable help. Special thanks go to the following: Katarzyna Kolendo, Dorota Kuta, Jacek Łodziński and Zbigniew Kocyek.

Photography Permissions
"Piękna" Agency, Jagiellonian Library in Cracow, Kórnick Library of the Polish Academy of Sciences, Warsaw University Library, Central Photographic Agency, Central Maritime Museum in Gdańsk, Collegium Maius in Cracow, Film Library in Warsaw, Chancellory of the President of the Republic of Poland, Gniezno Cathedral, Poznań Cathedral, Metropolitan Police Headquarters in Warsaw, Czartoryski Museum in Cracow, Diocesan Museum in Tarnów, Łódź Historical Museum, Cracow History Museum, Jan Kochanowski Museum in Czarnolas, National Museum in Kielce, National Museum in Cracow, National Museum in Poznań, Regional Museum in Jelenia Góra, Art Museum in Łódź, Museum in Wilanów, Museum of Warmia and Mazuria in Olsztyn, Museum of the Polish Army in Warsaw, Museum of Arms in Liw, Zamoyski Museum in Kozłówka, Maria Pałasińska, Photography Editorship of the Polish Press Agency, Warsaw Traffic Police, Road Traffic Department of the Metropolitan Police Headquarters in Warsaw, J. Baranowski, Jacek Bednarczyk, Maciej Bronarski, Father Tadeusz Bukowski, Andrzej Chęć, Renata Cichocka, Mirosław Ciunowicz, Alicja Firynowicz, Maja Florczykowska, Michał Grychowski, Stanisława Jablonska, Dorota and Mariusz Jarymowicz, Krzysztof Kapusta, Grzegorz and Tomasz Kłoszowski, Marek Kosiński, Beata and Mariusz Kowalski, Grzegorz Kozakiewicz, Jasusz Koziń, Stefan Kraszewski, Wojciech Kryński, Damazy Kwiatkowski, Janusz Mazur, Wojciech Mędrzak, Stanisław Micht, Jan Morak, Hanna and Maciej Musiał, Małgorzata Omilanowska, Henryk Pieczul, Tomasz Prażmowski, Ireneusz Radkiewicz, Wojciech Richter, Tomasz Robaczyński, Andrzej Rybczyński, Jakub Sito, Krzysztof Skalski, Andrzej Skowroński, Wojciech Stein, Wiesław Stępień, Wojtek Szabelski, Serge Tarasów, Jacek Urbański, Przemek Wierzchowski, Władysław Wisławski, Paweł Wójcik, Tadeusz Zagoździński, Jan Zych.

Picture Credits
Key: a=above; b=below/bottom; c=centre; f=far; l=left; r=right; t=top.

ALAMY IMAGES: David Crausby 350c; David Sanger Photography/David Sanger 315tl; P.E. Forsberg 356tr, 356br; Kevin Foy 315c; lookGaleria 9cl, 9br; Peter Adams Photography/Peter Adams 8cl; G. Owston (Poland) 355tl; Paul Springett 140clb; Krystyna Szulecka 314cl; Stanislaw Tokarski 344tl; Travel Pictures/Dallas and John Heaton 359c; BELVEDERE – CAFE ŁAZIENKI KRÓLEWSKIE: Pawel Traczyk 313c; BIKEONE: 361c; Courtesy of the CENTRAL MARITIME MUSEUM, Gdansk: Ewa Meksiak 245cla, 245cra; Courtesy of the CHANCELLERY OF THE PRESIDENT OF THE REPUBLIC OF POLAND: 55cra; COOL TOUR COMPANY: 361br; Cracow History Museum 31cl, 42tl, 51br, 144b; Czartoryski Museum in Cracow 28tl; Diocesan Museum in Tarnów 28tl, 41cr; Jagiellonian Library in Cracow 37t, 42bl; Jan Kochanowski Museum in Czarnolas 118bl; Museum in Wilanów 96cla, 97tc, bl; Museum of Arms in Liw 116c; Museum of the Polish Army in Warsaw 46tl, br, 51tl; Museum of Warmia and Mazuria in Olsztyn 280tl, bl; National Museum in Cracow 41tc, 48-49c, 51br, 131ca, 135cr, 137tr; National Museum in Kielce 45tr, 150b; Courtesy of PKN: 359bl; DK IMAGES: Michal Grychowski 141cla; Piotr Kozłowski 346cl, 361cr; Wojciech Kozłowski 347tl; Ian O'Leary 314-315; GETTY IMAGES: Henry T. Kaiser 340-341, 343tl, 358cl; Dariusz Zarod 342cl; GRZEGORZ GRABINSKI: 351c; DARIUSZ JEDRZEJEWSKI 8tc, 8br, 9tr; KLIF ARCHIVE, WARSAW: 328bc. KRAKOW AIRPORT: 353tl; POLSKIE KOLEJE LINOWE S.A: 164tr; PKO BANK POLSKI: 348tl, 348tr, 348bl; PKP INTERCITY: 354tl, 354cla; POLFERRIES: 353bc; POLSKIBUS.COM: 357tl; RACZYNSKI PALACE, Rogalin: 212clb; Regional Museum in Jelenia Góra 184c; STRAŻY MIEJSKIEJ M.ST. WARSZAWY: 346tl; Courtesy of the TOWN HALL Office Of Torun: Malgorata Litwin 270tr; WARSAW CHOPIN AIRPORT: 352bl; Warsaw University Library 24cla; Zamoyski Museum in Kozłówka 122; ZESPÓŁ PAŁACOWY, KUROZWĘKI: 154br.

MAP
FRONT COVER - SUPERSTOCK: age fotostock/Jan Wlodarczyk.

JACKET
FRONT - SUPERSTOCK: age fotostock/Jan Wlodarczyk.
BACK - DORLING KINDERSLEY: Olaf Beer clb; GETTY IMAGES: Jacek Kadaj bl, kryczka tl; SHUTTERSTOCK: BestPhotoByMonikaGniot cla.. SPINE - SUPERSTOCK: age fotostock/Jan Wlodarczyk t.

All other images © Dorling Kindersley.
For further information see: www.dkimages.com

SPECIAL EDITIONS OF DK TRAVEL GUIDES

Phrase Book

SUMMARY OF PRONUNCIATION IN POLISH

ą a nasal *"awn"* as in *"sawn"* or *"an"* as in the French *"Anjou"* but barely sounded

c *"ts"* as in *"bats"*

ć, cz *"ch"* as in *"challenge"*

ch *"ch"* as in Scottish *"loch"*

dz *"j"* as in *"jeans"* when followed by **i** or **e** but otherwise *"dz"* as in *"adze"*

dź *"j"* as in *"jeans"*

dż *"d"* as in *"dog"* followed by *"s"* as in *"leisure"*

ę similar to *"en"* in *"end"* only nasal and barely sounded, but if at the end of the word pronounced *"e"* as in *"bed"*

h *"ch"* as in Scottish *"loch"*

i *"ee"* as in *"teeth"*

j *"y"* as in yes

ł *"w"* as in *"window"*

ń similar to the *"ni"* in *"companion"*

ó *"oo"* as in *"soot"*

rz similar to the *"s"* in *"leisure"* or, when it follows **p**, **t** or **k**, *"sh"* as in *"shut"*

ś, sz *"sh"* as in *"shut"*

w *"v"* as in *"vine"*

y similar to the *"i"* in *"bit"*

ź, ż similar to the *"s"* in *"leisure"*

Emergencies

Help!	**pomocy!**	pomotsi
Call a doctor!	**zawołać doktora!**	zawowach doctora
Call an ambulance!	**zadzwonić po pogotowie!**	zadzvoneech po pogotovee
Police!	**policja!**	poleetsya
Call the fire brigade!	**zadzwonić po straż pożarną!**	zadzvoneech po stras posarnAWN
Where is the nearest phone?	**Gdzie jest najbliższa budka telefoniczna?**	gjeh yest nlbleezhsha boodka telefoneechna
Where is the hospital?	**Gdzie jest szpital?**	gjeh yest shpeetal
Where is the police station?	**Gdzie jest posterunek policji?**	gjeh yest posterunek politsyee

Communication Essentials

Yes	**Tak**	tak
No	**Nie**	n-yeh
Thank you	**Dziękuję**	jENkoo-yeh
No, thank you	**Nie, dziękuję**	n-yej jENkoo-yeh
Please	**Proszę**	prosheh
I don't understand	**Nie rozumiem**	n-yeh rozoom-yem
Do you speak English? (to a man)	**Czy mówi pan po angielsku?**	chi moovee pan po ang-yelskoo
Do you speak English? (to a woman)	**Czy mówi pani po angielsku?**	chi moovee panee po ang-yelskoo
Please speak more slowly	**Proszę mówić wolniej**	proseh mooveech voln-yay
Please write it down for me	**Proszę mi to napisać**	prosheh mee to napeesach
My name is...	**Nazywam się...**	nazivam sheh

Useful Words and Phrases

Pleased to meet you (to a man)	**Bardzo mi miło pana poznać**	bardzo mee meewo pana poznach
Pleased to meet you (to a woman)	**Bardzo mi miło panią poznać**	bardzo mee meewo pan-yAWN poznach
Good morning	**Dzień dobry**	jen-yuh dobri
Good afternoon	**Dzień dobry**	jen-yuh dobri
Good evening	**Dobry wieczór**	dobri v-yechoor
Good night	**Dobranoc**	dobranots
Goodbye	**Do widzenia**	do veedzen-ya
What time is it...?	**Która jest godzina?**	ktoora yest gojeena
Cheers!	**Na zdrowie!**	na zdrov-yeh
Excellent!	**Wspaniale!**	wspan-yaleh

Shopping

Do you have...? (to a man)	**Czy ma pan...?**	che ma pan
Do you have...? (to a woman)	**Czy ma pani...?**	che ma panee
How much is this?	**Ile to kosztuje?**	eeleh to koshtoo-yeh
Where is the... department?	**Gdzie jest dział z...?**	gjeh yest jawuh z
Do you take credit cards? (to a man)	**Czy przyjmuje pan karty kredytowe?**	chi pshi-yuhmoo-yeh pan karti kreditoveh
Do you take credit cards? (to a woman)	**Czy przyjmuje pani karty kredytowe?**	chi pshi-yuhmoo-yeh panee karti kreditoveh
bakery	**piekarnia**	p-yekarn-ya
bookshop	**księgarnia**	kshENgarn-ya
chemist	**apteka**	apteka
department store	**dom towarowy**	dom tovarovi
exchange office	**kantor walutowy**	kantor valootovi
travel agent	**biuro podróży**	b-yooro podroozhi
post office	**poczta, urząd pocztowy**	pochta, ooZHAWNd pochtovi
postcard	**pocztówka**	pochtoovka

stamp	**znaczek**	znachek
How much is a	**Ile kosztuje**	eeleh koshtoo-yeh
postcard to…?	**pocztówka do…?**	pochtoovka do
airmail	**poczta lotnicza**	pochta lotneecha

Staying in a Hotel

Have you any	**Czy ma pan**	chi ma pan
vacancies?	**wolne pokoje?**	volneh poko-yeh
(to a man)		
Have you any	**Czy ma pani**	chi ma panee
vacancies?	**wolne pokoje?**	volneh poko-yeh
(to a woman)		
What is the charge	**Ile kosztuje**	eeleh koshtoo-yeh
per night?	**za dobę?**	za dobeh
I'd like	**Poproszę**	poprosheh
a single room.	**pokój**	pokoo-yuh
	jednoosobowy	yedno-osobovi
I'd like a double	**Poproszę**	poprosheh
room.	**pokój**	pokoo-yuh
	dwuosobowy	dvoo-osobovi
I'd like a twin	**Poproszę**	poprosheh
room.	**pokój z dwoma**	pokoo-yuh z dvoma
	łóżkami.	woozhkamee
I'd like a room	**Poproszę**	poprosheh
with a bathroom.	**pokój**	pokoo-yuh
	z łazienką.	z wazhenkAWN
bathroom	**łazienka**	wazhenka
bed	**łóżko**	woozhko
bill	**rachunek**	raHoonek
breakfast	**śniadanie**	shn-yadan-yeh
dinner	**kolacja**	kolats-ya
double room	**pokój**	pokoo-yuh
	dwuosobowy	dvoo-osobovi
full board	**pełne**	pewuhneh
	utrzymanie	ootzhiman-yeh
guest house	**zajazd**	za-yazd
half board	**dwa posiłki**	dva posheewuhkee
	dziennie	jen-yeh
key	**klucz**	klooch
restaurant	**restauracja**	restawrats-ya
shower	**prysznic**	prishneets
single room	**pokój**	pokoo-yuh
	jednoosobowy	yedno-osobovi
toilet	**toaleta**	to-aleta

Eating Out

A table for one,	**Stolik dla jednej.**	stoleek dla yednay
please.	**osoby proszę**	osobi prosheh
A table for two,	**Stolik dla dwóch**	stoleek dla dvooh
please.	**osób proszę.**	osoob prosheh
Can I see	**Mogę prosić**	mogeh prosheech
the menu?	**jadłospis?**	yadwospees
Can I see the	**Mogę prosić**	mogeh prosheech
wine list?	**kartę win?**	karteh veen
I'd like…	**Proszę**	prosheh

Can we have the	**Proszę**	prosheh
bill, please?	**rachunek?**	raHoonek
Where is the toilet?	**Gdzie jest toaleta?**	gjeh yest to-aleta

Menu Decoder

baranina	mutton, lamb
barszcz czerwony	beetroot soup
bażant	pheasant
befsztyk	beef steak
bigos	hunter's stew (sweet and sour cabbage with a variety of meats and seasonings)
bukiet z jarzyn	a variety of raw and pickled vegetables
ciasto	cake, pastry
cielęcina	veal
cukier	sugar
cukierek	sweet, confectionery
dania mięsne	meat dishes
dania rybne	fish dishes
dania z drobiu	poultry dishes
deser	dessert
flaki	tripe
grzybki	marinated
marynowane	mushrooms
herbata	tea
jarzyny	vegetables
kabanos	dry, smoked pork sausage
kaczka	duck
kapusta	cabbage
kartofle	potatoes
kasza gryczana	buckwheat
kaszanka	black pudding
kawa	coffee
kiełbasa	sausage
klopsiki	minced meat balls
lody	ice cream
łosoś	salmon
łosoś wędzony	smoked salmon
makowiec	poppy seed cake
naleśniki	pancakes
piernik	spiced honeycake
pierogi	ravioli-like dumplings
piwo	beer
prawdziwki	ceps (type of mushroom)
przystawki	entrées
pstrąg	trout
rolmopsy	rollmop herrings
sałatka	salad
sałatka owocowa	fruit salad
sok	juice
sok jabłkowy	apple juice
sok owocowy	fruit juice
sól	salt
śledź	herring
tort	cake, gâteau
wieprzowina	pork
wino	wine

woda	water
ziemniaki	potatoes
zupa	soup

Health

I do not feel well.	Źle się czuję	zhleh sheh choo-yeh
I need	Potrzebuję	potzheboo-yeh
a prescription for…	receptę na…	retsepteh na
cold	przeziębienie	pshef-yENb-yen-yeh
cough (noun)	kaszel	kashel
cut	skaleczenie	skalechen-yeh
flu	grypa	gripa
hayfever	katar sienny	katar shyienny
headache pills	proszki od	proshkee od
	bólu głowy	booloo gwovi
hospital	szpital	shpeetal
nausea	mdłości	mudwosh-che
sore throat	ból gardła	bool gardwa

Travel and Transport

When is the	Kiedy jest	k-yedi yest
next train to…?	następny	nastENpni
	pociąg do…?	pochAWNg do…
What is the	Ile kosztuje	eeleh koshtoo-yeh
fare to…?	bilet do…?	beelet do
A single ticket	Proszę bilet	prosheh beelet
to … please	w jedną	v yednAWN
	stronę bilet do…	stroneh beelet do
A return ticket	Proszę bilet	prosheh beelet
to … please	w obie	v obye
	strony do…	strony do
Where is the	Gdzie jest	gjeh yest
bus station?	dworzec	dvozhets
	autobusowy?	awtoboosovi
Where is the	Gdzie jest	gjeh yest
bus stop?	przystanek	pshistanek
	autobusowy?	awtoboosovi
Where is the	Gdzie jest	gjeh yest
tram stop?	przystanek	pshistanek
	tramwajowy?	tramvl-yovi
booking office	kasa biletowa	kasa beeletova
station	stacja	stats-ya
timetable	rozkład jazdy	rozkwad yazdi
left luggage	przechowalnia	psheIIovaln-ya
	bagażu	bagazhoo
platform	peron	peron
first class	pierwsza klasa	p-yervsha klasa
second class	druga klasa	drooga klasa
single ticket	bilet w jedną	beelet v jednAWN
	stronę	stroneh
return ticket	bilet powrotny	beelet povrotni
airline	linia lotnicza	leen-ya lotna-yeecha
airport	lotnisko	lotn-yeesko
arrival	przylot	pshilot
flight number	numer lotu	noomer lotoo

| gate | przejście | pshaysh-cheh |
| coach | autokar | awtokar |

Numbers

0	zero	zero
1	jeden	yeden
2	dwa	dva
3	trzy	tshi
4	cztery	chteri
5	pięć	p-yENch
6	sześć	shesh-ch
7	siedem	sh-yedem
8	osiem	oshem
9	dziewięć	jev-yENch
10	dziesięć	jeshENch
11	jedenaście	yedenash-cheh
12	dwanaście	dvanash-cheh
13	trzynaście	tshinash-cheh
14	czternaście	chternash-cheh
15	piętnaście	p-yEntnash-cheh
16	szesnaście	shesnash-cheh
17	siedemnaście	shedemnash-cheh
18	osiemnaście	oshemnash-cheh
19	dziewiętnaście	jev-yENtnash-cheh
20	dwadzieścia	dvajesh-cha
21	dwadzieścia	dvajesh-ch
	jeden	a yeden
22	dwadzieścia dwa	dvajesh-cha dva
30	trzydzieści	tshijesh-chee
40	czterdzieści	chterjesh-chee
50	pięćdziesiąt	p-yENchjeshAWNt
100	sto	sto
200	dwieście	dv-yesh-cheh
500	pięćset	p-yENchset
1,000	tysiąc	tishAWNts
1,000,000	milion	meel-yon

Time

today	dzisiaj	jeeshl
yesterday	wczoraj	vchorl
tomorrow	jutro	yootro
tonight	dzisiejszej nocy	jeeshAYshay notsi
one minute	jedna minuta	yedna meenoota
half an hour	pół godziny	poowuh gojceni
hour	godzina	gojeena

Days of the Week

Sunday	niedziela	n-yejela
Monday	poniedziałek	pon-yejawek
Tuesday	wtorek	vtorek
Wednesday	środa	shroda
Thursday	czwartek	chvartek
Friday	piątek	p-yAWNtek
Saturday	sobota	sobota